Mastering Adobe Photoshop Elements 2023

Fifth Edition

Bring out the best in your images using Adobe Photoshop Elements 2023

Robin Nichols

BIRMINGHAM—MUMBAI

Mastering Adobe Photoshop Elements 2023

Fifth Edition

Senior Publishing Product Manager: Manish Nainani

Acquisition Editor – Peer Reviews: Gaurav Gavas

Project Editor: Rianna Rodrigues

Senior Editor: Aamir Ahmed

Content Development Editor: Grey Murtagh

Technical Editor: Aniket Shetty

Indexer: Manju Arasan

Presentation Designers: Aparna Bhagat / Pranit Padwal

Developer Relations Marketing Executive: Sohini Ghosh

First published: August 2018
Second edition: April 2020
Third edition: December 2020
Fourth edition: December 2021
Fifth edition: December 2022

Production reference: 2090123

Published by Packt Publishing Ltd.
Livery Place
35 Livery Street
Birmingham
B3 2PB, UK.

ISBN 978-1-80324-845-5

www.packt.com

*To my wonderful wife, Natalie, whose great love of life has continued
to be an immense source of encouragement to me
while working on the new version of this book...*

– Robin Nichols, Sydney, 2022

Contributors

About the author

Born in the UK, **Robin Nichols** has always had a great love for recording the world with a camera. After finishing school, he studied fine art, before moving on to study at Nottingham Trent University, where he gained a degree in creative photography. He subsequently worked in the advertising industry for several years, before emigrating to Australia in 1985. Robin has always worked in photography: as a black and white printer, a cameraman, a stock photographer, and a freelance photographer.

During the 1990s, Robin contributed to several photo-centric publications in Australia, New Zealand, Singapore, and the UK. This led to a full-time position as the editor of the Sydney-based *Commercial Photography* magazine, and later, *Australian Photography* magazine, a post that he held for 5 years.

In 1997, he founded the critically acclaimed *Digital Photography and Design* magazine. During this period, he also authored books for Focal Press and Octopus Press, lectured at seminars in Sydney, Melbourne, and Brisbane, as well as in Seattle and Chicago, and ran highly successful photographic workshops in Dubai for seven years.

In 2000, he started his own publishing business, launching what became Australia's best-selling specialist digital photography publication: *Better Digital Magazine*. With this he pursued the goal of presenting clear, well-illustrated information written in jargon-free English.

Two years later, he launched a second magazine, also a world first, called *Better Photoshop Techniques*. As a publisher during this period, Robin was lucky enough to interview some of the biggest names in photography, including Elliott Erwitt, David Doubilet, Joe McNally, Gregory Heisler, David Hobby, and even keen photographer and jazz legend Don Burrows, on one occasion.

Both magazines ran for more than 10 years, but as distribution and paper costs spiraled and access to free information on the internet exploded, he made the move into teaching. However, after ten years of teaching recent events, most notably COVID, forced an early retirement - and now Robin divides his time equally between his woodworking shop and his ever-changing home garden.

About the reviewer

David Asch lives in Haywards Heath, England. He works as a Content Designer and is also an artist with a passion for digital art and technology.

David has been working with digital imaging tools for over 20 years. In that time, he has authored several titles on Adobe Photoshop Elements and Adobe Muse, as well as numerous articles for digital photography publications and online resources. He is an Adobe Certified Expert in Photoshop CC and teaches Photoshop and Photoshop Elements.

Authored publications:

- *Creative Web Design with Adobe Muse (Focal Press)*
- *How to Cheat in Photoshop Elements (Focal Press)*
- *Focus on Photoshop Elements (Focal Press)*
- *Digital Photo Doctor (co-authored) (Reader's Digest)*

Table of Contents

3

The Basics of Image Editing   77

4

Getting Started with Simple Solutions   121

5

Easy Creative Projects 141

6

Advanced Techniques: Transformations, Layers, Masking, and Blend Modes 173

7

Advanced Techniques: Retouching, Selections, and Text   223

8

Additional Tools and Features   273

9

Advanced Drawing, Painting and Illustration Techniques 323

10

Exporting Work, Sharpening, and Plug-ins 373

11

Troubleshooting and Additional Techniques 411

12

Feature Appendix 435

Preface

Welcome to *Mastering Adobe Photoshop Elements 2023 - Fifth Edition*. This book is designed to take you on an image creation journey, from the absolute basics of photo editing all the way through to some of the most advanced and creative techniques possible using this comprehensive, powerful, and ever-popular image editing application.

Who this book is for

Mastering Adobe Photoshop Elements 2023 - Fifth Edition is written by a photographer for photographers of all skill levels. Its target audience is anyone with a thirst for knowledge and a desire to take control of their file organization while improving their visual creativity potential through the incredible power of photo editing.

Although novices are advised to start at the beginning, the book's structure is one that allows you to sample the chapters almost at random, depending on your skill level and the direction in which you might want to take your work.

It's certainly not an attempt to be the only book you'll ever need on the subject, but I hope it will entertain and inform those of you who want to escalate your level of expertise, from beginner through intermediate levels, and eventually toward being a professional in the fields of image creation, editing, photography, and even graphic design.

What this book covers

Chapter 1, Photoshop Elements Features Overview, firstly introduces you to the **new features** in this latest version. Not surprisingly, this includes several new **artificial intelligence (AI)** features - including animated graphics - that I'm sure you'll find useful.

To fully explain Elements, this chapter sets out how the program has been designed to operate and includes a typical **workflow scenario** as well as a clear explanation of the roles of all five sections of Photoshop Elements: the **Home Screen**, the **Organizer**, and, in the Photo Editor section, **Quick Edit** mode, **Guided Edit** mode, and finally, **Expert Edit** mode.

It also explains the importance of the application's organizational heart, the **Catalog**, plus its **panels**, **panel functions**, and the **Panel Bin**, along with the **Create**, **Share**, and **Enhance** menus. Finally, the chapter wraps up with a look at the relationship between Photoshop Elements and **Premiere Elements**, its video editing sibling.

Chapter 2, Setting Up Photoshop Elements from Scratch, helps you overcome the first hurdle of buying and installing the software. Your next move is to learn how to configure the application to produce the quickest and most efficient results. This chapter deals with how to prepare your camera (setting the correct **Color Space** in its menu), **best practices** for imaging computers (Windows and Mac), how to review all your media, as well as the all-important **media backup strategies**.

Following that is a description of the best ways to **import picture files** into the Organizer, plus all the techniques Elements provides for **organizing media**, using organizational tools such as **Star ratings**, **Keyword Tagging**, **Places**, **Events**, **People**, **albums**, **tags**, and **metadata**.

You'll also find a section on the different characteristics of the most **popular file formats**, **bit depth**, how to save your files, saving files as **Version Sets**, and **Managing Catalogs**. You'll also discover a new section on **digitzing photos** using a scanner and a camera. The final part of the chapter explains the basics of color management and screen calibration.

Chapter 3, The Basics of Image Editing, discusses the editing workflow and suggests a number of best practices. It illustrates how to get started with photo editing by covering a range of topics, including an in-depth look at **RAW file editing**, then 10 ways to get an image file opened in Elements, plus a look at **picture resolution** (and its impact on image quality). Other techniques discussed here include **cropping image files**, leveling photos with the **Straighten** tool, increasing or decreasing file size using a technique called **resampling**, applying "instant" **photo fixes** in the Organizer, and using the **Auto Correction** tools.

Besides getting up to speed with these basics, the chapter also covers how to master contrast, color, sharpness and clarity using the powerful **Levels**, **Hue/Saturation**, and **Shadow/Highlights** features.

At the end of the chapter, you'll discover how to create perfect skin tones using the **Smooth Skin** feature, plus basic but effective retouching techniques using the amazingly effective **Spot Healing Brush** tool.

Chapter 4, Getting Started with Simple Solutions. This all-new chapter sets out to answer some of the most popular photo editing queries. There are more than 15 examples - all of them have several possible solutions - these are ranked in order of simplicity.

Some questions include: '*What does the Histogram Do?*', '*How do I make a dull picture look great?*', '*How do I fix poor contrast?*', '*How do I make my shots look sharper?*', '*How can I remove someone from the image?*', '*How can I add a person from another image?*' and '*How do I make my photos look perfect in a print*' - and more.

Chapter 5, Easy Creative Projects. In this chapter, features covered include simple but effective "looks" using the massive range of creative **filters** found in Elements, including the range of **Artistic Effects**, creating a **Lomo Camera** 'look', an **Effects Collage**, making your own hand-coloring effects using the **Colorize Photo** tool, creating wide-screen and multi-deck panoramas with **Photomerge Panorama**, and delving into Elements' amazing **Photomerge Scene Cleaner** and its fun-to-use **Photomerge Faces Guided Edit** feature.

The chapter finishes with an overview of the easy-to-make **slideshow**, photo calendar, and greeting cards projects.

Chapter 6, Advanced Techniques: Transformations, Layers, Masking and Blend Modes, moves on from the basics described in previous chapters to turbo-charge your creativity.

The chapter introduces you to perspective correction, resizing pictures in pictures and warping shapes to make 3D shadows and text effects using **Transformations**. This is the place to discover the power of **Layers** as well as quick 'Pseudo' **Layer masking** effects, **Adjustment Layers**, **Adjustment Layer Masking**, and finally basic and advanced **Layer** techniques.

If that isn't enough, the chapter also demonstrates the power of layer based Blend Modes as well as Tool-based Blend Mode effects and Smart Objects.

Chapter 7, Advanced Techniques: Retouching, Selections, and Text, moves on from the power to Layers to look at fully understanding the use of retouching tools - in simple **beauty retouching**, using the powerful **Clone Stamp** tool, the magical **Healing Brush** and **Spot Healing Brush** tools, and the highly underrated **Burn**, **Dodge**, and **Sponge** tools. If adventurous you could go straight to the new **Advanced Retouching** section for greater in-depth features.

The chapter also highlights one of Elements' impressive retouching tools - the **Object Removal** Tool. We also tackle the complex world of **selections**, which, like layers, will transform how you edit images. There's also three of Elements' more esoteric, but highly effective retouching features: the **Blur**, **Sharpen** and **Smudge** brushes.

We also look at its effective **Subject Selection** feature, how to save your selections, **Feathering** selections, the **Refine Selection Brush** tool and the **Refine Edge** tool, before getting to grips with more advanced selection features like the **Marquee** and **Lasso** tools. We also take a look at the excellent **Magic Wand** tool, the **Selection Brush** tool, the **Quick Selection** tool, and the **Auto Selection** tools.

What many never appreciate is that Elements also features some great graphics tools, including the handy **Horizontal Type** tool—used, of course, to add text to images—plus all the different **type** and **font** options, as well as how to find, download, and use cool **custom fonts** for special projects.

Chapter 8, Additional Tools and Features, moves on from the power of **RAW file editing** and the basics of the **Levels** and **Hue/Saturation** tools and illustrates dozens more really excellent features to be found in Photoshop Elements. Some are **AI-driven**, while many others stem from the mightily handy **Guided Edit** mode.

In this chapter, you'll find a selection of more than 20 fabulous features that you might have passed by when performing routine edits. Some are **hugely visual** in their nature, some are designed for fixing photo problems, while others are there just for fun.

These include to **Adjust Color Curves**, the **Blur**, **Sharpen**, and **Smudge** brushes, the **Eraser** tools, **Smart Brush**, **Paint Bucket**, the **Gradient** tool, the **Haze Removal** tool, the **Content-aware Move** tool, the **Recompose** tool, the useful new **Extend Background** feature, the **Move and Scale Object** tool, **Moving Photos**, **Quote Graphics**, **Convert to Black and White**, **Duotone Effect**, **B&W Color Pop**, **Old Fashioned Photo**, **Perfect Landscape**, **Perfect Portrait**, the **Perfect Pet** feature, **Adjust Facial Features** (including its scary **Face Tilt** feature), and an equally scary but handy **Open Closed Eyes** feature.

Chapter 9, Advanced Drawing, Painting and Illustration Techniques, explains that Elements comes with a wide range of credible **graphics** and **illustration tools**, making it more of an all-around creative powerhouse than many might give it credit for.

To kick off this chapter, we highlight the best ways to master the handy **design** and **layout helpers** that you'll find under the **View** menu, plus the benefits of using **Brush** and **Pencil tools** (and their various **behaviors**).

This chapter also demonstrates the **Cookie Cutter tool**, the **Color Replacement Brush** and the **Impressionist Brush** - before moving on to cover some **basic drawing techniques**.

Elements has a large range of graphics tools - including scalable **Vector Graphics**, a handy **Custom Shape tool**, and a good selection of preset **Text Graphics**. We look at a basic DIY **custom greeting card project**, as well as **advanced vector designs**, **Texturizing** and other **Artistic Effects**. The back of this chapter encompasses **scrapbooking projects**, **Auto Page Layout** features, and amazing (free) downloadable **Custom Brushes**. The final section in this chapter takes you up another level with a **Photobashing** exercise demonstrating how to bring a wide range of photographic and graphic elements together to make your own custom illustrations. Finally there's a short section on **graphics tablets**.

Chapter 10, Exporting Work, Sharpening and Plug-ins. In this chapter, we look at the various resolution requirements for different social media platforms, as well as how to prepare files for print. Because so many photographers are now so reliant on the internet, it's important to get a handle on how to prepare pictures for display (using the **Save for the Web** feature), as well as how best to **sharpen** files for different print and online applications using the industry-standard **Unsharp Mask** tool, the excellent **Shake Reduction** tool, **High Pass Sharpening** effects, and the generic **sharpen filters**.

A new section deals with expanding the power of Elements by using third party **Plug-ins** - for sharpening your image files, for adding cool special effects - there are even plug-ins designed for converting your photographic images into something that looks a lot more like a painting. The sky's the limit!

Finally, this chapter takes a good look at how to export multiple instances of your work (with the **Export as New Files** feature), as well as how to bulk-process and even **copyright files** using the effective **Process Multiple Files** utility.

Chapter 11, Troubleshooting and Additional Techniques, deals with how to fix all the things that can go wrong when trying to manage a database of thousands, or tens of thousands, of images, and how to deal with image files that are not quite perfect. The chapter starts by explaining **file-saving protocols**: what options to go for. We also investigate what to do if files get **lost** or **disconnected** from the catalog, how to fully utilize the features of the powerful **Find** menu, adjusting dates for different time zones, as well as how to re-instate a lost or damaged **Catalog**. There's also information on how to fix resolution issues - typically when using low resolution files in print - using Resampling techniques.

You will also find a section on how to fix skin tone color (**Adjust Color for Skin Tones**), fix a color cast (**Remove Color Cast**), alter reality by adding **Lens Flare**, correcting **Lens Distortion**, creating your own **Depth of Field Effects**, plus how to **change eye color** and use the amazingly quirky **Liquify** filter.

Chapter 12, Feature Appendix, highlights all the tool features, panels, processes, and menus in Photoshop Elements. Use it to get more information on all the features in Elements, and check out the **author's personal feedback** on how effective or important many of these features might be for beginners.

To get the most out of this book

The point of this publication is that you don't need to have extensive experience before starting out in the world of photo editing. That was the premise of the original Adobe application many versions ago, and today, that idea, with the introduction of so many new AI-driven features, is stronger than ever.

That said, it would be immensely useful to have a fundamental knowledge of how computers operate, including Mac or Windows operating systems, and perhaps an inkling of basic image editing, just to get started. Also, be prepared to experiment with your images as much as you have the time for. It's the best way to learn.

Develop a network of friends or mentors who might be able to help you if you get stuck. To do this, you may find that it's a good idea to join a camera club in order to get help with both your photography and post-processing questions.

Above all, have fun, and experiment as much as you can.

Download the color images

We will provide all the color images and screenshots/diagrams used in the book for you to practice. You can download it here: https://packt.link/mCdiK.

You can also find the image bundle here: https://github.com/PacktPublishing/Mastering-Adobe-Photoshop-Elements-2023-Fifth-Edition.

Conventions used

There are a number of text conventions used throughout this book.

`Code in text`: Indicates code words in text, database table names, folder names, filenames, file extensions, pathnames, dummy URLs, user input, and Twitter handles. Here is an example: "TIFF files can end up being larger than the same file saved in the `.psd` format."

Bold: Indicates a new term, an important word, or words that you see onscreen. For example, words in menus or dialog boxes appear in the text like this. Here is an example: "Start the program and from the **Home Screen**, click the **Organizer** button."

> Tips or important notes
> Appear in boxes like this.

Get in touch

Feedback from our readers is always welcome.

General feedback: If you have questions about any aspect of this book, mention the book title in the subject of your message and email us at `questions@packtpub.com`.

Errata: Although we have taken every care to ensure the accuracy of our content, mistakes do happen. If you have found a mistake in this book, we would be grateful if you would report this to us. Please visit `http://www.packtpub.com/submit-errata`, selecting your book, clicking on the Errata Submission Form link, and entering the details.

Piracy: If you come across any illegal copies of our works in any form on the Internet, we would be grateful if you would provide us with the location address or website name. Please contact us at `copyright@packt.com` with a link to the material.

If you are interested in becoming an author: If there is a topic that you have expertise in and you are interested in either writing or contributing to a book, please visit `authors.packtpub.com`.

Share your thoughts

Once you've read *Mastering Adobe Photoshop Elements 2023, Fifth Edition*, we'd love to hear your thoughts! Scan the QR code below to go straight to the Amazon review page for this book and share your feedback.

https://packt.link/r/1803248459

Your review is important to us and the tech community and will help us make sure we're delivering excellent quality content.

Download a free PDF copy of this book

Thanks for purchasing this book!

Do you like to read on the go but are unable to carry your print books everywhere?

Is your eBook purchase not compatible with the device of your choice?

Don't worry, now with every Packt book you get a DRM-free PDF version of that book at no cost.

Read anywhere, any place, on any device. Search, copy, and paste code from your favorite technical books directly into your application.

The perks don't stop there, you can get exclusive access to discounts, newsletters, and great free content in your inbox daily

Follow these simple steps to get the benefits:

1.   Scan the QR code or visit the link below

https://packt.link/free-ebook/9781803248455

2.   Submit your proof of purchase

3.   That's it! We'll send your free PDF and other benefits to your email directly

Color keys

Hello reader,

I am excited for you to get your hands to this book and partner with you on this journey!

I wrote this book to include all the techniques I'd have loved to read and learn when I started off as a Photoshop artist. The book has been thoroughly updated with the latest features and techniques announced in PSE 2023 and I hope you enjoy reading and playing around with the tool as you progress and produce.

To make it easier for you to relate to the increasing complexity of the chapters, I've designed a color-key for this book. I've assigned a color stripe to every chapter to convey the difficulty level as follows:

Categories:	Skill Level Required
Photo Editing	Easy
Photo Editing	Intermediate
Photo Editing	Advanced
Projects	Easy
Illustration & Graphics	Intermediate to Advanced
Theory	Easy

Happy reading!

Robin Nichols

1
Photoshop Elements Features Overview

Adobe Photoshop Elements is a pixel-based graphics photo editing application that was first released in 2001. Its appearance followed on from an entry-level program called **Photoshop LE**, a light edition of Adobe Photoshop, which was a product made available mostly for students and teachers, though it was sometimes bundled with other hardware products at the point of sale. If you count its LE predecessor, Photoshop Elements 2023 is now in its 23rd version.

Initially, Photoshop Elements was released as a basic, entry-level product for consumer moms and dads trying to get their collective heads around digital technology. But over the years, it has dramatically expanded its feature set, inheriting many significant professional-level tools from its more complex sibling, Adobe Photoshop.

So, how different is Elements from Photoshop? Interestingly, Adobe maintains that the principle difference between the two is that Elements is still essentially a screen-based, **RGB** (**Red**, **Green**, and **Blue**) editing program, whereas Photoshop is not only a picture editing powerhouse—it's also designed to convert RGB files for work in the commercial **CMYK print space**—making it the go-to graphics application for all professionals working in print.

However, the market has changed significantly in the past 20 years, with so many more businesses trading online; therefore, the demand for print-ready conversions has reduced significantly. In my own experience, I have found that any good commercial print shop will gladly convert Elements' RGB files to its preferred CMYK color space, usually with only a nominal prepress charge, thus enabling everything produced using Elements to be commercially printed to the highest degree of quality.

In Elements 2023, you'll find a terrific range of sophisticated tools, features, and creative capabilities packed into an affordable editing package, making it a serious professional tool, as well as having the advantage of being simpler to use than Adobe Photoshop.

As you will quickly come to appreciate, this software is, in fact, made up of two separate applications, plus a number of different modes that are designed to address different user experience levels, all rolled into one bundle called Elements. Although it has technically evolved from other products, such as Adobe Photoshop LE and Photoshop Album, it's now an incredibly powerful and cohesive standalone tool designed for transforming photographic images, while remaining both affordable and, with each new version, increasingly easy to use.

What's important to learn in this chapter is that it's not necessary to know everything about Elements to succeed in editing your work—you can use just one, or a combination of its components to produce vibrant photo edits, or even impressive images from scratch, depending on your experience, creativity, and, indeed, your drive for perfection.

As you will see in the upcoming sections, this chapter is all about learning what each bit of Elements does—and therefore its relevance to your own picture creation workflow. And if you are indeed just starting out, the sections here will help you understand what's important right from the outset—and what can be tackled later, when you have more time and experience, to take more advanced features on board.

What you'll learn in this chapter:

- What's new in Elements 2023?
- How Elements is designed to work
- A typical workflow example
- The Home Screen
- The Organizer
- The Catalog
- The Edit modes: Quick Edit
- The Edit modes: Guided Edit
- The Edit modes: Expert Edit
- Panels and the Panel Bin
- Panel functions
- Create and Share menus
- The Enhance Menu
- Video and Premiere Elements

New: Peek Through Overlay

Sounds a bit corny, but this new Guided Edit effect is really neat, easy to use, and produces a very effective 'look' that, if you had to do it manually, might take hours to achieve!

What's New in Photoshop Elements 2023?

Unsurprisingly with this new release, you'll find a couple of nice new features that further expand its AI development. As with the previous version, its most notable new feature, Moving Elements, expands on its previously launched **Moving Overlays** to produce an animated GIF or MP4 video file. You'll also experience some housekeeping improvements—expanding its range of features such as overlays, backgrounds, templates, skies, and patterns, a beta version of Elements available anywhere via a Browser, plus improvements to the interface design including a Search function in the Guided Edit mode. Let's take a look at one of Elements' new features: **Moving Elements**.

Moving Elements

Ramping up the amazing range of cool features available via the **Enhance** menu, **Moving Elements** gives users the chance to animate their images—or rather, part of their images—through a relatively simple click, select, and (press) Play operation. Like most of Adobe's AI driven technology, this is actually a complex operation that's been rendered into a simple three-step process. And it actually works quite well—providing you choose the 'right' image (one where the part to be animated is easily distinguishable from the rest of the picture. Try this once and you'll see what I mean).

Adobe uses an image of a person gazing up at a waterfall—and the water appears to be flowing. It looks awesome but my version was not as good, as the water in my picture goes in two directions! I re-selected the water a second time and got a far better result. It's a fun feature to play with.

There's a new **Guided Edit Mode** feature called **Peek Through Overlay** that takes adding an overlay (i.e. a photo or graphic on a separate Layer) to new heights. With this fun addition you can add a range of (supplied) overlay images to one or all four corners to give, as the name suggests, the impression of peeking through foliage to see the subject (or a subject that's peeking out). Without the supplied artworks this probably wouldn't work (because you'd have to match image sizes and resolutions with the subject), but Adobe sensibly includes scalable overlays, plus a slider for changing the color (Hue), one for the color saturation, and, most importantly, the ability to perfect depth of field effects by blurring the top or bottom two overlays.

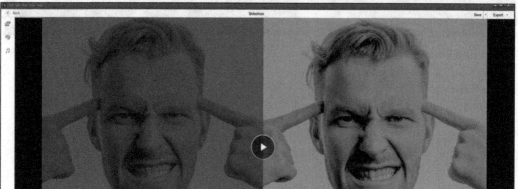

New Slideshow Themes: The original slideshow feature many versions ago was incredibly complex for an enthusiast application. The last version saw it being dumbed down so it was very easy to use. The 2023 version now boasts an expended preset theme list which is a welcome improvement. Creating a classy-looking slideshow is now easier than ever.

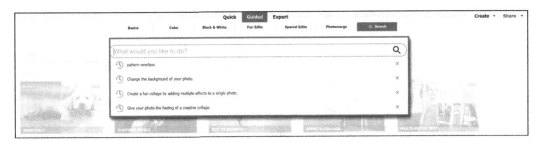

As with every new version release, you'll also note a few tweaks to the interface, including a new **Search** facility (highlighted here in red) in the **Guided Edit** mode, plus a bunch of productivity and performance improvements. I know a new Search menu sounds a bit lame, but as new features continue to be added into the Guided Edit Mode, it makes a heap of sense to put this Search engine front and centre. It works a treat.

Pattern Brush and **Replace Background** Though these are not new features—they now have a range of **new overlays**—just choose one from the extensive menu, choose to 'protect' the subject (Pattern Brush) and paint the effects into the image. The result is near instant and it looks great—AI technology at its best.

Mastering Adobe Photoshop Elements 2023

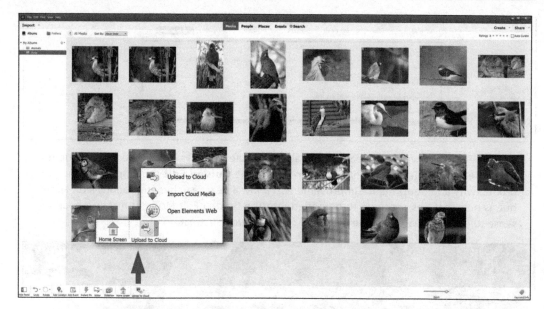

In Adobe's 2021 release of Elements, we saw the appearance of a **Save to Cloud** feature. At the time, it didn't attract much fanfare, and by the time Elements 2022 had been released, it had disappeared altogether. Now, as part of Adobe's Photoshop Elements 2023 release, the feature is back in the shape of 2GB of free cloud storage to subscribers (always nice to have) plus the ability to access a new browser feature. At the time of writing, this was just a beta version (offered only in English), but it's clear that by releasing this, Adobe plans to streamline its editing possibilities across all devices, thus making it considerably easier to share images and creations with family, friends, and work colleagues.

Above: Click the link in the Organizer (arrowed) or at the base of the Expert Edit window and select: Open Elements Web, Upload to Cloud, or Import Cloud Media.

Right: At the time of writing, you can only share images and videos, but there's also the ability to create slideshows as well as multi-image collages.

How Elements is designed to work

Elements' designers have produced an application that offers everything, from a comprehensive method of file organization (vital in such a media-rich environment), to a highly sophisticated level of editing prowess. It'll look a bit scary if you have not used this program before, but don't let this get in the way! Elements can be used in any number of different ways, from a super easy mode (see the new *How do I do that...* section), to super complex. It's entirely up to you which path you choose—and, of course, you can chop and change your editing style whenever the situation suits. Its "official" workflow might be something like the following:

With your images already transferred to a computer, install and start Elements. Start the program and from the **Home Screen**, click the **Organizer** button:

- Use the Organizer to import your media bit by bit so as not to overwhelm yourself—you can import stills, music, and even video clips.
- Sort your media into small, manageable groups using features such as **Albums**, **Keywords**, **Tags**, **Metadata**, **Face recognition**, and **GPS** co-ordinates—but there's no need to do this all at once. This is more a project for a rainy day.

Once your images are sorted, move on to the following:

- Perform basic edits on files displayed in the Organizer—using, for example, the **Instant Fix** tab (bottom left of the screen) or bringing them across to the Elements Photo Editor (a separate app from the Organizer). To bring them over, right-click the thumbnail image and choose **Edit with Photoshop Elements Editor** from the pop-out menu. This opens the file in either the Quick, Guided, or Expert Edit mode. (Note: you can easily change between these edit windows at any time.)
- Edit pictures using the **Quick Edit** mode. This part of Elements contains a wide range of easy, one-click photo fixes plus loads of special effects.
- Or, try editing your work using the more complex Expert Edit mode.
- Once finished, save the file as a `.jpg` (if destined for a photo book), a TIFF (`.tif`) file, or a Photoshop (`.psd`) file, if destined for print or more complex editing processes (such as retouching or adding text).

If you are not 100% sure of how to go about your picture editing, Elements offers the excellent **Guided Edit** mode, designed to hold your hand while it escorts you through the edit cycle in a clear step-by-step process. This is easy to follow and effective.

I hope that by reading through the various chapters and sections in this book, you'll begin to devise your own workflow. Remember, there's no right or wrong way to edit pictures, just the one that works best for you. Experiment with the different edit modes using the same file and you'll quickly come to appreciate what works for you—and what doesn't.

Guided Edit mode: The Guided Edit mode is as perfect for simple tone fixes as it is for more complex and creative project-type effects, like this striking **Painterly Effect**—which took me all of two minutes to complete.

Expert Edit mode: Even if you jump into the deep end and choose **Expert Edit**, many of its features, such as the excellent **Haze Removal** tool seen here, are easy to use and produce, in most picture examples, really impressive results (inset).

A typical workflow example

For your reference, here's how I use Elements.

First off, I always transfer images from a card reader directly into a pre-named folder on my computer or external hard drive (Mac or PC, whichever I am using at the time).

After each download, I try to remember to back up everything to a second drive—by dragging and dropping from one drive to the other (my external hard drives are formatted to be 100% readable by both PC and Mac computers—a tech term called ExFAT formatting).

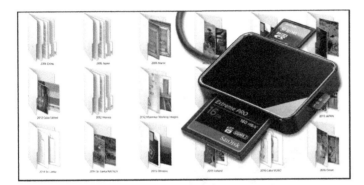

Card reader: Here's a glimpse of how I work with images. I manually download images straight into labelled folders. This is my **travel file**—so folders are labeled by year and destination. Inside each are more folders corresponding to each day of travel in that location.

Since I always specifically name folders each time I download a new batch of files, I don't need to use the Organizer a great deal—but I would recommend that beginners use it because, when it comes to making sense of all your work, you'll find it incredibly helpful.

I work almost exclusively in Expert Edit mode and always open images for editing using the keyboard shortcut *Ctrl/Cmd + O* to open files (PC/Mac).

Opening images for editing: From the **Open** dialog window, I navigate to the folder I'm after, then double-click the icon to open it, then double-click the image icon to get started. I'm lucky in that although I cannot always remember what I did last week, I can usually remember exactly where all my photos were saved. This somewhat old-fashioned technique has worked well for me for many years.

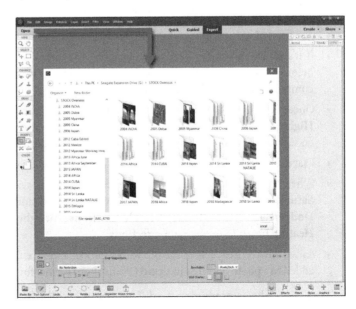

How I like to edit images

I've learned from years of picture editing that even though nearly every digital file might look fine on the camera's LCD screen, they are usually a bit lackluster once on the computer. This could be because the original lighting was poor, or because the computer screen is not calibrated. But it's most likely caused by the camera's operating software.

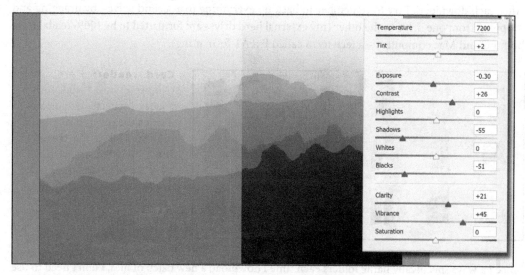

Editing Raw Files: Double-click a RAW file and it **must** open first in this special edit window. Here, you can achieve an amazing range of tonal improvements—from simple contrast and color boosts to noise reduction, cropping, and sharpening. The original is on the left, and the edited version (right) has had five sliders adjusted (in red) to add visual drama to the file.

Here's how I (try to) make each image pop on the page:

- The first thing is to correct the global tones in the file (using the contrast slider).
- If it's in the RAW file format, it opens in the Camera RAW window—see the preceding before/after image. (RAW files are large, and contain more picture information than the more commonly used JPEG file format.)
- Once there, I adjust the brightness and contrast, before fine-tuning the photo with the **Highlight**, **Whites**, **Shadows**, and **Blacks** sliders (but only if it needs it). This is normally enough to make the file look sharper, more contrasted, and more colorful.
- I save the file, giving it a proper name so it can be readily identified later.
- When editing non-RAW files, I use **Levels** for contrast and brightness adjustments, the **Hue/Saturation** tool to add/subtract color where needed, and, if required, I finish by using the **Dodge/Burn** brushes to exaggerate local darkness or lightness areas, plus sometimes the **Spot Healing** brush to remove imperfections.
- As with RAW files, I save the file with a proper name, either as a `.jpg` file (when it's being added to a photo book) or in `.psd` (Photoshop) format for when additional editing is required.

Let's move on to begin examining the different parts of this editing powerhouse.

The five faces of Adobe Photoshop Elements 2023

Here's a brief overview of the five main parts of Photoshop Elements that you'll encounter when working on your images—the **Home Screen**, **Organizer**, **Quick Edit**, **Guided Edit**, and **Expert Edit**. Generally, you might use just one or two of these windows—for example, the Organizer and the Expert Edit mode. But of course, you can freely swap between the editor and the Organizer, depending on your requirements—and skill level.

This is the **Home Screen**, the first panel you will see in Elements. Use it to gain inspiration from the range of auto creations, as a source of instruction (from the web links), or simply as a gateway to the other parts of Elements: the Organizer and the Quick, Guided, and Expert Edit modes.

This is the **Organizer**. Use this part of Elements to import and view all your pictures, Photoshop Elements projects, videos, and music clips. Use Organizer to sort your growing image collection into Albums, add Keywords, Tags, captions, and more. Or just use it as a jumping-off point to take images to one of the other three editing panels: the Quick, Guided, or Expert Edit modes.

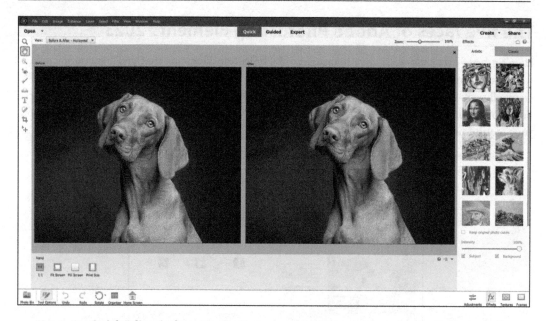

This is the **Quick Edit window**. Use this to make simple, impressive edits to photos brought directly from Organizer (or from folders). This shows the new **Effects>Artistic** looks that can be applied to any picture with just a simple click.

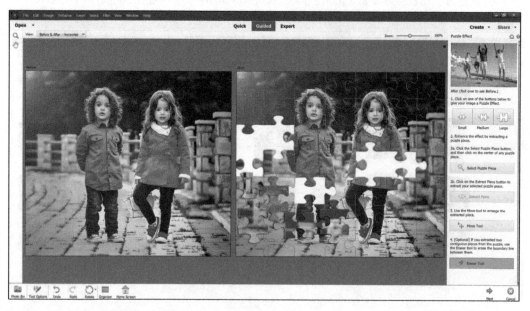

This is the **Guided Edit window**. Use this to transform your photos by following the step-by-step instructions displayed on the right-hand side of the screen. Here, I'm applying a jigsaw effect from the 'Fun' section in the Guided Edit menu.

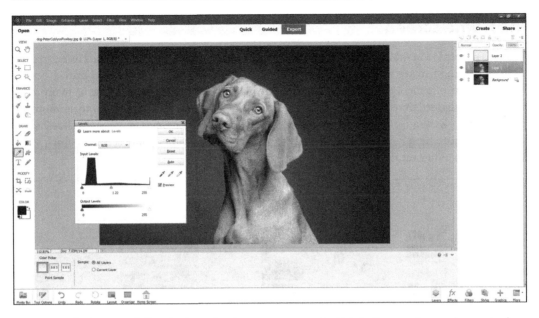

This is the **Expert Edit window**. As the name suggests, this is the most complex part of Elements because, unlike the Quick and Guided Edit modes, it has few instructions and even fewer one-button "fixes." You have to know what you want to achieve first—then you need to know what tools and techniques are required to make it all happen—so some prior experience would be of considerable benefit. Here it's showing the brightness and contrast adjusting tool, **Levels** (*Ctrl/Cmd + L* or **Enhance**>**Adjust Lighting**>**Levels**).

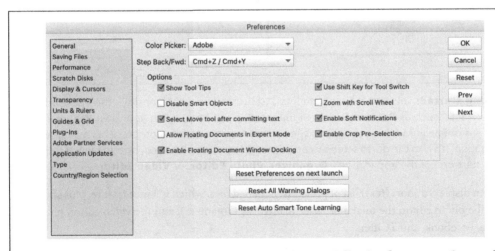

This is Elements' **Preferences** panel (*Ctrl/Cmd + K* or **Edit**>**Preferences**>**General**). It's not one of the five main panels, but it's worth knowing about—it does have its uses. Here, you can change things such as how files are saved, units of measurement, grid size and color, some key shortcuts, computer resources, transparency settings, and plug-in data.

The Home screen

What was referred to in Adobe Photoshop Elements 2018 as the eLive screen is now the **Home** screen. It's the first thing you see when Elements starts and, like its predecessor, is there to provide users with creative inspiration on how to edit images, embark on creative projects, and use its many auto creations (highlighted in red in the following screenshot). You can use it to learn how to accomplish basic editing tasks and for fun activities such as creating YouTube memes, automated slideshows, movies, and more, simply by clicking any of the pictorial links on the Home screen—which then takes you to an online tutorial.

Getting started: This is the new Elements 2023 Home screen. Over time, the application adds effects (such as **Pattern Brush**, highlighted in red here) using your own images and provides online links (along the top of the screen) to more creative processes as a source of inspiration. It's also the go-to screen to open previously edited files (icons on the lower right), or to start one of the applications: **Organizer**, **Photo Editor**, or **Video Editor**.

The screen displays a short (text) list of previously opened files, which is a nice feature, plus shortcuts to open the photo editor, the media browser (called the Organizer), and the video editor, plus links to Adobe, Facebook, and Twitter.

It's important to note that if you've not bought Elements and Premiere Elements together as a bundle, clicking the third icon, **Video Editor**, will prompt you to download and try Premiere Elements. Buying the bundle saves a fair chunk of money and makes sense because so many of us shoot video—plus you'll find several new features in Elements 2023 are now animated and so must be saved in a motion graphic file format such as .gif or .mp4.

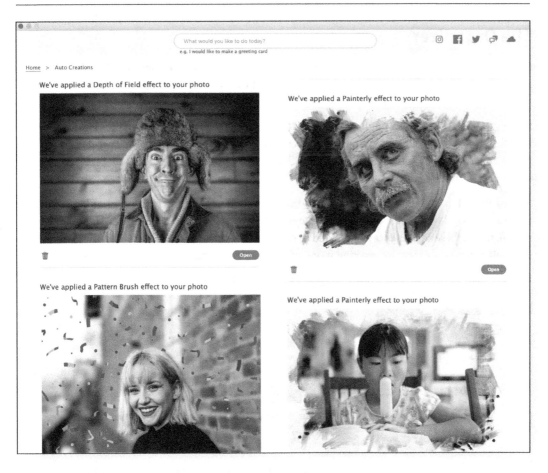

Auto creations are amazing—Elements picks random images from your Organizer collections and applies a selection of AI-driven features to them. I was quite surprised when I first saw this because I had forgotten that Adobe was doing the hard work for me! Though its image selection isn't always appropriate, it's still an effective preview feature.

If you are already using Adobe Premiere Elements 2023, you'll notice several new features, including the handy auto reframing feature, animated overlays, better shadow and highlight controls, plus easier file compression for refining image quality over a range of different display media. But that's a topic for another book...

Photoshop Elements users will note that to begin with, the handy **Auto Creations** feature on the Home screen remains blank until you import images to the Organizer.

Because the Home page is linked to Adobe's servers, it also provides access to the **Help** menu, plus thousands more pages of inspiration covering a massive range of topics, from basic tone enhancement and scrapbooking to pro-standard retouching techniques and much, much more.

The Organizer

One drawback of digital photography is that we accumulate **masses of images** and other assets like audio files and video clips. Keeping track of everything can be a nightmare, especially if you plan on upgrading your skill set from keen amateur status to something approaching a professional occupation.

Sorting everything into meaningful collections, therefore, is the main function of the Organizer. Once installed, note that it runs as a separate application, albeit one with almost inseparable ties to the photo-editing part of Elements, and, indeed, with its video-editing partner, Adobe Premiere Elements (often sold with Elements as a bundle).

Photos and other digital assets are imported into the Organizer and sorted into meaningful groups using a range of clever tools such as **albums**, **keywords**, **labels**, **place** and **people tags**, **star ratings**, and **metadata**. All these attributes can be applied to your files which means its organizational and file search capabilities are very extensive, making it one of the best asset management systems in the business.

The Organizer is also the place to go for quick fixes—called Instant Fixes—as well as a number of other creative activities, such as:

- Making collages
- Calendars
- Greeting cards
- Quote graphics
- Slideshows

We also use the Organizer for uploading our creations to the new (beta) Adobe web browser, as well as to social media platforms such as Vimeo, Twitter, Facebook, and YouTube.

The Catalog

Elements refers to your image files using **links**—nothing is ever physically moved into the application. When files are imported, Elements makes links to where the images are kept (normally this is in the `Pictures` folder but it could also be other hard drives in the computer or external drives). This linking information, along with all the metadata, image thumbnails, tags, attributes, and keywords—in fact, everything you do with the program—is what is saved in the all-important **catalog**.

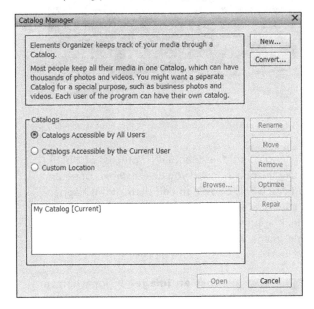

Occasionally, you will be reminded to "back up" this catalog. If you have simply downloaded and installed Elements and proceeded to get on with your image organization and editing, you might not even know that there was a catalog, or what it does. It's important from back up this catalog on a drive that's separate to where Elements is running. An external hard drive is a good choice for this task.

The **Catalog Manager (Organizer>File> Manage Catalogs)** provides the ability to monitor one or multiple catalogs. To start, I'd recommend just having the one catalog. Having multiple catalogs is a good idea if you share Elements with your partner, your kids, or perhaps your work colleagues, but, because you can only ever open one catalog at a time, it makes sense just to start with one.

Though your original high-resolution files are not stored in the catalog, copies of the files are. Catalogs should be backed up periodically onto a separate hard drive—preferably one that doesn't contain your original image file. We'll cover this in detail in *Chapter 2, Setting Up Photoshop Elements from Scratch*.

Tip:

Rotating your photos one at a time can be a drag. Select multiple images in the Organizer (Shift-Click to select multiples) then use the Rotate button (base of Organizer) to Rotate left or right and job done! It's an easy and fast technique.

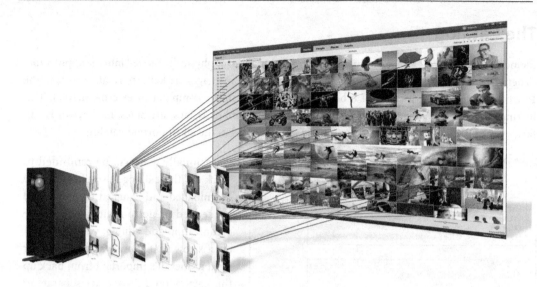

Links: As you can see from this illustration, "importing" files is actually a process of "linking" files—from their original location—to the Organizer window. If you delete, move, or rename any imported files, it will break the link and you won't be able to edit them. If this happens, Elements should immediately search for the missing file based on the name it imported with the metadata. If it locates the lost file, it automatically re-links it. If not, then you can manually search for the lost files. (A single image will have multiple links if it appears in multiple Organizer albums.)

Lost an image? If, for whatever reason, you lose a few files—something that does happen from time to time—Elements can be sent in hot pursuit of the errant images. When files are imported into the application, although it never copies the actual image files, it does bring in data such as file names, the metadata, and a thumbnail image—so Elements *does* know what that missing file looks like and what its name is. In my experience, provided that the missing files have not been renamed or deleted, the software will eventually locate them for you (**Organizer>File>Reconnect All Missing Files**).

Photo Editor: Quick Edit mode

Adobe presents its editing features in three different windows or edit modes located in Photo Editor, which is a separate application from the Organizer. If you are a newcomer to Elements, I'd suggest starting with the simplest editing mode—this is the Quick Edit mode.

Quick Edit 'before' and 'after': As you can see here, in the Quick Edit mode, the image being edited can be displayed in different view formats: a **before** view, an **after** view, or, as seen here, the more useful before-and-after view mode. The right-hand side of the screenshot displays some of the excellent single-click effects available in this mode (accessed by clicking the **Effects** tab, arrowed, at the bottom of the screen). In fact, there are 55 to choose from (5 variants of 11 originals), plus 30 new artistic looks (accessed at the top of the tab). This is a fantastic feature, producing one-click results, many of which are quite inspirational.

During the editing process, you'll use the Organizer to search for and find images that are then opened in one or, depending on your creative requirements, several of the three edit modes. After editing, they are saved and appear updated back in the Organizer. The process of getting images from the Organizer to the editor is dealt with in detail in *Chapter 3*, *The Basics of Image Editing*.

(Note that all three edit modes are interchangeable. This means that you can easily transfer an image from Quick, to Guided, to Expert, and back again, if needed.)

The Quick Edit mode enables users to make simple but significant improvements to any picture using a range of tonal adjustments. These are listed in a specific top-to-bottom order so as to produce the best editing workflow. Adjustments include **Smart Fix**, **Exposure**, **Lighting**, **Color**, **Balance**, and **Sharpness**.

This screenshot shows an enlarged view of the Quick Edit mode's Toolbar (top left) as well as its tool **Options** panel (lower left, set for the **Horizontal Type** tool), and its basic but effective **Effects** panel, far right—opened by pressing the **Effects** tab (enlarged, bottom right). Effects now encompass the original list of Classic Effects plus 40 new artistic "looks."

This mode's tools include the following:

- **Zoom tool**—used for enlarging/reducing the size of images onscreen
- **Hand tool**—used for moving a greatly enlarged image around the screen
- **Quick Selection tool**—ideal for selecting/isolating specific parts of the image
- **Eye tool**—specializes in removing red-eye and (green) pet-eye
- **Whiten Teeth tool**—selects and brightens teeth in one easy action
- **Straighten tool**—an easy way to level wonky horizons
- **Type tool**—specifically designed for adding text to an image
- **Spot Healing and Healing Brush tools**—powerful tools for retouching photos
- **Crop tool**—a ubiquitous tool for cutting bits off your image to recompose the frame
- **Move tool**—the ideal tool for repositioning elements such as text

The performance of each tool, throughout all edit modes, can be modified using the **Tool Options** panel, which pops up from the bottom of the screen when clicked.

Photo Editor: Guided Edit mode

As the name suggests, the Guided Edit workspace is packed with step-by-step instructions that guide you through a range of tasks—from tone fixes to far more complex processes such as panorama stitching and special type effects; there are 47 to be exact, presented in a beautifully designed and easy-to-use format. All you need to do is choose one of the effects and follow the step-by-step directions—easy!

Topics include **Basics, Color, Black & White, Fun Edits, Special Edits, Photomerge** (a mini-application designed for stitching images together into widescreen panoramas, among other things) and a new **Search** feature.

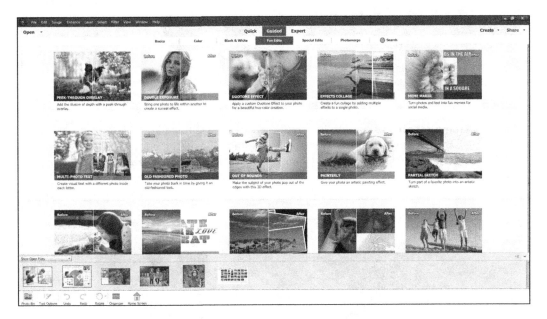

Guided Edit mode is a creative powerhouse. This screenshot demonstrates what the Guided Edit screen looks like (with the **Fun Edits** tab selected). Note that while this screen is visually quite busy, its interactive design makes it quite clear what each of these effects looks like when applied to the samples pictured. I think this is a greatly underrated feature.

All you do is swipe the cursor left or right over each thumbnail to reveal the effect in a before/after style. This is good, practical software design that should find its way into a whole range of other software applications.

The Guided Edit mode is a great source of creativity, more so perhaps than the current Home screen. For example, if you are a bit stuck with what direction to take your photo-editing in, just open a picture in this mode and try some of the effects offered; most of them are bound to get your creative juices flowing nicely.

Pattern Stamp magic: It's hard to illustrate the extent of Guided Edit mode because it's packed with so many great features, so where do you start? The preceding screenshot perfectly illustrates a feature (first introduced in Elements 2020) called **Pattern Brush**. This updated version contains 11 new patterns including, as you see above, a cloud brush.

Now you see it, now you don't: Another **Guided Edit** feature (introduced in Elements 2020) is called **Object Removal** (find it under the Guided Edit **Basic** tab). As with many Guided processes, this tool combines a complex editing action involving selections and object cloning, with nothing more than a swish of the cursor to make it work. Brilliant! More on this feature in *Chapter 6, Advanced Techniques: Transformations, Layers, Masking and Blend Modes*.

Photo Editor: Expert Edit mode

Having played with the Quick and Guided Edit modes, you might find this advanced editing workspace a little challenging, especially if you are a newcomer to photo editing.

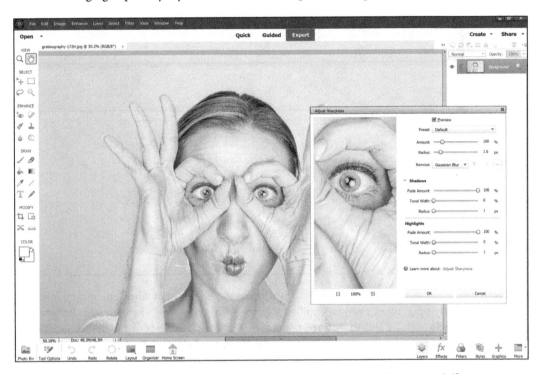

Expert Edit Mode: In this edit mode, most features are manually operated (for greater creative control), here showing the **Adjust Sharpness tool** (**Enhance**>**Adjust Sharpness**).

When using the Expert Edit mode, it's a good idea to have an editing plan—a basic idea of what you'd like to achieve visually once the image is open in the main window. Some experience with the tools is also important—but you'll have picked up a lot of experience using them from experience gleaned with the previous two edit modes. In some ways, the Expert Edit mode resembles Adobe Photoshop—although I'd add that it also contains a lot of processes that you will not find in Photoshop. We will cover this in greater detail in *Chapter 5, Easy Creative Projects*.

Don't let the name put you off; its basic tools (dealt with in more depth in *Chapter 3, The Basics of Image Editing*) are easily mastered, providing you with a raft of powerful creative options.

Essentially, everything offered here is more customizable than in the Quick and Guided Edit modes. Learning what everything does takes time and experience but, once you have played with some of the tools in the first two modes, moving into the Expert domain will be significantly easier.

Photoshop Elements Features Overview

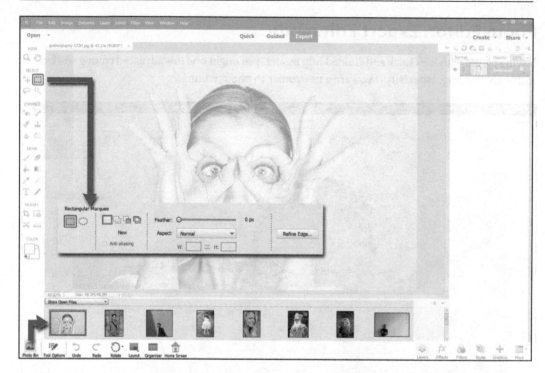

Photo Bin: As in all the edit modes, the main window has a Photo Bin (arrowed, bottom left), where currently-open photos can be shuffled into the main edit space. There are also **Rotate**, **Undo**, and **Redo** buttons, and an **Options** panel (here it's floating in the center of the screen) for the current tool (in this example, it's the **Rectangular Marquee Selection Tool**. This panel allows you to fine-tune the tool's performance—a very handy panel to familiarize yourself with because it allows you to finely control the efficacy of each tool—and therefore, hopefully, your results.

Once your images have been edited to perfection, you'll need to either incorporate them into a project, such as a slideshow or photo book, export them to a printer, or upload them to your favorite social media site. This is where the **Create** and **Share** menus come in very handy. Let's take a look at what these menus offer.

> **Tip:**
>
> When it comes to operating systems, don't worry about the old **Mac versus Windows** dilemma. After years of producing two different versions of this excellent software, Adobe finally settled its differences with Apple (over iPhoto). Now, the only difference between Elements running on the two operating systems comes down to the names of two keyboard keys (*Command* and *Control*) making life for those of us switching between Mac and Windows a breeze. As to whether one operating system works better than the other, that's a discussion I can leave to these two TV advertising rivals from 2009, on the left.

Working with panels and the Panel Bin

You'll find the most important panels in the Panel Bin, located on the right-hand side of the main screen in the Quick and Expert Edit modes. While they might not be the most glamorous part of this application, panels still play an important part in your day-to-day workflow.

Using Styles – drop shadows and more: Styles, third panel from the right (arrowed), contains a lot of special effects—from a simple **color filter** to something a lot more sophisticated, such as the plastic look yellow neon effect seen on my *La Habana*, Cuba text layer. One click on the thumbnail and the effect is applied. Easy.

The principle panels in the Quick Edit mode are the **Adjustments** panel (*Chapter 3, The Basics of Image Editing*), **Effects**, **Textures**, and **Frames** (*Chapter 4, Getting Started with Easy Solutions*). The Expert Edit mode has a wider selection of panels, including **Layers**, **Effects**, **Filters**, **Styles**, and **Graphics** (*Chapter 5, Easy Creative Projects*).

There are more panels to be found in the Expert Edit mode (**Actions**, **Color Swatches**, **Favorites**, **Filters**, **History**, **Histogram**, **Info**, and **Navigator**), accessed either by clicking on the **More** button (at the bottom and to the extreme right), or by using the **Window** drop-down menu (top of the page). Most panels have their own menus, designed to organize the features each holds and, most importantly, to help you find the stuff you really need.

Panels, Panels, Panels Everywhere! I've cheated a bit here—adding a bunch of panels onto the same screen to illustrate how many functions Elements has—there are hundreds of effects, graphics, styles, and filters available for your editing fun and creativity. Those used frequently can be dragged to the **Favorites** Panel found under the 'More' tab (arrowed) or under the **Window** menu at the top of the page.

Window
Images ▸
✔ **Tools**
Actions
Adjustments
Color Swatches
Effects   F2
Favorites
Filters   F3
Graphics   F7
Histogram   F9
History   F10
Info   F8
Layers   F11
✔ Navigator   F12
Styles   F6
✔ Panel Bin
Reset Panels

Tips:

- If you accidentally close a panel by clicking the **x** icon at the top-right of the panel on Windows, or the top-left of the panel on a Mac, it's easy to reinstate that same panel from the **Window** drop-down menu.

- Some panels can also be reactivated using a keyboard shortcut, which is listed to the right hand side of all drop-down menus.

- Although panels 'live' in the Panel Bin, you can drag them out of the bin and arrange them so they 'float' over the work area by choosing **Custom Workspace** from the tiny tab on the right-hand side of the 'More' panel (see arrowed above) then clicking, holding, and dragging the appropriate tab to reposition it over the main edit window.

Panel Functions

Elements has many panels, each providing essential help with certain aspects of the editing process. Some refer to the Quick Edit mode only (such as **Adjustments**), while others only appear in the Expert mode (such as the **Info** panel).

Here's an overview of what each panel offers:

- **Adjustments**: This provides sliders to adjust the **Exposure**, **Lighting (contrast)**, **Color**, **Balance**, and **Sharpness** settings.
- **Effects**: Provides the user with a great range of looks—automated effects recipes that can be applied to an image with a single click; it now includes 40 new "artistic" looks.
- **Textures**: Elements has a wide range of assets, such as surface textures, that, once clicked, are added to the file as an overlay. Good for backgrounds, web pages, and so on.
- **Frames**: Used mostly for graphic artwork. Click on an asset thumbnail in the panel and it downloads it from www.adobe.com, before automatically resizing and applying itself to the image. Clever stuff!
- **Filter**: The small thumbnails try to illustrate the effect of each FX filter. Click once on the thumbnail to apply the effect. Use the associated slider to vary the intensity of each effect. There are 98 different filters with millions of possible combinations.
- **Styles**: Single-click presets used to change an object, such as text, on its layer. Use **Styles** to add features such as drop shadows, bevels, glows, and patterns. Most are used for the purposes of design rather than to improve the image. This panel holds 176 different styles.
- **Actions**: An action is a small file of recorded instructions, an automated feature inherited from Photoshop. The supplied actions can be 'played' on images to achieve goals such as adding a border, resizing, and cropping. You can find more actions online. Download and import them into Elements to boost the paltry range supplied by default.
- **Graphics**: This panel contains a lot of (downloadable) assets: clip art, text effects, scalable vector shapes, and a huge range of picture frame styles—all of which can be applied through a single click. Because there are so many assets here, you can sort them according to **Type**, **Activity**, **Mood**, **Event**, and more. **Graphics** contains over 1,000 assets—most have to be downloaded first before they are ready to use.
- **Color Swatches**: These are used to choose colors for a range of features, from type of pencil, to paintbrush, to background colors. The panel allows you to make your own custom swatches for specific projects.
- **Favorites**: This is a big time-saver; you can keep your frequently used styles and graphics in one place by dragging the relevant thumbnail into the **Favorites** panel.
- **Histogram**: This displays the range of tones present in any image and, more accurately, where in the brightness range those tones sit (such as mid-tone, highlights, whites, blacks, underexposed, and overexposed).
- **History**: A useful panel that displays your editing steps—from opening an image to saving the new work. Click on any of the steps displayed to go back to a previous edit state, mouse click by mouse click. This is handy if you decide that you have edited the image a bit too much; just click back a few steps to a previous version.

- **Navigator**: This is another unsung hero of this program. The **Navigator** panel displays the image you have open in the main window. This is especially useful when the main window display is enlarged so that it is bigger than the screen, because it's then hard to know which part of the image you are seeing.

- **Info**: This is a useful panel that displays the RGB brightness values in any part of the image that you mouse over. The readout works regardless of the tool currently being used.

- **Layers**: Possibly the most important panel for advanced projects where text and multiple objects are added to a document, on separate layers, thus maintaining full editability throughout the production process.

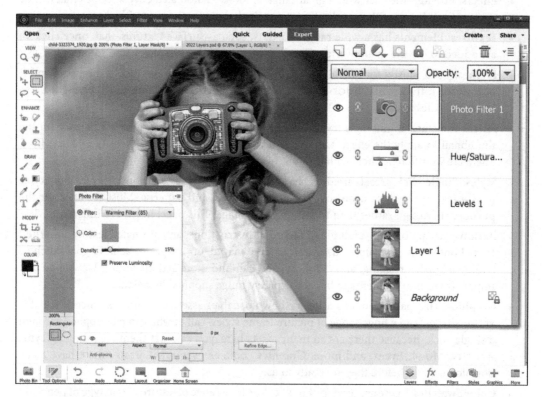

The **Layers** panel (enlarged, top right) is one of the most useful panels because it enables you to manage text, selections, images, and vector objects all in one (multi-layered) file. To preserve editability at every stage, layers must be kept separate in the one file and saved in either the Photoshop file format (`.psd`) or the TIFF file format (`.tif`) both of which preserve the layer integrity. The panel shows the original image layer (called **Background** by default), a copied layer (**Layer 1**), a **Levels Adjustment** layer, a **Hue/Saturation** adjustment layer, and a **Photo Filter** adjustment layer at the top of the stack. The white rectangles are editable masks, one for each layer—their white state indicates that they are currently transparent and are therefore not affecting the image. You'd use these to carefully limit each tonal change to very specific parts of the image by painting into the mask—more on this in *Chapter 6, Advanced Techniques: Transformations, Layers, Masking and Blend Modes*.

The Create and Share menus

When digital photography became mainstream 20 years ago, there were precious few things you could do with your images other than looking at them on low-resolution screens—digital printing was in its infancy, as were reliable computers, the internet, and editing software. It took programs such as Photoshop Elements to introduce us to the concept of doing something more than just looking at images on a screen. It began with a few creative projects and is now driving a huge range of activities, ranging from book printing to slideshows, scrapbooking, and custom stationery.

Effective automation: Creative projects are an excellent way to execute relatively complex actions with ease. In the screenshot here, all I did to complete this layout was find six different photos, open them, then choose **Photo Collage** from the **Create** menu (top right). The application automatically arranges the files according to the layout chosen in the right-hand panel, and it's done. A time-consuming process performed automatically here in seconds— that's genius! Even better news: the new 2023 version packs in twice as many templates, opening up your potential even further.

Running through both the Organizer and all three edit modes, you'll spot the highly useful **Create** and **Share** menus. The Organizer is used as a media browser for still images, music files, and video clips, so it's designed to work with both Elements and its consumer video-editing sibling, Premiere Elements. In it, you'll find a few additional features offered, in both the **Create** and **Share** menus, notably for producing video projects and uploading them to video-centric sites such as Facebook, YouTube, and Vimeo.

Some of its original projects provide the user with great creative options—for example, anything from making a slideshow, photo collage, photo book, to greeting cards and calendars. As suggested, its **Share** menu just provides you with the easy option of uploading your newly crafted work directly to Facebook, Twitter, email, Vimeo, YouTube, or the desktop.

It's possible to buy Photoshop Elements as a standalone photo editor but, as is often the case, it's also sold bundled with its moving-picture sibling, Adobe Premiere Elements, simply because the line between still images and video has become increasingly blurred.

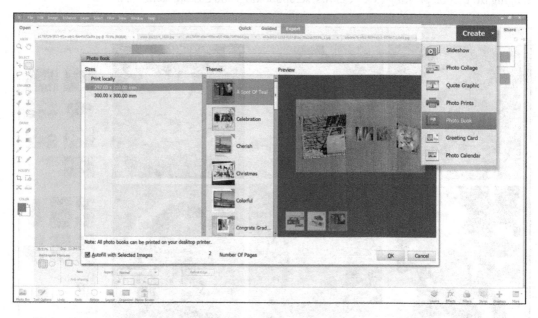

Create menu features: Use the **Create** menu to start a range of cool, creative projects—such as making a **Photo Book**. Choose the theme, size, and number of pages, then drag and drop your pictures into the automatically generated frames, add text, and print locally.

Otherwise, these two drop-down menus are identical, enabling users, after the editing is done, to incorporate them into one of the many creative projects offered, and then to share them immediately, directly out of Elements, with a range of social media platforms or local destinations such as the desktop. Interestingly, you'll also find a new feature lurking in this menu; it's called **Quote Graphics** (there's an example to the right) and is designed, as the name might suggest, to make it easy for you to add text—quotes or simple prose—into images or one of the many supplied graphics. Like many features in this application, **Quote Graphics** makes the often frustrating process of working with the **Type** tool a lot easier and more fun.

The Enhance Menu

Aside from the panels and easy-to-use single-click effects available scattered about the Elements edit modes, the application is also bristling with drop-down menus. These provide the basics—such as commands for a new document (**File>New Document**), opening an existing document (**File>Open**), and closing a document (**File>Close**), pretty much as you'd expect to find in other photo-editing applications. We deal with these menus in later chapters, as well as at the back of the book in the *Feature Appendix*.

I regard the **Enhance** menu as the most creative of all the menus—this is where you'll find many of Elements' excellent tools, both automated and manual.

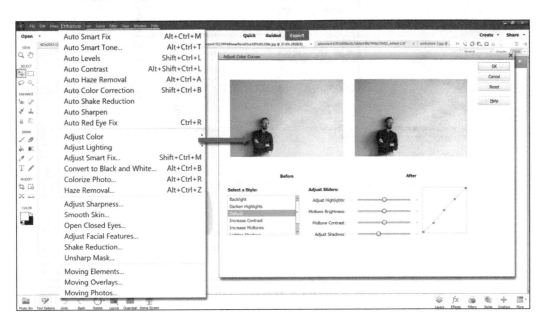

Try everything in the Enhance menu: One of the lesser-known tools, **Color Curves**, is a good color correction tool inherited, in a modified form, from Adobe Photoshop CC (see *Chapter 8*, *Additional Tools and Features,* for more on this tool).

Another impressive AI-driven feature, **Colorize Photo**, is one of my all-time favorites because it works so well on a wide range of image types.

Enhance is stacked with good stuff for the serious image editor. It has 30+ fantastic features—most of which are easy to use and produce outstanding results with little or no need for much previous experience.

Mastering Adobe Photoshop Elements 2023

Working with video and Premiere Elements

Adobe Premiere Elements targets the consumer video-editing market and, increasingly so, these two applications are often sold as a bundle, which incidentally should save you money of around 25% or more compared to buying the two applications separately.

Video timeline: As with most video editors, Premiere Elements 2023 features a non-linear timeline along which your clips are arranged. You can do this manually—or leave it to one of its auto video functions. It comes with a wide range of manual and automated features—many of which might look more at home in a top-of-the range professional application. Another very handy feature is its automated **Quick Movie** function—just find a few clips and the application edits them into a video in a matter of minutes!

We can use the Organizer to catalog still images, as well as HD video clips, **GIFs (Graphics Interchange Format** files used to record short animations), audio tracks, and music, together or separately, depending on the work planned. Once organized, files can then be opened in either application—Elements Photo Editor or Premiere Elements—depending on how they are to be used. I edit quite a lot of video, so I find this close relationship incredibly convenient, especially where I might need to use still images in a video project or video clips in a still image story that's, for example, to be exported to Facebook, Vimeo, or shared online with the new Adobe Web Browser. And as you'll see in Elements 2023, some of the new features, such as **Moving Elements**, are designed to use still images but export the animation as a .gif file.

Other new and innovative features include an **auto reframe** capability, allowing users for example to crop a horizontally-composed frame to display seamlessly vertically on a smartphone, serious **noise reduction** (a big problem with underexposed video clips), the same **artistic looks** that you find in Elements 2023 Quick Edit Mode, brand-new video slideshow **templates**, heaps more (free) music tracks and, very excitingly, an all-new **stop motion** feature (screen shot above).

Additionally, like Elements, Premiere employs some incredibly powerful features that include image stabilization; an amazing instant movie feature; a wide range of professional effect looks (a 'look' is a pre-recorded editing recipe designed to add a specific color, tone, or emotion to a video clip—they are great time-savers); sophisticated brightness, contrast, color, and sharpness tools; and an export function that allows you to easily upload any completed video project to social media effortlessly. The new version boasts some truly innovative AI-driven features, such as auto subject selection and tracking, video double-exposure, and animated matte overlays—features that, till now, were only ever found in high-end professional software.

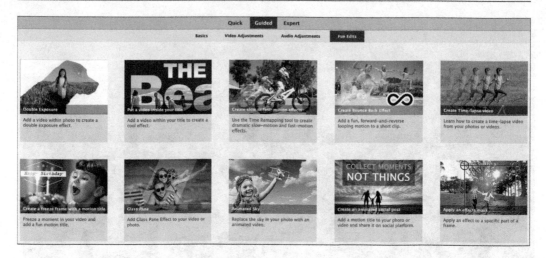

Like Photoshop Elements, Premiere Elements also has **Quick**, **Guided**, and **Expert** Modes. Guided Edit mode has all you need to take you step-by-step through the video-editing process, significantly speeding up the process of movie making.

To the novice, Premiere Elements might seem unduly complex. Being a video-editing application, it does deal with images and time together as a single process, but this application is very much like Elements' Photo Editor: you can skim through it using the automated video tools in Guided Edit mode, or explore its many professional standard editing features to produce a movie of outstanding quality.

The relationship between Premiere Elements and Adobe Premiere Pro, Adobe's high-end editing suite, is similar to that between Elements and Photoshop. It began as a simpler version of the high-end commercial product, but it's now one of the best video editors on the market.

If you are considering moving into video production, this is a very capable and professional tool with a great range of guided and automated functions that makes the often tedious job of editing video clips a breeze.

Create menu features

Elements' **Create** menu is stacked with great features—but watch out, the list of what's available is slightly different between what you'll find in the **Organizer** versus the **Editor**.

The **Create** menu (**Organizer**) contains links to the following:

- Slideshow
- Photo Collage
- Quote Graphic
- Photo Prints
- Photo Book
- Greeting Card
- Photo Calendar
- Video Story
- Video Collage

The **Create** menu (**Editor**) contains fewer links:

- Slideshow
- Photo Collage
- Quote Graphic (image below)
- Photo Prints
- Photo Book
- Greeting Card
- Photo Calendar

You'll see A LOT of keyboard shortcuts in the following chapters. My advice to all learners is to pick up maybe 10 to 15 of your favorites, and research the rest when the need arises. After all, no one can be expected to remember all the hundreds of published shortcuts.

Here are 10 of my favorite shortcuts:

Ctrl/Cmd + O (Opens a file).

Ctrl/Cmd + W (Closes a file).

Shift + Ctrl/Cmd + S ('Save File As' - this allows you to rename a file, if needed).

Ctrl/Cmd + Q (Quits or closes Elements down completely).

Ctrl/Cmd + N (Create a new, blank, document).

Ctrl/Cmd + L (Opens Levels - the best brightness and contrast adjustment tool).

Ctrl/Cmd + U (Opens the Hue/Saturation tool - the best color adjustment tool).

Ctrl/Cmd + A ('Select All' - selects the entire image).

Ctrl/Cmd + C (Copies whatever is in a selection and places it in the clipboard).

Ctrl/Cmd + V (Pastes the clipboard content into the currently open document).

Summary

In this chapter, we have learned about the different parts that make up the Photoshop Elements image-editing application. We have also taken a peek at some of the great new features found in this 2023 version. This innovative software package not only offers a comprehensive suite of truly professional editing tools, but its Organizer, running as a separate application to the main edit modules, can be used to catalog all our media assets and display them in one place: as stills, music, clips, and even HD videos. We have also discovered that you can even start editing your work in the Organizer. fixing the color and contrast at the click of a mouse, as well as adding your work to a range of very neat step-by-step fun projects via its very handy Create Menu. Even so, its basic function is to help you get your stuff into some kind of order.

Once done, depending on the level of editing required, and your experience, it's relatively simple to jump from the Organizer into one of the three Edit Modes to achieve complex edits—in many cases using one of the semi-automated AI-driven processes seen in the Quick Edit mode.

We have also seen that, as Adobe continues to develop its artificial intelligence capabilities, there's a move from the realms of pure image editing to producing social media-ready animated graphics that can be uploaded directly to your favourite Sites, and it's something that's further enabled through its association with its sister application, Adobe Premiere Elements.

If project-based exercises are not your thing and you feel you want to take your editing up a notch, we now know that it's also possible to take far greater control by exploring the powerful Expert Edit mode in greater depth, harnessing the power of Layers, Selections, Masks, Blend Modes, text and graphics.

The next chapter highlights the best way to set up a powerful editing computer, how to import images and other media into the Organizer, how to work with the Organizer's important Catalog backups, and how to get all your media into a cohesive order using Albums, Tags, Metadata, Keywords, Attributes, and its powerful search facility. As you should now realise, one of Photoshop Elements' main strengths is its ability to offer all-comers the opportunity to create something really special, and in the upcoming chapters you'll get to appreciate just how good this program really is.

2

Setting Up Photoshop Elements from Scratch

If you are new to Photoshop Elements, then this is the chapter for you. Here, we'll be looking at how to set up your camera, computer, monitor, data storage, and media backup—all of which are vitally important steps toward developing the perfect editing workflow. Getting your setup correct from the outset will enable you to plunge straight into the learning process without having to waste time renaming files or folders, go looking for lost images, or worse, losing materials because it never occurred to you to back up your original files in a timely fashion.

This chapter also discusses how to import your media, how to back it up safely, plus how to start sorting through the thousands of images in your collection using a terrific range of organizational tools, such as Keyword Tags, Star ratings, Events, People, and Places (GPS).

And even if you are not new to Elements, take some time here to check that your camera settings, screen calibration, photo import, and backup workflow are optimized. You never know, this might save you a lot of grief later on.

What you'll learn in this chapter:

- Setting up a photo editing computer
- Importing media into the Organizer
- Reviewing Media
- Media Backup
- Organizing your work: Star rating
- Organizing your work: using Metadata
- Organizing your work: Keyword tags
- Organizing your work: Places

- Organizing your work: Events
- Organizing your work: People
- File formats
- Saving Files
- Saving Version Sets
- Managing Catalogs
- Scanning photos
- Screen and print calibration

Setting up a photo editing computer

Although we take the multi-use characteristic of computers for granted these days, using such a machine to store, process, and edit high-resolution stills and video data requires a totally different set of features compared to a machine that's only used for web browsing, social media, emailing, or downloading music.

Although the compatibility of Windows and Mac computers used to be very minimal, their operating systems are now far more user-friendly, both in the way third-party hardware interacts (such as external drives) and in that most software is now shared between the two systems.

Operating system wars: Is there really a difference between running Elements on a **Windows** or **Mac** computer? The answer to this question can get you into a lot of hot water, depending on the technical leaning of the person being asked. I have used Windows and Mac desktops and laptops for a long time and find that, when editing images, there's really no big difference in performance between the two operating systems. In the early years, Elements was a different application on a Mac because Adobe was in contention with Apple over **iPhoto** (being the default image browser), but that's all sorted now. Macs are certainly beautifully designed, but provided that you have the same processing power, RAM chips, graphics card, and screen resolution set, you'd be hard-pushed to pick out any real performance difference. However, you will experience a significant **cost difference** between the two platforms. Macs have always sold at a premium compared to Windows gear.

An imaging computer needs to have a very fast processor (the **central processing unit (CPU)**). This is the bit that does all the calculations. A computer with one of the latest CPU chips installed will certainly future-proof your investment for several years to come. That said, I don't advise you to purchase the very latest technology, simply because you'll pay an absolute premium for it without necessarily gaining a commensurate speed advantage. Such is the downside of being an early adopter.

It's better to buy something that is just about to be replaced—which means it might only be five months old—and spend the cash saved on installing additional memory (also called **random access memory (RAM)**). The more memory installed, the more images, video clips, and applications you can have running at the same time without the computer visibly struggling. I'd recommend at least 16GB of RAM to start with, and more if you can afford it.

Screen resolutions are ever-increasing, with 4K resolutions (3,840 x 2,160 pixels) now becoming 'the norm'. Some companies even produce 5K and 8K screens (at 5,120 x 2,880 pixels and 7,680 x 4,320 pixels respectively) which sets the quality bar higher still. Since some of these screens are curved, they are not so good for image editing as they will never provide accurate feedback when trying to adjust for perspective and proportion. A flat screen is therefore your best choice for image editing.

Screen performance is not all about pixels—you also need a **graphics card** strong enough to display all those pixels with perfect contrast and brightness. Powerful cards are essential for gamers and video producers as well as still image makers. Many pre-installed graphics cards are powerful enough to drive HD and 4K screens sufficiently although it always pays to check if a more powerful card might produce better image quality results. You'll certainly need to upgrade your graphics card if you opt for a 5K or 8K monitor.

Monitor quality: The best image editing computer monitors are made by **Eizo**—these have superb edge-to-edge brightness, are easily (color-) calibrated, come with a hood, and produce reliable, accurate color. They are expensive, so are only practical if you plan on running a business. If you want to save some money, look at buying a monitor from Dell, BenQ, or even LG, three companies that produce pretty good display products that are considerably more affordable.

To keep prices competitive, most computers sold off the shelf contain the minimum amount of RAM. For maximum performance, it pays to increase your RAM, either at the point of purchase or later, where you might save money buying from a local computer shop or online. Increasing the amount of RAM significantly improves computer performance—even in an old computer it can be hugely beneficial—almost giving it a new lease of life. Note that not all computer mother boards can be upgraded as it depends on how many free slots there are on the main board to accommodate extra RAM modules, so check with a professional first.

If it's an entry-level video card not suited to a high-resolution output, you might encounter a lot of screen flickering, which can be quite disturbing. Check carefully before you buy.

Small but sweet—SSDs: For absolute speed freaks, **solid state drives (SSDs)** are the best option—both as an internal drive in your Windows or Mac and also as an external option. Expensive and not as high in capacity as their older SATA drive companions, SSDs are small and light, require no additional power, and are incredibly fast.

Then there is the very real problem of storage. Most photographers are prolific shooters and, with consumer camera resolutions generally passing the 25 megapixel mark at present, it won't take long to fill the computer's hard drive with media.

My advice is always to use a desktop computer, Windows or Mac, because, though large and bulky, they are significantly cheaper than laptops.

Removable desktop hard drives: The device on the left is a single hard drive unit from LaCie (the is company has a unique Porsche-style design for its products). A single drive, such as this 6TB model, would suit most beginners. The Western Digital My Book Duo, shown in the middle, is a RAID drive containing two hard drive units in the one box. This offers a mirroring feature, where it backs up two copies of everything, or it can be programmed for extreme speed if this is needed. The unit on the right is by a company called Drobo—this is another RAID storage-style drive suited for heavy users. Drobo claim its drives are significantly smarter than standard RAID drives (RAID technology has been around for more than two decades), providing sophisticated backup for professional image makers and small businesses. The idea behind this type of system is that it is integral to your workflow and can grow with your requirements. A device such as this is a must if you are starting your own imaging business.

Apart from that, their size (notably for Windows PCs) permits the addition of further internal hard drives when more storage is needed and even the upgrading of internal components, such as video cards and motherboards for improved performance. Mac desktop computers are a little harder to upgrade internally, partly because of their design, and partly because, if you do, you might void your warranty.

Desktop hard drives are the perfect way to keep up to date with backups—they are relatively inexpensive for the capacity offered, and if one fills up, it's easy enough to buy another. There are a number of excellent devices currently available from Seagate, LaCie, and Western Digital, to name a few.

The best practice is to install just your operating system and software applications onto the computer's hard drive. Everything else—photos, music, and video—should be saved to an external hard drive, or drives. That way, your computer can run at its optimum level while accessing your photo library on an external drive. Once that external drive is full, it's simple enough to carry on with a second, or even a third, external hard drive.

Other software: I appreciate suggesting "other" photo editing software is not a favorable thing to do in a book written about Photoshop Elements. But in fact there are many other software apps on the market that can do certain things, such as **HDR (high dynamic range)** image making, far, far better than Elements. To give you an idea, three products come to mind that will extend your image making capabilities significantly:

HDR: **Aurora HDR Professional** (by Skylum)

Painterly effects: **Dynamic Auto Painter** (by MediaChance)

Best plugin range: (see section on plug-ins in *Chapter 10, Exporting Work, Sharpening and Plug-ins*).

Laptop issues: If you absolutely have to use a laptop (and a lot of photographers are entirely mobile these days), this is also a good option, although its storage space, computing power (CPU), and screen size will all be compromised unless you spend a lot of money. One answer is to buy several external storage drives and a large desktop screen that can be hooked up to the laptop when you are working locally in the home office.

Laptops are designed to be lightweight and compact, so there's never much storage space in them for all your ██. Typically, we would buy a portable USB-powered hard drive for backups while traveling. Once home, it might make better sense to transfer all your work from the USB-powered hard drive to a physically larger desktop drive—these are usually cheaper, have a far greater data capacity, and are (mostly) more reliable.

Importing media into the Elements Organizer

As mentioned in *Chapter 1, Photoshop Elements Features Overview*, when images are imported into the Elements Organizer, they are not physically copied into the application; they are just linked from the place where they are stored (typically, this is the `Pictures` folder) in the Organizer. Should Elements or your computer develop a technical issue and you have to delete and reinstall the application, you just need to reinstate the catalog from the backup version, and it automatically re-links all files. Sometimes, it's necessary to actually point the program to the hard drive where the images are stored, but as often as not, Elements will search and find every image that was previously linked in the catalog. It's a clever program.

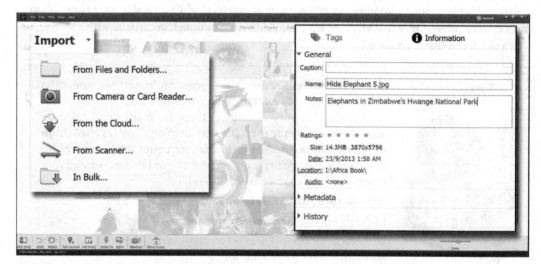

Import: Using the **Import** button (in the top left-hand corner in the Organizer), you can bring images, audio, or video clips into the Elements Organizer directly using the **From Files and Folders...** option. These files can physically reside anywhere—locally, on the computer, or externally on a drive. There are also options to import files directly from a camera or a card reader, or in bulk from pre-organized folders. The panel on the right-hand side of the main window holds both keyword and metadata information about each file. Click the small **Keyword/Info** button in the lower right-hand corner of the main screen to open/close this panel.

Because of this linking process, it's not advisable to rename or move files that have already been imported into Elements. If files are moved or renamed using the Windows **Explorer** or Mac's **Finder**, the next time Elements starts, it will prompt you that the file is missing and immediately start a search for the file. This is fine if the name remains the same, but if it has a new name, it will have to be re-imported. You can leave Elements to complete the search, or do it yourself, if you know where the file was moved to. How long Elements takes to locate a moved file depends on how big your photo collection is.

The import process is fast because Elements only copies thumbnails and the metadata (essentially text) when it forms a link to the original files. So, to avoid wasting time searching for files that have been renamed or moved after they were imported into the Organizer, it makes sense to sort out the storage hierarchy on the computer or external drives before importing to the application.

We all have different ways in which we organize our busy photographic lives. Some prefer to store files by date, while others prefer to name everything according to events in their lives. There's no right or wrong way to do this. The best method is the one that you are going to remember.

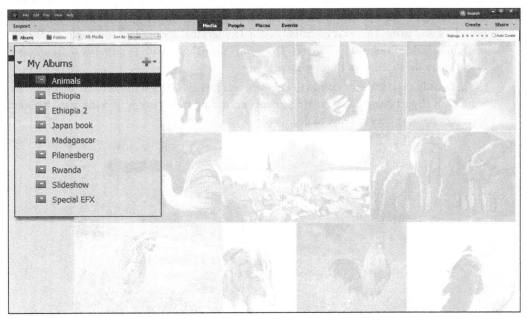

Making albums: In the preceeding screenshot, I have created an album called **Animals**. Selecting the album on the left-hand side of the window will display the contents of that album in the main window. As with most features in Elements, an album can be renamed at any time. The huge advantage of creating albums, apart from enabling you to easily compartmentalize your work into smaller, more practical collections, is that you can have the same image or images in multiple albums without increasing the space taken up on the storage drive.

Tip:

Before you import a second batch of images, it makes sense to sort out the first batch, because if you continue to import folder after folder of images, before long, you'll have thousands displayed in the main screen, and that can get very confusing. Once imported into the Organizer, you can see exactly where on your hard drives those imported files reside through the **Folders** menu in the left-hand bin.

That said, there are basic rules I can suggest that will make the editing process flow better:

- Download and organize your files into pre-made folders as often as you can. If you download on a regular basis, it will help you keep abreast of the Elements imports and will also ensure that you don't accidentally overwrite files on a camera memory card.

- Always add keyword tags to freshly imported files. The longer you leave organizing your work, the more confusing it gets.

- Divide your images into events—these might be "work," "trips," "family," "weekends away," and so on. Create an album for each big trip, an album for a conference, an album for the kids' birthdays, and so on. These are essentially virtual folders that are used for compartmentalizing image files inside Photoshop Elements. Dragging image thumbnails to populate these albums doesn't alter the location of the originals.

- Use keywords, tags, and star ratings to help you sort images into a sense of order that you can work with (I particularly like ranking images according to keywords and the star attribute hierarchy because they are easy to do).

Auto Curate: Photoshop Elements has a number of quite powerful but often overlooked features—including this one, called **Auto Curate**, arrowed at the top right of screen, which picks the top 500 images from the Organizer. The results might surprise you. With your media displayed in the main window, check the **Auto Curate** box and watch as Elements finds 50 of the best images from anything up to 20,000 images (according to Adobe). As I think most of the images in my test media are good anyway, it's a mystery how it finds 50 (or any number you choose) of the best. Nonetheless, this is worth a look for a quick, frustration-free selection.

- Give everything a proper name once it is edited.
- As new images appear in the Organizer, they show up in the main window as thumbnails. Make the thumbnails bigger/smaller using the zoom slider at the bottom right-hand side of the screen. Use the edge-of-screen sliders to scroll down the page to see more thumbnails, or just use the *up/down* keyboard arrows.
- All the details of this filing system (albums, tags, keywords, thumbnails, original files, and so on) are part of the Elements catalog, which is something that needs backing up to a location different from where the original files are stored.

Some photographers prefer to divide image collections into multiple catalogs. For example, wedding photographers might have a separate catalog for each client. For most of us, one catalog is enough because you can only open one catalog at a time anyway.

Nearly all DSLRs and mirrorless cameras use the JPEG and RAW file formats. Most of the cheaper point-and-shoot type cameras only use JPEGs. That said, JPEGs can be opened and read by a very wide range of applications—photo software and even Microsoft Word and PowerPoint. RAW files are far less universal and require specific software to work. In Elements, this is called Camera RAW. As each new camera model produces an entirely new type of RAW file, Elements has to be updated reasonably regularly so it can keep up to date with all the new stuff coming onto the market. If you have just bought a new camera, don't be surprised if Elements cannot read its RAW files. You might have to wait till the next Adobe Camera RAW update before the application can open them. In the interim, you can always use the software that came with the camera to open RAW files or download the free Adobe DNG file format converter, convert your RAW files to the DNG format, and edit from them until the new software is ready.

Tip: What's a .PSE file?

In your experimentation in and around Photoshop Elements' many creative features, you might notice that your projects appear in the file browser (Mac or PC) as **.PSE** files. These are quite different from the usual .jpg, .psd, and .tif files that photographers are more familiar with. So, what's the difference? A .pse file applies to any Elements **project**, such as a greeting card project (found under the Create Menu in the Organizer and Editor). Its job is to keep all the components for that project linked and in one place—the photos, clip art, text, etc., that make up the card, for example. If you accidentally delete the .pse file, you don't lose the components, but you will have to re-create the project again from scratch.

Reviewing the media

Looking at your media in the Organizer couldn't be easier. The main window displays all media files in a mode called **Grid View**—these are adjustable thumbnails. But note that if you create and populate albums, the main window will only display the contents of each album.

Compartmentalizing a photo collection into multiple albums, therefore, is an effective way to break up what would otherwise be a confusing mass of files populating (or flooding) the main screen into smaller, more visually digestible quantities.

Small thumbnails or big thumbnails: One tip for anyone wanting to sort through a lot of images is to maximize the thumbnail size (using the slider—arrowed) so the screen effectively only displays one image at a time, as seen in this coastal seascape, then use the *up/down* arrows on the keyboard to scroll through the latest import while examining each file full size. Every time you find an image that you want to keep or think needs editing, you can classify it simply using the **number keys** to add one, two, three, four, or five **stars** (see the *Organizing your work: Star rating photos* section later in this chapter). Use these keys to sort and search for images. (Pressing the number zero on the keypad removes all star attributes.) You can also see that once expanded to full screen, you can type in a caption for the displayed image and play any associated sound (that is, if it's a movie clip). Even better, there are no restrictions as to how many albums you can create and, since they are essentially virtual folders, they don't take up much storage space.

Media backup

As we expand our image and media collection, we'll not only need large capacity hard drives, but also data **backups**. It's important to perform backups in case the original drive corrupts, or suffers a mechanical failure. Nothing is forever and even though the drive might be a premium brand, things can still go wrong, usually when you least expect it.

There's no point in backing up images, or your Elements Catalog, to the place where the originals are also stored—typically your computer's hard drive. If it becomes corrupted, everything is lost. Consider a large-capacity hard drive that is used only for backing up your data: images, music, Elements' Catalog, and so on. Most PCs have room for additional internal drives. If you use a Mac, you'd be better off buying an external hard drive.

If you are using a Mac, backing up your data is easy using a pre-installed Apple application called **Time Machine**. Windows users also have it easy because most quality external drives (such as Seagate and Western Digital) come with automated backup software included.

This software takes only a few moments to set up. Once done, you can forget it, because it automatically backs all your new material up every hour, day, or week (depending on how you initially set up its preferences). Another viable option is to back up to the cloud. In many ways this is the most secure option as those companies spend an awful lot more on **data security** than any individual photographer! Some cloud storage companies worth a look include Dropbox, Backblaze, Google Drive, Apple, Box, and Microsoft OneDrive.

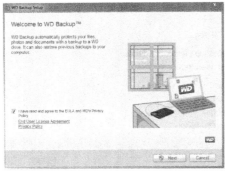

Above: This is a standard **desktop hard drive** with a massive 8TB storage capacity, of the type easily purchased online or from most good computer stores. This is the perfect solution for data backup. Devices are not expensive and come in a wide range of storage capacities—and if that fills up, it's easy enough to buy more to add to the library.

Left: Auto Backups The two screenshots here show **Western Digital's** free auto backup software (available for Mac and Windows) at the top, and under that, Apple's excellent **Time Machine**, an auto backup feature that comes preloaded on every Mac.

Organizing your work: Star rating photos

Some of you might be familiar with the Windows operating system's star ratings. This is a feature that allows you to award a file one to five stars, depending on their merit. You can then search for files (in this context, images) that are displaying *X* number of stars.

You might give your best images five stars, and those that need editing three stars—that kind of thing. Ratings appear in a wide range of photo editing applications, including Adobe Bridge, Lightroom, and Camera Bits' Photo Mechanic image browser, and for good reason—it's a system that's easy to implement and effective in its organizational potential. Here's how to get this happening:

Step one: Right-click an image in the **Organizer**.

Step two: From **Ratings** in the contextual menu, slide over the number of stars you'd like to award that image (from one to five). Or select one or more images in the main window, and hit any number key between *1* and *5* (use the top of the keyboard, not the number keypad) to add a rating.

Step three: To search for an already-rated image, click the appropriate star symbol in the **Ratings** search field (top of the screen just under the **Create** tab), and everything in the main screen with that star rating remains. Everything else is hidden until you click the same star rating again to clear the search.

Note that this search can be refined by clicking the tiny symbol to the right of the word **Ratings** to set **Greater than, or equal to, Less than, or equal to**, or **Rating is equal to**. It can make a big difference to your search results. This is an exceptionally intuitive system that's easy to set up, easy to modify, and very efficient in its search results—just use that pop-out menu to lower, raise, or delete the rating if required.

Contextual menu help: While sorting through recently imported images, get into the habit of right-clicking a thumbnail. This reveals a contextual menu that offers many options, but in particular reference to sorting images, you can choose from any of the following: **Delete from Catalog...**, **Edit with Photoshop Elements Editor...**, **Edit with Premiere Elements Editor...**, **Adjust Date and Time...** (good for when you cross different time zones), **Add Caption...**, **Ratings** (1-5 stars), **Add a Person** (identified in the image for later searches), **Create a Slideshow** (when more than one image thumbnail is selected), and **Show File Info** (that is, view the file's metadata). All good stuff.

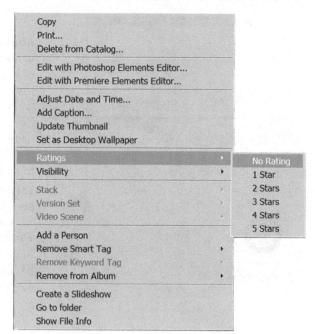

Organizing your work: Picture search using Metadata

Metadata is little more than a small text file that records all your camera details at the time a photo is taken. We rarely read the metadata unless we specifically look for it or, in this context, use it to search for images. Metadata records camera and lens details, date, time, size, resolution, filename, and, if your camera has the feature, a set of GPS coordinates.

The advantage of metadata is that the information already exists, so we can use **Organizer** to search our image database using any of those pre-recorded metadata details for a fast result.

You might think that the **Find by Details (Metadata)** search field looks a bit confusing because it offers so many ways to search for images. You can also use this dialog box to save frequently used searches—a real time-saver. It can also be used to search for images by the date and time captured (this is especially useful if you holiday in different time zones).

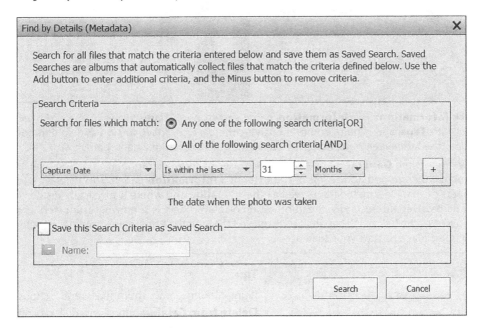

Metadata search: By selecting **Find>By Details (Metadata)**, you see this screen. By default it opens with **Search for files which match any of the following search criteria** (by capture date—which you choose using the drop-down menu). This is a very wide type of search but as you'll discover, you can click that left-hand menu to see 36 other search options. As I write a lot about camera technique, I often search for specific things such as aperture (f-stop), ISO setting, focal length, and White Balance, which makes the task of trawling through hundreds of potential image files a breeze.

Another criterion I use a lot is to search for **camera type**, or the **date taken**—but if you are more interested in searching for people, for example, you can also access all of Elements' other methods of search, including **People tags**, **Event tags**, and, of *course*, keywords. If what you find in the menu is not specific enough, add a second or a third "search rule" by clicking the **+** button that sits to the right of the **Search Criteria** window.

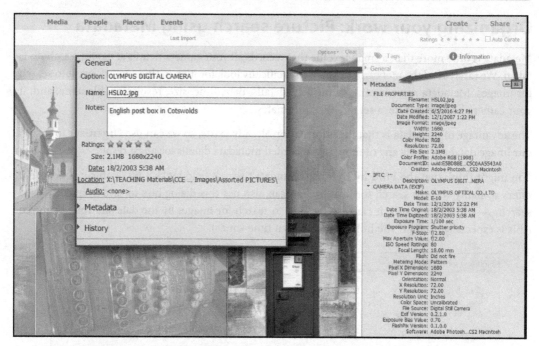

Quick information: The **Information** panel shown here shares space in the right-hand panel with **Tags**, and is quite comprehensive—there's a compact version and an extended version (the latter seen here, currently occupying the entire right-hand panel).

Above that is the **General** menu (for the purposes of this illustration, it's floating over the thumbnail picture grid, to the left of the extended **Information** panel). This displays a few snippets of that file's metadata, as well as the star rating and where it physically resides on your hard drives. Interestingly, the information displayed here is somewhat truncated when compared to the full search capabilities displayed through the **Find** menu—but nevertheless, it's a good place to start your search.

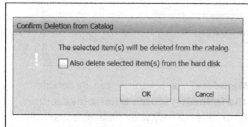

Tip:

Right-clicking any thumbnail and choosing **Delete from Catalog** brings up a dialog window asking whether you also want to physically delete the original file from wherever it might be stored. This is handy if you think it really needs to go!

Tip:

You can take your keywording as far as you have the time and patience for by being increasingly specific. For example, I could also keyword my holiday pictures with the words "beaches," "restaurants," "funny signs," "people," "markets," "night life," "sunsets," "palm trees," and "cocktails."

If you add multiple keywords, separate them with a comma (,) to avoid confusing the search engine. Limit keywords to five or six per image. Too many keywords can be counter-productive.

Organizing your work: Keyword Tagging

One of the best features in Elements is its ability to sort out hundreds, thousands, or even tens of thousands of images using the tested method of **keyword tags**.

While viewing a newly imported batch of pictures, select a file by clicking it once and, in the bottom right-hand corner of the screen, type in a keyword.

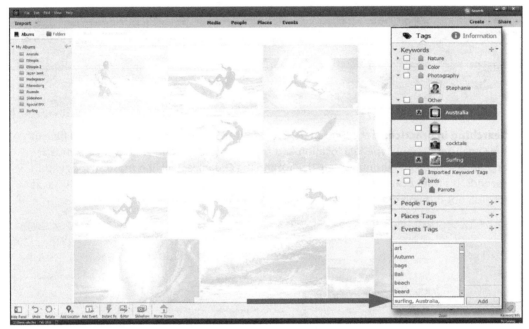

Keyword tagging: You can see that, in the red arrowed field, I have added the words 'Surfing' and 'Australia'. If I import and add keywords to hundreds of surfing images in the Organizer, all I need to do is click on the **Surfing/Australia** tags (both highlighted in blue here) to find those images—they can then be placed in an album called 'Surfing'.

I think keywording is one of the most important setup features in this program. Get into the habit of adding a keyword, or keywords, to everything you import into the Organizer and you will be able to search, and find, almost any image weeks, months, and even years later. It's an incredibly efficient and effective system of image retrieval.

Let's say you have got back home after a vacation. Select all the images from the vacation and type the name of the place you visited. If you went to Australia, for example, all images could be keyworded as 'Australia'. But if half that time was spent in the mountains around the town of Katoomba, re-select those images of Katoomba alone and add 'Katoomba' as the keyword. If three days in Australia were spent surfing, select those images only, and add the keyword 'surfing'. This takes only a few minutes and, with a little forethought, you'll quickly be able to keyword all the important events in this album (named "Holiday in Australia") so that, months or years later, you can search for "Australia," "surfing," or "cocktails," for example, and Elements will locate those images (almost) instantly.

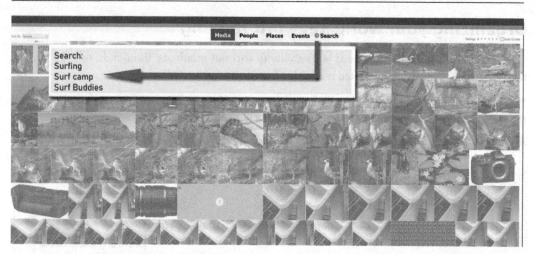

Searching in practice: In the **Search** field (the blue magnifying glass icon, arrowed here in the Organizer screen), type in a location and maybe an event using whatever keywords are appropriate (such as "Surfing" or "Australia"), and the Organizer will find those images within seconds. It's fast because it only has to sort through its database (which is essentially a text record), not through gigabytes of high-resolution RAW files.

Personalizing Tags: In this screenshot, I right-clicked my **Surfing** keyword tag in the right-hand bin and chose **Edit** from the contextual menu. This brings up the **Edit Keyword Tag** window (above, on the left). You can edit the name of the tag and add comments. Clicking the **Edit Icon** tab brings up another, larger window, into which you can load a surfing picture to make that group instantly recognizable. It's a cute feature, but it won't really improve your workflow.

Keywording is an easy process, but the real magic only really begins when you try to search for specific images shot on that trip.

Keyword tags are written into the file so that, for example, if I sent a bunch of my (tagged) images to a third party, they would be able to sort them using my attached tags. Elements' tags can be read by a range of other image editing software programs. An album, on the other hand, is a purely Elements-only feature.

If you create a new tag in the right-hand tag bin, you can apply it to any image simply by dragging that tag onto the photo thumbnail. Easy. If you have a hundred images that need the same tag, select all of them first, drag the newly made tag onto any one of the selected thumbnails, and it will automatically apply that tag to all selected images. Very smart!

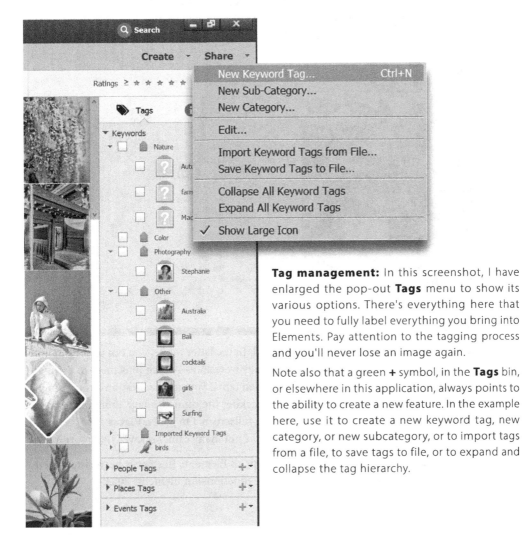

Tag management: In this screenshot, I have enlarged the pop-out **Tags** menu to show its various options. There's everything here that you need to fully label everything you bring into Elements. Pay attention to the tagging process and you'll never lose an image again.

Note also that a green **+** symbol, in the **Tags** bin, or elsewhere in this application, always points to the ability to create a new feature. In the example here, use it to create a new keyword tag, new category, or new subcategory, or to import tags from a file, to save tags to file, or to expand and collapse the tag hierarchy.

Organizing your work: Places

The Organizer has a huge range of features designed to help photographers keep track of, and search for, their images. I think there are too many search features—but that's just my opinion.

The **Places** feature has been in Elements for many years. Its principal use is to automatically put any image that contains **GPS data** onto an internet-driven world map so that users can identify pictures simply by seeing the locations where they were actually shot.

In earlier versions of this program (several years ago), few cameras had GPS capabilities, so the only option open to you if you needed this kind of display was to drag images from the grid on the left-hand side of the screen onto the map to 'pin' them in place instead. You can still do this.

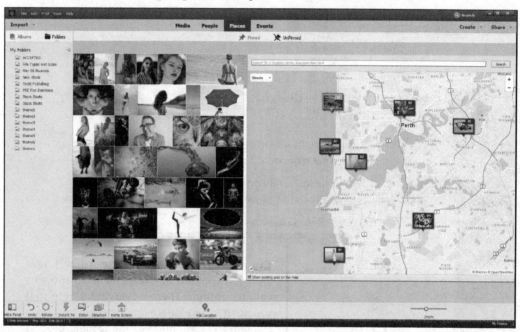

The feature has two view modes: **Pinned** and **Unpinned**. In the latter mode, you can select single or multiple images and drag them to the location where they were shot—which pins them to the map. Once pinned, they automatically appear under the **Pinned** tab. If you get the location wrong, simply drag the pinned image(s) to a new location. Double-clicking the pinned image thumbnails opens them in **Grid** view. Double-click again and they open in fullscreen. On paper, **Places** appears to be a nice feature, but it's still not widely used; I suspect because not many cameras save GPS information.

Note: Since 2018, **Places** stopped working in old versions of Elements (it's never been clear exactly why). But that's all sorted now, so you'll find Places fully functional in Elements 2023.

Organizing your work: Events

The **Events** category is, I think, more useful to everyday photographers. Why? Because **Events** starts off by using dates as a way to categorize images. We might take a bunch of shots over a family weekend or on our 12-day trip to Bali. Using the **Events** feature, these images can be grouped into either events dictated solely by the data or read from the metadata, or they can be grouped and renamed into something more memorable, such as `Family Weekend, 2019`, or simply `Bali Vacation`.

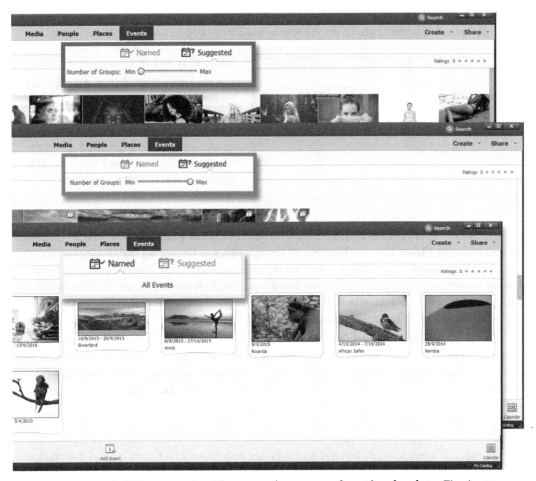

Events at work: This screenshot illustrates the power of **sorting by date**. The bottom window shows **Events**, with the **Number of Groups** slider positioned to the left-hand side (highlighted in red). Everything is pushed against everything else because the search engine is effectively compressing time. The middle window (highlighted in blue) shows how, if the slider is pushed to the right, images are displayed on an almost day-by-day basis, making it easier to find photos from a day shoot, or some other short-running function. The front window illustrates what the named events look like in the **Named** tab (highlighted in orange). Events can be modified.

Events has two view modes: **Named** and **Suggested**. I normally dislike anything that *suggests* things to me (such as predictive text), but in this case, it presents all your images grouped by date. This is quite useful because it instantly orders everything in the main window, whether from an album, folder, or all media. That's a good start.

To delete an Event, right-click and choose **Remove this Event**. This pop-out menu also allows you to edit the event (that is, to add/subtract images from the event), to use **Set as Cover**, which makes the displayed image the default front page, and to use **Create a Slideshow**, which takes all the files in that specific event stack and puts them into a slideshow that can be saved for further editing in the Organizer, or directly uploaded to social media via the **Share** menu (top right-hand corner of the Organizer).

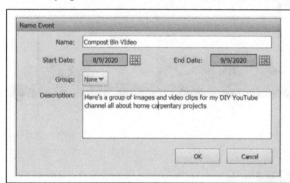

Name that event:

Once selected, click the **Add Event** button at the base of the page and, in the dialog box that opens (at left here), give the event a proper name, check the dates to ensure you have grabbed the right sequence, select a **Group** if that's needed, and add a **description** if required, then click **OK** to lock it in.

It's a good idea to award albums and folders real names, rather than going on just the dates—the same can be done using **Places**. Shift the **Number of Groups** slider so the setting that displays your **event** does so in one group of images (that is, selecting just the weekend, or just that week). Physically select all those images (do this by holding the *Shift* key down, and clicking the first and then the last image in the group). They are now all selected. If the images you need are in more than one group, it's easy to select multiple groups by drawing a marquee around those groups.

But what happens to the proper names this group of pictures was just awarded? Click the **Named** tab at the top of the screen and you'll see all the images that were custom-grouped and named now appear as stacked thumbnails. Sliding the cursor over a group displays its contents. Double-clicking an event stack reveals the individual images it contains. Clicking the **Back** button in the same screen moves those spread-out images back into a stack format.

Tips:

When drawing a marquee, click and drag the cursor so it draws a rectangle over all the images you need. Blue check marks appear in all those that are selected. If you accidentally miss one image, add it by holding the *Ctrl/Command* key down while you click the mouse once (Windows/Mac).

By the same process, if you select too many by accident, you can hold *Ctrl/Cmd* and click the file to deselect it.

As your image collection grows, you can further refine a search, or just what's displayed in the main window, by selecting different dates from the calendar that's posted on the right-hand side of the screen. You can also create a new event in the media window. Click the **Add Event** tab at the bottom of the page, then drag those images you'd like into the new event to the right-hand side bin. Give it a proper name, check the date, and click **OK**.

Organizing your work: People

Elements' **People** mode is really all about using face recognition, an algorithm that analyzes images in the background as they are imported into the **Organizer** for the first time.

If it detects a face in an image, it presents it as a circular thumbnail in the main **People** window. If it *thinks* that there are several of the same person in the import, they will be automatically stacked like a deck of cards. You can view the results in the **Unnamed** panel. Every image will appear with the label **Add Name** underneath the thumbnail to begin with.

If you recognize the person depicted, click in the **Add Name** field and type in the name. As soon as you click the check symbol to the right of the field to lock it in, the thumbnail stack disappears.

This is the **People** window—you can let Elements run through your image collection to identify images with people in them automatically. It works really well—but it will also make mistakes, so some curation is usually necessary to get it looking perfect.

Where's it gone? Click into the **Named** window and there you'll see the newly named stack. Hover the cursor over the stack and you'll see the words **Faces** or **Photos** appear. Click **Photos** to reveal the full image in which the face was detected, or click **Faces** to reveal just the face or faces in that group.

Elements' **People** window will find images of your friends—but it also finds every image that looks like a face, including pictures in posters and abstract backgrounds. These can easily be discounted by right-clicking the icon and choosing **Don't show again**. As soon as an image gets a proper name, it's automatically moved into the **Named** tab and stacks with similarly named images. For those of us that prefer to identify our images based on the content, and specifically on the people depicted in the files, you'll find the **People** feature very handy.

Setting Up Photoshop Elements from Scratch

Organizing your people: Like the keywords feature, the **People** feature, shown in this screenshot, allows you to subdivide your found faces into smaller categories, or groups, as seen on the right-hand side of the screen. Elements starts you off with **Colleagues**, **Family**, and **Friends** but, of course, clicking the green plus (**+**) symbol allows you to add new group categories when needed.

Like most organizational tools in Elements, you can choose to work simply by adopting just keywords, or maybe the ratings, or you can use a combination of everything covered in this section to create a sophisticated and deep searchable database. The best advice is to make up your mind regarding which way is best for you before you start; that way, you can streamline your workload from day one rather than having to go back over everything that's been imported into the Organizer because you changed your mind about how to organize your images.

Preplanning will save you a lot of time and effort.

Tips:

You can merge one stack into another simply by click-dragging one file over another. You can further refine the sort process by adding stacks to groups—such as **Family**. Click the **Groups** tab on the bottom right-hand side of the main window, and either use one of the default groups, or make a new one by clicking the green **+** symbol. As with most Elements features, there's no limit to the number of groups you can have.

If you discover an "inappropriate" face in the stack, right-click the Faces icon, and choose **Not...**, or just rename it, it places it out of that stack into its own, new stack. You can also use this pop-out menu to assign that image as a profile photo (this is the default top of the stack). Finally, there's the **Don't Show Again** command, which hides that image from ever appearing in the **People** view again.

Understanding JPEG and RAW file formats

Nearly all digital cameras can shoot and record two types of picture file: **JPEG** and **RAW** files. Some models can also record a third file type called DNG (digital negative) another type of RAW file. We'll look at them later in this chapter.

The difference between JPEG and RAW files is simple: JPEG files are 8-bit picture files. These are processed in-camera and then compressed (squashed) to maximize storage space, before being saved to the memory card.

RAW files are usually 10-bit files that have little or no processing applied in camera, and they are not compressed before being saved to the memory card. The result is a file that is several times larger than a JPEG, but one that can be edited to a far higher degree of accuracy than the humble JPEG.

Although each camera manufacturer shares the same three-letter suffix across all of its camera range, RAW files produced by different models are quite different from each other; that is, RAW files from the Nikon D7000 are different from the Nikon D7200, D800, and D850 RAW files. This is why it takes companies such as Adobe several months to provide an update for the different RAW file types designed for each new camera make and model. If you are an early adopter, waiting for Adobe to catch up and release a compatibility update can be a source of frustration.

RAW files have to be edited in a specific RAW edit window, called **Camera RAW**, which is separate from the regular **Quick**, **Guided**, or **Expert** mode windows. Once edited in this space, a RAW file must be either closed (there's no **saving** with RAW files—it automatically records all the edits applied to it), or it can be saved in a more universally acceptable file format for storage, backup, or later distribution.

Such formats include JPEGs, TIFF files, digital negative files, or even Photoshop files. But what's the difference between these formats and when would be the best situation to use them?

Choosing the right format in which to save your edited work is an important decision because it can have direct ramifications on both final image quality and your backup and archiving practices.

Physical file sizes: To illustrate the different properties of image files, I saved the same photo in **six different file formats**. Because JPEGs are compressible, their saved state is considerably smaller than everything else, hence their popularity in social media, the web, and emailing. Compressed to the maximum (the smallest saved file size) reduces them to only 800 KB—less than one megabyte—but that compression level would seriously damage the quality. Despite my original Canon `.CR2` RAW file being 28.99 MB, the `.png` file is larger (39.9 MB), followed by the slightly compressed (though lossless) TIFF file (46.5 MB), the Photoshop file (62.9 MB), and the uncompressed TIFF file (63.3 MB).

- **JPEG** (`.jpg`): This is a compressed *lossy* format (*lossy* means it loses quality when saved and compressed) that's ideal for emailing, photo books, web, social media, and photo lab printing (note: most photo book companies only accept JPEG and PNG files).

- **RAW**: RAW files are untouched data straight from the camera. They contain four times more picture data than a JPEG, are good for shooting in any light, plus they take any amount of editing without loss of quality.

- **DNG** (`.dng`): A digital negative file is a universal RAW file, retaining all of the benefits of regular RAW files while retaining a wider accessibility than regular RAW files. Adobe Lightroom, for example, is opimized to work best with DNG files.

- **PSD** (`.psd`): These have no compression and can store extra (Photoshop) data within the file itself, such as layers, paths, and selections, thus retaining a high degree of editability. This is good for preserving the best quality for complex editing and commercial print projects.

- **TIFF**: Similar to .psd files, TIFF files can be compressed by up to 25% with no loss of quality. TIFF files preserve features such as selections and layers. Good for preserving best quality, editing, and commercial printing. TIFF files can end up being larger than the same file saved in the .psd format.
- **PNG**: Portable Network Graphics files are used primarily for website design and in photo books where background transparency is a requirement.

1-Bit
2 colors
black + white

4-Bit
16 colors

8-Bit
256 colors

24-Bit
16.7 million
colors

Bit depth relates to the amount of color information held in a file. The higher the bit depth, the more color information it contains. More information produces smoother tonal gradation, which in turn produces a more realistic image.

Single-bit color is made up of two colors only—black and white, rarely used in photography other than in the creation of masks. 8-bit color produces 256 tones, which was considered an acceptable number for the photograph—until, that is, 24-bit color came along and produced 16.7 million tones. No need to count them; they just look good. Top-of-the-range cameras can now record 10-bit and 12-bit files.

Too much JPEG compression? Of all the file formats available in Elements, the one that's perhaps the most useful is JPEG. The close-up of this bespectacled gentleman displays the problems over-compressing JPEG files, on the left, will create. Don't get me wrong—JPEG files are great because they can be compressed. However, if they are squashed too much (that is, **set to level 7 or lower** in the **JPEG Options** dialog), you'll see a significant deterioration in image clarity and color (the left half of this composite image was set to **Quality**: 0, producing a tiny file).

Too much compression, or repeated saving (and therefore repeated compression), will generate ugly **image artefacts**, for example, in the form of **posterization** (banding) seen mostly in the smoother tones. Over-compression will also create inaccurate color, and might even introduce blocky-looking pixels when compared to the minimal compression level 12 setting, as seen on the right of the illustration above, producing a larger saved file but with smoother, more accurate tones.

Saving Files

It's important to note that, when saving JPEG, TIFF, PSD, or PNG files, if you choose the **Save** option (**File>Save**), some older applications might write the new file **on top of the old one**, effectively deleting the original and saving the (hopefully) improved new version instead. Not so with Elements as it always asks whether it's **OK** to overwrite the previous version of this file—a face-saving feature in some cases.

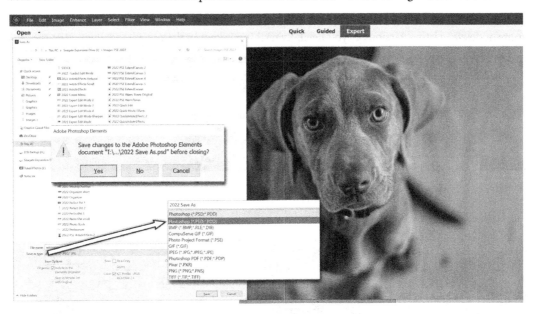

If you open a file, do nothing to it, then choose **File>Save**, nothing happens because there's been no change so there's nothing to save. However, if you make any kind of alteration to the file, then choose **File>Save**, you'll see the **Save As** panel appear. This allows you to do the following:

- Save your progress.
- Change the file format if needed.
- Include that saved file back in the Organizer.
- Save it as a copy (as in NewPortrait copy.jpg).
- Save it into a Version Set (see overleaf).
- Save it with a specific Color Profile.
- **Save to the Cloud**—this handy feature announced in Elements 2021 and removed in 2022, is back in Elements 2023. Head to the **Organizer** or **Expert Edit** windows to access this feature (Note: You can use this cloud browser to make slideshows and collages—at the time of writing it's a beta version in English only).

For added security, if you change anything in the file then quit Elements or try to close the file (*Ctrl/Cmd + W*), Elements throws up the warning panel (inset above, with a warning symbol) asking whether you want to quit without saving: select **Yes**, **No**, or **Cancel**.

Saving Version Sets

Other options in the **Save As** dialog window include **Save in Version Set with Original** and **Save as a Copy**. What the first feature does is save the new version of your (cherry blossom) shot with the original file for safe-keeping. In Organizer, you only see the original image, but if you right-click it, you can choose to see all the different versions you might have made from the original.

This is called a **Version Set**—single photos stacked into one file like a deck of cards. You can add more or delete existing versions as you need. Everything is kept in the one file, saving screen space.

I like to experiment with all sorts of special effects—and there's more than enough potential to do this using Elements' **Effects** and **Adjustments** tools. So, Version Sets might be just the feature you need to keep all those variations on a theme safely stored in one file till you decide which one to use.

Managing catalogs

The Catalog Manager (**Organizer>File>Manage Catalogs**) is used for several tasks. These include the following:

- Create new catalogs.
- Rename existing catalogs.
- Convert a previous, older version of an Elements catalog to the new version of the software.
- Optimize a catalog—this helps reduce its size, making it more efficient.

While a software-driven data backup is a good procedure to set up for all users, it might not back up your Photoshop Elements catalog. And even if it did, it wouldn't be in a format that Elements can recognize, should you need to restore it after a software mishap.

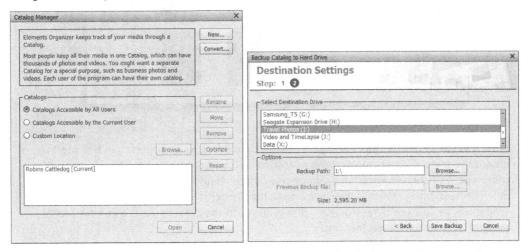

Back up the catalog: It's important to ensure that your backed-up catalog is saved to a location different from where the default catalog is stored. For most, this means saving it to a different drive—in the screenshot above, there are **five** different drives available for backup.

Tip:

If you purchase a **RAID drive** (multiple hard drives in one box), you can program it to back up once to each drive, essentially giving you two complete backups in one operation, so if one drive fails, you still have a second copy to use. Another use of the RAID drive is to split the backups 50/50. This greatly enhances the read/write speeds of the device but, in this mode, if one drive goes down, you lose everything because the process actually splits files rather than putting one file on disk A, then the next file on disk B, and so on. Nothing in digital imaging can be 100% safe, but if you use a reliable RAID system it should still give you years of good service.

What's actually inside the catalog? Although Elements' backup process can be a lifesaver, it's not the same as a regular Windows or Mac operating system backup. With Elements, the backed up files are referenced in a completely different way from those that are copied to a different hard drive—which is why if you open the Elements backup file, everything appears scrambled, as you see here. However, if you reinstate the catalog via the correct process, everything reappears in perfect order.

The catalog is where all your hard work is stored: tags, keywords, albums, captions, places, maps, and events; as well as your images, as RAW, JPEG, TIFF, PNG, or PSD files; plus a lot of other stuff that helps Elements be as efficient as possible.

The files' proper names are reinstated once a **Catalog Restore** function is completed. Generally, we only access an Elements backup if the original has been compromised and we need to restore the entire catalog's contents.

In an emergency, you can still open the Backup folder and pull out images, if need be. If you have issues with the current catalog, it's easy enough to choose **File>Restore Catalog** from the **Organizer** and reload the entire catalog from its backup location.

The logical way to perform a catalog backup is to choose **File>Backup Catalog** in the **Organizer** and follow the prompts. Make sure that the location of the backup is not on the local drive—put it on an external drive. Elements insists on a full backup to begin with, then a partial backup if you are just updating work as you go.

Digitizing Photos with a Scanner

There's a general assumption in the photography community that we only produce images using a camera or smartphone. While this might be partly true, there's also a sizeable proportion of image keepers who produce digital images using a dedicated scanner—although you can of course use a regular camera to scan artwork which we'll look at later.

Scanner types

Basically there are two types of scanner: the **flatbed** type, designed specifically for scanning paper documents and artwork (note: some of the more expensive flatbed models incorporate a lamp in the scanner lid thus enabling them to scan film) and the dedicated **film scanner**, designed to scan all kinds of negative or positive film (slides).

Above, left: Epson's current top-of-the-range flatbed and film scanner. **Centre left:** An innovative film scanner for smartphones. **Centre right:** A simple Kodak film scanner and, **at right:** a high quality dedicated film scanner. There are dozens of scanner brands to choose from for both film and flat art. How much you pay depends on your output quality requirements as well as the size of the job. If it's a really big project (i.e. hundreds of scans) it's better to buy a more efficient and fast machine. If you only need a few scans then you need only spend $20-$50.

So, what's the difference between the two? Ten years ago I'd have said the main difference was price. Flatbed scanners cost a few hundred dollars while dedicated film scanners ran into the thousands. It's roughly the same now—in my country I can buy a cheap flatbed scanner from the post office! Though today, prices have dropped quite dramatically while the output quality, even on the most basic models, has increased quite significantly. And that's a good thing for anyone wanting to scan valuable family pictures before they fade and get lost forever.

Scanner Specs

Scanned image quality can be measured in terms of:

- **Scan resolution**: measured as dots per inch or just DPI.
- **Dynamic range**: measured as the D-Max number (4.0 represents excellent quality)higher numbers enable the scanner to record faint details in the very light and dark parts of the image which might otherwise be missed by a lesser specified device.
- **Operating speed**: if you have ever used one of these in the past, you'll know that they tend to be slow operators. No problems for a few scans, but if your project involves digitizing a lot of records, you'll need a fast one. Generally, the more you pay, the better its features, including scan speed (check manufacturer's specs).
- **Included software**: all scanners ship with Windows/Mac software. While most are quite good, some have better features than others including extras like **optical character recognition** (this converts a scanned text document into an editable text document), batch scanning, **dust and scratch removal**, **color restoration**, and more.

Flatbed Scanning Tips

Essentially, scanners are quite simple to use:

- Connect the device to your computer and install the scanner software.
- Lift the lid and place your document face down on the glass platen, lining it up with the edges carefully. If the prints to be scanned are small, scan several at the same time.
- Run the software and click Scan (or just press the Scan button on the device). Most flatbed scanners can scan straight to an SD card, print, or the computer and the resulting file can be saved in a range of file formats for later use.
- Always clean the print and glass platen with a soft cloth before scanning to remove loose dust. This will save a lot of time when it comes to cleaning up the dust and scratches.
- Match the output size requirement to an appropriate resolution. Print resolution is 300dpi. This means that a letter-sized document at 300dpi produces a 24MB file which will produce a perfect reproduction of the original **at the same size**. If you set the resolution to 600dpi (or '200%'), the scan will take longer but with no apparent increase in print quality, despite its huge 42MB file, but it will print perfectly at twice its size. Most old family snaps were small— 3x4-inches or so—which, scanned at 300dpi, will produce a small 3MB+/- file. But scan the same print at 4800dpi and the resulting file could be printed as big as a poster.
- Scanning a 35mm film negative/positive on a flatbed scanner (with its film adaptor) requires a high resolution because the original negative is so small, and this is where having an efficient and fast machine can really help your production.
- For smartphone users, there are a number of quite good scanning apps available. These can produce reasonable results providing the lighting is appropriate and you have a steady hand.

Dedicated Film Scanner Tips

High end film-capable flatbed scanners are probably the best option if you are looking to scan different film formats (ie. 35mm, 120, and 5x4-inch film) and prints.

- Dedicated film scanners are ideal if that's all you need to digitize. They are also less expensive (The more you pay, the better the quality and the higher the resolution produced).

- Because film negatives are so (relatively) small they have to be enlarged significantly. Which means that any dust, scratches, fingerprints—and even drying marks left from the original chemical processing—will show up in the scan. Clean the film carefully using an anti-static microfibre cloth, taking care not to add your own marks, especially on the emulsion (matt) side of the film. A blower brush is a good tool to use.

- One way to save time retouching blemishes in Photoshop Elements later is to use the included **dust and scratches removal software** during the scan. Compare the result with a straight scan, then see if you can do better using Elements.

- Open the scanned file in Elements, then run the **Dust & Scratches filter** over it (**Quick/Expert> Filter>Noise>Dust & Scratches**). It's a very aggressive filter so try a setting of '1', '2', or '3' Pixels first. It does an excellent job of removing the very small specks. Save the filtered file, then remove the larger marks using the Spot Healing Brush Tool.

Digitizing Photos with a Camera

Digitizing your precious family photos or artworks with a camera might not be a first thought to some, but, when done properly, it can produce outstanding results, even with an inexpensive compact camera or a smartphone. The easiest way to copy any document is to place it on a flat surface, access your smartphone's camera, line it up, and take the shot. You can do the same with a compact camera, or a DSLR, but if accuracy is required, you'll be aware that lining up the print, getting close enough, overshadowing and uneven lighting, and pop-up flash can all make a copy look amateur in its execution. Here are some tips on how to produce professional-looking copies:

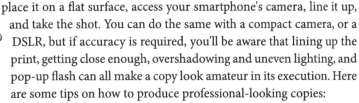

- Always use a camera (or smartphone) **stand**. Shooting indoors, unless the location is brightly lit, produces slow shutter speeds and potentially camera shake. Supporting your camera/ phone on a tripod produces much sharper results, regardless of shutter speed. You can buy a small DSLR or smartphone **tripod** online for less than $20. Some even feature a Bluetooth trigger for vibration-free operation. Perfect!

- Never copy originals in bright sun: cameras and smartphones cannot capture such a wide dynamic range so leave you with no detail in the highlights. Find an evenly lit, shady place, preferably indoors, to make your copies.

- If you need **lights**, consider using two similar-powered table lamps placed either side of the flat artwork at 45 degrees. That's all you need.

- Set the camera to the **low ISO setting** (ie.100 or 200 ISO) for best image quality, the aperture to f8 or f11, and shoot in **Aperture Priority Mode**.

- Use the camera's **self-timer** or a **bluetooth remote trigger** to take the shot—that way you don't touch the camera and run the risk of adding camera shake.

- If the prints being copied are not flat, stick them down using Blu Tack.

- A zoom lens is ideal for copying different-sized pictures as it allows you to reframe each shot rather than having to fiddle around with the height/position of the tripod support.

- If you have slides or negatives to copy, consider buying a **digital slide copier**, a device that screws onto the lens. It is a very simple yet effective device, but check the specs to see if it will work with your specific lens.

For more on how to perfect your scans, turn to *Chapter 4, Getting Started with Simple Solutions*.

Above: I often use an old wooden dressmaker's t-square to help me line up pictures if I'm copying a lot of work. It speeds up the copy process and it also means I waste less time when doing the final edits in Elements. All that's needed is some cropping and tonal enhancement. If shooting down onto a table top it's a good idea to tape the zoom ring in place with a piece of masking tape because zoom rings tend to move of their own accord when pointed down!

Color management: Understanding color spaces

Cameras, all monitors, and most printers can display only a limited range of colors—this is called the **color space**. The industry standard space is called **sRGB color** (Standard, Red, Green, and Blue), but there are many other *spaces*, such as **Adobe RGB (1998)** and **ProPhoto RGB**, to name just two.

Most color spaces correctly claim to encompass a broader range of color than sRGB. While this is certainly true, actually being able to see an increase in the range of colors with one of these wider-ranging spaces, on both a computer screen and in print, is a characteristic that's hard to evaluate because most screens and printers cannot recreate the number of colors captured by the camera regardless of what color space it was recorded in.

Most consumer cameras can only function in the **sRGB** or **Adobe RGB (1998) color spaces**.

I think the best practice for amateur photographers is to choose sRGB. This matches the range of colors that most monitors can display. Plus it matches the gamut, or range, of most consumer photo inkjet printers. That said, some commercial lithographic print businesses now require files to be Adobe RGB (1998) in order to match the high-end print machines they use. If you are considering a move to commercial photography, then Adobe RGB (1998) is the best color space setting. That said, a good color prepress business should also be able to make these space conversions for you, for a fee.

Keep it current: Elements is fully compatible with most RAW file formats, provided that your software is up to date. To ensure this is the case, go to the **Help** menu at the top of the Organizer, or any of the edit screens, and choose **Help>Updates**. This normally works perfectly but occasionally it doesn't load the latest software update. You'll notice this when trying to open a RAW file from a new camera. Elements will state that it **does not recognize that format**. Try updating the software through the **Help** menu. If that fails, go to the Adobe site and follow the prompts to download the update and install it manually.

Adobe Photoshop Elements Add-on Utilities 2023

Adobe RGB 1998 versus sRGB color space: Camera menus tend to be different from each other—refer to your camera's manual to find the option of color space in the menu setup.

In the illustration, compare the color range difference between Adobe RGB and the narrower sRGB space. For many, the fact that sRGB has a smaller range of colors makes no difference—it's only when asked to reproduce very specific colors (for example, clothes in a catalog) that you need to consider spaces such as Adobe RGB 1998. Whatever your choice, it's important to always calibrate the monitor so you know that what you see onscreen is an accurate rendition of the original.

Adobe RGB

sRGB

Color management: Color settings

It's a sad fact that all image editing is virtually worthless if the monitor on which you make all your creative decisions doesn't actually represent the correct color, brightness, and contrast accurately.

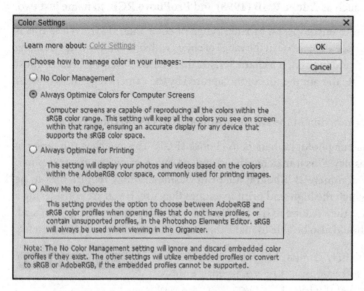

Color management—the process of making sure that what you see onscreen is both accurate to life and will be correctly reproduced online and in print—is, I think, an unnecessarily complex operation. Although Elements' calibration is not nearly as controllable as that found in Photoshop CC, it's presented in a reasonably easy format that should work well in most situations. And if you are sending your work into a commercial print environment, you can always let them handle the finer complexities of color reproduction, which allows you to pay more attention to the editing process.

What you'll find in the program's **Color Settings** dialog box are four simple options:

- **No Color Management**
- **Always Optimize Colors for Computer Screens**
- **Always Optimize for Printing**
- **Allow Me to Choose**

Essentially, this means that if you choose to ignore any color management, Elements will discard existing color space settings, but if you choose to optimize colors, the color range will be kept within the existing sRGB color range.

If you go for the printing option, it would be best to set Adobe RGB (1998) in your camera. The **Allow Me to Choose** option permits the user to make a choice between sRGB and Adobe RGB (1998).

Color Management: Screen and printer calibration

Another important technique for ensuring that what you see onscreen is accurate is to calibrate your monitor with a hardware calibration device.

These third-party sensors plug into the USB outlet on the computer and hang over the screen. Run the associated software and the sensor will determine whether the RGB colors displayed onscreen really are 100% red, green, blue, white, gray, and black. If the screen is different from the known values for these colors, the software adjusts the brightness and color to make it display correctly. This is a far more accurate method of color management than using the human eye to gauge the settings. As a general rule, screens need calibrating every six months or so, especially if they are used a lot.

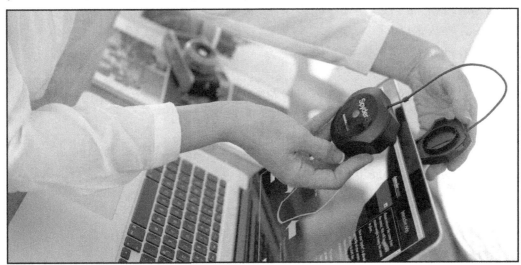

Screen calibration: Attaching a USB-powered hardware calibrator to the laptop or desktop screen is easy. Pictured is the (reasonably inexpensive) ColorVision Spyder5 device. This process needs to be done (probably) once every six months or so, to ensure that what you see onscreen is a realistic representation of the original image. It does not ensure print accuracy—that's the job of another device (see below).

Printer calibration: Making what comes out in print look exactly the same as what's seen onscreen is a slightly trickier and more expensive operation.

For this you need another scanner that can read both screens and test prints. It takes longer to print and scan the resulting chequerboard of colors, but once done, the accuracy of screen-to-printed paper is exceptional.

Organizer keyboard shortcuts

I always provide my students with a list of 10-20 keyboard shortcuts. I can usually see that most are not happy with having yet more stuff to remember. But if you train yourself to use some of these, instead of relying on the mouse all the time, you'll not only reduce the risk of RSI, but you'll also find many repetitive tasks so much safer and faster to execute. Two hands are always better than one.

Operations and their respective Windows/Mac shortcuts are as follows

- Undo last operation: *Ctrl/Cmd + Z*
- Redo last operation: *Ctrl/Cmd + Y*
- Copy: *Ctrl/Cmd + C*
- Paste: *Ctrl/Cmd + P*
- Select all: *Ctrl/Cmd + A*
- Deselect: *Ctrl/Cmd + Shift + D*
- Rotate image 90 degrees left: *Ctrl/Cmd + Left Arrow*
- Rotate image 90 degrees right: *Ctrl/Cmd + Right Arrow*
- Adjust date and time: *Ctrl/Cmd + J*
- Edit in Expert Edit Mode: *Ctrl/Cmd + I*
- Edit in Premiere Elements Editor: *Ctrl/Cmd + M*
- Zoom in: *Ctrl/Cmd + +*
- Zoom out: *Ctrl/Cmd + -*
- OK: *Enter*
- Cancel: *Esc*
- Display metadata properties: *Alt + Enter*
- Add caption: *Ctrl/Cmd + Shift + T*
- Update thumbnails: *Ctrl/Cmd + Shift + U*
- Set photo as desktop wallpaper: *Ctrl/Cmd + W*
- Open Color Settings dialog box: *Ctrl/Cmd + Alt + G*

Summary

It's always been something of a dry subject, but setting up a computer for quality photo editing tasks is not as simple a task as many might imagine—and of course, it's far more demanding on your equipment than simply writing a few emails and surfing the internet!

This chapter explained the basics of setting up a computer: adding memory, choosing hard drives, considering backup drive options, as well as learning about color spaces, and calibrating the monitor so that what we see onscreen is an accurate depiction of what we photographed. It's a big topic but once understood, it will send you out into the editing universe well prepared.

We also took note of the many tools found in Elements Organizer that are designed to help us keep track of our ever-increasing photo and video media collections. And again, although this is often seen as being as exciting as cleaning the bathroom or filling out a tax return, once done, you'll find yourself on top of the image cataloging process, thus making future expansions to your image collections significantly less problematic.

And we haven't even edited an image yet! Coming up in the next chapter, you'll find a heap of great information about adding a range of basic and easy edits to images—all of which can produce brilliant results: dealing with RAW files, saving files, cropping, straightening, lightening, darkening, and a great deal more. It doesn't take long to produce truly impressive results with this editing application.

3
The Basics of
Image Editing

To many, image editing, or more specifically, the word *Photoshop*, conjures up ideas of fantastical landscapes, or of portraits of impossibly beautiful people retouched to the brink of plausibility and beyond.

If you are not interested in taking your creativity into the realm of photo illustration or image composites, you'll more than likely use photo editing to make your digital photos look exactly as they appeared when the shutter button was first pressed.

But why would we need this sort of artificial aid in the first place? It's a frequently asked question, and the simple answer is that **what we see is not always what our camera records**. This is because we have a brain that can be very flexible when it comes to processing the visual information it receives from any scene, whereas a camera simply responds to the light it is pointed at with essentially a rather limited ability to translate that information into a faithful, realistic reproduction of any scene.

One of the biggest drawbacks of image editing is its apparent complexity. No one wants to spend hours slaving over a keyboard with little to show for their toil. In this chapter, you'll discover the basics of how to make your photos look as good, if not better than when you first pressed the shutter button.

But you'll also learn how to generate some exceptionally cool effects and creative 'looks', all with very little time and effort, it's that easy. And, of course, that might leave you with extra time to go out and shoot more great pictures!

And if you are a RAW file shooter, you'll also be able to take control of those files and learn how to transform them into something that better resembles a perfect picture using the tools and techniques covered in this chapter.

In this chapter, we'll learn about the following:

- The editing workflow and best practices
- Editing RAW files: Overview
- Editing RAW files: Basics tab
- Editing RAW files: Sharpening
- Editing RAW files: Noise reduction
- Editing RAW files: Profile browser
- Editing RAW files: Other features
- 10 ways to open a photo for editing
- Understanding picture resolution
- Cropping for better composition
- The Straighten tool

- Increasing/Decreasing resolution: Resampling
- Instant photo fixes using the Organizer
- Auto tone correction tools
- Mastering contrast: using Levels
- Mastering contrast: using Shadow/Highlights
- Mastering color: using Hue/Saturation
- Simple retouching: Smooth Skin feature
- Simple retouching: Spot removal

Use the **gamut warning** feature to discover what tones you might inadvertently miss in your edits using the power of the Camera RAW utility.

The editing workflow and best practices

Nearly all digital camera images need some form of adjustment to make them appear as the scene did when the image was first captured. What many might not immediately appreciate is that there will always be a visual difference between a RAW file and a JPEG file once they are downloaded onto a computer.

This is because the former is neither compressed nor processed in-camera, while JPEG files are compressed and processed in-camera. JPEGs are also 8-bit files, which contain considerably less picture information than a 10-, 12-, or 14-bit RAW file.

Here are two working examples of how in-camera JPEG file processing can initially produce a significantly better-looking version of the same shot (on the right) when compared to the **14-bit (Canon) RAW file** on the left. Because this was shot inside a poorly lit church, there's some underexposure present, but worse than that, there's overexposure in the highlights, typical of any photo taken in a dark place that has little ambient light and a lot of artificial lighting. Most of the lost detail in the shadows and highlights should be recoverable from the RAW file in Elements but not if you try editing the JPEG file.

Best practices for editing files are as follows:

1. **Download** your images to a computer, if this is your default storage place. If not, download them to an external drive.
2. **Back up** the files on the computer to a hard drive, a second drive, and/or the cloud.
3. **Open** a file (see *10 ways to open a photo for editing* later in this chapter).
4. Crop the image to the desired shape or format (be aware that cropping removes pixels, which in turn reduces the printable size of the file—see the *Cropping for better composition* section later in this chapter).

> **Note:**
>
> If you had the option to Save to the Cloud in the 2021 version of Elements, it disappeared in the 2022 version, but it's now back—go to the **Save to Cloud** button in either the **Organizer** or the **Expert Edit** window. Registered users get 2GB cloud storage and access to the new web browser.

5. Check and adjust the **white balance**. For RAW files, do this in the special **Camera RAW** editing window. You can reset any camera's **White Balance** setting from **As Shot** to **Shade**, **Cloudy**, **Indoors**, **Fluorescent**, or whichever setting you have in your camera. If the color is wrong in a JPEG, you can also force it to open in Camera RAW (**File>Open in Camera RAW**) or use one of Elements' seven color adjustment tools (**Enhance>Adjust Color**) to make things appear better.

6. Check and adjust **Brightness** and **Contrast**.

7. Adjust the color intensity using the **Saturation** and/or **Vibrance** tools.

8. Fine-tune the color using tools such as the **Adjust Color for Skin Tone** tool.

9. Apply **Retouching** where needed.

10. Add special effects, text, images, and so on.

11. Adjust **Sharpness**, fine-tuning it to the file's ultimate usage: web or print.

I don't know if any photographer has ever done a comparative study between the success rate of a RAW file versus a JPEG file. I know that at the beginning of the digital imaging revolution, a lot of so-called professional photographers would say that using RAW files was akin to some sort of religious experience and anyone contemplating JPEGs should be barred from civilized society. Maybe I exaggerate a little, but there was, and to a certain extent, there still is, a degree of negative press against the JPEG file format. That being said, here's a clear example of the type of shooting situation where a RAW file really does lord it over a JPEG result. Night-time photography is contrasty—the JPEG overexposes and loses detail in the precious highlights, as illustrated in the red overlay in the top right. The JPEG, at the bottom, looks punchier in terms of color, but is missing most of the lighter tones, while the RAW file at the top reproduces something a lot closer to what the human eye experiences.

Overview: editing RAW files

RAW files produce the best photo-editing results because they contain about four times the image data of an 8-bit JPEG file. But this extra size can be annoying, as it uses up more hard drive space, so files can't be emailed, and initially, they look rather drab compared to a JPEG file. That being said, some **quick editing** in the Elements' native Camera RAW utility will usually produce an image that looks a lot better than most JPEGs.

One aspect of RAW files that might confuse beginners is that they can only be opened/processed using the **Camera RAW** utility, which is quite separate from the **Quick/Guided/Expert** edit modes. It's a bit like having a specialist application within the parent application, which is Photoshop Elements Photo Editor. If you double-click any RAW file icon, it has to open in the **Camera RAW** window within Elements rather than opening inside the **Quick**, **Guided**, or **Expert** workspaces (double-clicking any JPEG, TIFF, PNG, or PSD file will open it directly in **Quick** or **Expert** mode).

Camera RAW utility: At the time of writing, Camera RAW was version 14.4 (note, you might have to download the RAW utility the first time it's used). Double-click any RAW file and this application is what opens—for some photographers, this is the only software that they ever need to make their images look great. Clicking **Open Image** (bottom right-hand side) closes the **Camera RAW** window and takes you to the main **Quick, Guided** or **Expert** edit workspace, where it can be further edited or saved in a more usable file format such as Photoshop, TIFF, or JPEG. If you make an edit, then click **Done**, Elements saves your changes automatically in a **separate file**—a bit like a set of instructions—so that when that same file is opened again, it refers to that file first so it can apply your last set of changes as it opens. If that special file gets deleted, once clicked, the RAW file simply reverts to its original, unedited state.

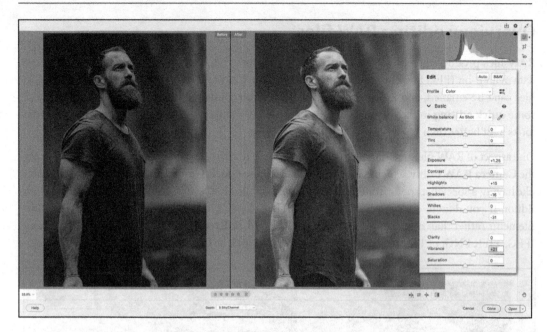

Edit the file: In Camera RAW, photographers can start with the **Edit** tab (here, enlarged on the right-hand side of the screen) to edit **White Balance**, plus make adjustments to **Exposure** (brightness) and **Contrast**. Other adjustments include: **Highlights**, **Shadows**, **Blacks**, **Whites**, **Clarity** (an increase of the mid-tone contrast levels), **Vibrance** (which delivers a boost to weaker-looking color in the file), and, of course, **Saturation**, a slider that boosts all the colors in the file across its entire spectrum. Set this to a negative value and the file eventually turns black and white. Camera RAW 12.3 has been simplified in that the previous **Edit** and **Detail** tabs have been amalgamated into just the one menu, making the workflow somewhat easier to follow.

Sharpening should be the last step in the editing process and is essentially only undertaken when you know how the image is to be used. For example, different amounts of sharpening are applied to images that are to be printed or uploaded to social media. We generally add about 25% more sharpening to files that are to be printed because the print process of ink on paper produces a slightly softer-looking result.

And perversely, once the sharpening effect is added to the image, you might see more digital noise, which can be very annoying visually, so Elements incorporates not one, but two noise reduction filters, **Luminance Noise** reduction and **Color Noise** reduction, in the **Camera RAW** edit workflow.

Tip:

Don't forget to keep your copy of Elements updated so that the RAW processor can read and edit RAW files from the latest camera models released. If you are not sure if you have the latest version of Camera RAW, navigate to **Help**>**Updates** to check.

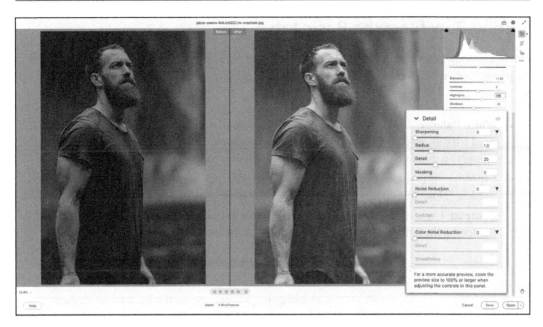

Sharpen the file: Once you're happy with those processes, you can sharpen the file using the **Detail** tab. This deals with sharpening and noise reduction. The reason these two features are at the end of the processing list is simple: there's no point in sharpening a picture if it's too dark or garishly colored because you won't be able to see the sharpening action effectively. Get the tones and color right first, then apply sharpening.

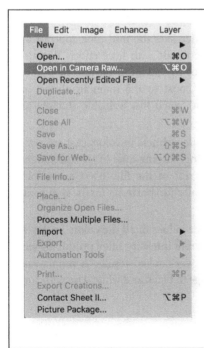

Tip:

You can also force non-RAW files, such as JPEGs or TIFFs, to open in the **Camera RAW** processing window by choosing the **File>Open in Camera Raw...** command first, allowing you to use RAW features on non-RAW files.

Even humble JPEG images can benefit from this feature. I do this quite a lot, so I can use the excellent **Unsharp Mask** and **Noise Reduction** features, which I find often can work better than the ones located under the Photo Editor workspace's **Filter** drop-down menu. It's **White Balance** sliders are also a reliable way to color-correct almost any tonal inconsistency.

Having said that though, if your JPG file is significantly over- or under-exposed, those highlight or shadow tones will have been lost forever. So, even bringing them into Camera RAW will not be enough to rescue the situation. Expose more carefully or shoot RAW files...

Editing Raw files: the Basic tab

This section includes a more detailed description of what the many Camera RAW tools offer the photographer. To achieve significant changes and improvements to your images, concentrate on the following:

- **White Balance**: Using this, you can easily reset your white balance setting to whatever you need (that is, reset from **Shady** to **Daylight**, **Tungsten**, **Flash**, or even back to **Auto**). It also allows you to refine the color using the blue/yellow or magenta/green sliders.

- **Exposure**: This is also called brightness. It's used to brighten/darken the initial exposure if needed. (Note: this does not recover tones if the file is grossly over or underexposed.)

- **Contrast**: Quite different from **Exposure**, **Contrast** darkens the darker parts of the file while lightening the lighter parts of the image, resulting in fewer midtones.

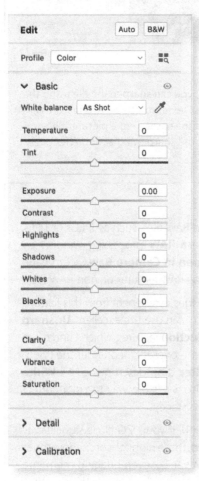

Use it to add visual *punch* to your images. Too much contrast loses valuable details in the shadows and highlights—keep an eye on the RGB values in those marginal tonal areas.

- **Highlights/Shadows/Whites/Blacks**: Separate and adjust those tonal zones using these four sliders. They allow you to increase/decrease contrast and boost the sharpness without the need for creating time-consuming masks or selections. These sliders can make a significant improvement to almost any file.

- **Clarity**: This slider increases the mid-tone contrast and produces a **dramatic result** with little effort. **Warning**: too much *clarity* is not a good look, but just enough can add a much-needed boost to the tones in almost any image; too much and you'll lose valuable shadow and highlight detail.

- **Vibrance**: Increases the richness in colors that are not so colorful while, amazingly, doing little to enhance already bright colors in the rest of the file. It's a great color-boosting tool, especially for portraits (as in skin tones) and landscapes.

- **Saturation**: Boosts the values of all the colors in the file, regardless of their current intensity, often producing what I call *candy-colored*, over-cooked results. A minus value reverts the color image to black and white. Use with some caution.

Editing RAW files: the Detail (sharpening) tab

Sharpening is all about contrast—and in particular, edge contrast. If you make the darks go darker and the lights go a bit lighter, you add contrast—and the image appears clearer and sharper. A little sharpening can even make a (slightly) shaky-looking shot appear a bit clearer, and it can make an already clear image look really stunning.

It's also very important to sharpen for specific output requirements. Sharpening for print is different from sharpening for social media. It's even slightly different for different types of paper stock (such as glossy or matte) because each has a varied absorbency characteristic.

The **Detail** (**Sharpening**, or more correctly, **Unsharp Masking**) tab offers some adjustments that don't make a lot of sense until you understand how a sharpening *mask* actually works:

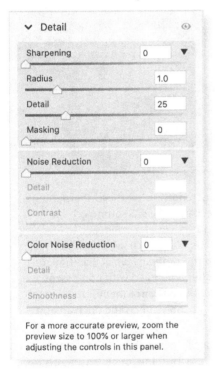

For a more accurate preview, zoom the preview size to 100% or larger when adjusting the controls in this panel.

- **Sharpening**: Adds the amount of sharpening effect to the file. Set it to 100 and move on to refine the look by tweaking **Radius**, **Detail**, and **Masking**.

- **Radius**: The sharpening process looks for **edges of contrast** to which it applies its effect. The radius dictates how far, either side of the found edge, it looks for that contrast difference. A setting of 1.0 to 1.5 pixels works well.

- **Detail**: This is used to emphasize the found **edge detail** in the image. Hold down the *Alt/Opt* key when shifting this slider to see the precise edge detail being added to the image.

- **Masking**: This feature should be under **Amount**, not at the bottom of this list. If you hold down the *Alt/Opt* key, then shift the **Masking** slider, you'll see a black and white mask appear onscreen (*see the screenshot on Page 11*). Anything that's black is *protected* or masked, so no sharpening is added. Everything white is not masked and is sharpened accordingly.

By adding a **mask**, in this case set to a value of 86, I have limited the effect of the sharpening to the white areas in the mask only. The black areas in the mask are opaque, and therefore protect that part of the image from change.

> **Tip:**
> Holding the *Alt/Opt* key down while sliding the **Exposure**, **Highlight**, **Shadow**, **Whites**, or **Blacks** sliders to the left or right displays the **gamut warning**, a feature which highlights loss of detail due to overexposure or underexposure. This is an excellent viewing technique for assessing just how far to go with your brightening or darkening adjustments.

Never over-sharpen your work: By applying near full strength to all these sharpening settings, you'll see a lot of grittiness in the skin tones, especially if the ISO setting is high (for most cameras, that is over 800 ISO). Too much sharpening is never a good idea, because it can make a (portrait) subject appear older and less glamorous than they really are, as you see in the right-hand portrait example here. By using the mask, the program can concentrate on just the important bits of the face in this example and not get entangled with non-essential details. If you use the excellent **Smooth Skin** feature (under the **Enhance** menu), you'll note that the smoothness effect, even when applied at full strength, only affects the open areas of skin and not the eyes, nose, lips, eyebrows, and so on.

Another tip when sharpening is to avoid sharpening a file more than once. Layering sharpness in multiple passes can significantly damage a file and once an image is over-sharpened, it's very difficult to go back to the way it originally looked.

Tip:

Besides just sharpening an image file, a second, but equally as important, thing to consider is the end result—what's the file going to be used for? Sharpening for print should be more aggressive than if it's just being used to display on social media—unfortunately, there's really no one setting that fits all when it comes to sharpening photographs.

Revealing the (unsharp) mask: By holding down the *Alt/Opt* key while shifting the **Masking** slider, Elements reveals the "mask" in stark black and white. The black areas are protected by the mask and the white areas are affected by any manipulation of the **Amount**, **Radius**, and **Detail** sliders. The idea in this portrait example is that you do not want to sharpen the pores in the skin—but you might want to accentuate the lips, nose, eyebrows, and hairline. In this example, that's exactly what the unsharp mask does—it's a perfect tool for all portraitists, but it's also effective for general photography.

Below: The following example has been softened slightly using the unsharp mask—now it needs some of the excess noise levels reduced.

Editing Raw files: Noise Reduction

Digital noise is the bane of any photographer's life. It's caused (mostly) by using **high ISO settings** while shooting in poor light. Ironically, high ISO in good lighting usually has negligible noise effects. Smaller sensor cameras are particularly prone to this horrible side effect. Sharpening can also increase the look of added graininess in the file, so we have to use a little **Noise Reduction** to keep the result looking clean and clear of noise.

There are two kinds of noise: **Luminance** and **Color** noise. Both are horrible to look at, but perhaps color noise is worse:

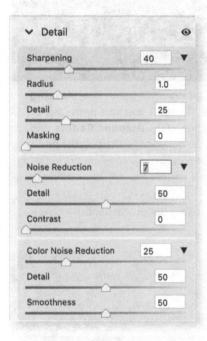

- **Luminance** noise is just a graininess in the image, seen especially in the darker, underexposed parts of a scene. The higher the ISO rating, the more it appears. Underexposure will also show noise far more than if shooting in daylight. The **Luminance** noise slider softens the texture of the picture. Too much, and the image might take on a slightly surreal, airbrushed look. The **Luminance Detail** and **Luminance Contrast** sliders help reintroduce a bit of sharpness without adding more noise, but in practice, I find that they have only a limited influence on the end result.

- **Color** noise is significantly uglier than luminance noise because we, as photographers, are perhaps more used to film grain (present in the super-fast films of 20 years ago), but color specks in our digital pictures? This is an all-digital phenomenon that just never looks nice. Shifting the slider turns color noise into black and white noise, which, I think, looks far more acceptable than the color version.

The **Color Detail** and **Color Smoothness** sliders are there to help make the noise removal process less obvious. I use the Luminance and Color noise removal sliders all the time, but find the other four to be almost too subtle in their actions to have a visual benefit for my images.

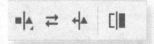

Raw view modes: Pressing one of the three small tabs in the bottom right-hand corner of the main window, you can view before and after versions of your labors. Once you begin editing, you can move the already-edited display to the left-hand window by pressing the second tab. The third tab allows you to transfer edits from the left to the right so you can carry on adding edits. The fourth icon gives you a straight before/after view.

Noise reduction is the second part of the **Detail** panel and should only be used if you think the image requires it. Remember, any noise reduction filter action will end up softening the image. How much to add really depends on your requirements and how the image is to be exported, be it online or destined for print. Here's a picture I photographed in a cave church in Ethiopia. I had to use a high ISO (3200) because it was so dark—and once the image was onscreen, I could see it was suffering from a lot of color noise (left-hand image). I use Canon cameras, and they seem to have a lot more color noise than equivalent Nikon cameras. In Elements' Camera RAW utility, I can then reduce that color noise to almost nothing. The fixed right-hand image is pretty good, although the tones are beginning to look a bit soft—the negative effect of too much filtering...

Tip:

It's interesting to note that over the years, file types (`.jpg`, `.tif`, `.psd`) have not changed much—apart from one new format, **HEIF (high efficiency image format)**. This is supposed to contain twice as much image data than a same-sized `.jpg` file with no loss of quality and is currently the go-to format for Apple smartphones. This is a derivation of the HEVC (video) format, which uses the highly successful H.265 codec. Adobe Photoshop Elements 2023 is supposed to be compatible with HEIF and HEVC files. On a Mac I have found this to be the case, but on a PC, depending on how the application was first downloaded, you might have to download a special HEIF extension - from Adobe or Microsoft.

Editing Raw files: Other Features

Camera RAW is not just all about making your images lighter, darker, or more colorful. It's packed with an entire editing suite of tools, features, and processes all designed to make the job of editing images that much more streamlined and professional. Features include cropping, histogram adjustments, tonal information, over and underexposure control, as well as a sophisticated **Profile Browser** for applying some awesome color and mono looks:

Cropping: One of the many advantages of using RAW files is this: once the image has been cropped, the RAW file still retains **all the original pixels**—meaning it's easy to go back to it and re-crop. Pixels are **never discarded**. The nature of the edit is recorded either in the file itself or in a "sidecar `.xmp`" file (which is little more than a text file). Make another change to the image and a new set of instructions is recorded. If you delete the `.xmp` file and the RAW file reverts to its unedited form.

Expanded view of the Profile Browser: This houses a comprehensive color management and special effects feature located just beneath the histogram window. Click the tiny Profile Browser button to the right-hand side of the **Profile** drop-down menu to view the entire selection of RAW profiles in Elements. As mentioned earlier, you might decide that this is too complicated and just go with the Adobe defaults. (Note that these profiles can also be applied to JPEG files.)

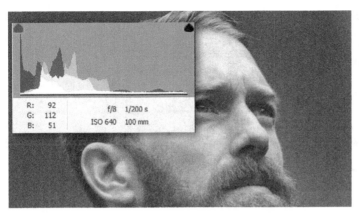

The **histogram** is often overlooked. This small window displays the distribution of tones in any image with shadows and blacks on the left-hand side, and whites and highlights on the right-hand side, making it easy to see, at a glance, whether the image is over or underexposed.

Use this readout to check the **camera shooting settings** (ISO, aperture, shutter speed, and the **focal length of the lens**). A useful feature of the histogram is its RGB values readout, here reading R: 92, G: 112, B: 51. Move the cursor over any part of the image to see how dark or light it really is as an RGB value. Zero indicates you can't see any detail, while 255 means that it's so white (overexposed) that you can't see any detail there either. This measurement bypasses the accuracy of the screen display (which might be wrong). What it displays is an accurate measurement of the brightness levels in the file, so it can be used to assess the influence of your editing on the file.

The histogram keeps on giving: By clicking either, or both, of the triangles at the top left and top right of the histogram window, you can switch on the **Shadow** and **Highlight** warning feature. If the image is over-brightened or over-darkened, you'll see a warning color highlighting the affected tones. In the example on the left, you can clearly see that the highlights are red, indicating **dramatic overexposure**. Like the RGB value display, this can be an invaluable and instant visual feedback tool on a monitor that might not be properly calibrated.

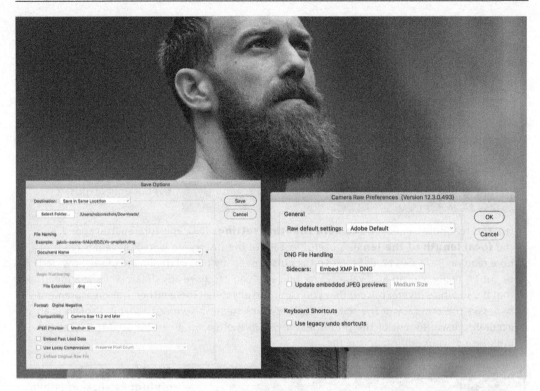

Camera RAW Save Options + Camera Raw Preferences: These two panels are opened from the top right-hand side of the Camera RAW main screen. **Save Options** offers the user choices as to where the edited file can be saved (if not back in the location it came from). You also use this panel to rename files and even to change the saved format—to DNG (digital negative) format. **Preferences** is the panel that allows you to choose between saving your edits as an XMP file separate to the RAW file and saving as the RAW file itself—a safer option. I think most Elements users never even look at the features—you really don't need them unless you have a specific application for one of the features mentioned here.

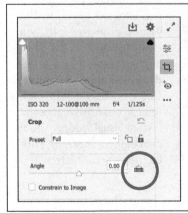

Did you know?

Aside from having an effective cropping features, Camera RAW also includes the **Level Tool**.

It's icon is the same as its cousin's on the Tool Bar: a builder's **spirit level**. It also works in the same way—click and drag the stretchy line across the horizon where you imagine it should be, click a second time and it rotates and crops your image to align with the new level.

10 ways to open a photo for editing

You can choose any of several different ways to get an image from the Organizer into any of the three editing modes to start creating magic:

- Right-click any thumbnail in **Organizer** and choose **Edit with Photoshop Elements Editor** (panel to the right).

- Select a thumbnail in **Organizer**, then select the **Photo Editor** option from the **Editor** button pop-up at the base of the page (inset, on the right).

- Click/select a thumbnail in **Organizer**, then drag it directly into the edit window (into **Quick** and **Expert** modes).

- Click the **Open** tab (top left-hand side in **Expert**), then navigate to the image files. Double-click the file name/icon.

- Choose **File>Open recently edited file** in the **Quick**, **Guided**, and **Expert** edit modes.

- Drag an image (icon) from a Windows/Mac **Finder** window into the **Quick** or **Expert** edit window.

- Use the **File>Open** menu command.

- Use the *Ctrl/Cmd + O* keyboard shortcut.

- Click/select a thumbnail in **Organizer**, then press *Ctrl/Cmd + I* (opens in **Expert** mode).

- Using *Alt/Opt + Ctrl/Cmd + O* (**Quick** or **Expert** modes), navigate to the appropriate RAW, JPEG, or TIFF file, and click **Open** to bring it into the **Camera RAW** window.

Left: Don't miss the pop-up tab at the bottom of the Organizer to access three editing applications: **Photo Editor**, **Video Editor**, and **External Editor**.

Final thought: Don't forget that right-clicking any image icon in either **Windows Explorer** or the **Mac Finder** also provides an opportunity to open the file. If it opens in something other than Elements, change it to Photoshop Elements via the file's Properties. Do this once, then all files of that type will automatically open using that same software.

Understanding picture resolution

Resolution, and in particular, **photo resolution**, is a feature that confuses many. This shouldn't be an issue because the resolution of a camera is a **fixed quantity** and only changes when you physically choose a different picture size in the camera menu—or if you **crop the file** on a computer.

To be pedantic, resolution is not only about the number of pixels in the camera, although this is important. Resolution is also influenced by the quality of the **glass elements** in the lens, the camera's image stabilization technology (indirectly), and the shooting technique employed by the photographer.

The biggest point of confusion arises from the way the number of **pixels per inch (ppi)** can vary widely from camera to camera. In the printing world, **dots per inch (dpi)** is the same as ppi, which in turn is the same as **lines per inch**.

Different resolutions = different viewing sizes: Demonstrating resolution can be daunting—the web is a low-resolution medium and unsuited for exhibiting high-resolution files. The only difference between these two images is that one is a lower resolution than the other (5Mp compared to 32Mp). Clearly, the more pixels in the image, the larger it can be displayed, both onscreen and in print, while appearing to have the same clarity.

Of course, in photography, we have the tools to crop and enlarge and resample files—all of which can make it hard to keep track of quality. If I were to enlarge a small 5Mp file to the same size as a 32Mp file then print it, this is what you'd see: a very clear left-hand portrait and a soft-focus, low-resolution result in the right-hand portrait. The latter has gone soft because there are not enough pixels in the file to fill the area it has been enlarged to. You'd think that in this case you'd see the pixels, but digital print technology adds a feature called dithering when enlarging image files, and in particular, when printing, so the sharp edges of the pixels are blurred slightly to blend the expected raggedness. This works well for small enlargements, but in this case, all that happens is that the resulting image looks soft.

Tip:

When printing, you need all the pixels you can get. A 24Mp RGB file, for example, will print clearly up to A3 and maybe even bigger if the image quality is exceptional. However, if I were to crop a small bit out of that same file, then enlarge it to A3, the result would be very soft because there would not be enough pixels to produce a detailed, photo quality result.

To make matters somewhat more confusing, different cameras produce different dpi characteristics. For example, a 24Mp Canon might produce files that, when examined in Elements, are set to 180dpi, while a 24Mp Nikon might have its files set to 300dpi. What's the difference? Actually, there's no real difference because both have the **same number of pixels** and are therefore the same resolution—the Canon's files are just programmed (in the camera's software) to be spread out over a larger physical area, but once the Canon image is set (using Elements' **Image Size** feature) to 300dpi, it will come out the same size as the Nikon. That dpi number is just an arbitrary figure set by the camera's designers—it can be changed at any time.

Tip:

There's little to no advantage of printing an image at a resolution higher than 300 dpi because at that setting, the pixels reproduce the look of continuous tone (that is, no pixels are actually visible). Once it is a continuous tone print, adding more pixels does not increase quality—it just has the effect of slowing down the print process (because the file is that much larger and takes longer to transfer from computer to printer). When resampling, software such as Elements can also add dithering, a process in which pixels are blended into each other to give the effect of a smooth tone—inkjet printers are especially good at this. You don't necessarily choose it; it's just part of the process. Although a 300 dpi file produces a smoother, continuous tone because of this dithering process, even files set to 100 dpi can look very good.

Cropping for better composition

Cropping is an editing feature that allows you to trim off parts of the image that you don't like—it provides an opportunity to recompose the shot after it has been taken.

However, one vital point to remember is that cropping **discards pixels** and therefore lowers file resolution. I love photographing birds, but unfortunately, they always tend to be too far away, even with a 400 mm telephoto lens, so I have to crop the edges off the file to make the subject appear larger. If I crop 50% from a photo, it then looks as if I have shot the subject with an 800 mm lens, not my regular 400 mm lens. Cropping has saved me a lot of money so that I do not have to buy an even more powerful (and thus very expensive) lens. But the inevitable compromise is that, in that example, I have lost half the pixels in the file—no problem if I only ever post the image online, but will be a restriction if I hope to have it printed large.

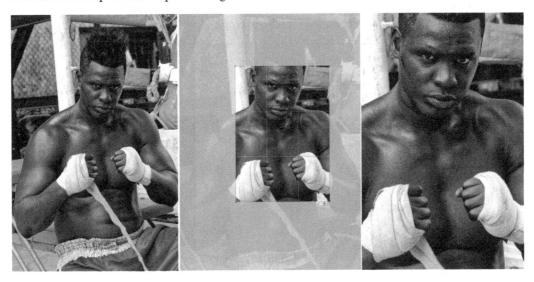

Left frame: This screenshot shows the image's full frame.

Middle frame: I have dragged the **Crop** tool over the boxer to go in close over his face and fists—the gray overlay indicates this portion of the file (about 70% of it) will be lost once I click the green **OK** button located on the cropping overlay.

Right-hand frame: The final cropped result looks pretty good, but once this is enlarged to the same size as the original, it does appear a little soft—because I have chopped out 70% of the pixels and then expect it to look really good at the same size. If this were destined for online use, there'd be no loss of quality because both versions have more than enough pixels to display clearly at 72dots per inch (screen resolution).

Inset: Printed at this size, the cropped version appears as sharp as the original, albeit somewhat smaller.

Crop is one of the easiest tools to use. Here's how it works:

Step one: In **Quick** or **Expert** mode, press *C* on the keyboard to engage the **Crop** tool or select it from the toolbar (make sure it's the **Crop** tool and not one of the other tools on the same peg: the **Cookie Cutter** or **Crop Perspective** tools).

Step two: Click and drag the cursor anywhere over the image. This draws a **Crop Marquee**. When you press the green check mark at the bottom of the marquee, the parts of the image inside that marquee are kept, while the outer pixels are discarded. Clicking the red symbol cancels the cropping operation, as does pressing the *Esc* key.

Step three: If your initial attempt is not the shape, size, or rotation you want, release the mouse and grab one of the edge handles (the little square tags in the center, or corners, of the marquee) and adjust the proportions of the crop edges. Note that if you slide the cursor over the edge of any corner to the outside of the marquee, the cursor changes from a **diagonal shape** to a **curved shape**, meaning that you can now **rotate** the entire crop marquee. Use this to crop and rotate at the same time, for example, to get a horizon level. If you find this fiddly, try the **Straighten** tool first (see the *Straightening horizons* section later in this chapter), then crop it.

Instant photo framing: One neat feature of the **Crop** tool is it works: to **add a border** to any image. To do this, all that's needed is for you to first drag the crop marquee across the entire image. An easy way to do this is to drag from outside the image (over the pasteboard area) diagonally to the opposite corner. Now that the entire image is covered by the **Crop** tool, drag it a second time over the pasteboard—as seen above and on the left. The crop marquee spreads out away from the picture edges. When you have the desired width and height, click the green check mark and Elements adds pixels to the image. Note that the resulting border color is based on the current **background color**. If you need a different color border, the background **Color Picker** must be chosen before the **Crop** tool is engaged.

Elements has a number of excellent additional cropping features to help the compositional process, such as **Rule of Thirds** and a **Grid** overlay. These are included to help you recompose shots into more dynamic-looking compositions. There are also four **preset crop shapes offered as potential cropping suggestions**—click the image thumbnails in the **Crop Options** panel to initiate them.

If you intend to crop your files to a specific print dimension, use the preset drop-down menu in the **Options** panel. It offers classic print sizes, such as 4 x 6 inches, 5 x 7 inches, and 10 x 8 inches, which is handy when you have a lot of files to crop to the same size. But if you are cropping to a size that's different from the presets, type the dimensions into the width and height fields, making sure you add cm, px, or in (centimeters/pixels/inches) after the width and height measurements; then, when you crop, it resets the resolution at the same time. If the file happens to be smaller than what you have chosen to crop to (that is, a file from a low-resolution camera or smartphone), Elements adds pixels to the image to bring it up to size using a feature called **resampling**. It might make the end result appear softer, but it works pretty well.

The **Crop** tool panel also features the **Cookie Cutter** tool, which I will deal with in *Chapter 7, Advanced Techniques: Retouching, Selections, and Text*.

Proportional viewing: Ever wondered about the resolution seen on **freeway billboards**? As a rule, most of these images are the same resolution as a double-page spread in a glossy magazine. Sounds implausible—but it's all to do with **viewing distances**. We generally read a magazine at a distance of around two feet. A freeway billboard will be viewed at 50 feet, maybe more—and usually at speed. To achieve that immense size, billboards can be printed at a tenth of the resolution (dpi) of a magazine—about 30 dpi—and still produce acceptable clarity. But get out of your car and approach the poster and you'll see that it is not nearly as sharp as it appears from the freeway. **Viewing distance is everything**. (Refer to the upcoming section in this chapter, *Increasing or Decreasing File Size: Resampling* to read about how to add pixels to an image to make it significantly larger.)

The Straighten tool

Alongside the **Crop** tool, I rate the **Straighten** tool highly. Few photographers can shoot a landscape, for example, and get the horizon 100% level. Many photographers, myself included, also have serious problems getting verticals, well, 100% vertical. Here's how this tool works:

Step one: Open an image that needs its horizon leveled.

Step two: Choose the **Straighten** tool (cunningly, its toolbar icon is a builder's spirit level).

Step three: Click once on the horizon and, while holding down the mouse button, drag the *elastic* line that appears from that first click point across the horizon and let go. You do not have to stretch the line along the entire horizon—a few inches is enough. The program immediately rotates the image to make this line the new horizon. If you get it wrong, click **Undo** (*Ctrl*/*Cmd* + *Z*) and try again.

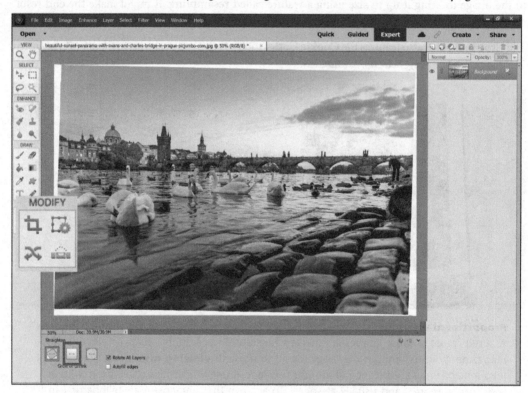

Trimming the rough bits: With the first option at the bottom left of the screen, if the image is rotated to straighten the horizon, pixels are added to the parts that overlap the pasteboard (seen here in white on each side of the image). These bits can be cropped off or, if you choose the second option here (highlighted in red), the software automatically crops it for you. Alternatively, you can check the **Crop to Remove Background** option (in red). This automatically removes the blank edges with pixels copied from inside the image. Clever stuff. If it's only a small amount of fill, the results are usually seamless, but the more space it has to fill, the more likely you are to see auto retouching errors.

Increasing or decreasing file size: Resampling

As we mentioned in the *Cropping for better composition* section, **resampling** is the process of adding or subtracting pixels to any file to make it larger or smaller.

Now, you might think, if this is the case, then your dreams of producing very high-resolution files have just been answered. But there's a catch. Resampling is a mathematical algorithm that can be used to upsample or downsample files effectively, provided that the original is of the highest quality.

In practice, this means that if you try to resample a 1 Mp file so it can be printed as a poster, it's not going to look very sharp. But if you start with a lot more image data—let's say, a 24 Mp file—this can be resampled to 30, 40, or 50 Mp with almost no loss of quality. It could go as high as 200 Mp before it really looks soft.

Further sharpening after the resampling process will help to reverse the softening that adding extra pixels might have created. Also, bear in mind the viewing distance. We might hold an A4 print at arm's length to appreciate its quality, but for a poster, you'd probably stand 6 feet away to get the best view, and therefore would not be so aware of any softening due to resampling.

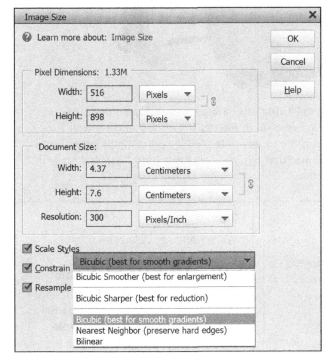

How do we enlarge (or reduce) the size of a file?

Follow these steps:

Step one: Open the file in Elements' **Expert** mode.

Step two: Open the **Image Size** feature (**Image**>**Resize**>**Image Size**).

Step three: Check the **Resample Image** box, at the bottom of this panel.

Step four: Select the resampling method from the drop-down menu at the base of the panel (see the following explanation to learn what each resampling method should be used for).

Step five: Click **OK** and watch as Elements resizes the file. Save the result.

There are several types of resampling offered:

- **Bicubic Smoother**: Best for enlarging a file
- **Bicubic Sharper**: Best for reducing the size of a file
- **Bicubic**: Good for producing smoother tonal gradients
- **Nearest Neighbor**: Perfect for upsizing hard-edged graphic images, such as the screen captures used in this book
- **Bilinear**: Far better than **Nearest Neighbor,** but still not quite as good as bicubic resampling

I'm taking a bit of a visual liberty with this illustration of a large-format inkjet printer. However, if you start resampling with a very high-resolution file (let's say, shot with a Nikon D850, producing a 45 Mb file), it's entirely possible to resample the file several times larger, up to 1 gigabyte and higher. And with a file size that big, you can easily print large posters with no trouble.

Tip:

For best results, do the following:

- Ensure the file is well exposed (that is, not too dark or light) and clear (that is, not blurred).
- Leave the sharpening process until after you have resampled the file.
- Upsampling works best if you keep the enlargement to between 10 and 50%. Any more than that and you'll notice it becoming softer.
- Once resampled, make adjustments to the brightness, contrast, and sharpness if needed.

Tip:

While Elements' default resampling method (Bicubic) generally works well, choosing the specific **Bicubic Smoother** or **Bicubic Sharper** method should produce a better-looking result. Remember to reset your **Resample** method in the **Image Size** panel if you move on to resample hard-edged graphics. Resampling with the wrong method can lead to poor quality— usually in terms of overall sharpness.

Instant photo-fixing in the Organizer

The **Instant Fix** feature found in Elements' Organizer is a good way to produce quick and highly visual effects without the need to transfer the file from the **Organizer** to the **Quick**, **Guided**, or **Expert** modes.

Here's how:

1. Find an image in **Organizer** that you'd like to edit.
2. Select it (click once).
3. Click the **Instant Fix** button at the bottom of the page.
4. Use one or more of the tool or process icons that appear on the right-hand side of the screen.

The tools available are **Crop**, **Red Eye**, **Effects**, **Smart Fix**, **Light**, **Color**, and **Clarity**. You'll find that not all of them are *instant*. The **Crop** tool, for example, requires you to choose a crop ratio first, then position it over the appropriate part of the image, then resize it, if needed, before clicking the green check mark to execute the process. But I'm being pedantic.

Once you are happy with the result, click the **Save** button at the base of the page to apply your awesome edit to the file. I tend to save my files with a different name (such as `cherryblossomFinal.jpg`) so that, months later, when I am looking for that very file, I can recognize it easily from its name.

Using Auto Correction tools

If you don't like the Organizer's rather brief **Instant Fixes**, Elements has a stack of other automated editing tools located within the **Quick** and **Expert** modes. These effects are designed to make your picture editing go faster and with less stress. Some, I think, are nothing short of beautiful, while others might not be so impressive.

There are hundreds of visual possibilities achievable with these features and if some don't work, there will be many others that do. Some of these auto features have several processes wrapped up into the one tool, so while most work admirably, some might do little or nothing to your shot. If this happens, just undo the last action and try another auto tool.

Here's a screenshot of the tone correction tools in **Quick** edit mode, set to a **warmer** color temperature on the right. Use the slider to fine-tune the effect, or just hit one of the nine tone thumbnails to select a different effect recipe.

Tip:

The best file formats to save an edited RAW file are as follows:

JPEG: These are the most common. Used for emailing, in digital photo books, and for social media.

TIFF: A robust file format designed for more aggressive editing or high-end printing.

PSD (Photoshop): An excellent format if you are creating masks, selections, multi-layered edits, adding text, and more.

PNG: Produces larger files than a JPEG—perfect for any project where you need a transparent background. Also used online where the quality of the image is paramount.

Here's how to use the auto correction tools using the **Quick** edit mode:

Step one: From the **Organizer**, select an image and press *Ctrl/Cmd + I* to open that file in the **Editor** window. It opens in whatever edit space you were last using. If this is **Expert**, click **Quick** at the top of the window to switch it to the easier-to-use **Quick** edit space.

Step two: At the bottom right, you'll see the **Adjustments**, **Effects**, **Textures**, and **Frames** tabs. Click **Adjustments** to open that panel, and note the **Smart Fix**, **Exposure**, **Lighting**, **Color**, **Balance**, and **Sharpen** tools that slide out of the right-hand panel. To use these effectively, start at the top (**Smart Fix**) and click **Auto**. If this doesn't help, slide the cursor over the tiny thumbnails to select another strength of the **Smart Fix** effect.

Step three: Then move on to the **Exposure** setting and repeat the same process, if needed, or jump ahead to try one of the other features on offer.

Auto correction in the **Expert** edit space (above left) is quite different from the Quick Edit version (above right). Some of the features offer no adjustment, while others, such as **Auto Smart Tone**, are not really *automatic* at all because they're fully adjustable. Even so, these features are effective to use.

Here's how to use the auto correction tools using the **Expert** edit mode:

Step one: Open an image from **Organizer** in the **Expert** window.

Step two: Starting at the top, click the **Enhance** menu and try the **Auto Smart Fix** or **Auto Smart Tone** features. (Note that **Auto Smart Fix** might not do much, but if its effect is too strong, use the **Adjust Smart Fix** feature, which, weirdly, is located 11 items further down the menu. In my mind, this should be part of the top-level **Smart Fix**.) **Smart Tone** has its own adjustment window. Then continue to run through the rest of the auto tone-fixing features:

- **Auto Levels** will adjust both contrast and color.

- **Auto Contrast** will adjust only the black and white tones in the frame (not the color).

- **Auto Haze Removal**, as the name suggests, is ideal for hazy days, dust, fog, mist, and sea spray. It adds clarity while sometimes making the image darker with more contrast. Often, this action is too harsh—be careful not to overdo it!

- **Auto Shake Reduction** sounds too good to be true, but it can reduce the appearance of blurriness quite effectively. Note that the **Shake Reduction** feature, second from the bottom in this menu, gives you greater control over how this tool works and might prove to be the most effective way to go with not-very-sharp pictures.

- **Auto Sharpen**, amazingly often, hits the spot nicely, adding just a bit more *snappiness* to the edges of your subject and making the image appear crisper than it was before. Like all the **Auto** tools, though, **Auto Sharpen** can often leave you wishing for a stronger version—which, of course, you will find with the **Adjust Sharpness** and **Unsharp Mask** tools seen further down the menu.

You'll see how **Haze Removal**, **Shake Reduction** and other sharpening tools work in greater detail in: *Chapter 8, Additional Tools and Features (Haze Removal), Chapter 10, Exporting Work, Sharpening and Plug-ins (Shake Reduction, Unsharp Masking and more...).*

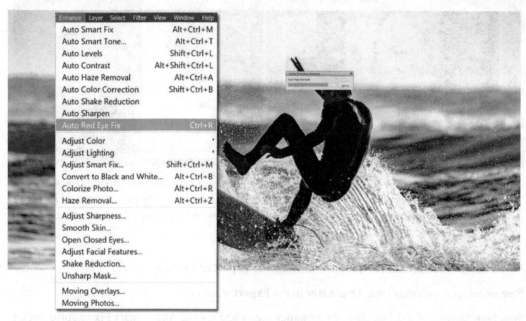

This is the **auto correction** range of tools from the all-important **Enhance** drop-down menu in the **Expert** edit space—with **Auto Haze Removal** highlighted.

Mastering contrast: using Levels

Contrast, or more specifically, a lack of contrast, is often the most noticeable fault in many pictures. This is partly because cameras are designed to capture images with a slightly lower contrast than what was actually present in reality—and in doing so, they capture a slightly wider range of tones than if they were recording higher contrast from the get-go.

JPEGs are processed in-camera—which is why, when compared with a RAW file, they will always appear slightly more colorful, but you can always extract more tonal range from a RAW file. It just needs a little more work.

The best tool to begin editing any non-RAW image (such as a JPEG, TIFF, PNG, or PSD file) is **Levels** (*Ctrl/Cmd + L* or **Enhance>Adjust Contrast>Levels**).

Levels is used to adjust the tonal distribution in any image. You'll recognize this when you see the **histogram**—this is the same display that you'd see on your camera's LCD screen when replaying a file (to make the histogram appear, press the **Display** or **Info** button on the back of the camera). Some cameras do not display the shooting information by default—it has to be turned on via the **Camera** menu.

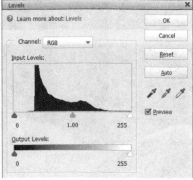

Digital files typically display in low contrast (that is, the black tones usually look a bit washed out). Although this is a very cute-looking kitten, its tones are a little washed out or low contrast. In the **Input Levels** panel, if you see a flat area to the left or right of the tonal *mountain* shape, it most likely needs *fixing*.

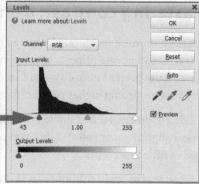

As soon as the shadow slider is shifted to the right (in the **Input Levels** scale), the darker parts of the image go even darker and might lose detail, even though it actually appears clearer and sharper. To maintain all the tonal range in the file, restrict yourself to stopping at the edge of the tonal mountain, as is illustrated in this screenshot.

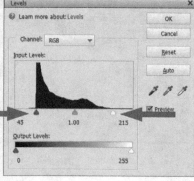

I shifted the shadow and highlight sliders to the right and left, respectively, stopping just at the edges of that central mountain shape. The shadows are darker and the highlights are brighter. In general, this is all the editing needed to make them pop with tonal interest. The shape of the tone mountain doesn't make any difference to the result.

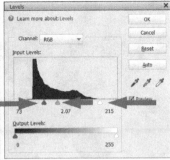

Here, I dragged those sliders too far toward the center of the **Input Levels** scale. This produces a contrast boost (which has also affected the color values). The black is now absolute, preventing you from seeing any detail; the whites are also too bright. The **Output Levels** scale is used to lower the brightness of the shadows and highlights, which in turn, drops the contrast.

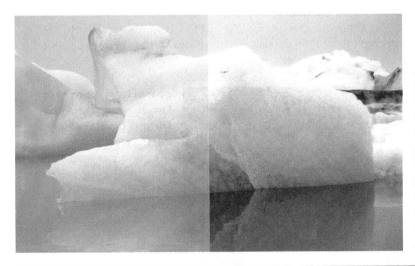

As you can see in this image, the left hand side is very lacklustre with flat contrast and no black tones at all. It's not nice to look at. A quick contrast boost using Levels, on the right hand side makes the the image really pop off the page.

> **Tip:**
>
> In general, an **Auto Levels** adjustment works quite well—but it adjusts both contrast and color in one action, which might not be what you want. I advise against using **Auto Levels** because what do you do when this doesn't work the way you want it to? You have to come up with a **plan B**—and this requires more time and effort.

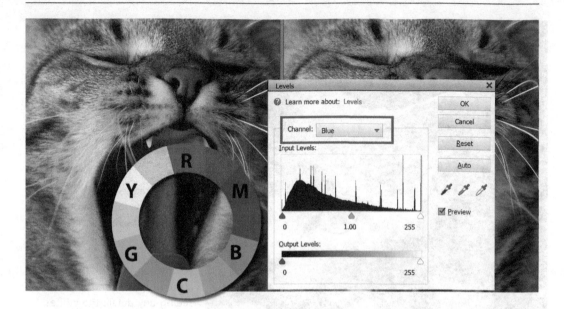

General adjustments using **Levels** are good for perfecting the contrast range in most files. These are **global adjustments** that are applied to all three channels (red, green, and blue) at the same time. If you make adjustments to just one color channel, you can shift the image color quite considerably. I use these color channels to add a warm tint to any shot, to correct a color cast (that is, from a white balance mistake), or just to add a color accent to the image. As you can see in this screenshot, the **Channel** drop-down menu now reads **Blue**. The blue histogram is a different shape than the three-color RGB histogram. Move the slider to the left to add blue and to the right to add the opposite color: yellow. The color wheel displays RGB and their opposite colors: cyan, magenta, and yellow.

Lowering contrast: Levels has a second scale, **Output Levels**, which is used for reducing the black density and the highlight brightness, as you can see with this dramatic black and white image. The original is on the left, while the right-hand version shows distinctly lowered brightness in the highlights, essentially dulling the image significantly.

Mastering contrast: Shadows/Highlights

You'll note that under the **Enhance>Adjust Lighting** menu, there are two other tools worth mentioning: **Brightness/Contrast** and **Shadows/Highlights**.

The former does exactly what **Levels** does, but without the benefit of being able to see that tone mountain, which for most photographers is enough encouragement not to use this feature. It's also regarded as being a destructive form of editing—too much use might damage the pixels irreparably, so I'd not recommend using it.

The **Shadows/Highlights** tool can be very useful for rescuing tones that might appear lost in the highlights and the shadow areas, for boosting details in the darkest parts of the file. Some care must be taken with this feature because too much will make the result appear fake.

Remember that if you are doing this on a JPEG file, it has already been processed in-camera, so if there appears to be no tone in the lighter parts of an image, you might not be able to recover them at all, but it's certainly worth a try. You'll have more luck using the shadow-recovering part of this slider, revealing details that might be hidden in an over-darkened part of the file. Although the photographer deliberately hid some of the darker details in this striking portrait, it's interesting to see how the image can change radically just by lightening the shadows only (on the right-hand side).

Mastering color: using Hue/Saturation

Elements has several color adjusting tools—the most commonly used perhaps being **Hue/Saturation** (*Ctrl/Cmd + U*).

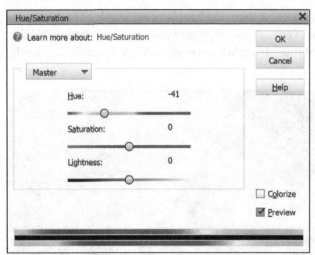

Hue describes the color values of the pixel. Use this slider to reassign different color values from what's in the file (that is, changing red to yellow). Used solo, it works **globally**, so not only do the red tones change to yellow, but all the other colors shift their hues as well, often producing wildly surreal and not very useful color results.

Saturation controls the intensity of the color value in the pixels. So, if you set the slider to a minus amount, it loses color, or *desaturates*, eventually turning black and white. Shifting it to the right increases the color values, making the picture richer in color. As it's a global change, everything in the file gets more or less colorful.

For me, **Lightness** isn't very useful. The slider adjusts the maximum and minimum black levels in the file, essentially helping you fine-tune the global contrast in the file. It does the job, but I find using the **Output Levels** scale of **Levels** to be far more effective.

All these effects are **global**, which, most of the time, isn't what we want. For example, an image might just need the red tones to be brighter and nothing else. Elements has the answer:

- Choose the **Hue/Saturation** tool (**Enhance>Adjust Color>Hue/Saturation**).
- From the **Master** drop-down menu, choose the color that you'd like to adjust (that is, reds, yellows, greens, cyans, blues, or magentas). Note: these are Adobe colors—to make your color selection more accurate, move the cursor off the **HSL** tool and over the picture; then click the exact color you want to change. You might see the color bars along the bottom of the panel shift as you sample the color in the photo rather than picking the "canned" Adobe red.
- Moving the **Hue** slider now reassigns red to another color. **Note**: you can also make use of the eyedroppers at the bottom of the window to fine-tune a color selection. Use the left-hand dropper for a general color selection, then either the minus or plus droppers to add/subtract different tints from the initial selection.
- Move the **Saturation** slider to minus 100 and anything red in the image will turn black and white; move it to a plus value and just red will increase in intensity.

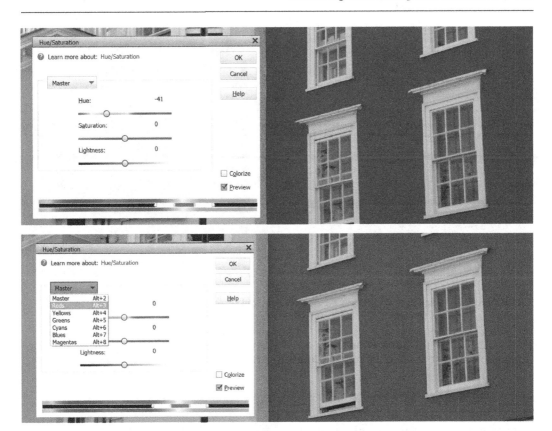

- If there are multiple red objects in the frame (and you only want to change one of them), you will have to make a **basic selection** using one of Elements' excellent selection tools to limit color changes to just that one object. Using this tool will also teach you a lot about the components of specific colors—how much the color yellow is a part of the color green, for example.

- To make your eyedropper's color selection even more specific, you can try shifting the tiny white pins along that rainbow-colored color picker located at the base of the HSL panel. The two inner pins limit how broad the color selection is—the narrower these are, the more specific the color choice. The gap between the inner and outer markers fades the initial color selection from that specific color with the new color, blue. The further apart these pins are from each other, the softer the gradation from the chosen color to the color that's next to it. This sounds more complex than it really is. Move the pins to see how they affect fading from one color change into another.

Warning: Although radical adjustments to the saturation values can make your image look amazing, very few home inkjet printers can reproduce the intensity of color that this creates. They will look OK once uploaded to social media but if the saturation levels are higher than about +25 saturation, the color is not reproducible in print.

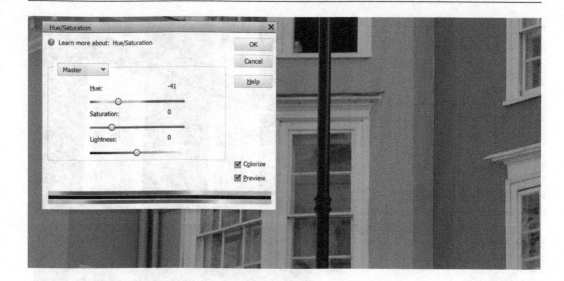

Olde worlde effect: A final tip is to use the **Colorize** feature (check this at the bottom right-hand side of the tool). This instantly renders any color image as a monochrome file with a colored tint—the color (hue) is controlled using the **Hue** slider (naturally). Its intensity can be adjusted with the **Saturation** slider. You can also achieve this look using **Guided** Edit's old-fashioned photo preset or the new **Duotone Effect**, which is also in **Guided** Edits.

Left: Another good example of where the color selection process, via **Hue/Saturation**'s **Master** drop-down menu, can radically improve just about any image. I was happy with this shot but felt the red breast of this bird needed a bit of a boost. By selecting **Red** from the menu, then clicking on the red in the image with the dropper, I could increase the strength of the red without affecting much else in the frame. I also did this using the **Yellow** drop-down option, thus making the fish appear a little more appetizing to the bird.

Simple retouching: Smooth skin feature

One effective retouching feature in Elements is the **Smooth Skin** feature (no guesses for what this does). It's one of those (quite) complex processes that have been simplified by the Adobe software designers to the point where it's dead easy to use—and yet still produces great results.

Here's how easy it is to add a significant improvement to your portraits. Open an image, apply the feature (**Enhance**>**Smooth Skin**), and make an adjustment in the (smallish) window that appears onscreen (see inset panel above). Smooth Skin works very well, provided that the artificial intelligence driving this feature can first identify a face in the picture. It doesn't work so well for profiles or shots where the subject isn't looking more or less directly at the camera. It does work, however, with pictures that feature multiple faces. The blue circle is the "active" face—in photos with multiple faces, click a face to make it active, add the effect, then click another face and repeat.

Tip:

Use the square brackets to enlarge/reduce the size of the brush. Use *Ctrl/Cmd + +* and *-* to increase/decrease the image size to get right into the areas that need attention. *Ctrl/Cmd + 0* (zero) returns an enlarged/reduced image to fit the entire screen.

Simple retouching: manual spot removal

I clearly remember when **Spot Healing Brush** was first announced by Adobe. It was at the launch of Adobe Photoshop 7.0 in 2002, and once the presentation was over, there was a stampede to the back of the auditorium to buy the product (which was the *thing* to do in those days), such was the impact it had on all those portraitists, wedding shooters, and retouching gurus. Overnight, their lives had changed because no longer did they have to make careful selections, feather that selection, then copy and paste the selected area from one part of the shot to another, then line it up directly over the skin blemish before blending the copied pixels into the background using **Layer Opacity** settings.

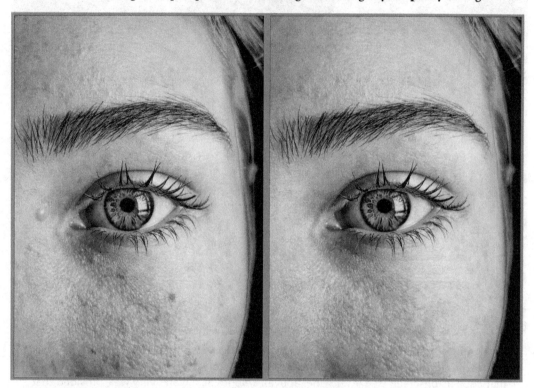

This before and after example took about three minutes to complete—that's how easy the **Spot Healing Brush** tool is to use. Set the brush diameter a little larger than the blemish area. Click it once, and the blemish disappears.

It seemed like magic at the time it was launched, but now this tool is totally synonymous with retouching, and can be found in a huge range of photo editors, including Elements. This tool is exceptionally good for cleaning up the smaller blemishes in our lives. If there's a large object that needs removing—or if the blemish is among other textures that you need to keep—then the **Healing Brush** or **Clone Stamp** tools would be more appropriate because they can be set to copy from a custom source area.

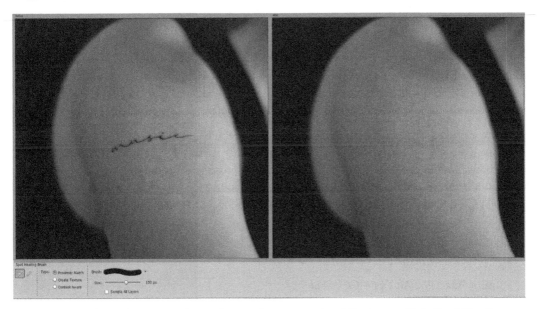

This screenshot of a tattooed man is a perfect example of the type of job **Spot Healing Brush** is good for. The blemish is relatively small, and the source, the area used to sample good pixels from, is large, limiting the possibility of retouching mistakes happening.

Retouching Troubleshooting Tips:

Despite being a superb tool, the retouching process doesn't always go to plan. It can smudge the image, blur details when it's not supposed to, and even copy and paste inappropriate bits of the image back into the frame rather than out of it! Here are some troubleshooting suggestions:

Instead of the **Spot Healing Brush** tool, try the regular **Healing Brush** tool—the main difference between the two is that while the former is principally a click-and-forget action, the latter offers better control over where the source information is coming from, which is especially useful if you are retouching small, confined areas.

Position the cursor over the area you want to sample (the **source**), hold down the *Alt/Opt* key, and click once. Release the *Alt/Opt* key.

Reposition the cursor over the area to be fixed (the **target**) and click once, or click, hold, and drag to copy continuously from source to target.

How much is transferred is controlled by the brush's **Opacity** setting (so, if set to 50%, you'll have to click twice on the target area to transfer all the pixels from the source area to cover the damage entirely).

Lowering the brush's opacity is helpful because clicking multiple times can assist in blending mismatched tones together more convincingly.

Reselecting the source area again and again from different parts of the image is one way to work with a limited source area. Another way to do it is to check the **Aligned** checkbox in the tool **Options** panel. This leaves the target exactly where it was first clicked. Clicking and dragging makes the source move with the target, but just clicking repeatedly does not.

Additional resources

Using keyboard shortcuts has several significant benefits for photographic editors, regardless of their skill level. Firstly, they take the pressure off your mouse hand. If every function is performed using only the mouse, you will tire more easily. It can also lead to greater physical strain, which in turn could lead to all sorts of medical issues (such as stiffness, arthritis, and even carpal tunnel problems).

Therefore, using a few keyboard shortcuts will not only help to alleviate the physical stresses of just using one hand to edit images, but they'll also significantly speed up the editing process and make your actions more efficient. Elements has a huge range of possible keyboard shortcuts—far too many for most of us to remember, let alone to use effectively—so to keep things as simple and as practical as possible, here are a few of the most **relevant shortcuts** for this chapter.

The descriptions and their shortcuts are as follows:

- Create a new, blank file: *Ctrl/Cmd + N*
- Auto Smart Fix: *Alt/Opt + Ctrl/Cmd + M*
- Adjust Smart Fix: *Shift + Ctrl/Cmd + M*
- Auto Smart Tone: *Alt/Opt + Ctrl/Cmd + T*
- Auto Levels: *Shift + Ctrl/Cmd + L*
- Auto Contrast: *Alt/Opt + Shift + Ctrl/Cmd + L*
- Auto Haze Removal: *Alt/Opt + Ctrl/Cmd + A*
- Auto Color Correction: *Shift + Ctrl/Cmd + B*
- Auto Redeye (removal): *Ctrl/Cmd + R*
- Convert to black and white: *Alt/Opt + Ctrl/Cmd + B*
- Haze Removal: *Alt/Opt + Ctrl/Cmd + Z*
- Levels: *Ctrl/Cmd + L*
- Hue/Saturation: *Ctrl/Cmd + U*
- Open a file: *Ctrl/Cmd + O*
- Close a file: *Ctrl/Cmd + W*
- Close all open files: *Alt/Opt + Ctrl/Cmd + W*
- Save As (that is, to give your edited file a proper name): *Shift + Ctrl/Cmd + S*
- Open in Camera RAW (used specifically if you want to open a non-RAW file in this editing window): *Alt/Opt + Ctrl/Cmd + O*

Summary

In this chapter, we have looked at introducing you to the **best editing practices** in Elements so as to streamline your creative photographic workflow, which in turn will make your output more efficient, giving you more time to shoot pictures. It's also been a comprehensive introduction to the use of **RAW files,** and most importantly, how to edit them using Elements' **Camera RAW** utility—an important step if you are to develop and maintain a high level of professionalism in your creative careers. We should also now have a good understanding of **image resolution** and file **resampling** when it comes to reducing or enlarging image files.

We have also seen how easy it is to come up with a stunning look for your images by editing them using one of Elements' many instant preset **special effects** and **image fixes,** just as you might when applying an Instagram filter online. It's important for beginners to see how easy it is to produce beautiful effects with no previous experience. These effects not only work with very high-resolution images but also provide a far greater depth of choice. We have also made ourselves familiar with: tasks of controlling **brightness**, **contrast**, and **color** using two of Elements' most important non-RAW editing tools for **Levels** and **Hue/Saturation**. They might sound gimmicky, but they actually do the job surprisingly well.

Chapter 5, Easy Creative Projects, highlights a number of what I call "Easy Creative Projects." On paper, this sounds really impressive, and when you discover just how powerful these features are, they should certainly impress. We look at using filters, auto AI-driven photo colorizing, panorama stitching, how to remove clutter from your images, and making slideshows—just to name a few of the upcoming features. These are not only fun to play with, but you'll also discover how easy it is to attain great results.

4

Getting Started with Simple Solutions

For many, the real difficulty in learning how to make your photos look awesome is not by learning what functions **all** the features and tools have, it's much more about being able to match a specific feature to fit your realistic picture editing requirements.

If you don't do this, you could spend hours trying all sorts of things before you find the one that works. And if it's such a random search, chances are you won't remember what the solution was next time you need similar help. Searching for answers online can help of course, but I think most readers will agree when I say you can also waste a heap of time looking, but not finding. It is far better to head straight to the specific problem first, then deal with the process. And that's really what this chapter is about: providing answers to some of those awkward questions we all ask that begin with "How do I do that...?"

I have compiled several **common photo editing issues**, complete with a brief description on the tools and technique best suited to fix the 'problem' and set you on the road to image-making stardom!

And if there's more than one solution (and let's face it, there's usually multiple possibilities to any image editing question, more if you take your search online), I have supplied solutions - in the form of a list of where to begin with. These solutions are more or less ranked in order of complexity - the first suggestion is usually a simple auto fix, but as you move through the options you'll find that the solutions become more involved and sophisticated. But don't be put off, you might find that the first suggestion might well produce the best result! Let's start!

What's that strange-looking graph?

Cameras and editing software use a **Histogram** to display the distribution of tones in the picture. Is this important? Actually it's very useful—the histogram acts a bit like a **graphical exposure meter**. The shape of what I call the black 'mountain' is not as important as its position in relation to the baseline axes, that the mountain is sitting on. The left hand side of the graph represents **shadows**, while the right hand side represents the **highlights**. The middle section represents the **midtones** (greys).

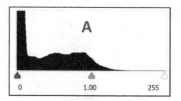

Graph A is from a very dark photo—a lot of the tones are slumped against the left hand (shadow) axis, resulting in detail lost in the dark areas of the photo.

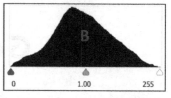

Graph B is from a near perfect picture while Graph C is very overexposed.

You'll find this display in several places in Photoshop Elements— the Camera RAW utility and Levels for starters, as well as in your camera's viewfinder (check the camera manual if it's not visible).

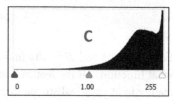

Photo problems fixed in this chapter:

- What does the Histogram do?
- Make a dull-looking photo appear better (Brightness/Contrast)
- Fix a flat, greyish-looking photo (Auto Contrast)
- Fixing washed-out color (Auto Color Correct or Vibrance and Saturation)
- Boring looking photos? (Try Classic or Artistic Effects)
- Perfecting skin tones (Spot Healing Brush)
- Lose a bit of weight? (Liquefy Filter)
- Change people's facial expressions (Adjust Facial Features)
- Clean up dusty scans (Dust and Scratches Filter)
- Remove people or objects from a picture? (Guided Edit>Object Removal)

- How do I move something in a picture to make a better composition? (Guided Edit>Move and Scale Object)
- My picture is messy—how do I clean it up? (Photomerge Scene Cleaner)
- How do I level the horizon in my photos? (Straighten Tool)
- My photo needs trimming (Crop Tool)
- How can I soften a background so it's less noticeable? (Guided>Replace Background)
- How do I add a person from another photo into my picture? (Clone Stamp Tool)
- How do I make my pictures look sharper? (Auto Sharpen)
- How can I print perfect color? (Screen Calibration)
- How can I make my scanned images look perfect? (Spot Healing Brush)

How do I make a dull-looking photo appear better?

While there are many things that can go wrong in our picture making, you'll come to appreciate that a simple brightness and contrast boost might be all that's needed to make your picture look stronger/brighter—even punchier. Here are a few suggestions on how to get this done:

Firstly you might try the simple to use **Brightness and Contrast** tool:

- Guided > Basics > **Brightness and Contrast** (includes step-by-step instructions).

This scene (inset, right) is tonally quite accurate—the evening atmosphere was slightly misty, producing a very soft light. I wanted to add more **visual drama** to the scene so, I purposely darkened the file using the basic but effective **Brightness/Contrast** sliders and voila, the color intensified, producing a more dramatic result.

Other tools you can try include:

- **Auto Smart Fix**, or **Auto Smart Tone** (both of these are located under the Enhance menu in either the Quick or Expert Edit modes).
- The **Adjustments Panel** (located in the Quick Edit mode). This provides a slightly wider range of tonal control over the Auto tone tools but is still visually easy to use.
- Guided > Basics > **Lighten and Darken** (includes step-by-step instructions).
- Expert > Enhance > Adjust Lighting > **Brightness and Contrast** (same tool as photo above).
- Guided > Basics > **Levels** (includes step-by-step instructions).
- Expert > Enhance > Adjust Lighting > **Levels**. My favourite—this is the best way to enhance brightness and contrast and almost guarantees positive results.

My contrast looks 'greyish', what's wrong?

A lack of contrast (i.e. no deep black or bright whites) usually produces flat-looking, lacklustre images. This is usually fixed quite easily with a simple contrast boost.

Low contrast photos are more common that those that are too dark. It's usually caused when the light meter 'overreacts' to the scene brightness. In this picture, taken at a local wildlife park, the slightly darker than average scene forced the meter to over-expose, and that's why the koala looks paler than he really was. Here, Auto Contrast (Quick/Expert Edit>Enhance>**Auto Contrast**) provided an instant fix, leaving a near perfect result. And a happier looking koala!

Here are some other 'instant' contrast fixes that are well worth trying out:

- Quick/Expert Edit > Enhance > Lighting > **Levels**. Start by trying the **Auto** button to improve the tone. If that doesn't work, manually shift the shadow, highlight or midtone sliders.
- Quick/Expert Edit > Enhance > Lighting > **Brightness and Contrast**. This simple tool features easy-to-use sliders for adjusting the tone.
- Quick/Expert > Enhance > **Auto Haze Removal**. Perfect for really hazy landscapes but it also works on most other images that need a boost.

My colors look weak or 'desaturated'

If the brightness and contrast have been improved but the colour still looks 'underwhelming', try increasing the **colour intensity** using one of the following possible fixes:

I had to smile when I tried this first fix, **Auto Color Correct**, as Photoshop Elements transformed my late afternoon sunset to an early morning look. The color in the fixed version is good, just not the result I was after. I then tried the **Vibrance and Saturation** sliders under the Quick > Adjustments > **Color** panel and struck lucky, forcing the color enhancement you see below. Although you could enhance the color more, if you take it too far, it produces a richness than can not be printed accurately. Worth considering.

Here are a few more color fixes worth noting:

- Quick > Enhance > **Auto Color Correction**
- Quick > Adjustments Panel > Colour > **Saturation/Vibrance**
- Quick/Expert > Enhance > **Adjust Hue/Saturation**. This is probably the best way to improve the strength of color (includes a neat Colorize function).

Getting Started with Simple Solutions

My photo looks boring – how can I add interest?

Chances are adding a **tonal filter effect** might be just the boost to make your shots appear more professional, 'different', and unique. You'll find some of the best ones in the Quick Edit mode.

- Quick > Effects Panel > **Classic** or **Artistic**. There are more than 40 single-click visual effects or filter 'looks' to choose from. It's also an excellent place to get inspiration for future projects.

Another fantastic color booster to try is this:

- Quick/Expert > Enhance > **Colorize Photo**. This feature adds a gorgeous old-fashioned hand-colored look to the picture at the click of a button.

This is an old post office and general store dating back to 1894 so I thought my snap needed to reflect that age somehow—I chose one of Elements' 50 or so **Classic Effects** from the Quick Edit mode to give it that little extra color boost. The problem with this feature is it's very hard to know when to stop!

I want to make my complexion look better

Use the excellent **Spot Healing Brush** to click-and-remove small blemishes instantly.

- Guided > Special Edits > **Scratches and Blemishes**. Effective with easy-to-follow instructions for fixing small blemishes.
- Quick/Expert > Tool Bar > **Spot Healing Brush (J)**. This is the same as the Guided Edit Mode technique but with no step-by-step instructions.

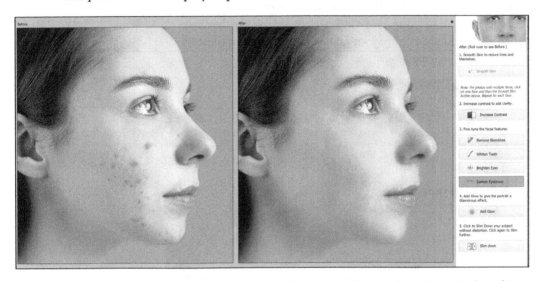

The **Perfect Portrait** tool incorporates a host of cool retouching tools and was the best fit to improve this model's complexion (Guided>Special Effects>**Perfect Portrait**). This took a couple of minutes to perfect.

I look a bit overweight in photos. Help!

OK, we've all encountered this issue at one time or another and Elements has the solution: the **Liquify Filter!** (Quick or Expert > Filter > Distort > **Liquify**).

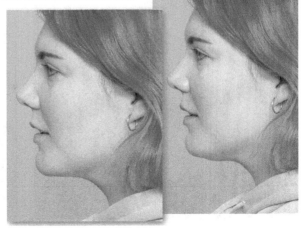

At right: Here I used Liquify's **Shift Pixels Brush Tool** to give the model a more shapely curve under her chin. A little adjustment goes a long way. Liquify sort of treats pixels like wet oil paint that can be pushed back and forth for the perfect weight loss and beautification result.

4

Getting Started with Simple Solutions

128 | My kid looks too serious in family photos. Help!

My kid looks too serious in family photos. Help!

Sometimes its just too hard to get everyone smiling in your pictures. Either develop some funnier jokes to get them laughing, or use this amazing Photoshop Elements feature—you'll find it under: Expert > Enhance > **Adjust Facial Features**.

As the name suggests, use this tool to auto - isolate then, modify the major facial features of your subject, one at a time. Quickly adjust lips, eyes, nose and face shape and angle using the sliders. It's easy. Make your subject smile or frown, lose a little weight or look like they have put on a few pounds. Change your family photos, or change history with a cheekier looking Mona Lisa!

I want to remove people from my picture

How often does this happen to you? You wait for ages for folk to move out of your shot, but they don't, so you give up and take the snap. Now there's an easy way to remove people digitally!

Use the superb **Object Removal** utility (Guided > Basics > **Object Removal**). Note: This feature works well providing that the object being removed is not overlapping or touching important parts of the subject. If this is the case, use the manually operated **Clone Stamp Tool**.

- Expert > Tool Bar > **Clone Brush Tool**: use this the same way as the Healing Brush. Hold *Alt/Opt* and click on some 'good' pixels to copy that area before moving to the damaged area, and clicking a second time to paste the copied pixels over the bit you want covered up.

For large areas, you could also first carefully select the offending object, then either paint over it (Brush Tool) or cover it up using pixels from another part of the same image, or even another picture.

This is a cute stock shot of a few kids messing about at the edge of a lake but it demonstrates how effective this feature can be. Relying solely on the power of the **Object Removal** tool (actually the Clone Stamp Tool working in the background), just select the 'offending' object/person and when ready, click 'Remove'. The software assesses the scene, then copies and pastes pixels from a different part of the image over the object you want gone. It works best if the object you need removed is not near the main subject otherwise the utility might remove some of the subject as well. This is an awesome feature.

I want to move a person/object to make a better composition

- Guided > Basics > **Move and Scale Object**. A powerful feature for selecting, then cutting out part of an image, before moving and pasting it to another part of the picture. The space left by the cutting out action is automatically filled in. This process works really well, especially if the person/object is not too close to the main subject.

- Expert > Select > **Subject**. Like most auto select features, this works well if the subject is clearly delineated. Elements selects the subject which can then be moved (using the Move Tool) and/or have its size changed (a process called Transformation—see *Chapter 6, Advanced Techniques: Transformations, Layers, Masking, and Blend Modes*).

Move & Scale Object

After (Roll over to see Before.)

1. Use one of the Selection Tools to choose the object you want to move or duplicate.

Auto   Quick

Brush Size:

Use add/subtract mode to refine the selection.

 Add   Subtract

2. Click the Move or Duplicate button and drag the selected object to desired position. Drag the corners to scale the selected object.

Move   Duplicate

- Guided > Special Edits > **Recompose**. Includes a step-by-step demo on how to stretch the background to change or improve the composition.

- Expert > Tool Bar > **Recompose Tool**. Essentially the same as the process mentioned above. Paint the main subject to 'freeze' the pixels, then grab and stretch the rest of the image to give a new look (note that though this sounds good, it doesn't work with every picture).

As with the previous example (Removing People), any process that involves complex actions like selecting, cutting, moving, pasting, then Cloning over the space left by the cut and paste operation, is subject to problems. It works well providing the subject being selected, then moved, is separate from the rest of the image details. This shot has clearly delineated figures so it was easy to select the figure, copy it, resize it, move it along the beach and then Elements cleverly fills in the gap left by the cut and paste operation.

My picture looks 'messy'—how can I clean it up?

How often have you visited a famous location wanting to get a great shot only to be frustrated by the number of other people wanting exactly the same shot? Here's a neat way to clean up your image to make it look like you are the only person left on the planet: it's called **Scene Cleaner**.

- Guided > Photomerge > **Photomerge Scene Cleaner**. Note: this process only works if you remember to shoot a series of images, of the same scene, at suitable intervals while you are actually there. Snap a shot, wait for people to move a few feet, snap a second, wait till they've moved on, and repeat. Try and shoot without moving position—a tripod is really helpful.

Photomerge Scene Cleaner replaces people with empty spaces created by waiting for the crowds to move. The trick is to remember to take the shots while you are still on location. See *Chapter 5, Easy Creative Projects* for more information on this technique.

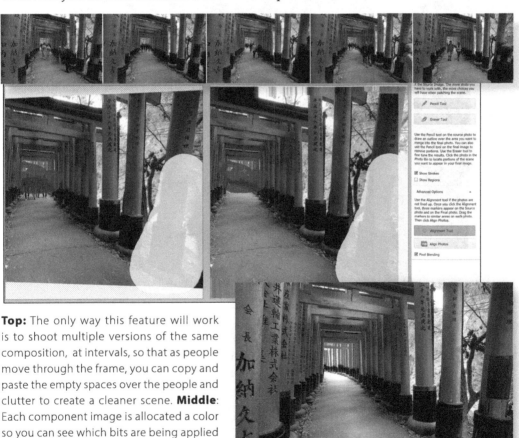

Top: The only way this feature will work is to shoot multiple versions of the same composition, at intervals, so that as people move through the frame, you can copy and paste the empty spaces over the people and clutter to create a cleaner scene. **Middle**: Each component image is allocated a color so you can see which bits are being applied to the master image file. **Right**: This is the now magically depopulated Japanese temple at Fushimi Inari, Kyoto.

My pictures never look 100% level

Most people lean slightly when taking a picture, right? You might not be aware that this is the case until you look at the photos on a computer screen. Fixing this slight error is easy. First, check your camera. Many feature an inbuilt **digital level** originally designed for use on a tripod. Ensure this feature is switched on and keep an eye for it in the viewfinder, or on the LCD screen when shooting. If you still get wonky horizons, it's easy to fix with software.

- Quick > Tool Bar > **Straighten Tool**. Click and hold the cursor on the horizon, then drag the cursor across where the horizon should be, and when you release the mouse button, the picture is automatically rotated to make your stretched line the new horizon.

The **Straighten Tool** (the icon resembles a builder's level) allows you to make a very quick click, drag, and release action that 'tells' Elements that the line you have drawn is the 'new' horizontal, and then the picture automatically rotates to give you a perfectly level horizon. If there's no visible horizon (i.e. it's too hazy to distinguish the real horizon), you can try first and if it doesn't look so good, UNDO, and try again.

Note that the **Options Panel** has a function to crop off the pixels (seen in white, above) that get added to each corner as a part of the auto rotation process.

The **Autofill edges** check box (highlighted in yellow) is important. If checked, Elements will use its **Content Aware Fill** technology to fill in all the gaps left by the rotation process. Sometimes this works perfectly, but at others it can make a mess copying the wrong bits of the image into the empty spaces. But it's worth trying.

My photo needs cutting (cropping)

Photographers use the **Crop Tool** to remove bits of the picture that they don't like. It's easy to do but don't forget, a downside of cropping is that you **lose pixels**, therefore receive a lower resolution. This might negatively impact how large the photo can be printed and still appear sharp. If you've never cropped a photo, here's a good place to start:

- Guided > Basics > **Crop Photo**. This mode provides step-by step directions on how it works. Otherwise I'd recommend going directly to the Crop Tool located on the Tool Bar.
- Quick/Expert > Tool Bar > **Crop Tool (C)**. Same as above but manual operation.

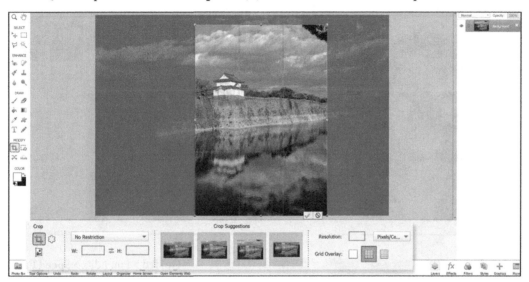

Once the Crop Tool is selected, a crop marquee (grid) appears over the image. You can also customise the color around the outside of this marquee to make it easier to see (here, it's done in red). Mouse-click one of the marquee edges or corners to resize and reposition the grid. Clicking the green check button on the marquee (or pressing *Enter* on the keyboard) executes the crop action. Everything inside the marquee is retained, while anything outside the grid is deleted. Note that by moving the cursor carefully to the **outside** of a corner point, you can also rotate the marquee—another way to make horizons level. You can vary your crop shape by choosing one of the presets in the **Options Panel** (enlarged, above). The Expert Edit mode also has a special **Perspective Crop Tool** and the fun **Cookie Cutter Crop Tool** designed for trimming your shots into an irregular shape. There are hundreds of shapes to choose from.

My background looks too clear (sharp)

Use Elements to simulate the look of a **shallow depth of focus** by selecting and blurring the background details. There are several ways to achieve this:

- Guided Edit Mode > Special Edits > **Replace Background**. A simple tool, enabling you to select the main subject, then replace whatever else is in the frame with a flat color, a texture, or one of your own photos. This makes a complex operation seem easy; providing you choose simple images, the results are stunning—import one of your own out-of-focus shots or, as this process adds the new background on a seperate layer, blur it afterwards in the Expert Edit mode!

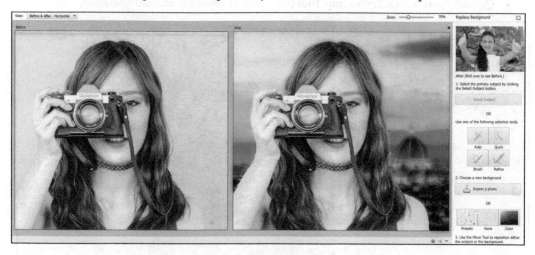

- Guided > Fun Edits > **Speed Pan**. This feature protects your subject while blurring the background to exaggerate the look of fast-moving subjects.
- Guided > Fun Edits > **Zoom Burst Effect**. Protects the subject while adding a zooming effect to the background.

Left: Tilt Shift (Guided > Special Edits > **Tilt Shift)**. This interesting process selects the background area and blurs it radically, softening distracting detail while creating a **miniaturization effect** in the foreground area. Does not work for all images but when you find the 'right' image it looks fantastic!

How can I add a person from another picture?

This is where we get a bit ambitious. If you are OK with basic retouching (using the **Healing Brush Tool** and the **Clone Stamp Tools**), you'll find copying from one image to a second reasonably easy. Best results come from choosing what I call 'simple' images, ones that don't have complex detailed backgrounds—this makes selecting one subject to paste into another image that much easier. Also make sure that the two photos are the same orientation (i.e. vertical/horizontal) and the same, or similar resolution (i.e. two 24MB files). If you use wildly different resolution files, what you paste into the second photo might be too big or too small. To rectify this, open the first image and change the resolution (**Image > Resize > Image Size**) to match the second image.

Open both files, and from the **Window menu**, choose **Window > Image > Tile**. Click the source image once, select the **Clone Stamp Tool**, hold the *Alt/Opt* key and click part of the image you want to transfer. Then move to the second image, click the second image's tab to select it, go to the Layer Palette and click **Create a New Layer**. This adds an empty layer above the target image. Now click into the target image and you'll see the cloned image appear in the frame. Drag the cursor to continue cloning the image across from the source. Unless you are a superhero with the mouse, you'll probably also clone some of the source's background into the target file. So, once the figure is fully copied over, select the **Eraser Tool** and use it to remove the unwanted pixels, leaving just the subject. It's fiddly, but can produce great results.

Advanced users can follow a similar process but instead of cloning, use a selection tool to first copy the entire figure, then paste the contents into a second image in one go.

Mastering Adobe Photoshop Elements 2023

My picture doesn't look sharp

Sharpness has a lot to do with contrast so, if you increase the image contrast (see the contrast enhancing techniques earlier in this section) you'll most likely see the photo looking sharper and clearer. But Elements does have a great range of **sharpening tools** that work well providing the picture is not hopelessly out of focus:

> Quick/Expert > Enhance > **Auto Sharpen**. If it doesn't sharpen enough, try repeating it.

- Quick/Expert > Adjustments > **Sharpen**. Use the slider (or click one of the nine thumbnails) to add your required degree of sharpening. Don't add too much!

- Quick/Expert>Enhance> **Shake Reduction**. This feature is designed specifically to 'save' a slightly blurred-looking picture, but it also works on normal images.

- Quick/Expert > Enhance > **Adjust Sharpness**. A more complex tool for those wanting more control over the process.

- Quick/Expert > Enhance > **Unsharp Mask**. Probably the best tool for those wanting more control over the process.

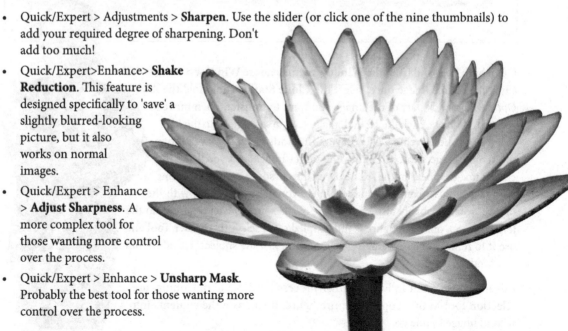

My picture looks great on screen but dark once printed

Computer screens look bright and colorful, especially when set for video replay, gaming, and HDR. Because most just keep photos online, it can be a shock to see what happens once it gets printed, in a lab or at home on an inkjet printer. Here are a few tips on how to get the most accurate printing results.

To begin, a simple, non-technical technique to represent 'true' color and brightness is to slightly darken the brightness level of your monitor.

- On a Mac, set the screen brightness slider three clicks less than full. This should provide a good reference point of how bright an image might print.
- On a PC, go to the **Control Panel** and then **Display** to make a brightness adjustment (Note: access to this setting might vary depending on the PC operating system, plus the make and model of your monitor (check manufacturer's specifications).

Re-edit the brightness of your photo once you have adjusted the screen brightness, then make a test print. If it's still dark, make a further screen brightness adjustment, and test again. This takes time, paper, and ink, but once set, should produce reasonably faithful printing results.

- For a professional result, buy or borrow a **screen calibration device**—load the dedicated software and follow the setup steps. It usually takes around 20 minutes to complete.

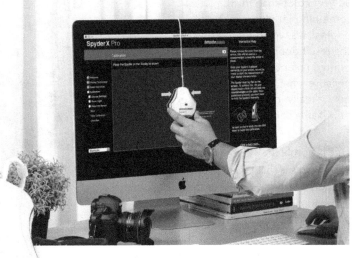

The device measures the actual brightness of the screen, and balances that with the ambient light, the age of the screen and the display requirements. Note: it doesn't calibrate an inket printer—that's done with another USB device, but it does guarantee that what you see on your screen will be very close to what is printed by any photo lab that also runs a calibrated color system (and most do). Once calibrated, make a test print on your home inkjet printer and you should find the result is far more accurate.

How can I make my scans look perfect?

I admit that I scan my artwork first then perform all my repairs using Photoshop Elements, ignoring the accompanying scanner software. It's just sometimes easier and faster to do everything in one application. This is doubly true when using specialist tools that are not part of the scanning suite, like the **Burn and Dodge Brush Tools** and even the **Shadows/Highlights** tool (Enhance > Adjust Lighting > **Shadows/Highlights**). Use these to darken or lighten shadow, highlights, or the important mid-tone contrast.

If the scanned file contains uneven tones—and many do due to poor storage conditions, fading, and chemical staining—use the Burn and Dodge Brush Tools (**Tool Bar > Burn/Dodge**) to 'paint in' darkness or lightness where required. Fine-tune the tool via its Options Panel. Go slow: always set the speed of the tool (called Exposure) to a low value to avoid leaving tell-tale retouching marks.

At right: Here's a good example of how a **color restoration filter** in a scanner application can transform a badly faded 50-year color snap into something far closer to the original. It's worth noting that if the result doesn't look as if it were printed recently, it might just be because what you get is exactly how it really looked when printed new, half a century ago!

One big problem when copying old pictures is that you copy the memories as well as some of the dust, scratches, and age spots that mar the surface of old prints. Here are a few tips on fixing the problem:

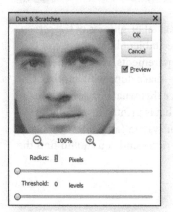

Remove larger blemishes using the **Spot Healing Brush**.

(Guided > Special Edits > **Scratches and Blemishes**—good step-by-step instructions for general repairs). Use the same process directly out of the Quick or Expert mode > **Tool Bar (J)**.

For small stuff, use the **Dust and Scratches** filter (Filter > Noise > **Dust and Scratches**). This filter (set its Radius to 1, 2, or 3, Threshold 0) removes most of the tiny dust specks and even fine scratches from a scanned print, but it softens the image, so don't overdo it. Another good fix is Perfect Portrait (Guided > Special Effects > **Perfect Portrait**).

Consider trying the **Auto Smart Fix** or **Auto Smart Tone** features first. Both would be useful to replace the brightness and contrast lost in old, age-faded prints. (**Quick/Expert > Enhance >** Auto Smart Fix or **Auto Smart Tone**).

Use the Sponge Brush Tool (same location as **Burn/ Dodge**) to enhance local color if, for example, a sepia-toned print has lost some of its original color.

TIP: Most old prints have very little shadow and highlight detail so take great care not to over-brighten/ darken these areas while editing otherwise you'll lose precious detail forever.

In this example, the entire surface was covered in small blemishes—some scratches, dust, and even chemical stains. The **Dust and Scratches filter** might have helped here but I preferred to use the excellent **Spot Healing Brush Tool**—it involved a lot of clicking to remove every speck but, as you can clearly see in the finished version, it now looks as good as it was when first printed in 1910!

Summary

In this chapter, we have seen how simple photo editing can be. In so many examples, all that's needed is the click of the mouse to bring about a radical tone or color change. And, of course, being such a mature application, Photoshop Elements provides not one but several possible solutions for your creative requirements.

You will also now appreciate that the first technique is not necessarily always the best solution—inevitably there are three or four other ways of achieving a similar result and it's up to you to choose the one that works best for your style.

One thing that I have found after years of teaching is that photographers tend to choose a certain tool or editing technique not so much because it's deemed to be 'the best' but more often because they can do it using the mouse, or they can do it *using a keyboard shortcut*—or because *it was the first thing they tried and they prefer to stick with 'what works'*. I never like to say 'this is the way it must be done' because, in so many ways, these personalised habits make perfect sense. If you are happy doing it 'your' way, and it works, then that's usually the best way.

The next chapter combines what I determine to be quite complex image editing effects with the genius of Adobe's software designers who render visual ideas—like panorama making, colorizing photos, making greetings cards, calendars and more—in a tantalizingly simple step-by-step format, ensuring creators at any level can produce solid, colorful and beautiful results.

Now that you have the answers to some of the most commonly experienced picture editing questions, it's time for you to take your image creation skills up another level.

5
Easy Creative Projects

In this chapter you'll discover a fantastic array of semi- and fully automatic special effects, most of which can be mastered with little or no previous experience. Even better, each effect produces a different style, significantly pushing your creativity in directions you may never have considered before.

I have always liked Elements' slightly alternative approach to photo editing because it includes a lot of project-based activities rather than concentrating on just the skills of picture editing. However, over the years, this has changed—Elements now boasts some of the most sophisticated editing features—tools that you'd normally expect from the top end of town—while still retaining awesome project based features, such as panorama stitching, calendar making, and photo slideshows.

This chapter highlights a number of features that anyone can use to produce truly great results—without having to climb that steep learning curve (that curve begins at *Chapter 6, Advanced Techniques: Transformations, Layers, Masking and Blend Modes*).

What you will learn in this chapter:

- Using filters
- Artistic Effects
- Lomo camera FX
- Effects collage
- Colorizing images
- Photomerge Panorama
- Making a multi-deck panorama
- Photomerge Scene Cleaner
- Photomerge Faces
- Making a slideshow
- Creating calendars
- Creating greeting cards

Bring life back to those old photos—try out Elements' impressive **auto colorize** feature: it's easy!

Simple visual effects: using Filters

Elements is heading in the direction of the smartphone. By this, I mean that the visual effects achievable are increasingly preset-driven. Open a file, check out a range of special effects, and apply one to your snap by clicking the thumbnail image. Nothing could be easier, and while doing this doesn't teach you how the effect is really achieved, it makes enhancing your work simple, fast, and approachable for the majority of camera users not wanting to spend hours in front of a screen.

As there are over 100 filters in Elements, they are carefully subdivided into collections: Adjustments, Artistic, Blur, Brush Strokes, Distort, Noise, Pixelate, Render, Sketch, Stylize, Texture, and Other. To make it easier to use the filters, Adobe supplies a mini-program called the **Filter Gallery**, which displays the filter effects in a large window alongside the various sliders that can make it look really good, or not. You might not like all of the filter "looks" on offer but don't forget, if the result doesn't appeal to you, you can modify what the automated process throws at you to make it more to your taste.

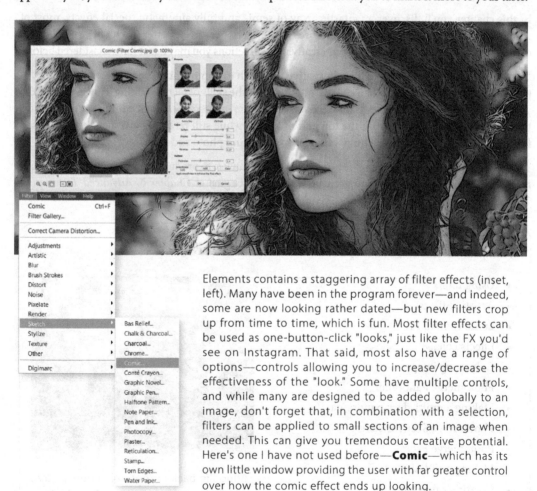

Elements contains a staggering array of filter effects (inset, left). Many have been in the program forever—and indeed, some are now looking rather dated—but new filters crop up from time to time, which is fun. Most filter effects can be used as one-button-click "looks," just like the FX you'd see on Instagram. That said, most also have a range of options—controls allowing you to increase/decrease the effectiveness of the "look." Some have multiple controls, and while many are designed to be added globally to an image, don't forget that, in combination with a selection, filters can be applied to small sections of an image when needed. This can give you tremendous creative potential. Here's one I have not used before—**Comic**—which has its own little window providing the user with far greater control over how the comic effect ends up looking.

The Filter Gallery: The preceding screenshot shows the **Filter Gallery** with a few of the effects filters represented in thumbnails on the right and their individual options in the column on the far right (the puppy has had the **Poster Edges** filter added). Sometimes, the effect is a bit ho-hum. I find that if you cancel the filter, then brighten the file using **Levels**, and maybe increase the color saturation using **Hue/Saturation** when you add the same filter effect once more, it gives a far better result.

Cleaning up a spotty scan: One of my favorites is the **Dust and Scratches** filter. It's not an effects filter as such, but, as you can see above left, if you have a damaged, dusty, or scratched (scanned) print file, the filter can remove nearly all of the small dust marks. I had the filter set to **Radius 3 pixels** to produce a nice "cleaned up" result. If I'd set it to **5** or **6** pixels, the softening effect would have blurred the bride's features too much. **Threshold** affects how selective it is in searching for things to fix. Both sliders have to be used with care to avoid losing precious detail. The large damage marks should be manually removed first using the **Spot Healing Brush** tool.

Instant Artistic Effects

New to Elements 2022 was this neat feature called **Artistic Effects**—you'll find it in the **Quick Edit** mode, sharing a Panel with the regular **Classic Effects** that have been in Elements for several versions now. Its regular Effects are already brilliant—choose a tonal "flavor," click the thumbnail image, and it applies that recipe to your photo in seconds. There are more than 50 variations to choose from. The difference between these and the new **Artistic** effects, apart from the obviously very colorful palette that they display, is that you can auto-select the subject or the background before you add the arty effect. If the effect goes over the subject, it can obscure features with too much color and texture.

Uncheck the subject from the panel first and you get an amazingly accurate subject selection before the effect is applied. This is another feature that can produce fabulous effects with no need for prior experience. Just click and go!

On the right: The regular **Effects** panel (arrowed) comes loaded with over 50 different one-click "looks," each of which is global—the effect is applied to all of the image.

Below: If you opt for the default setting, the new **Artistic** effects are also globally applied—which can work well, depending on which effect is chosen and the nature of your subject (there are 30 to choose from).

Above: The main difference between **Classic** and **Artistic Effects** is that if you uncheck **'Subject'** in the **Artistic** tab (arrowed above), the effect is applied to the **background only**, producing, in my opinion, a more agreeable result than if it were slathered across the entire picture. Of course, this depends on your subject choice and artistic intent. You can also apply the effect to the subject only by checking the **Subject** tab and unchecking the **Background** tab. Either way, this is an effective feature that's both easy to use and produces great results (below).

Lomo Camera Effect

I saw my first Lomo camera in a **GUM** store in Warsaw, shortly after the Berlin Wall had come down in 1990. It was, in fact, the only camera on sale in that huge store, and it piqued my interest. Lomo cameras were made in the Lomo factory in St. Petersburg (along with a lot of other specialized optics—for telescopes, cine cameras, microscopes, and more). Its 35 mm **Lomo LC-A** film camera was adopted by a group of enthusiast photographers who used to take pictures almost randomly—from all manner of angles, locations, and subjects. **Lomography**, as it is called, often spawned huge exhibitions of images, mass-printed and displayed almost like wallpaper.

The Lomography movement started in Vienna in the 90s and continues today, although not quite with the mass appeal of the last century. Elements' **Lomo Camera Effect** produces a soft, heavily vignetted effect similar to that produced by the LC-A and the **Diana** toy camera, and many more unsophisticated types of film cameras, those with few features and a plastic lens—you can still find a lot of these iconic toys online today.

Although you can reproduce this kind of heavy vignette look using selections and other tone-changing tools, **Guided** Edit's **Lomo Camera Effect** is by far the easiest and most effective way of adding a cool look to almost any style of image. Click the **Lomo Camera Effect** button once or more if you feel it needs beefing up, then do the same with the **Vignette** button. Again, this can be hit several times so that the background almost entirely disappears into blackness. A nice, fun effect that's ready in seconds.

Effects Collage

This **Guided Edit** feature, located under **Guided Edit>Fun>Effects Collage**, is impressive because it can add a collage and coloring effect to your images in seconds, where it might take most of us over an hour to do this manually—which quite probably we'd never bother trying. Elements is full of these clever little effects that compress an often tedious manual process into an automated feature that works a treat.

Open your image, go to **Guided Edit>Fun>Effects Collage**, choose from a two, three, or four-panel effect, and click the **Style** tab to view, and choose, a color effect. It's easy and if it's not what you expected, undo the previous action and try a different combination, such as the picture-in-a-picture effect seen below. Use the **Opacity** slider to reduce the effect intensity if needed.

Colorize: AI-driven creativity

One feature that Adobe has been developing is its use of **artificial intelligence** (**AI**), something that is perfectly demonstrated in this epic feature: **Colorize Photo**. You'll find it under the **Enhance** menu in the **Expert Edit** window.

Initially, I was drawn to this effect because I have actually spent many years hand-coloring black-and-white images for sale around the city I live in. It's great fun but involves a lot of printing, coloring in, erasing, ripping up prints, and starting again. The oils used added a permanence to the print, so they naturally lasted a long time—I'm sure you'll find a few hand-colored photos among your family albums. Before color photography was an affordable thing, this was the only way to get a color print!

To use this feature, all that's needed is a black and white image (in this example, I started with a sepia picture) and choose one of the colorized "looks" from the panel on the right-hand side of the window.

Then, I noticed that Adobe has included a manual override mode in this new AI-driven feature. Brilliant, because this was not looking good. **Manual** mode allows you to elect different bits of the image for a color change—one at a time. Do this using one of the two selection tools offered: **Selection Brush** or **Magic Wand**. The problem with this image is that there's no distinct separation between the soldier's uniform and the background, thus making a clean selection nearly impossible. As you select one object in the photo, add a **droplet**—this means that any tint chosen floods the selected area with color. You choose the tint and the depth of color from the drop-down color checker and it adds automatically. If it is too light or dark, just choose another color, then move on to select another part of the image, add a droplet, and then add another color.

1. Select the area to be colorized.

Add

2. Add a droplet within each selection to mark the area to be colorized.

Droplet Tool

3. Click below to change the color of marked area.

Color Palette

All Applicable Colors

In **Manual** mode, the **Selection Brush** tool proved most effective for this picture—especially for the skin tones, as they were so bright. But the uniform color bleeds into the background a bit. It's not really an accurate result, but it definitely looks like a genuine, hand-colored vintage photo.

This is a brilliant tool because, as with most of the other examples you see here, the automatic, AI-generated, select-and-color process actually works beautifully. I found that the result from the sepia print of the soldier, although appearing different to how I'd imagined it would be, looked great—and that's the cool thing about many of these AI effects: they might not be 100% accurate, but they do provide a raft of interesting creative options, many of which you might never have thought of.

Try all the versions on offer: Next, I tried using this feature (set to **Auto**) on this Hollywood promo shot of a Hepburn-esque model, and not surprisingly, all four AI-driven examples produced very acceptable results. The thumbnail strip shows a realistic colorization, then a warmer, then a greener, and finally, a cooler version. The second might be a bit over-tanned, but mostly, they are quite acceptable.

I then tried to improve what Adobe Sensei had produced in its **Auto** mode with my own manually painted version. It took around 20 minutes, and although it's certainly a lot "cleaner" in terms of painting accuracy, unless you blow it up to 400%, you'll probably not appreciate the added work. As a tip, don't always accept what the program produces. If one result looks "sort of" OK, but it's not light or contrasty enough, boost the brightness/contrast using **Levels**. Same with color—the over-tanned version at the top of the page is too much, but with **Hue/ Saturation**, you can reduce the saturation so it becomes more acceptable. There's no right or wrong way to use these tools, just the way that works best for you.

In this close-up, you can see four different **droplets** on the model's face. Each denotes a differently selected part of the photo (and therefore a differently colorized region). The "active" droplet, the one currently being colored in, is highlighted in blue. In the final version, I added small areas of color to her lipstick, earrings, and the necklace. The combination of using a quality picture and the colors selected produced a result that looked very much like a professional promo shot from the '30s. I included the original black-and-white version as a comparison (previous page).

These photos show how well this auto-coloring-in process works with no user intervention. It worked brilliantly on these old family snaps (scanned prints). To get the most out of this effect, use the **Sponge Brush** tool (in both **Desaturate** and **Saturate** modes) to remove/ boost color in small parts of the scene. If the colorize effect still doesn't work, revert the image to its original state (**Edit**>**Revert**) and try adjusting the contrast using **Levels** (*Ctrl/ Cmd + L*) and try again. To learn more about scanning prints refer to *Chapter 2, Setting up Photoshop Elements from Scratch—Digitizing Photos with a Scanner*.

Photomerge Panorama

Everyone likes a panorama—which is why smartphones and compact cameras have an inbuilt fully automated panorama feature. These usually work well—I find myself using my iPhone for this all the time because it's so convenient. But if you only ever look at the results produced by a smartphone, and its small screen, you'll never get to fully appreciate what a bunch of high-resolution images and Elements' Photomerge Panorama can offer a serious photographer.

Save a file and display it on a large screen, and you'll begin to appreciate how much better multiple high-resolution sections assembled using Photomerge can be. It's a powerful feature.

We all visit beautiful places on our travels, many of which are too large or too majestic to warrant just one snap. A panorama is the perfect answer. **Above: Ait Ben Haddhu**, **Morocco**. This shows a five-frame panorama, complete with a black border and Arabic-style text. Architecture is quite hard to stitch together, but if it's shot at a reasonable distance, as I was doing here, Elements can usually produce a flawless, distortion-free result.

Expansive vistas: This is a six-frame panorama of **Himeji**, Japan's best-preserved castle.

This panorama was taken at the **Imperial War Museum, Duxford**, one of the UK's best aviation museums. There were about 10 aircraft, some on the ground, some suspended from the ceiling. Getting a clear shot of just one plane was hard enough, but the entire hangar? The best option was to shoot multiple frames, and then use Elements to stitch them together.

I still create panoramas using a DSLR camera and Photoshop Elements because the finished product is far better than one that's produced with a smartphone—plus, if Elements makes a mistake matching up the different sections, it can usually be fixed.

To stitch together a panorama, Elements must use its AI to line up and match each section. To enable this, the software distorts each frame to make lines, angles, and tones in each section match. When it works well, as it mostly does, this is a very impressive bit of technology.

Panorama shooting and stitching is not a fully automated process; it's best to do a bit of preparation work to set up a panorama. Here's what I suggest:

Step one: With the camera set to **Program** mode, point the lens at the scene and take a **test snap**. Use the **Exposure Compensation** feature on the camera to make the image lighter/darker, if needed.

Step two: If you are happy with the look of the exposure, delete the test and snap a picture of your left foot.

Step three: In your mind, divide the scene very roughly into five vertical sections and start snapping (use more sections if necessary). Start at the left-hand side and take a shot, shift the viewfinder to the right, overlapping the frame by up to 20%, and take a second shot. Repeat until you've covered the entire scene.

Step four: Finally, take another picture, this time of your right foot. This should help you when it comes to finding those panorama sections among all of those other images shot around the same time—which might be months or even years later.

Step five: Open just those sections in Elements.

Step six: Navigate to the **Guided** edit workspace and choose **Photomerge>Photomerge Panorama** from the top of the screen.

Step seven: Select all of the panorama sections through the **Photo Bin** first, and then click the **Create Panorama** button on the lower right-hand side of the **Photomerge** window. Elements goes into action, selecting all of the images, matching edges, and then arranging all of the sections into one widescreen image, blended together using a series of clever black-and-white masks.

Final steps: At the end of the stitching process, Photomerge will ask whether you want the blank edges filled. You inevitably see blank patches like this because the sections were shot with a wide angle lens, or because the software has bent the perspective to achieve a better fit. It's a small price to pay for a perfect panorama. If you click **Yes**, Elements uses its **content-aware AI** to fill the empty spaces with pixels. If you elect not to do this, then you'll have to crop the image to remove any unevenness around the edge. Save the panorama as a Photoshop (`.psd`) file In case you need to come back to it to make final edits. Alternatively, to make it smaller, **flatten** the multiple layers (**Layer>Flatten Image**), and then save it as a JPEG file.

The result: Having asked Elements to fill the edges, this screenshot was the result. You can clearly see the dotted selection lines that delineate where Elements has added pixels to the composition. It's a reasonable result—although on closer inspection, there are some weird additional reflections on the floor where there should be none, and the yellow tail fin at the back of the hangar has been copied and pasted above itself. In this example, I used **Edit>Undo** to remove the AI pixels and cropped the file at the top and bottom. Sometimes this auto-fill works a treat, while other times, it doesn't.

Making a multi-deck panorama

One of the problems you will encounter when stitching a panorama is that, if it's too wide, it's nearly impossible to print. Although it might be 48-inches wide, it might only be 8 inches high, especially if all of your sections were shot horizontally. One fun and creative answer to this is to zoom in first and shoot **multiple decks** so that, even after cropping, the image quality isn't compromised.

City of Fes, Morocco: Don't think that you have to shoot horizontally all of the time. This is like a jigsaw, comprising 37 sections, shot in three decks, from left to right. I love the fact that, although Elements does an amazing job of lining up all of the images near-perfectly, it's not put off by having images at an angle, horizontally, vertically, zoomed in, or shot at wide-angle settings.

It handles such a challenge with ease (although this took 20 minutes to process). If you think you have missed a section while still in the field, it's best to shoot a few extra frames to cover any possible "bald" patches. I love the randomness of the edges in this technique, so I'm happy to leave them uncropped for effect. The final version was well over 1 gigabyte and could print over 2 meters wide.

Tips for shooting panoramas:

- Always **shoot vertically**; that way, if you have to crop the image because the sections were not on the same level, it isn't so problematic in terms of the overall proportions of the panorama.

- Use a **tripod**, making sure that the panning head is 100% level (most tripods have a bubble level built into the tripod head to help with alignment).

- Choose subjects that aren't too close together. Close subjects, especially ones that contain a lot of detail, make it harder for the software to align.

- **Zoom in** with the lens slightly. It's better to take more shots than fewer wide-angle shots. Wide-angle images will distort, making it tricky for Elements to line up accurately.

- Shoot JPEG or RAW—RAW files will always produce better, but larger files.

- **Auto Stitch** will work most of the time, but if not, try the other stitching settings to see whether they come out better.

Photomerge Scene Cleaner

Elements began by offering Photomerge Panorama on its own, but within a few versions, the designers came up with a number of other useful applications for Photomerge technology, including the ability to remove random people and objects to "clean up" a scene with ease.

Busy or clean? **Scene Cleaner** is an efficient, automated copy-and-paste feature designed to clean up heavily populated and cluttered scenes with the least amount of hassle. Important note: This only works if you take multiple images (two or more) of the same scene preferably without moving the camera.

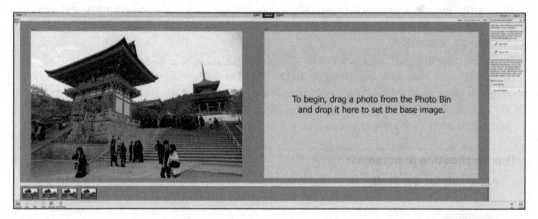

To begin, drag a photo from the Photo Bin and drop it here to set the base image.

Step one is to open all the images shot on location (there are four here) and open **Photomerge Scene Cleaner** from the **Guided** menu. Note that **Scene Cleaner** has its own separate panel showing one image on the left and an empty space on the right. Choose the least cluttered image from the thumbnails at the base of the screen and click-drag it up into the right-hand window. Don't worry if it's the same as the default left-hand image—it can be changed easily by clicking on any of the other thumbnails. The right-hand image is your "working" image. As with all **Guided Edit** features, just follow the excellent onscreen instructions on the right-hand panel, and you are good to go.

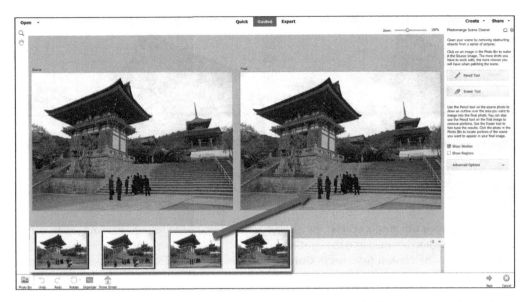

Step two: In this screenshot, I dragged the third image (highlighted in green) from the **Photo Bin** to the right-hand pane. This is the "base" image. As it's the same shot in both windows, I need to substitute the left-hand one with a snap in which the businessmen are standing in a different location so I can "clean" them from the right-hand screen. Elements **color codes** each image— a brilliant bit of practical design that will become evident once you copy empty bits from different pictures to clean the scene. The four sections here are color coded: blue, yellow, green, and red.

Step three: The new photo I have chosen (for the left-hand source) has no one standing where the businessmen are on the right-hand side. Take the **Pencil** tool from the right-hand menu and draw around this empty space (here, it's in thick red ink because it's from the red-coded image). Although it states it's a pencil tool, it's really a **selection tool**.

Step four—now the magic starts: The pixels encompassed by the red circle are automatically copied, pasted, and blended into the right-hand scene, effectively covering up the businessmen. This is one of the coolest features in **Guided Edit** because you don't need any experience with selections, blending, feathering, or editing for that matter. It just does it. You can see my red pencil line is wobbly, yet the application handles the transfer of pixels wonderfully (we'll look at exactly how selections work in much greater detail in *Chapter 7, Advanced Techniques: Retouching, Selections, and Text*).

Step five—cleaning up the rest of the scene: The next frame I chose had no one on the steps at the far left, so a quick scribble with the **Pencil** tool and the girl climbing the steps in the right-hand image is gone. You'll quickly realize whether you have shot enough frames for this technique to work—I could have shot a lot more base frames on location, but I wasn't prepared to wait 20 minutes for the gang of school kids at the top of the steps to move. Even as it is, the scene has become far less populated with people. If you like the result, press **Next** (bottom right of the screen) and save the file. If it needs fine-tuning, move on to the next step.

Additional tools: I mentioned color-coded images—this applies to all the photos used for the scene-cleaning operation. Images in the **Photo Bin** are highlighted in unique colors that correspond with your pencil marks. Click the **Show Regions** checkbox (on the right-hand menu) to view the bit of the picture that has been copied and pasted over that right-hand frame. This is handy if you are working with multiple shots and need to fine-tune your selections with the eraser. To do this, identify the color area on the right screen, and then click the corresponding left-hand color thumbnail to bring it back into the main left-hand window. If the selection "grabs" too much, go back to the source on the left-hand side, and using the **Eraser** tool, rub out some of the pen marks so it grabs fewer pixels as it updates. If this doesn't work, I erase the original pencil lines entirely and start over with a much thinner pencil tip. You can also just add a small blob to the image—which will grab an even smaller selection. Bear in mind that this is a bit of a rough-and-ready process—I doubt you could copy and paste someone's eyes from one image to another using this tool; it's too fine a job (but you could do this using a tool called **Open Closed Eyes**, see *Chapter 8*, *Additional Tools and Features*).

Shooting tip:

I know most folks consider a tripod an unnecessary hassle—but carrying one for this kind of photography can make a significant difference to the clarity and accuracy of scenes shot for the **Scene Cleaner** process, or any other Photomerge feature. Plus, it's useful for a range of other shooting scenarios—such as landscapes, still life, and sport. These days, you can buy carbon fiber tripods that are a fraction of the weight of the older-style aluminum tripods. Many are designed to pack away into a small package, making them perfect for travel. This particular tripod is fitted with a ball-and-socket head—you only need to adjust one knob to move the camera in any direction, which is a huge advantage over the older pan-and-tilt heads. Note that it also has twist-lock legs. These are far superior to the more common lever lock style because they are streamlined, whereas lever lock legs tend to snag on everything, thus raising the frustration level of the user!

Lining up features: Another good feature of all Photomerge tools is the software's ability to line images up so that when you copy pixels from one frame and paste them over another, they paste over the correct spot, thus producing a realistic-looking result. This is especially useful for hand-held shots—if you use a tripod, you won't need to use the **Alignment** tool. Elements aligns your pictures automatically when you start **Scene Cleaner**—you might notice that the finished image needs cropping a little, because due to the auto-line-up process, some of the originals have shifted from the vertical or horizontal. If the auto-alignment process is not working well, try the **Alignment** tool. The way this works is you position three line-up **target symbols** in the left-hand frame on specific, non-moving parts of the image. Note: I have enlarged symbol #2 in the left-hand window as an example. Then, arrange the targets on the right-hand side **on those same points**, click **Align Photos**, and Elements will work its magic—usually very accurately.

The trick with the **Scene Cleaner** is to remember to shoot the raw material—multiple frames of the same scene over a time period—while you are on location. However, unlike panorama sections, the idea is to position yourself quietly in one place without moving and snap between three and five shots of the same scene over a short period of time, ensuring that people move in between frames.

Left: Kyoto's famous Sagano bamboo grove with and without crowds of tourists thanks to the Photomerge **Scene Cleaner**.

Photomerge Faces

Ever taken a snap of friends only to discover, after they have all gone home, that one of them is looking in the wrong direction, has their eyes closed, or just looks a bit grumpy?

This is a common photo-taking error that many experience. Before Photoshop Elements came along, the only remedy was to get your friends back together to reshoot, or to spend time selecting, copying, and pasting figures from one picture to another. This was a time-consuming and complex process, so no one bothered.

By leveraging the power of the Photomerge AI technology, Elements has three fantastic features: **Photomerge Faces**, **Photomerge Compose**, and **Photomerge Group Shot**, all designed to fix compositional errors, however heinous they might appear. The **Faces** tool enables you to remove a face from one image and transfer it to another, all without the need for making complex selections—in much the same way that Scene Cleaner works when copying and pasting one part of the shot over another. You'll find these features next to **Photomerge Panorama** in **Guided Edit** mode.

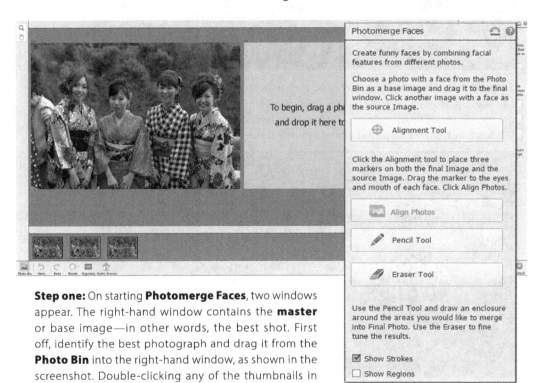

Step one: On starting **Photomerge Faces**, two windows appear. The right-hand window contains the **master** or base image—in other words, the best shot. First off, identify the best photograph and drag it from the **Photo Bin** into the right-hand window, as shown in the screenshot. Double-clicking any of the thumbnails in the **Photo Bin** will load it into the left-hand pane. This is the source image from which we can select a better facial expression, angle, or look.

The only provison with this feature is that you must have more than one image of the group available. If you're using the more specific **Photomerge Faces** function, you'll need a second or third face to copy and paste. I generally advise anyone shooting snaps of their family to use the camera's drive mode and to take at least two or three images because someone is bound to have their eyes closed or be looking away when the shutter is pressed.

Step two: Here's what I considered to be the best shot on the right-hand side, but as you can see, the woman on the extreme right is looking off to her left while the woman in the orange kimono is looking down. I just caught them at the wrong moment. The image on the left has a better version of the woman on the right-hand side.

As with **Photomerge Scene Cleaner** and **Photomerge Group Shot**, all that's needed is to draw around the "good" face or figure in the left-hand window, and it copies and pastes into the right-hand window, hopefully in perfect registration, so it replaces the person's face seamlessly, rather than sitting to one side, which happens if the two images are not aligned correctly. I had to add a bit extra to the pencil line to ensure the top of her head was copied over completely.

Fine-tuning the final result: The amazing part of this process is that you don't need to be 100% accurate. Sketch a mark in the area you want to copy, and Elements will transfer that marked area to the right-hand window. If only part of the face is transferred, draw around the *donor face* a bit more and wait for the update. It's a great process, but remember, it only works if you remember to take additional shots when in the field. Sometimes it makes sense to work with a thinner pencil line or even just add dabs of color. The auto-selection process is generous—sometimes too generous, so you'll find yourself going back again and again to trim down the line thickness to reduce the amount selected. As with all the Photomerge products, Elements uses a clear color-coding system that allows you to identify which picture each face comes from—especially useful when you're working with multiple originals. I think you'll find the color coding very helpful.

Tip – perfecting the process:

- Use the effective **Alignment tool** if multiple images don't line up precisely. This is an excellent feature and makes the subsequent face replacement process much more accurate.

- Use the program's **Eraser** tool if you overdraw around an object and too much copies across.

- Use the **Show Regions** checkbox to highlight in the aligned color what has been copied into the right-hand pane and from which image.

- If the software is copying too much in one hit, try just dabbing the **Pencil** tool onto the source image. A single brush tip mark might be all it needs to work optimally.

- Don't forget, you can also use this feature to create funny results, copying and pasting heads onto the wrong bodies. Your family snaps might never be the same again!

- Use the **Reset** button (arrowed in red, top right) if it all goes horribly wrong—and start over.

Creating Slideshows

A slideshow in Elements is not quite what I was used to as a child when my parents would drag out the Kodak projector and screen to view various snaps that were taken that summer holiday. A slideshow these days is a **multimedia event**, normally presented as a video file that can be replayed on a computer or uploaded to a range of social media sites.

If you already have images in your **Organizer**, and you look at the home page, chances are you'll see that Elements has already created a slideshow through its **Auto Creations** feature.

Making a slideshow in Elements is quick and easy. Previous versions featured a far more sophisticated slideshow-making utility, but it was both complex and time-consuming to use. It then got dumbed down too much—but I'm happy to see that the 2023 version has a larger set of theme presets from which to make a show. As with previous versions, making a half-decent show is easy to do—and fast.

Save and Export: The menu on the right-hand side of the slideshow screen allows you to save the file with a unique name. Next to that is the **Export** option—use this to send the video to a folder somewhere on your computer (such as **Export to Local Disk**) or upload directly to Vimeo or YouTube.

Here's how to create a simple, but effective, slideshow in only a few minutes:

Step one: Select the pictures you want to include. Because of its final video format, it's best to choose **horizontally orientated images**.

Step two: Best practice would be to create a specific **album** in the **Organizer** for your slideshow images.

Step three: Select all of the images (you can always add or delete images later).

Step four: With the images selected in **Organizer**, click the **Slideshow** button at the bottom of the page, or go to the **Create** menu (top right) and choose **Slideshow** from there—it's the same process.

Immediate feedback: The slideshow renders almost immediately as a preview. You might have to wait a minute or so, depending on how many photos you have included. Once rendered, it then automatically plays. If you don't like the music or the default theme, pause the slideshow and access the tiny menu at the top left-hand side of the slideshow screen. In Elements 2023 there are 18 themes to choose from, and 28 royalty and copyright-free music tracks to select. You can also use this menu to import more images, video clips, and sound clips, when needed. Right-clicking any thumbnail allows you to remove/rotate that particular slide. There's also a checkbox for adding captions or text slides. When you play the slideshow, these captions animate into the frame, a nice touch.

Copyright Alert: If you plan on publishing the slideshow video into the public domain, note that it shouldn't contain any images, music, or video that are not your own. There are plenty of free image and music sources online where you can download completely copyright-free material for use in personal, and in some cases, commercial, projects.

Because most of Elements' project-based features are semi-automated or powered using Adobe Sensei (AI), once one project is mastered, almost everything else seems far easier. Let's move on and see how easy it is to make calendars and greeting cards.

Mastering Adobe Photoshop Elements 2023

Creating Photo Calendars

A calendar is a marvelous gift for family, friends, and even work colleagues. What's more, it's also a great way to show off your prowess as a photographer, and creating a calendar has never been easier. Once again, Adobe has packed some incredibly complex imaging actions into a simple-to-understand, single-click operation, and on the whole, it works very well.

My only niggle with the slideshow feature is that I don't really like the offered templates - but that's a matter of personal taste. If you are of the same view, you can customize the calendar using the Advanced Mode (selectable once the calendar style has been chosen) or make your own design by adapting some of the techniques you'll discover in *Chapter 9, Advanced Drawing, Painting and Illustration Techniques.*

Step one: It saves time to sort through your work first and save potential calendar images to an Organizer Album.

Step two: Choose **Photo Calendar** from the **Create** drop-down menu, at the top right-hand side of the **Organizer**, and check out the range of calendar styles presented in the next stage.

Step three (above): Pick out a **design style**. This is one of the weak points in the calendar-making process. It's hard to see exactly what you get with each of the designs because they are so small. Monitor resolution has steadily climbed over the past 5 years, but the preview window remains painfully small!

Tip:

Choose one of the 31 layouts, set the start month and year, and click **OK**, making sure that the **Auto Fill with Selected Images** checkbox is unchecked. It's simple enough to load the right pictures onto the correct pages later. (You might have to wait a while as the templates for that particular design physically download from Adobe.)

Step four: Start by navigating to the front cover if it's not already on the main screen. If you have taken the time to put your calendar-bound images into an **Album**, you'll see the images at the base of the page in the Photo Bin. Click and hold and push an image into the gray image holder. It automatically resizes and rotates to fit whatever shape the image template is for that calendar design.

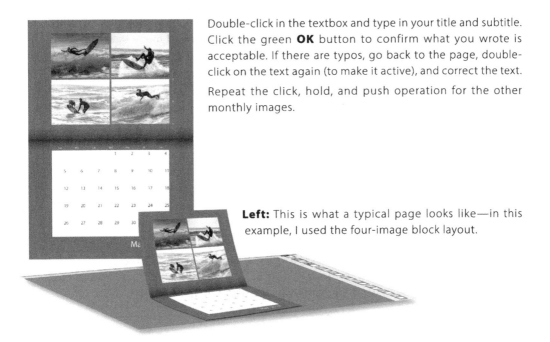

Double-click in the textbox and type in your title and subtitle. Click the green **OK** button to confirm what you wrote is acceptable. If there are typos, go back to the page, double-click on the text again (to make it active), and correct the text.

Repeat the click, hold, and push operation for the other monthly images.

Left: This is what a typical page looks like—in this example, I used the four-image block layout.

Mastering Adobe Photoshop Elements 2023

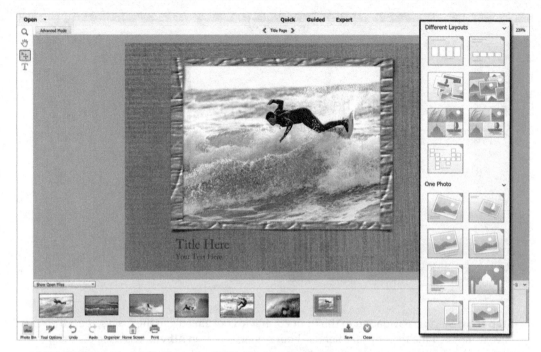

Step five—customize: If you don't like the **number of images** on a particular page or the **photo orientation**, they can easily be changed by opening the **Layouts** panel, in either the **Advanced** or the **Basic** window.

Once there, replace what's being used with a new design by double-clicking the thumbnail in the panel. It's easy. You can do this for one image, or for all of them. You can even get into the complexities of manipulating the individual layers in **Advanced** mode but that's, well, advanced, and not for this chapter.

Once the calendar is complete, save the file; it's ready for printing. You can do this on a regular photo inkjet printer—12 pages, plus a cover page—then take it down to your local office supplies shop to get it **spiral bound**, ready to send off to your friends or family.

Tip:

Working with text in Elements is not as easy as, say, Microsoft Word or Apple Pages, especially if you are adding more than a few comments to any Elements project or document. The best way to work with text is to create your document in whatever your favorite text editor might be, and then copy and paste the content from the word-processing application into Elements. One good point to this is that most, if not all, of your formatting will copy over to Elements, which will be a great time-saver.

Creating simple greeting cards

To make a greeting card, the process is almost identical to that of the calendar, except that you are making one page, not 12. Image placement and proportions are controlled through the menu.

Step one: To make a greeting card, arrange a few images into an **Organizer Album**.

Step two: Select one, two, or three images from this album (depending on how many you'd like to put into the card) and choose **Greeting Card** from the **Create** menu.

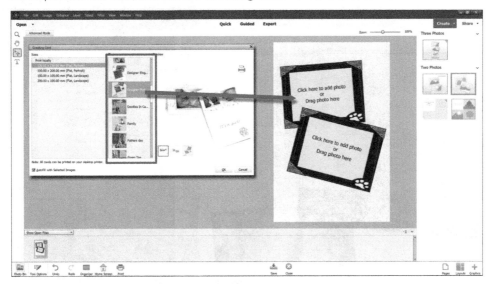

Step three: From the tiny **theme menu** that opens (outlined in red), choose a style and click **OK**. The graphic downloads and you then click, or drag, an image from the Photo Bin into the card art. Note that, on the right-hand side of the Greeting Card window is a panel of design layouts, which includes the ability to choose how many images are to be displayed on each page.

Working tips:

I have a few problems with using this particular utility—to begin, it's only designed for single-sided printing. I think this is probably because not everyone has a home inkjet printer that can duplex print (that is, print on both sides of the paper), but most of the templates are more like flyers than cards.

- As mentioned, the tiny window illustrating the card styles is both small while its content is, in my opinion, very dated. For this reason, I think it's far better to make your own custom designs manually.

- If I were to use this, I'd only place one or two images into the design and add them to the bottom half so that, once printed and folded in half, the front is where the image is and the back is blank.

- Use matt inkjet paper—this produces excellent color results, but it's also the best surface to bend and score flat. Some of the glossy papers, although more luxuriant in their thickness, are far harder to fold neatly.

- I suggest either using a blunt knife to score the spine prior to folding or using a professional card bending tool (usually found in a craft store).

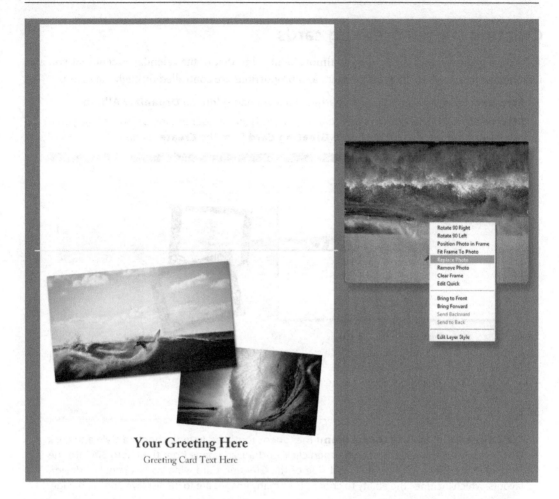

Step four: Once your chosen design has downloaded, try shuffling the images around if they have auto-loaded into the wrong part of the card. Do this by right-clicking the image itself and choosing either **Replace Photo** or **Delete** and find a replacement (above right).

Step five: Move the image holders to the best position. If you're printing these at home, you need to bear in mind the **fold line** through the center (here in yellow). The Adobe designs run the images over the middle of the document, which can be annoying if you want to fold it in half. I deleted the one at the top, and then moved the other two below the half-way line using the **Move** tool.

Note that if you mouse just to the outer edges of any image, the double-headed arrow changes into a **rotating arrow**—meaning that you can click, hold, and drag the orientation of the image to a different **rotational value**. Use the green tick (check) button to confirm your image movement before moving on. Save. When you save one of these projects, it creates a unique file format (`.pse`). This type of file holds all the information in one place—text, images, clip art, and color. Unlike the Photoshop file format, PSE files are only readable in Elements. The only other format that this can be saved as is **PDF**, which is universally readable.

Summary

Adobe Photoshop Elements started life as very much a scrapbooking-type, project-based photo editor, and while that *feel* has been somewhat replaced by an increasing number of hardcore image-editing features, it continues to surprise with the types of clever instant and automated features we discussed in this chapter. But for many, these automated processes, while extraordinarily useful, also have finite practicality—you can only go so far with them.

In this chapter, we have seen the power of Adobe's AI develop further with its semi-automated processes, such as its all-new **Artistic Effects** located in the **Quick Edit** mode, as well as its equally fantastic **Colorize Photo** feature, the clever **Photomerge Scene Cleaner**, plus its equally cool siblings, **Photomerge Faces** and **Photomerge Panorama** functions, a newly-expanded **Slideshow** feature, automated greetings card designs and DIY calendars, plus Lomo camera effects and effects collages, and, of course, there's a whole lot more—just check the listing in the **Create** menu.

These are all tools designed to help the user, novice, and advanced learners alike, pick up their images and get impressive results right from the get go. That's the power of this amazing program.

In the next chapter, we'll start looking at some of the **advanced editing features** that can be found in this application: **Layers, Selections, Adjustment Layer Masks,** and more. Once you've grasped these features, you will be able to significantly power up your editing skills.

6

Advanced Techniques: Transformations, Layers, Masking, and Blend Modes

This is the chapter where you'll move up a notch, from practicing the basics of good, but essentially fairly simple image editing, to learning the art of greater creative control over your work output in Elements' **Expert Edit** mode.

That said, for many grappling with the concept of Layers and Masks, this might seem counter-intuitive. Indeed, when I first started to learn Photoshop Elements, it took me months of self-persuasion before I was ready to make an assault on the concept of Layers, such was its perceived complexity.

I was lucky in that, at that point, I had always worked in photography—from commercial audio-visual production to printing in a pro lab—so the concepts of **dodging**, **burning in**, **masking**, and **exposure** were all familiar.

Even so, I still found Layers a little bit tricky, but after a few weeks of messing about, it became one of my all-time favorite features simply because it opened my eyes to a completely new range of creative possibilities.

Hopefully, this chapter will do the same for you...

The chapter begins with an introduction to **Transformations**—what this is, their features and options, and of course, how to use them. Once mastered, you'll find the Transform command will open doors to things you previously thought were too hard, or impossible.

The same goes for the sections on **Layers**, **Adjustment Layers**, and **Layer Masks**—picking up these techniques should make a massive difference to how you work with images—opening up a whole new world of image making.

Plus, you'll find a bunch of handy information on getting the most from Elements' range of Layer and Tool **Blend Modes**.

What you'll learn from this chapter:

- Transformations: Correcting perspective

- Transformations: Pictures in a picture

- Transformations: Warping shapes

- Transformations: Warping text

- Introduction to Layers

- Layer features explained

- Pseudo Layer masking

- Adjustment Layers

- Layer Masking basics

- Advanced Layer Masking

- Blend modes

Transform your image-making skills by learning all about the amazing power of Layers and Layer Masking.

Transformations: Correcting perspective

Because most of us photograph from ground level (and therefore point the camera upward at tall structures), our pictures often suffer from increased **optical distortion**. By packing more information into a small frame, the optical system cannot help but distort some of the vertical and horizontal lines. The best way to avoid such distorted perspective would be to shoot horizontally, from an upper floor, opposite a tall building, which means that you're less likely to suffer from optical distortion because there's less reason to tilt the camera. But we are rarely in a position where we can do that, so it's back to street level and optical distortion.

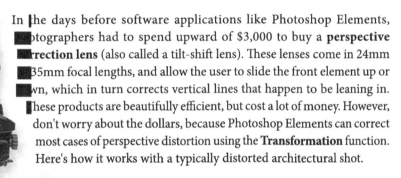

In the days before software applications like Photoshop Elements, photographers had to spend upward of $3,000 to buy a **perspective correction lens** (also called a tilt-shift lens). These lenses come in 24mm and 35mm focal lengths, and allow the user to slide the front element up or down, which in turn corrects vertical lines that happen to be leaning in. These products are beautifully efficient, but cost a lot of money. However, don't worry about the dollars, because Photoshop Elements can correct most cases of perspective distortion using the **Transformation** function. Here's how it works with a typically distorted architectural shot.

Step one: Open the offending picture. In this case, it's a magnificent vaulted ceiling supported by plenty of stone columns; you can clearly see that the wide-angle lens has added a fair bit of optical distortion to the columns, which we need to fix.

Free Transform
Scale
Free Rotate Layer
Skew
Distort
Perspective
Warp
Rotate Layer 180°
Rotate Layer 90° Right
Rotate Layer 90° Left
Flip Layer Horizontal
Flip Layer Vertical

Step two: I often use the **Grid** feature (**View > Grid**) on images like this as it provides a more accurate idea of what's vertical and what's not. Note if the Grid is too busy, reduce the gridline frequency and change their color via the **Preferences Panel** (**Edit > Preferences** or *Ctrl/Cmd + K*).

You can transform a single background layer, but if your distortions involve pushing the edges of the frame inwards, it will reveal a transparent background (not always desirable). It's usually best to first duplicate the layer (**Layer>Duplicate Layer**). To activate the **Transform** feature, choose **Image>Transform>Perspective**). The typical corners ('handles') of the **Transform** tool appear at the edges of the picture frame. **Ctrl/Cmd + T** also activates the Transform tool, but it opens into its **Free Transform** mode (see top of the pop-out menu panel above). To select a different mode, either right-click inside the image, and pick one from the pop-out menu or pick one from the tool Options Panel.

Step three: Grab one of the top corners and drag it horizontally outward, away from the image, and note that in doing so, the opposite corner is also dragged out, mirroring your movement. Essentially, you are making the top of the image wider. Keep an eye on the **Grid** to make sure everything is as symmetrical as possible.

On paper, this technique must read like a dream because all those architectural shots with the building looking as though it's leaning backward can now be corrected. One of the downsides to this technique is that, if the correction is dramatic, you'll also lose a fair amount of the original image as it drags the edges off the picture area. Next time you're out shooting architecture, take a few steps further back to encompass more of the surrounding area so that, once edited in Elements, you won't lose so many vital details in the transformation process.

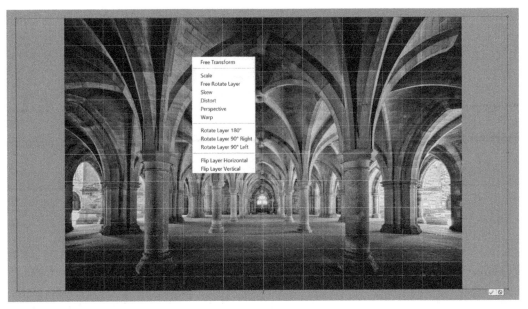

Step four: You'll note that the process of widening the top of the image not only loses a few pixels off the side of the rectangular photo, but it also makes it appear to be squatter. I usually finish off by committing that transformation first (click **OK**, or hit *Enter*), then change the **Transform** feature from **Perspective** to **Scale**, then I drag the top-center handle upward to stretch the image higher, and therefore closer in proportion to the original, but without the added distortion. You will lose more of the image doing this, but that's inevitable bearing in mind the pixel manipulations going on! Click the **OK** button, and it's done.

Left: By right-clicking inside that transformation rectangle, you'll notice other modes, which include the following:

Free Rotate Layer: As the name suggests, if you move the cursor to one of the corners, you can click and rotate the entire image or image layer.

Above: Skew is an interesting distortion effect. In this mode, if you click and move any of the central handles (not the corners), you'll see that they only move (skew) left or right (or up and down). This is a perfect mode to use on buildings that appear to lean away from vertical. That tower in Pisa, Italy, needs to lean no longer.

Below: I use **Distort** a lot when creating illustrations - such as 3D text and for Photobashing projects (see *Chapter 9, Advanced Drawing, Painting and Illustration Techniques*). Grab a corner and pull - true to its name, It distorts any frame in whichever direction you drag it. It's a handy tool to use, especially when none of the others do the job. The final Transform mode is Warp and works like a combination of Distort and the **Liquify filter**. You can see how this works later in the chapter (***Transformations: Warping Shapes for a 3D Shadow***).

Transformations: Pictures in a Picture

Another great way to understand how layers work in Photoshop Elements is through creating a **multi-image poster**. By adding multiple photos to a single file, you can then resize those pictures and move them so that they sit side by side rather than sitting on top of each other.

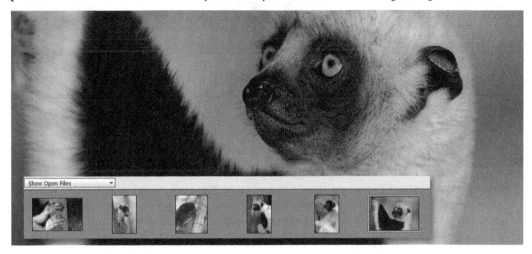

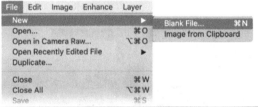

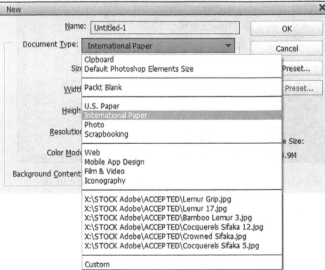

Step one: First off, open the pictures you want to incorporate into the project. Note that their thumbnails appear in the Photo Bin at the bottom of the main screen (pictured above).

Step two (left): Then, create a new document to the dimensions of your poster by going to **File**>**New**>**Blank File**.

Step three: The **New** panel that subsequently appears onscreen allows you to type in the vertical and horizontal dimensions of your new document, along with its base resolution. You can also quickly choose one of the preset document dimensions from the **Document Type** drop-down menu (such as A4, A3, US letter, HD Video, and so on). If the poster is to be printed, I suggest setting a resolution of 200 or 300 dpi. Click **OK**. The new, white Background Layer will appear onscreen.

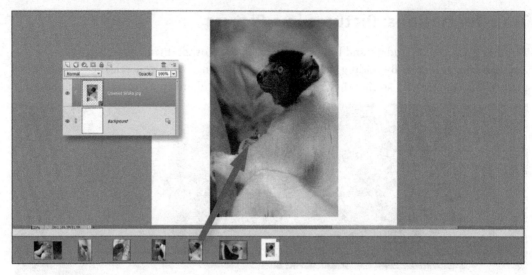

Step four: With the white new document displayed on the main screen, drag and drop one of the image thumbnails from the **Photo Bin** onto the main image. You'll see it appear on top of the white document. Check the **Layers** panel when you do this to confirm the arrival of a new layer containing your photo on top of the white background. Save the document in either the Photoshop (`.psd`) or TIFF (`.tif`) file format. Remember, JPEGs cannot contain any extras, such as selections, layers, or masks.

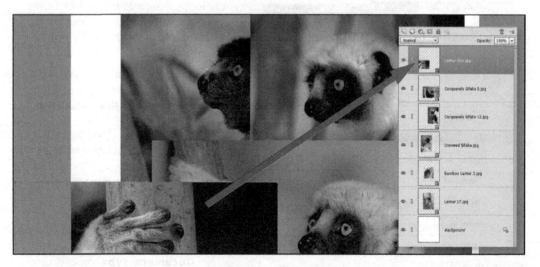

Step five: Follow the same process with the other images that you want to include in the poster, checking every time to confirm that the new image being pushed into your master document appears in the **Layer** panel (arrowed) . Inevitably, each image being copied into the master document will cover the previous one (as you can see in the screenshot here—it can be a bit of a jumble!), but don't worry about this because we are about to reposition everything for a better design. Save your work and move on to the next stage.

Step six: The easiest technique for changing the proportions of any item, pixel-based or vector, on an individual layer is called a **transformation**. To begin this process, choose **Image**>**Transform**>**Free Transform** (use the *Ctrl/Cmd + T* keyboard shortcut, or simply click and push the corner of the selected image with the **Move** tool). Once this is selected, you'll notice a grid appear across that single image with what Adobe refers to as corner **handles**. If you click, hold, and drag a corner handle inward, you'll reduce the size of that image proportionally. Dragging a midpoint handle (there's one on each side, inset, above) will shrink the size of the image, while also distorting it. Avoid this. Once the image has been resized so that it is smaller onscreen, you'll see a green checkmark appear at the bottom right-hand side of that image. Click this if you're happy with the resizing operation, or click the red icon if you want to cancel and retry the transformation process.

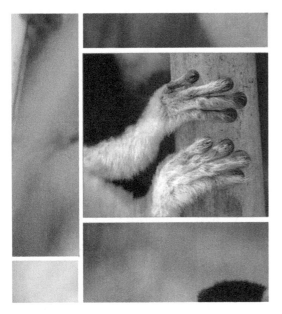

Step seven: Repeat this transformation process for the other images in the Photo Bin, resizing them so they fit the layout of your choosing. Whenever a file is resized (larger or smaller), Elements waits for you to 'OK' that action before allowing you to move on. This is a good feature, but if you are not paying attention, getting stuck without knowing why can be frustrating. Either confirm by clicking the green **OK** symbol (or press *Enter* on the keyboard), cancel the operation by clicking the red no entry symbol, (or press the *Escape* key (*Esc*) to cancel most operations in this application.

The advantage of working with layers is that the document remains **completely editable**. But save it as a JPG file and you lose control as all its' component layers are flattened into one file.

Advanced Techniques: Transformations, Layers, Masking, and Blend Modes

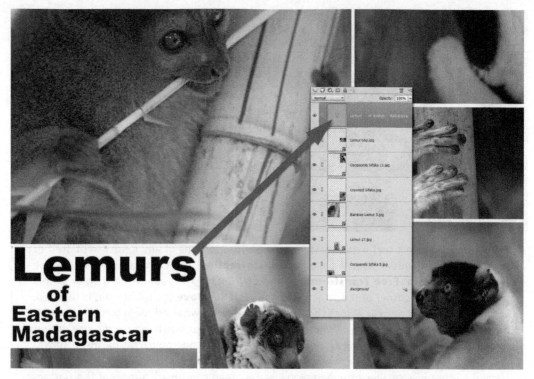

Step eight: To add text, choose the **Horizontal Type** tool from the **Tool Bar** (or press the *T* key) and click once in the document to automatically create a new text layer (check the **Layer** panel to confirm); note the type insertion point blinking just where you clicked in the image. Begin typing and the program will probably pick up the font and point size that was selected the last time the Type tool was used. By clicking once in the document to start the Type tool, it will allow you to type a sentence.

A really easy way to add text to any image is to use one of the **text presets** found in the **Graphics** panel. For more information on getting the most out of the **Type** tool, check out *Chapter 7, Advanced Techniques: Retouching, Selections and Text.*

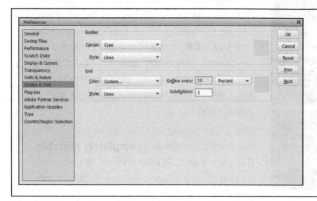

Use the View menu to open the Rulers or better still, use the Grid (See more on the Grid in *Chapter 9, Advanced Drawing, Painting and Illustration Techniques*). The default Grid is too busy - simplify it by reducing the gridlines via the Preferences Panel. Gridlines and Rulers do not print.

Transformations: Warping shapes for a 3D Shadow

This is a feature of the Transform tool that I have used for years, but it has only been available in Photoshop, until now. Finally, this feature has been added to the list of Transform commands that we just looked at over the last few pages (that is, **Image**>**Transform**>**Scale/Rotate/Skew/Distort/Perspective**, and now **Warp** modes). Let's take a look at how powerful this new Elements feature really is:

Step one: I copied and pasted the subject image into a blank document then resized the layer so it was smaller than the base document (**Image**>**Transform**>**Scale**). I then duplicated Layer 1 to produce two identical layers (above).

Step two: To make the drop shadow layer, I selected Layer 1, then used the **Output Levels** slider part of the **Levels** tool (*Ctrl/Cmd + L*), moving the pin from the far right to the far left. The image goes black (at right).

Step three: With the **Move** tool, I dragged the shadow layer down and to the right hand side, thus simulating the drop shadow's final position. I also changed the shadow layer's opacity to 50% (arrowed). You can change this later if the "shadow" is too light or dark.

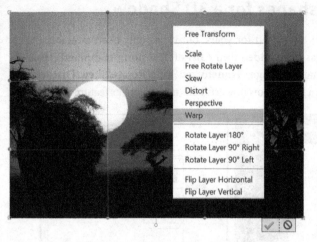
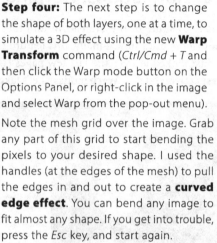

Step four: The next step is to change the shape of both layers, one at a time, to simulate a 3D effect using the new **Warp Transform** command (*Ctrl/Cmd + T* and then click the Warp mode button on the Options Panel, or right-click in the image and select Warp from the pop-out menu).

Note the mesh grid over the image. Grab any part of this grid to start bending the pixels to your desired shape. I used the handles (at the edges of the mesh) to pull the edges in and out to create a **curved edge effect**. You can bend any image to fit almost any shape. If you get into trouble, press the *Esc* key, and start again.

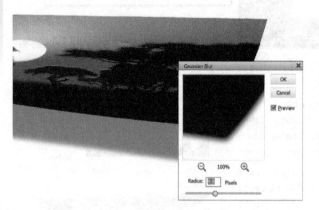

Step five: To give the drop shadow a greater authenticity, we need to soften the shadow layer. I used the **Gaussian Blur** filter (**Filter**>**Blur**>**Gaussian Blur**). The "higher" the subject is to appear above the background, the lighter and fuzzier the shadow needs to be. In this example, I settled on **9 . 8** pixels. You can fine tune this at any time along with the opacity of the layer.

Step six: To finish, I rotated the top photo layer anti-clockwise so the warped shadow underneath the image appears even more offset—adding to the 3D "look" I was trying to achieve.

Transformations: Warping text

Warping shapes is not the only thing that you can do with this feature—I use it a lot for warping images, as you saw in the last couple of pages—but don't forget **Warp** also works on text too. In fact, text warping has been in Elements for a long time, hidden away in the **Horizontal Type** options panel.

Just for fun: May your family snaps never look normal again! Here are three preset warp variations: **Inflate**, **Squeeze**, and **Twist**. All the presets you see on the pop-up menu below can be used as is or modified by grabbing the handle attached to the mesh frame and dragging. Hours of fun can be had messing with your pictures or, as you see below, warping text layers

Introduction to Layers

Layers is a powerful feature found in Elements that, once understood, should dramatically change the way you approach editing your pictures. More importantly, it should also dramatically expand your *creative potential*.

Layers are used when we want to include more than one element in a file, such as photos, text, clip art, or graphics. They're also important when we want to edit individual parts of an image without affecting the rest of the picture—for example, making one layer more colorful than all the others in the file. Aside from retaining **complete editability** of all layer components, a layered file must be saved in a special file format—typically a Photoshop (.psd) or a TIFF (.tif) file. These file types can also retain **selections** and never add **compression artefacts** (something JPEGs can suffer badly from), plus they have the unique ability to contain multiple versions of the same image within the same file. Let's take a look at some examples of Layers working in practice:

Layers example #1 - The traveler's journal: This is a project I undertook a few years ago. It's made up of more than **50 individual elements** located on **40 or more layers**. It's a busy image made from a few of my photos; everything else has been sourced from the internet. Because all the elements are (mostly) on their own layers, everything can be moved independently of everything else—the passports, stamps, tape, and postcards can all be shifted if the composition requires it. And thanks to the power of layers, I can 'hide' bits of picture elements by carefully positioning them under other objects—such as the stamps and passport under the diary.

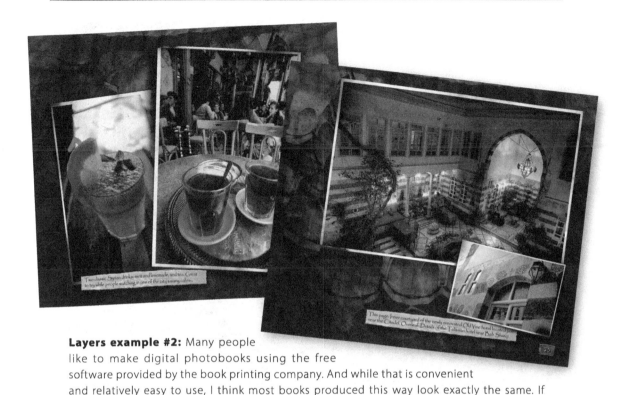

Layers example #2: Many people like to make digital photobooks using the free software provided by the book printing company. And while that is convenient and relatively easy to use, I think most books produced this way look exactly the same. If you want to add a unique 'look' to your next book production, consider custom designing the pages one at a time. Begin by creating a single new document the same size as your commercially printed digital photo book (in this example it was 10x8 inches), then add your own elements to the page. **Right:** Here's a 3D breakdown from one of this book's pages featuring a dark background image plus four texture layers (all set to different Blend Modes), text, text label, a straight photo, and even page numbers embossed into a bar of soap (this location is a major producer of laurel soap). Doing it page by page takes a long time but I think the results speak for themselves.

Layers example #3: Another book cover, this time a view over the old part of Havana, Cuba. In this image I wanted to reproduce the look of a photo from the early 50s—the days of the revolution—so added multiple textures, color tints, and text overlays to give it a faded, old look strikingly different from the straight shot (inset).

Layers example #4: On a slightly simpler note, this is a picture of two leaves that have been scanned, cut from their respective backgrounds and pasted over a color background image.

The red leaf layer was duplicated once, then the layer was flipped using the Transform command to provide the symmetry.

Layers has its own panel and, when there's more than one, the layers are displayed like a deck of cards. Each layer, be it text, graphics, or an image, can be shuffled up or down the layer panel. Those that reside on the top of the stack overshadow those beneath unless those at the top are smaller, or have a reduced opacity so data shows through. More on this later.

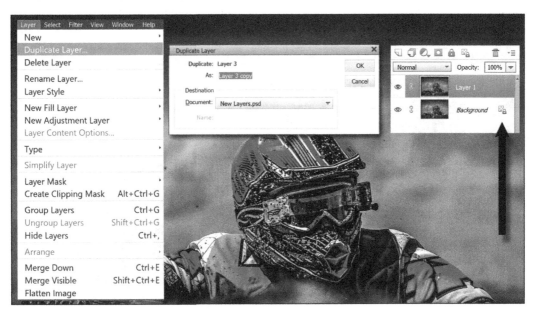

Let's take a look at some Layers basics.

Layers #1: Hover your cursor over the **Layer** menu (inbetween Enhance and Select), choose **Duplicate Layer...**, and then click **OK** in the **Duplicate Layer** panel that opens (above, center). Get into the habit of naming your layers—it'll help you identify layers if you come back to that file at a later time. There are now two identical layers in the **Layer** panel (above, right). One is highlighted in blue—this means that it's the **active layer**, so anything done to this file (that is, changes to the color or contrast) will only appear on this layer, not the one beneath it. When duplicating a layer, nothing changes in the main screen because you have simply covered the original picture with an exact copy, and since it's identical, you won't see a change. The duplicated layer will always sit above the original—this is called the **Background layer**. The **Background layer** has a small **padlock icon** to the right of its name (arrowed). This means that this layer is partially locked and cannot be moved, or made smaller. To remove the padlock, click the icon once—it automatically becomes **Layer 0**; then it can be moved (or choose **Layer>New>Layer from Background**).

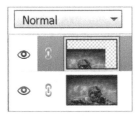

Layers #2: If you copy/duplicate a layer, then push it aside with the **Move tool**, you'll see a chequerboard pattern in the Layer panel - around the part of the layer no longer covered with pixels. This indicates **transparency** - but, look at the image in the main screen and you'll see, by shifting the image on the top layer, what's on the layer directly beneath it.

To get the best understanding of the power that Layers brings to the photographer and graphic artist, let's start by looking at the **layer components** and how they can be employed to jump start your creativity.

A photo, irrespective of its dimensions, resolution, or color mode, occupies a **single layer**. It's usually made up of pixels. If it's text or some type of graphic, it will be made up of things called **vectors** (see *Chapter 7, Advanced Techniques: Retouching, Selections, and Text,* and *Chapter 9, Advanced Drawing and Painting Techniques*).

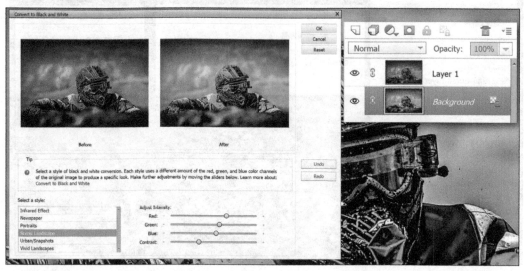

Layers #3: Here's a visual way to describe how layers work: if I were to select the **Convert to Black and White** feature from the **Enhance** drop-down menu (above), then click **OK** (no need to spend any time choosing a black-and-white style), I'd see that the active layer

turns black and white (as well as the tiny thumbnail in the **Layer** panel, above, right). However, although the **Convert to Black and White** feature shows it turning black and white, the main image remains in color. Why? It's because the active layer (blue, highlighted) is underneath the color layer. Since the color layer is opaque, it effectively stops us from seeing what's going on in the layer stack. But we can always see what's happening if we look at the layer thumbnails. To view the B/W version, make the top layer invisible by clicking the tiny **eye icon** to the left of the thumbnail in the active layer. Turning the visibility of that layer "off" means that we can see the content in the layer below it—the newly converted B/W version. A red line through the eye icon means that layer is invisible. Knowing which layer you are actually working on can be a bit confusing, but as long as you keep monitoring that **Layer** panel, you should be fine.

Layers #4: To make the color layer smaller, I can use the **Transform tool** (*Ctrl/Cmd + T*) and push one of the square photo corners inward to shrink it down. As you make that upper layer smaller, it reveals the original color version behind it. When transforming any object on a layer, Elements needs you to confirm or cancel the action by either clicking the green checkmark (OK), or the red symbol (cancel) before you can proceed with more editing (more on the **Transform** tool later in this chapter).

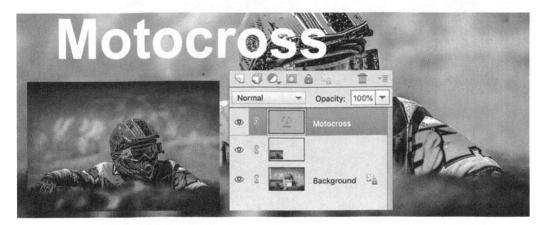

Layers #5: If text is added to a file, it creates its own **text layer**. This is made up of vectors, not pixels. The main difference between a vector and a pixel layer is that the former is a mathematical formula that can be enlarged to any dimension with no loss of quality (because it's just an algorithm), while the latter, the pixel-based layer, has a finite range of enlargeability that it can move through before it loses quality. When you shrink or enlarge an image on a layer, Elements uses clever interpolation or **resampling** algorithms to calculate how many pixels are needed to make the image larger or how to remove them to make it smaller. It's an excellent process, but it also involves a lot of **dithering**, a process that softens the edges of pixels (to avoid obvious pixelation), which makes the resulting resized image softer.

Layers #6: After spending some time practicing with layers, you'll find that adding text is a relatively easy operation, and you can then embark on a range of text-based creative projects, from posters to flyers and even business cards. I changed the regular-looking font, **Myriad Pro**, to something a little rougher to match the energy of the sport. I used a font called **SoulMission** in red, then added a drop shadow (from the **Styles** panel). There's more on using the **Type** tool in *Chapter 7*, *Advanced Techniques: Retouching, Selections, and Text*.

Other vector layers that you'll find in Elements include **custom shapes**, such as text boxes, copyright stamps, and other graphic symbols, which can be combined into any document. Like all the pixel-based photo layers, text can also be edited independently of the rest of the image, which makes it a great feature if you're as bad a typist as I am.

Layers #7: Drop shadows do a great job of giving the effect of 'lifting' text off the surface of the image underneath it. They add depth and improve legibility, which is particularly important when adding text on top of an image like this. The busier the image is, the harder it might be to read.

Font choice is also vital to the success of any multimedia document that might incorporate text. Understanding how font choice, font style (bold, italics, and so on), and point sizes work can make or break a good project (see the next section on custom fonts). As we'll see in the section on graphics coming up in *Chapter 9*, *Advanced Drawing, Painting and Illustration Techniques*, you can also add text boxes behind the text itself to make the typeface 100% legible. You can also reduce that text box's opacity so that some of the image shines through so that it's not a solid block of color on the image.

Other features on the Layers panel

The **Layers** panel (located on the right-hand side of the main window in the **Expert Edit** mode) features a number of useful productivity shortcuts in the form of **buttons** along the top of the Layer panel. From left to right, these include the following:

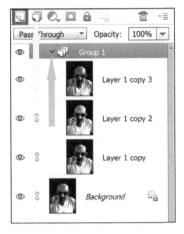

Create a New Layer: Here the icon is highlighted in **red**. Click this to add a new layer to a document. It will have nothing on it, so it appears clear, so you will see a chequerboard background.

Create a New Group (yellow arrow): When you are working with multiple layers, bunch similar layers together into a **Group** folder to help clean up the **Layer** panel. Grouped layers can be moved, transformed, and masked as a single entity. Here, three versions of the background image have been grouped together. Clicking the tiny chevron icon (green arrow) opens/closes the grouped folder.

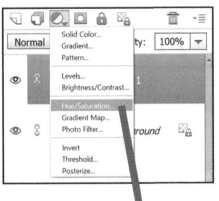

Create a New Fill or Adjustment Layer (left): Here's where you can add a range of **non-destructive edits** to a specific layer. They are termed "non-destructive" as they don't affect the pixels in the target layer. Adjustment layers come with an attached mask (the white thumbnail), which can be used to add the effect to parts of the target layer only. Very handy—see the *Adjustment Layers* section in this chapter. In this example, a **Hue/Saturation Adjustment Layer** is in place. Note also that to the right of the Hue/Saturation feature is a blank, white mask used for when you need to add an HSL adjustment to only a small part of the image. As we see in the **Layer Masking** section, this is an incredibly sophisticated way of selectively editing any part of any image.

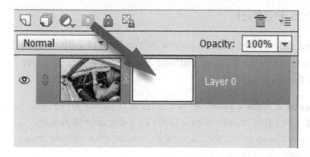

Add a Layer Mask (left): Layer masking is fully explained elsewhere in this chapter. Masks add tremendous editing control over different parts of any layer by using a black or white brush to hide/reveal different parts of the image. If nothing changes in the original, then the mask is inoperative. But make a small change, such as a color boost, and then any painting in the mask will show/hide the new color (see below).

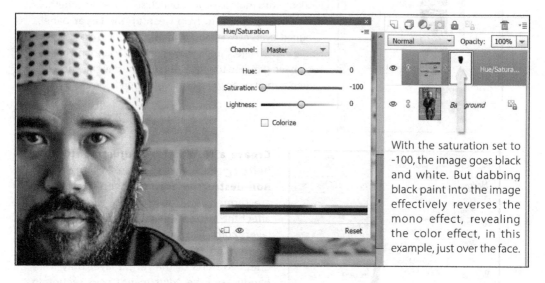

With the saturation set to -100, the image goes black and white. But dabbing black paint into the image effectively reverses the mono effect, revealing the color effect, in this example, just over the face.

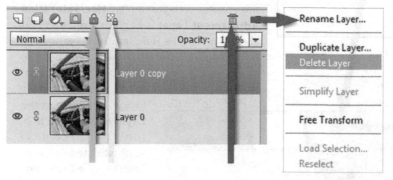

Lock All Pixels (green arrow): Use this feature if you want to prevent further changes to the layers.

Lock Transparency (yellow arrow): This prevents you from accidentally losing the transparent sections of the document (for example, by painting over them). **Delete Layer** (red arrow): Take out the trash! I think this feature is self-explanatory. You can also delete a layer by right-clicking the layer itself and choosing **Delete Layer** from the pop-out menu.

Layer opacity

As the name suggests, use the **Opacity** feature to change the density, or **opacity**, of an individual layer. One way to blend one layer into another is to reduce the top layer's opacity. Another reason for lowering the opacity is to check what's underneath that layer if you needed to reposition the top layer precisely above an object below it. Once repositioned, you can reset that layer's opacity to 100% and carry on with the edit.

Here, I have reduced the **MAGAZINE** text layer to 50%. Generally, if you are going to create this kind of look, it pays to have all elements saved as separate layers, otherwise in this example the header '**Classic Car**' would also fade, ruining the intended effect.

Merging layers

Apart from the buttons and menus on the **Layer** panel, if you click the tiny icon to the right of the trash can (arrowed), you can access the same features as the **Layer** menu at the top of the main screen, including the ability to integrate one (active) layer with the one below, a process called **Merge Down**.

Merge Visible is different as it flattens all the visible layers into one layer. The more useful **Flatten Image** command merges all the layers into one layer. If you try to save a multi-layered Photoshop format file (`.psd`) as a JPEG file, watch the **Layer** panel as Elements flattens the layers, saves it as a JPEG file, then unflattens everything as it returns to its former multi-layered `.psd` format state, leaving you with the original `.psd` file, plus a flattened `.jpg` file.

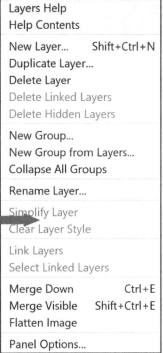

Layers Help
Help Contents

New Layer...   Shift+Ctrl+N
Duplicate Layer...
Delete Layer
Delete Linked Layers
Delete Hidden Layers

New Group...
New Group from Layers...
Collapse All Groups

Rename Layer...

Simplify Layer
Clear Layer Style

Link Layers
Select Linked Layers

Merge Down   Ctrl+E
Merge Visible   Shift+Ctrl+E
Flatten Image

Panel Options...

Pseudo Layer Masking

While I'd really like to think I coined the term **Pseudo Layer Masking**, I'm sure there are others who thought of the idea before I did. But what does pseudo masking mean?

Masking, as the name might suggest, is a technique where we can use an editable layer to 'protect' parts of the image while it's being changed/adjusted. The really neat thing about true Layer Masks is that they are a bit like an infinitely editable stencil - you can paint into the mask to add whatever change you want to the image, locally. The beauty is that the mask can be infinitely adjusted: if you make a mistake, it's no problem to keep adjusting the mask back and forth till you have the perfect result!

Pseudo masking is far simpler—you use a duplicated photo layer (rather than an editable black and white mask) and make changes to that layer, even when you might only want to enhance a small area in the picture. In this example, I want to enhance the tones in the bird, not the background! Here's how it works:

Step 1: Open your photo and duplicate the layer (**Layer>Duplicate**). Make sure that the top layer remains the active layer (highlighted in blue).

At right: This is what the original file looked like—good, but in need of some brightness control to reveal more detail in the feathers.

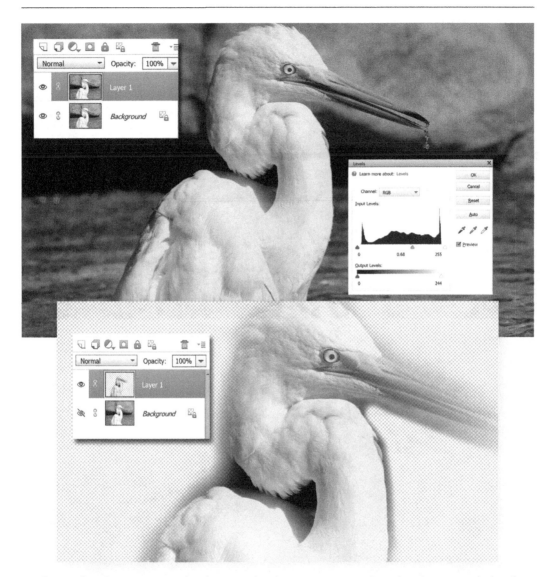

Step 2 (top): In my example, the egret has been overexposed so there's not much detail showing in its feathers. I chose to use the **Levels** tool (*Ctrl/Cmd + L*), although the **Brightness and Contrast** tool (**Enhance>Adjust Brightness>Brightness and Contrast**) would also do the job nicely. I darkened the **top layer** using the **Input Levels** sliders, ignoring the brightness of everything else in the frame except for the bird.

Step 3: Now the fun starts—choosing the regular **Eraser Brush Tool**, slowly remove all the pixels on that layer around the bird. Use a soft-edged brush but note that, if you select a super-large brush, the erasing action spreads a considerable distance. As you move closer to the bits you want to keep, reduce the brush size. The chequerboard pattern means that there are no pixels on that bit of the layer—they are visible here because the Background Layer's visibility has been turned off.

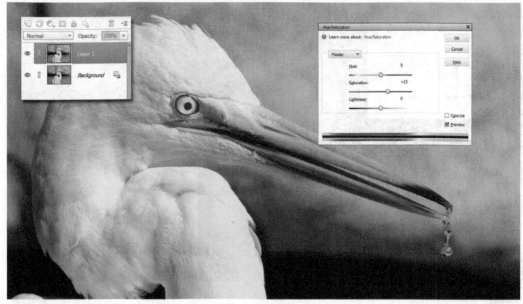

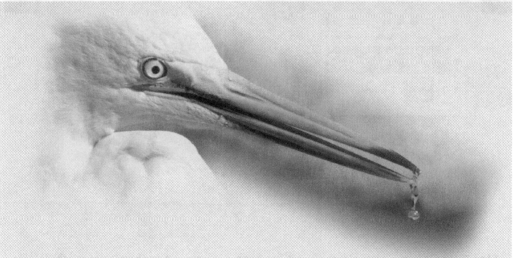

Step 4 (top): To edit another part of the frame, flatten the layer down (**Layer>Flatten Image**), then make a new duplicate layer and move on to the next local edit. In this case enhancing the color in the bird's beak, using the Hue/Saturation feature (*Ctrl/Cmd + U*). Again, you must ignore the rest of the image when you make the adjustment. Click OK and move on to the erase stage.

Step 5: In this screen shot I have already begun to erase the pixels I don't want (i.e. everything but the beak). Note that I have used a large, very soft brush, which is perfect for the edges but not so good when erasing close to the important bits as there's a danger of erasing too much. Avoid erasing the bits you need by reducing the brush size the closer you get to the detail.

Step 6: If I'd left a fuzzy edge around the bird's beak, the colour adjustment would bleed into the background and look incorrect. I swapped the fuzzy brush tip for a sharp edge and carefully etched my way around the beak to produce a far more accurate edit and a more realistic result (**below**).

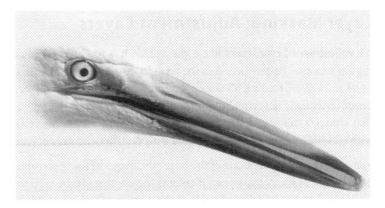

Pseudo Layer Masking Pros and Cons

Pseudo Layer Masks are easy to create, quick to execute, simpler to grasp than true layer masks, and can be a very effective way to add a quick boost to small parts of any image.

Disadvantages include: Unlike proper Layer Masks (see *Layer Masking: the Basics* in this chapter), this process has a limited repeatability; it's a one-way street and it relies on the user's manual skills erasing with a mouse.

Layer Masking: Adjustment Layers

An **Adjustment Layer** works like a *ghost layer*. It is used to make non-destructive tonal changes to regular images. The clue here is in the term "non-destructive." Editing files, especially JPEG files, can be *destructive*, especially if it's done over-enthusiastically, repeatedly, or not very well. In such cases, the image (eventually) loses quality, unless it's a RAW file, which is always a copy of the original. I may add that, although this non-destructiveness claim certainly sounds impressive, it's actually hard to quantify with real-life examples when compared with destructive forms of editing.

For many photographers, one of the huge advantages of using an **Adjustment Layer** is that it can also be used as a mask. A mask is an Elements feature that can be used to limit the effect of any change, tonal or otherwise, to **selected parts of the picture**. It's an incredible way to lighten, darken, saturate, or desaturate bits of an image, while leaving the rest of the photo untouched. What's more, a mask is a relatively simple feature to create. Here's how it works:

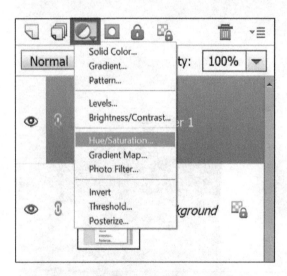

Step one: An **Adjustment Layer** can be added to any picture—either via the icon on the top of the **Layer** menu (here in red), or via the **Layer** menu, along the top of the main screen.

From the menu, you can choose a range of different Adjustment Layer effects:

- **Solid Color**
- **Gradient**
- **Pattern**
- **Levels**
- **Brightness/Contrast**
- **Hue/Saturation**
- **Gradient Map**
- **Photo Filter**
- **Invert**, **Threshold**, and **Posterize**.

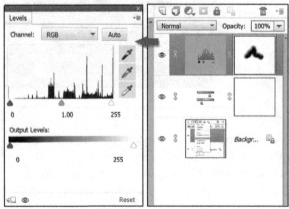

Step two: In this example, I chose the **Levels Adjustment Layer**. The idea is to make a **Levels** adjustment, paying attention to only the part of the scene that needs added brightness and/or contrast—ignore the rest, even if it begins to look too light or dark.

The Adjustment Layer's mask is located to the right of the **Levels** adjustment icon (I have started to paint into the white mask using black paint).

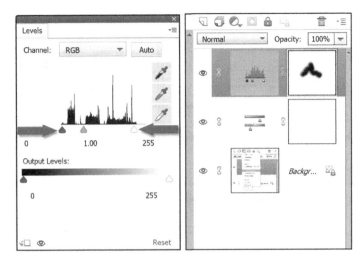

Step three: By pushing the two small sliders on either side of the tone histogram, I increased the contrast in the scene. Once done, you can leave the Adjustment Layer as is (it then has to be saved as a `.tif` or a `.psd` file) or you can move on to use the white mask to limit the tone changes to certain parts of the image only, not all of it.

Aside from making fast tonal changes to your work, Adjustment Layers are also all about **masking**—let's take a look at a **practical application** for an Adjustment Layer:

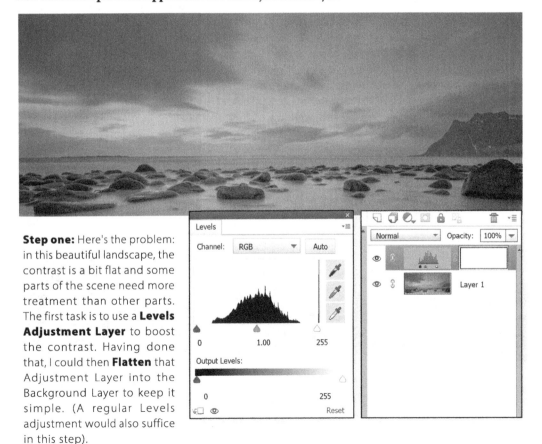

Step one: Here's the problem: in this beautiful landscape, the contrast is a bit flat and some parts of the scene need more treatment than other parts. The first task is to use a **Levels Adjustment Layer** to boost the contrast. Having done that, I could then **Flatten** that Adjustment Layer into the Background Layer to keep it simple. (A regular Levels adjustment would also suffice in this step).

Advanced Techniques: Transformations, Layers, Masking, and Blend Modes

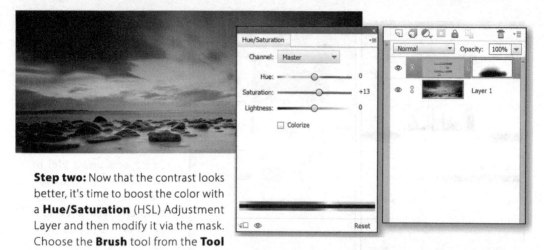

Step two: Now that the contrast looks better, it's time to boost the color with a **Hue/Saturation** (HSL) Adjustment Layer and then modify it via the mask. Choose the **Brush** tool from the **Tool Bar** with a soft brush tip. To ensure that you get black paint (and not some other color), first press *D* ('Default' color setting—black in the background and white in the foreground). Press the *X* key to swap black with white. Press again to swap it back to black.

With the white mask thumbnail highlighted in blue (click once to do this), paint directly into the image on the main screen, and see the color effect created by the HSL adjustment is removed as you paint black onto the white mask (black makes the mask opaque). Check the thumbnail and you'll see that your black brush marks appear in the thumbnail. The more you paint, the less the adjustment appears in the image. If you make a mistake painting black onto the mask where you shouldn't have, press *X* (to swap black with white) and paint over the black paint to make that bit of the mask transparent again. You can go backward and forward, fine-tuning the position and accuracy of the tonal change, as many times as you like. It's infinitely editable.

Here's a comparison between the flat and dingy original image, above left, and the improved image, with local contrast and color added into the mix, mostly across the shoreline, lower right to create a far more dynamic looking picture.

Layer Masking: the basics

Most photographers will agree when I say that you can only take your editing so far using Elements' **global tone-changing tools**. In this book, we have seen how effective the global tools are, but sooner rather than later, you'll realize that you need to develop skills to edit small parts of your picture, rather than the entire file.

Layer masking is one of the keystone features of all photo editing applications for the simple reason that it allows you to make significant changes to very specific parts of any image. Once set up, it's easy to do and is infinitely editable. This is achieved by first making a global edit (using a tool such as **Levels**); then, with the mask active, painting black makes the layer transparent, thus revealing the original state of the image. Painting white makes the mask opaque, thus covering the original image with the newly edited version.

The magic of this technique becomes apparent if you make a mistake and paint over something in the mask so that part of the image returns to the original—when you really wanted it to remain enhanced. If this happens, tap the *X* key to flip the background to the foreground color (white to black). Magically, the mistake is erased with the application of white paint on black. This backward/forward masking is infinite—which is what makes it such a great editing technique.

Step one: Setting up a **Layer Mask** is easy. Begin by opening an image. This is part of the old town in Kyoto featuring centuries-old wooden houses. It was a dull day, so the resulting image was the same. It needs a little selective help. Duplicate the layer; this stage is not vital to the editing process, but out of habit, I've always kept the original layer intact and operated on, or edited, a duplicate so that I can easily return to the original in the same file by switching the editing layer's visibility to **off** (by clicking the eye icon).

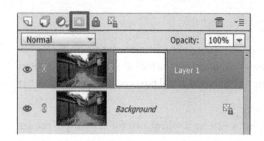

Step two: Ensure that the **Layer** panel is fully visible and check that the top layer—the duplicated layer—is the active layer (highlighted in blue). Above that layer sits a row of buttons that are specific to layer editing. The feature that we are interested in here is the **Add Layer Mask** button. Click this and note that a white thumbnail appears at the right-hand side of that layer's photo thumbnail. You have just created your first Layer Mask on its own. A white Layer Mask is transparent, so at this stage, it has no effect on the image.

Step three: Make a tone edit to the layer. As an example, let's brighten the image using **Levels** (*Ctrl/Cmd + L*). You could use an Adjustment Layer although here I am using a regular Layer Mask. Before you start painting into the mask, make sure that the photo thumbnail, and NOT the mask thumbnail, is highlighted.

Double-clicking the thumbnail selects it, and you'll see that the thumbnail becomes highlighted in light blue. Adjust the image contrast and/or brightness. Everything looks 100% normal; the white mask is still fully transparent, so all we see onscreen is the adjusted version. Some parts look good, while others might be too bright.

Step four: Now comes the magic. Clicking the white layer thumbnail (I highlighted it in red here) will make it active (highlighted around the edges in **light blue**). Select the **Brush Tool** (making sure it's the real brush, and neither the **Impressionist Brush** nor the **Color Replacement Brush**, choose black from the **Color Picker** (the two small color squares under **Modify** at the bottom of the **Tool Bar**). A quick way to do this is to press the *D* key, which sets a default of white in the foreground and black as the background color. Press the *X* key—this automatically flips the foreground to the background color (to give you black paint).

Step five: Paint over the object in the image that you want brought back to the original brightness, and as you paint onto the image (actually onto the mask) with a brush loaded with black paint, note that the original brightness and contrast returns. Release the mouse and the black paint mysteriously appears, not on the main image, but in the mask thumbnail.

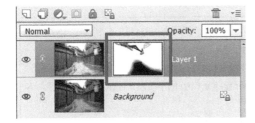

Step six: Each time you stop painting and release the mouse, the state of masking is updated in the mask. So, if you keep an eye on this feature while you create your mask, it will keep updating and you can get an idea of the true coverage of the mask—and indeed if you have missed sections (easy to do).

Don't forget that you can further refine this technique by changing the size, shape, opacity, and softness of the brush that you're using. This gives the designer or photographer infinite levels of control in terms of adding subtle changes to any image.

Advanced Techniques: Transformations, Layers, Masking, and Blend Modes

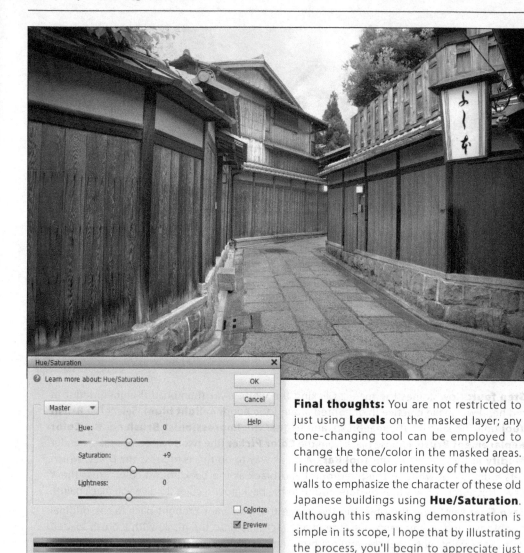

Hue/Saturation

Learn more about: Hue/Saturation

Master

Hue: 0

Saturation: +9

Lightness: 0

☐ Colorize
☑ Preview

OK
Cancel
Help

Final thoughts: You are not restricted to just using **Levels** on the masked layer; any tone-changing tool can be employed to change the tone/color in the masked areas. I increased the color intensity of the wooden walls to emphasize the character of these old Japanese buildings using **Hue/Saturation**. Although this masking demonstration is simple in its scope, I hope that by illustrating the process, you'll begin to appreciate just how powerful this technique can be.

Layer Mask Tips

- Always make sure that the mask is active (highlighted in blue); otherwise, any painting will land in the image, not the mask, and cause irreparable damage to the pixels.
- Remember to use the *D* key to reset the Color Picker to a white foreground over a black background.
- Use the *X* key to change between foreground and background colors.
- Don't forget that the image thumbnail must be highlighted in order to add tone effects.

Layer Masking: advanced techniques

Hold on to your hats, this section is likely to take you to yet another creative level. As we just saw in the previous sections, simple tonal corrections using basic Layer Masks is actually quite easy.

Finished image: This project involves taking two stock images (and other objects) and blending them together as seamlessly as possible using Layer Masks, contrast, 3D shadows and color tweaks.

Before we get into the next project, let's recap on the main points:

- A Layer Mask is attached to its own layer and appears as white in the Layer Panel.
- In its unedtited form, it's white. White = opaque. If it's black it's 100% translucent.
- To make a custom mask, select the mask first (i.e. click it to highlight its edges) then paint into the main image (NOT the thumbnail) using the Brush Tool.
- Set the Color Picker to black (foreground) and white (background) and paint over the object to be masked in the main window.
- Pressing the **D** key resets the Color Picker to the Default black/white color. Pressing the **X** key swaps foreground color with the background color.
- If you make a masking/painting 'mistake', press the **X** key and paint over the mistake to reverse the masking action. This forwards/backwards technique for painting the perfect mask is infinitely repeatable (unlike the Pseudo Masking technique previously demonstrated).

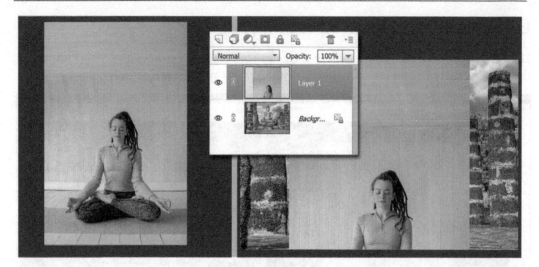

Step One: Two different photos need to be in the same file. Open both, then tile them (**Window>Images>Tile**), select and copy the model file (*Ctrl/Cmd + A*, then *Ctrl/Cmd + C*)), move to the second image tab, and click to make it 'active', then paste the selected image into the Buddhist temple file (*Ctrl/Cmd + V*). Resize (**Transform**—*Ctrl/Cmd + T*) the top layer so the image fits the background. It can be resized later.

Step Two: Cut out the yoga model - Add a Layer Mask to the top layer (circled), make sure it's selected (click the mask to highlight it: here in yellow), grab a soft-edged Brush, choose black from the Color Picker then paint into the main image to start drawing the mask to remove the background. Monitor your mask drawing progress by checking the black paint in the mask in the Layer Panel.

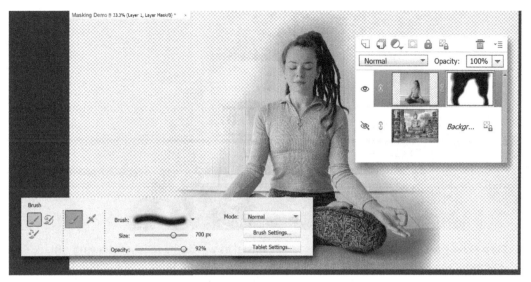

Step Three: As a working tip, switch the bottom layer off (by clicking the eye icon in the layer Panel) to make viewing your mask painting easier. Also, when working on a Layer Mask, note that the name of the file is automatically appended with these words: (Layer x, Layer Mask/8).

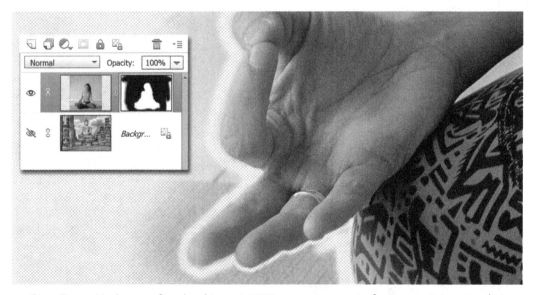

Step Four: Masks are often hard to get 100% accurate; most of us are not very good at drawing with a mouse. Remove the obviously redundant pixels around the outer parts of the subject first, then reduce the brush size dramatically—this produces a cleaner cut line, compare the mask around thumb and forefinger with a cut line around the index finger. Another tip is to use the *Shift*, click, Shift, click drawing technique (featured in the **Basic Drawing Techniques** section of *Chapter 9*). This enables you to draw straight and even curved lines very quickly and accurately.

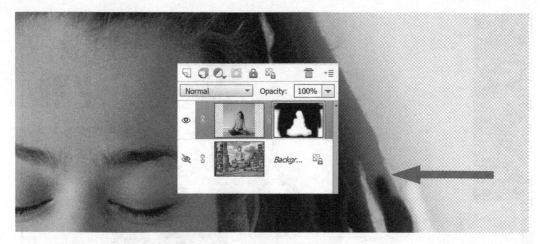

Step Five: Even when using a graphics tablet, mistakes will be made when drawing a mask. Here you can clearly see that I have erased the area around the subject's head but, because the soft brush was too large, it also partially removed pixels in the hair (arrowed). This is where the power of Layer Masks becomes apparent. Press the **X** key to swap black with white (in the Color Picker) and paint over the problem area; the lost hair returns as if by magic.

Step Six: Don't forget to turn the bottom layer's visibility on and off occasionally to see how well your masking is going. This looks OK but there's still some background fuzz around the subject's top. Don't forget, if you have accidentally chewed off some of the subject, it's easy to replace by swapping your paint color from black to white.

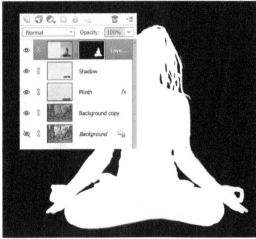

Step Seven: Because the subject layer in this example is vertical, you'll see gaps either side of the layer as it sits on a horizontal background. Fix this by extending your mask—painting past the frame edges. Note that if the top layer is reduced in size (to fit the composition), you'll have to go back and paint in more mask to those edges. Another thing to watch out for is to check the gaps, such as in clothing and hair. Tending to these small details, though fiddly, makes the end result that much more authentic.

Step Eight: The mask at left looks OK, but to be honest, you don't always see missed bits as they might be the same color as the background or they are too faint. To view a mask full size hold *Alt/Opt* and click once in the mask thumbnail (in the Layer Panel). The mask is displayed in the main window, making it much easier to spot mistakes. You can still use the Brush Tool to fix the mistakes. Hold *Alt/Opt* and click the mask thumbnail a second time to turn the large mask off.

At left: Right-clicking the mask thumbnail opens more options such as **Disable Layer Mask** (temporarily turn it off), Apply layer Mask (converts mask and image to just the masked subject with no mask), **Add Mask to Selection** (adds a selection line around masked subject), while **Subtract Mask from Selection** and **Intersect Mask with Selection** subtracts/adds the subject selection with an existing selection covering part of the masked subject.

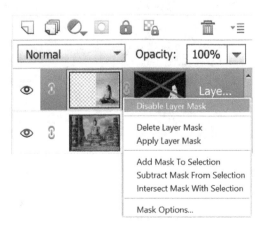

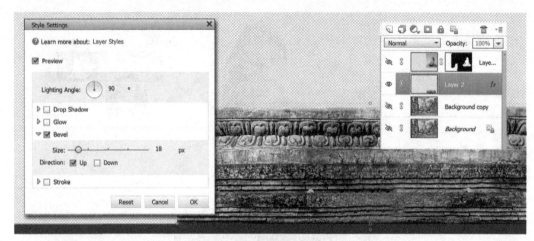

Step Nine: At this stage you should be able to appreciate that Layer Masks are a powerful tool. But if the elements you are trying to bring together do not match, no amount of masking is going to work. Placing the yoga practitioner in the scene kind of works but she really needs something to sit on. I searched online for a plinth (or similar) to use and came up with nothing so simply copied some of the brickwork in the pagoda, resized it and cloned out some of the details so it looked a bit different from its source. As the new pedestal sits on its own layer, I added a small **Bevel** effect (from the Styles Panel) to give the copied brickwork a little more depth.

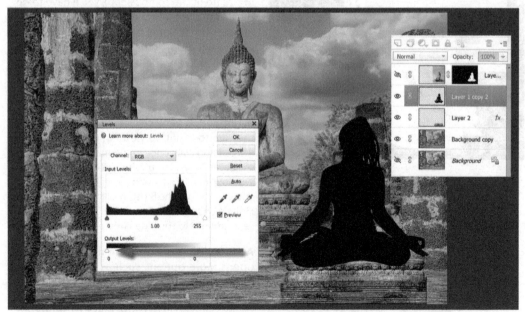

Step Ten: In an attempt to make the subject fit the background more convincingly, I duplicated the masked layer, clicked its mask thumbnail once (to make it active), then right-clicked the mask and chose Apply Layer Mask from the pop-out menu. This left me with just the figure on a clear background. This is then turned black by radically adjusting the Levels **Output Levels** slider (see arrow) - then its blurred using the Gaussian Blur filter for effect (see over).

Step Eleven: This screenshot shows the duplicated, darkened and blurred shadow layer in place. If it's a real shadow, it needs to fall on the pedestal under the subject—this is easily shaped by erasing all the shadow pixels apart from the lower part of the body. You can transform the shadow layer to any shape so it fits the scene. As it's just fuzzy, black pixels, you can bend it in any direction without worrying about damaging the pixels (below, left). I also copied the brick plinth, reduced its brightness (Levels) and added a **Gaussian Blur** (Filter>Gaussian Blur) to simulate another shadow, then used the **Transform>Distort** command to bend it into the right shape (see bottom right).

Final thoughts: In a perfect world, you'd choose picture elements that have matching brightness, contrast, color, sharpness and lighting—that's hard to achieve. For all those combinations where there is a difference, you need to adjust the tones using **Levels**, **Brightness/Contrast** or **Hue/Saturation**. I also added local darkening using the **Burn Brush Tool**—one of Elements' most underrated features.

Blend Modes

Underneath the **Layer** panel's row of buttons sits another drop-down menu with 24 settings—these are the **Blend Modes**. They only become active when two or more layers are present in the document. The default setting is **Normal**. It's almost impossible to provide a clear description of what Blend Modes actually do, other than to say that different Blend Modes affect the way the top layer *blends* with the one below it. Some appear to do nothing, while others have a radical effect.

In the following screenshots, I have created a masthead for a fake publication, **Classic Car Magazine**, and have changed the Blend Mode on the text layer (in this exercise, some made no change to the look of the text, so have been left out).

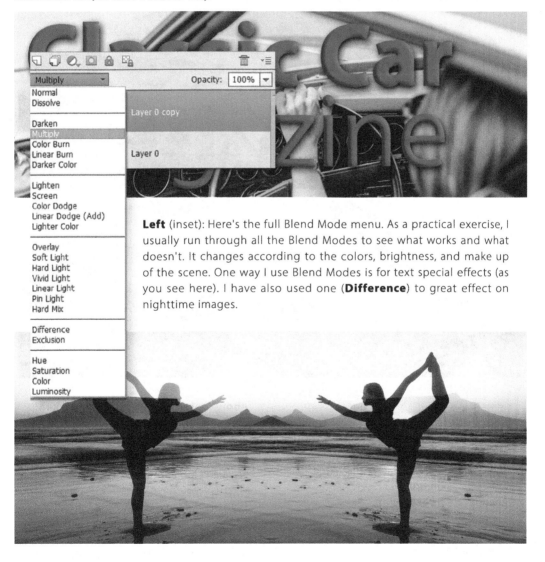

Left (inset): Here's the full Blend Mode menu. As a practical exercise, I usually run through all the Blend Modes to see what works and what doesn't. It changes according to the colors, brightness, and make up of the scene. One way I use Blend Modes is for text special effects (as you see here). I have also used one (**Difference**) to great effect on nighttime images.

The best advice is to try them yourself, then decide whether they are improving your edit or not. Note that most of Elements' brush-based tools can also be set to operate in a specific Blend Mode. If you take a paint brush and set that tool's Blend Mode to **Exclusion**, for example, any subsequent brushing will produce a reversed-out color from the one you see in the image above.

Above, listed from the top: the **Darken**, **Linear Burn**, and **Overlay** Blend Modes in action.

Previous page, bottom: Another way to use Blend Modes is to duplicate the image layer (so you have two identical layers), then flip the top layer horizontally so it's back to front, then change the Blend Mode for the top layer from **Normal** to **Overlay** to produce this double-image effect.

Above, from the top: In these examples, the **Difference**, **Color**, and **Saturation** Blend Modes made the most noticeable differences to the norm.

Right: In some cases, changing the Blend Mode makes little or no difference, while others can produce extreme graphic color effects, such as these flowers. The posterized effect is created by changing the top Blend Mode to **Hard Mix**—it's an instant Andy Warhol-esque result!

Tool Blend Modes

Most of us using the tools in Photoshop Elements take them 'as is'. What I mean by that is the tool operates much as you'd expect it to: the Brush Tool 'paints' a color into the image, the Clone Brush Tool copies and pastes pixels from one spot to another, and so on. What many might not appreciate is that most of these tools also work in a range of Blend Modes. Blend Modes, as we have seen in the section on Layer Blend Modes change the way pixels on one layer react when placed on top of another pixel layer. Place two opaque images one on top of the other and you lose sight of the base image as the top one covers the one underneath. But if we change the transparency of the top image, we begin to see what's underneath. Simplistically, that's how Layer Blend Modes work and it's the same for the tools. Let's take a look at how this can be used to your creative advantage:

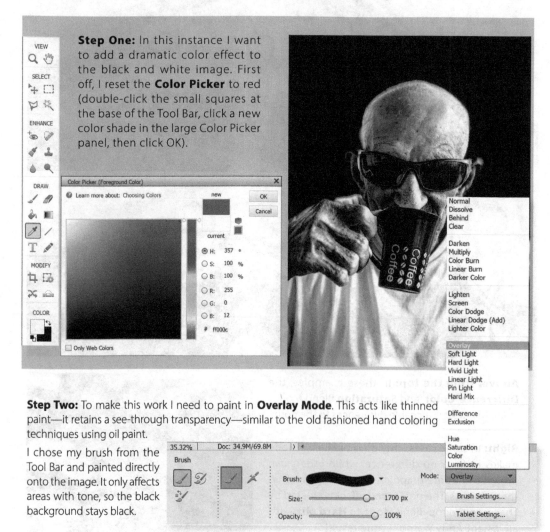

Step One: In this instance I want to add a dramatic color effect to the black and white image. First off, I reset the **Color Picker** to red (double-click the small squares at the base of the Tool Bar, click a new color shade in the large Color Picker panel, then click OK).

Step Two: To make this work I need to paint in **Overlay Mode**. This acts like thinned paint—it retains a see-through transparency—similar to the old fashioned hand coloring techniques using oil paint.

I chose my brush from the Tool Bar and painted directly onto the image. It only affects areas with tone, so the black background stays black.

Step Three: To jazz it up even more, I then added yellow and purple—adjusting the size and opacity of the brush with each color. This is a fun and fast way to add a little **visual intensity** to your work.

Layers: Smart Objects

It's important to note that the process of click-pushing an image from the **Photo Bin** into any (new) master document (in the main edit window) converts a pixel-based image into a feature called a **Smart Object**. You can also import an image by using the **File>Place** command.

Smart Objects are essentially non-destructive layers. This means that you can resize them at will and not damage the pixels—as you might when you resize a pixel-based image layer. They can be used in conjunction with Adjustment Layers and masks.

You can't perform operations that alter pixel data (such as painting, dodging, burning, or cloning) directly on a **Smart Object** layer unless it's first converted into a regular layer in a process called **Simplify Layer**—this changes its status from smart to pixels.

For many processes, a Smart Object has to be converted back to being just a pixel-based image—in fact, Elements will tell you when this is needed, but you can also do it by right-clicking the image later and choosing **Simplify Layer** from the pop-out menu.

In this screenshot, I have placed the black-and-white portrait of the man into the weightlifter shot. In the **Layer** panel, you can clearly see the smart layer above the background layer—it has a special Smart Layer symbol on it at the bottom right-hand side.

I can stretch the image corner handle in or out to increase or decrease its size—as this is happening, Elements refers back to the original file and updates the quality of the image, depending on whether it's getting larger/smaller. This preserves the image quality, regardless of the magnification applied to it.

Keyboard shortcuts

As with most editing, you can lose sight of the image-making process and become too immersed in the more complex editing functions. Keyboard shortcuts are there to help spread the load, reduce RSI, and generally speed up your workflow. I use the first three of the following list repeatedly. It's beneficial to memorize some of the tool access keys (single letters) to make it easier to jump from process to process. Some of these are shown in the following list:

- Duplicate the (active) layer: *Ctrl/Cmd + J.*
- Use this to deselect or remove any active selection: *Ctrl/Cmd + D.*
- Use this to transform objects on the active layer: *Ctrl/Cmd + T.*
- Merge down: *Ctrl/Cmd + E.*
- Merge (all) visible layers: *Shift + Ctrl/Cmd + E.*
- Burn, Dodge, and Sponge tools: *O.*
- Selection brushes (Quick Selection, Selection Brush, Magic Wand, Refine Selection, and Auto Selection): *A.*
- Lasso tools (Freehand Lasso, Polygonal Lasso, and Magnetic Lasso): *L.*
- Clone Stamp tool (also the Pattern Stamp): *S.*
- Spot Healing and Healing brushes: *J.*
- Brushes (Brush tool, Impressionist Brush, and Color Replace Brush): *B.*
- Eraser brushes (Eraser, Background Eraser, and Magic Eraser brushes): *E.*
- Paint Bucket tool: *K.*
- Gradient tool: *G.*
- Enhance>Select Subject: *Alt/Opt + Ctrl/Cmd + S.*

Out of the hundreds of possible keyboard shortcuts published for this program, I consider those on this page to be the most important. They sum up the most practical features in this program and, once learned, they will advance your understanding and editing proficiency tenfold.

Summary

As you may well now be aware, it's possible to spend your entire working life immersed in the realms of commercial photography and professional retouching.

All the tools are abundantly present in Photoshop Elements, but if you need to take the control you require to a higher level, this was certainly the chapter for you.

In this chapter, we ramped up the knowledge that this book has explored so far by introducing you to Transformations and how they can help reshape your images, then on to Layers, Warped Layers, Adjustment Layers, and full-on Layer Masking.

You also learned how to enhance images and create powerful graphic effects using Blend Modes, have fun with tool Blend Modes, and much more.

Learning how to use layers like this will enhance your creativity tenfold.

Coming up in the next chapter, we'll take a close look at the intricacies of beauty retouching using the **Clone Stamp** and **Healing Brush** tools, as well as learning how to improve images with the amazing **Burn**, **Dodge**, and **Sponge Brush** tools.

The next chapter also covers how to work with another powerful Elements tool: **Selection**, used to limit the edit process to specific parts of the image only. The final part of the chapter takes you in the direction of the graphic designer with the use of **text**, and all its different applications, using special effects.

Advanced Techniques: Retouching, Selections, and Text

With the experience of working with Layers now safely saved to your repertoire of editing skills, it's time to tackle the often confusing world of retouching. This chapter introduces you to the power of the Spot **Healing Brush** and **Clone Stamp** tool - you will have seen examples of how this is used to 'perfect' images earlier in this book but here we shift the emphasis from beauty retouching to complex repair jobs that need multiple tools to create the perfect result.

You'll also find a section on what I regard as two of the best image modifiers: the **Burn** and **Dodge Brush Tools** - simple brushes that can transform a tired looking image into a dynamic picture - just with the stroke of a brush!

But this chapter is also about simplifying selections - highlighting excellent tools like the **Subject Selection** and **Object Removal** features.

And then we focus on the power of selections, describing all of Elements' many fantastic **selection tools** in practical examples.

And finally there's a chance to move into the world of graphic design with an introduction to the expansive **Type Tool** - how to add simple text to an image and furthermore, how to add some very nice special effects to that text using Elements' many and varied presets. The final section is one after my own heart - revealing how easy it is to find , download and use an awesome range of **custom fonts**. Let's get started!

In short, this chapter is designed to build on the lessons of the previous one. We'll be building up and focusing your editing, and in particular, your retouching skills, so, with the right inspiration, you can create almost anything with this awesome software.

Here's what we will learn in this chapter:

- Retouching: Spot Healing Brush and Clone Stamp Tools

- Advanced Retouching Techniques

- Retouching: Object Removal Tool

- Retouching: Burn, Dodge, and Sponge Brush tools

- Retouching: Blur, Sharpen, and Smudge Brush tools

- Subject Selection tool

- Advanced Selections: Selection features

- Advanced Selections: Saving Selections

- Advanced Selections: Feathering

- Advanced Selections: Refine Selection Brush

- Advanced Selections: Refine Edge Tool

- Advanced Selections: The marquee and Lasso Tools

- Advanced Selections: The Magic Wand Tool

- Quick Selection Tool

- Auto Selection Tool

- Basic Text: Text Styles

- Basic Text: The Type Tool

- Basic Text: Styles and Effects

- Advanced text: Using Custom Fonts

Now you see him, now you don't. In this chapter, we learn all about the power of **retouching**.

Retouching: Spot Healing Brush and Clone Stamp Tools

In this section, we'll look at how to correct the tones, imperfections, and the *look* of a simple beauty shot, step-by-step.

During this process, you'll learn how to use both the **Spot Healing Brush** tool and the powerful **Clone Stamp** tool, one of the original and, in my opinion, best retouching tools in Elements. The **Clone Stamp** tool was inherited from Adobe Photoshop in the years before Photoshop even contemplated being part of Creative Cloud.

In effect, the **Clone Stamp** tool is little more than a **copy-and-paste tool**. It works in a similar way to a word-processing application, where you might copy and paste a paragraph of text from one part of a document to another, except that it copies pixels rather than text.

The key point to remember when using either the **Clone Stamp** or **Spot Healing Brush** is that you first need to identify a clear **Source** area. This is an area where the "good" pixels are copied from. If you can find an area in the image that closely matches the color, texture, and brightness of the damaged section (called the **Target** area), it will make the copy-and-paste retouching action 100% easier and significantly more convincing.

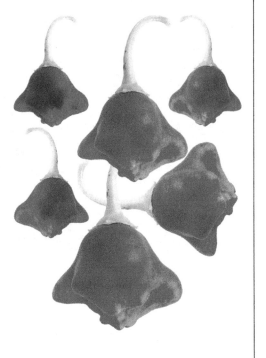

The **Clone Stamp** cannot easily blend pixels in the way the **Spot Healing Brush** can. So, if your source area is a little more textured or darker/brighter than the target area, any attempt at trying to retouch seamlessly is going to fail. In fact, you'll discover that, in most instances, there simply might not be enough pixels of the same color/texture/brightness to make it work at all. Although this sounds like a disastrous PR exercise for the **Clone Stamp**, bear in mind that there are occasions where copying precisely from point 'A' to point 'B' might just be what's needed. For example, you might want to make your chili harvest look a little more productive. In this example, I photographed one chili on a plain white background, then, using the **Clone Stamp** tool, copied and pasted it several times onto separate layers so they could be resized and rotated to fit. I now have a much more prolific chili harvest! Not so realistic perhaps, but a fun and quick exercise.

Most commonly, beauty retouchers use the **Clone Stamp**, set to a **low opacity value**, to copy and paste pixels again, and again, and again, while moving around the target area slightly with each mouse click—this effectively softens the target area, brilliant for smoothing out skin tones to create a porcelain-like appearance that's harder to achieve using either of the Healing Brushes.

To familiarize ourselves with retouching, we'll be using an unedited file (seen in the following screenshot) to practice on. It needs help—as you can appreciate, it's dark and murky, plus it has quite a few other problem areas that need fixing: stray strands of hair, shiny skin, and camera sensor spots. When working on any retouching job, it's a good idea to **plan your editing steps** in the order in which you want them done. For example, there's no point in trying to perfect the color until the brightness has been fixed, and if the image is dark, you won't see all the blemishes that might need removing.

In the following set of images, I'll demonstrate how to edit such a picture, and while the actions are specific to this model shot, the issues are common. As a result of these actions, we should be in a position to radically improve the look of the sample image.

Step one – identify the problem areas: I have circled some points in the preceding image that we might want to edit. First, the photo desperately needs brightening. Then, even though the model has excellent skin, we might want to provide a little minor retouching, skin smoothing, and localized lightening. We can also fix up any small strands of hair that the stylist might have missed. Irrespective of the subject matter, the more you enlarge an image, the more imperfections you'll see, so it pays to consider the **final viewing size** before you spend too much time editing parts of the subject to a level of detail that no viewer will ever appreciate.

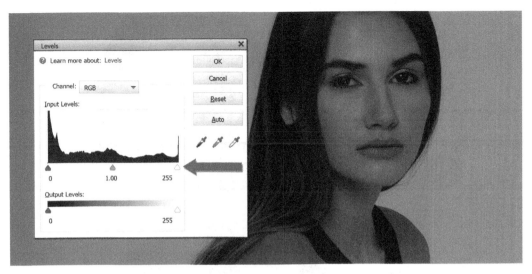

Step two: As with most editing projects, I like to **duplicate the layer** first. It's not essential, but it's often good to have a 'spare' as a reference. Choose **Layer**>**Duplicate**. I used **Levels** (*Ctrl/Cmd + L*) to brighten the image. You can try pressing the **Auto** button, or push the right-hand **Input Levels** tab (arrowed above) to the left to lift the brightness.

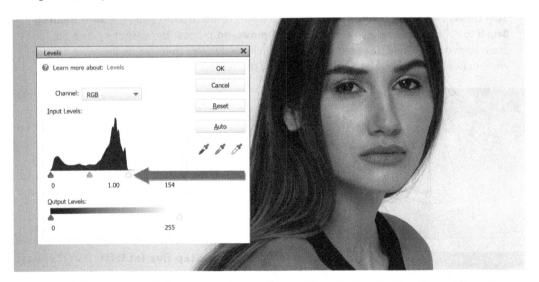

Be careful not to over-lighten your pictures by pushing the highlight or the midtone tab too far. With the image now considerably lighter, you might see more blemishes, or at least **sensor spots** that are most noticeable against light backgrounds. You can have the camera sensor professionally cleaned or you could buy a set of **sensor swabs** and do it yourself. The quickest and most economical method of removing these spots is to use the **Spot Healing Brush**. For an easy complexion fix, use either the **Perfect Portrait** feature (found in the **Guided Edit** mode) or the **Smooth Skin** feature that you'll find in Elements' **Expert Mode**. Here, we'll use the powerful **Spot Healing Brush** and the **Clone Stamp** tools.

Step three, above: Removing the sensor spots would be my first job using the **Spot Healing Brush** tool. This should be an easy **click-and-move-on** process because the brush copies pixels from outside the brush shape (usually a circle) and pastes them inside the brush shape, while matching those pixels' tone and color. It's the perfect tool for this step.

Step four: Moving closer in, I held the mouse button and dragged the cursor along some straggly hair on the right-hand side of the face. Even though my action was wobbly, it covered the required bits and, because the background is nice and even, the stray hair was banished instantly.

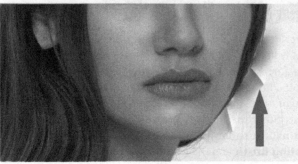

Step five (at left): Don't be lazy! Trying to speed things up, I chose a large brush, hoping to retouch the remaining stray hair in one swipe. But, as you can see, the model now has two weird growths. The larger the brush, the further the software "looks" for pixels to work with—running too close to the model's face created pixel mayhem.

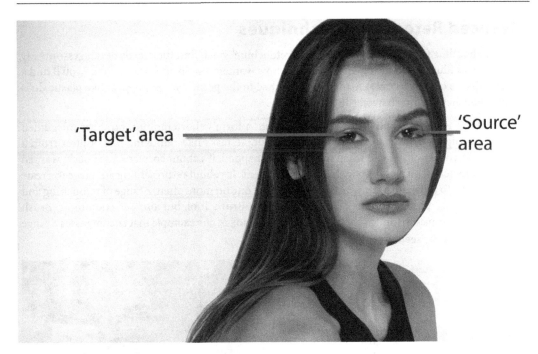

'Target' area — 'Source' area

Step six: Cloning is a different type of retouching process compared to the **Spot Healing** and regular **Healing Brush** tools. With the **Clone Stamp** tool, although it's still a copy-and-paste process, *it does not match the pixel's color, tone*, or *brightness*. If you paste light pixels over dark pixels, it shows up as light on dark. So, how is this going to be helpful? Follow these steps to find out.

Firstly, choose the **Clone Stamp** tool (by using the '*S*' key or by selecting it from the **Tool Bar**>**Enhance**). Choose a soft brush tip, setting its **opacity** to around 50–75%, then ensure that the **Alignment** checkbox in the tool's **Options** panel is set to **Off** (Note: Alignment forces the pasting action to follow the initial selection angle. With it **Off** the retouching can be a bit more random).

What I did here was copy the highlight in the model's right eye and pasted it over the (less bright) highlight in the left eye (as indicated in the screenshot). With a brush tip about the same size as the subject being copied, I held the *Alt/Opt* key down, then clicked the right eye. This is referred to as the **Source area**. The program copies the pixels into the computer's **virtual memory**. Release the mouse button and move the cursor from the source area to the area to be fixed. This is referred to as the **Target area**. Click once. In this case, the tool was set with an opacity of 75%, so it only transferred 75% of the highlight pixels from the right eye.

Retouching tips:

Make sure that the brush tip is approximately the same size as the blemish, or a little larger. If it's too big, it might copy over parts of the image you don't want to use for the repair. Too small and it might just leave a smudge. Note also that you can click-hold-drag the cursor across and around the blemish to create a larger retouch area.

Advanced Retouching techniques

If you search online for images using the word 'retouching' you'll find thousands of images—mostly of women. This illustrates a misogynistic view on how women should appear in public - you'll find a good few images of men too, also made and retouched to the point that they appear like plastic dolls with no blemishes and no character to boast of.

But retouching is not just about correcting the human form's shortcomings, however misguided that concept might be. It's also about performing simple tasks like removing bits of litter from a landscape that you'd not noticed when the shot was snapped, it's about correcting seriously warped perspective created when shooting with a wide-angle lens, it's about re-presenting an image to create a different look. To fully retouch any image, you can use one or, more often, a range of retouching and manipulation tools, principally: the Clone and Healing Brush Tool, but also Selection tools, Brush tools, layer transformations and even masks. Let's take a look at one example that encompasses a range of tools to achieve the seemingly impossible.

Main image: Here's the challenge—you have just invested in some real estate but need to see how that investment might appear once it's been fully renovated. So it's off to the retouch lab we go. Or is it to the painter?

One tip I use when it comes to retouching a file is to carefully analyse the image first and then decide, in advance, what tools or techniques are best for the different jobs at hand.

If you are simply removing a small blemish then the obvious tool of choice would be either the **Healing Brush Tool** or the **Clone Brush Tool**. In this example, I can easily remove some of the more isolated patch marks using the **Spot Healing Brush** - but then the larger patched areas make the task significantly more complex.

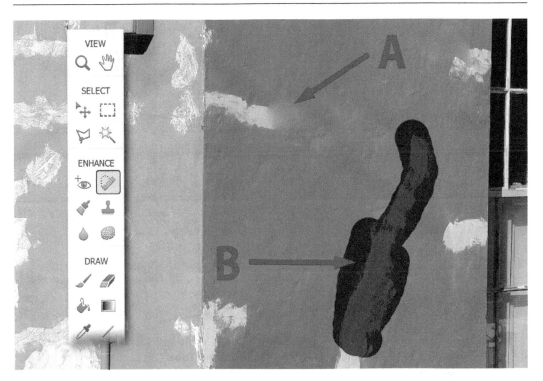

Step One: Although the **Spot Healing Brush** appears to offer an easy blemish removal process it can also cause problems if the object you hope to remove is too close to an object you want to keep. Because it copies pixels from around the brush shape and then pastes and blends them inside the brush shape, getting too close to objects can produce a smudged result (**example A**)

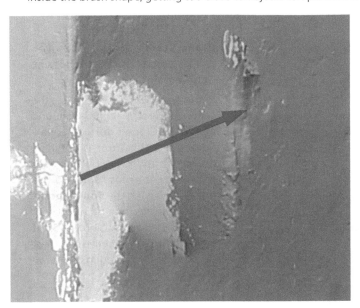

or it copies a bit you don't want to another part of the canvas. This looks odd and just creates more work to get it fixed. But if you click, hold and drag the cursor over an entire object, then let go, you might get a better result (**example B**), again, providing that it's not too near something important. In the example, at left, I clicked too close to the corner of the house and the brush copied some of that corner and pasted it over to the right hand side. Not a good result. It's time to **UNDO** (*Ctrl/Cmd + Z*) and try another tool.

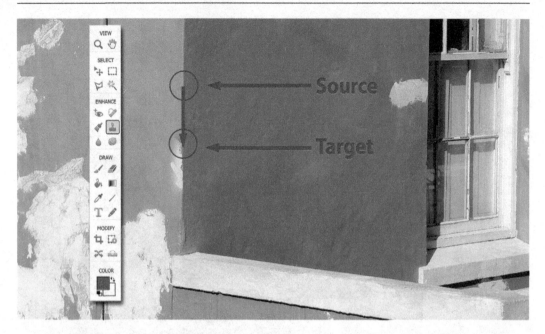

Step Two: When you need to cover up pixels in a tricky position - such as those at right angles on the corner of the building, use the **Clone Stamp Tool**. This requires you to first select a **Source point** (where the pixels are copied from). Do this by holding *Alt/Opt* and click once, then move the cursor, in this example, down the image, over the white paint and click a second time so it pastes the clean pixels over the white paint pixels (the **Target area**). I continued clicking as I moved the cursor down the corner of the wall, copying the corner tones as I went. As with most tools, you can regulate the speed of this copy and paste process by increasing or decreasing the brush size and its opacity.

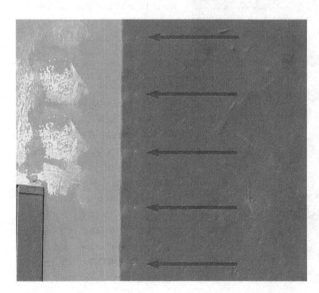

Clone Stamp errors: When you continuously retouch from the same **Source point**, errors occur.

In this screenshot at left, notice the same specks appearing again and again as I Cloned down the wall. Sometimes this error is so small it's not worth fixing - but if it does look weird, it needs fixing. Do this either by varying the **Source point** to mix textures up a bit or go over the damaged areas using the **Spot Healing Brush** to remove or at least break up that distracting step-and-repeat cloning pattern.

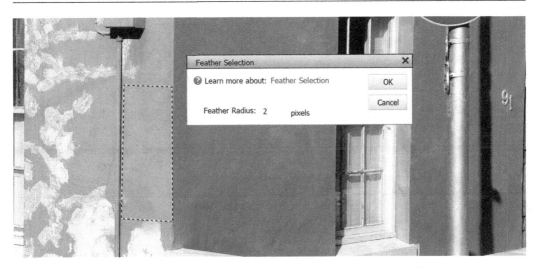

Step Three: The rest of the house has too many large patches on it to be effectively removed using the **Spot Healing** or **Clone Stamp** tools—in this case I selected the only bit of 'clean' wall and used the copied pixels to cover up the messy white paint marks to the left. As this is a 20Mp file, I added a 2 pixel Feather to the selection—this softens the 'cut' line very slightly. If you don't add a **Feather** amount when you start pasting selected pixels, it often shows up—a soft edge usually works best.

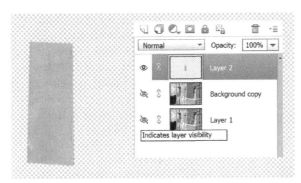

At left: Because this is a high resolution image, I can use the **Transform** function (*Ctrl/Cmd + T*) to enlarge the wall selection so it covers more of the painted surface. As I am just using it to cover up parts of the wall, I can also stretch it into any shape if needed. This is what it looks like with the background layer visibility turned off.

Step Four: If the pixels copied are lighter or darker than the pixels on either side, use a tool like **Levels** to make the 'patch' the same brightness.

Note that once this patch was in position, I reduced its opacity to around 70%—I could then see the features beneath—meaning I could then erase parts of the patch so unpainted sections, like the white window ledge, is revealed, adding to the accuracy of the retouching job.

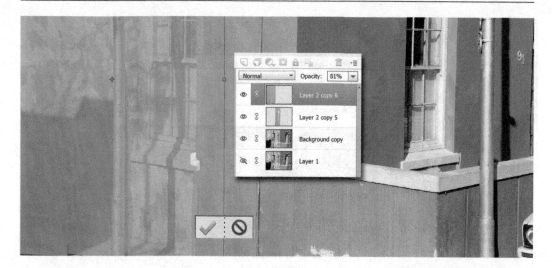

Step Five: If your **Source** area is similar in tone and color to the **Target** areas, you can copy and paste multiple samples into one large "blanket"—this is what I did here placing it over approximately half of the image on the left. I set the layer opacity to 80% so I could see what was underneath. The technique then is to use the **Eraser Brush** to remove those pixels covering something important in the image beneath it—like the lamp post, windows,

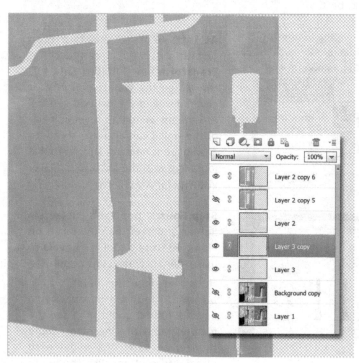

etc. To make your life easier when cutting out regular-shaped things like the lamp post, click once with the Eraser tool, then hold the Shift key down, move your cursor along the object and click again - the tool erases in a straight line.

Left: This is what the paint 'blanket' looks like with the background layer's visibility turned off. Note that, as this is a complex retouching job, I have duplicated the **Background Layer** as well as the paint blanket layer, just in case I need a spare.

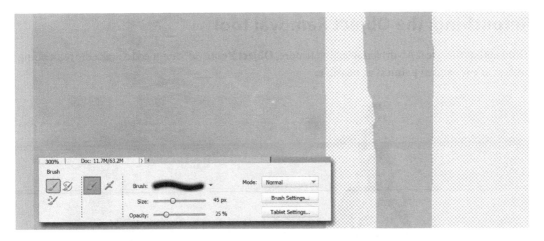

Step Six - Brushing for victory: In this example, my retouching technique also includes use of the regular **Brush Tool**. Because the "blanket" of blue pixels is tonally quite irregular, I used the brush tool with a very soft tip and a low opacity (25%) to smooth out some of the lumpier coloration in the copied plaster. You have to be careful not to make things worse by making the color too dark or too light. The low opacity helps to blend the paint job - similar to thinning paint. It takes a bit of time, but it does produce results.

Final result: Now the house is ready for the real estate agent to price the house! This exercise demonstrates that skilled retouching techniques can be applied to any image requiring a specific 'look'.

Retouching: the Object Removal tool

Elements has this great AI-driven selection feature, **Object Removal**, designed to make the retouching process as easy and as painless as possible.

Step one: Choose the feature (**Guided Edit>Basics>Object Removal**).

Step two: Choose one of the selection tools to match the type or accuracy of selection needed—in this example, I used **Selection Brush**, which lays a red mask over the painted area. You can modify the accuracy of this brush by choosing the **Add** or **Subtract** buttons. My "selection" was a bit over-generous, but once **Remove Object** is pressed, the magic happens. In this example, the surfer in the background disappeared seamlessly in a matter of seconds.

Tip:

Although **Guided** Edit's **Object Removal** feature is a great feature, Adobe has developed another sophisticated AI-driven selection tool simply named **Select Subject** (**Select>Subject**).

As its name suggests, its job is to select the subject in the image automatically. In this feature, you don't even have to draw roughly around the subject; Elements finds it for you. Really. And the good news is that in most of my test images, this worked seamlessly.

Local Retouching: the Burn, Dodge, and Sponge Tools

The **Burn**, **Dodge**, and **Sponge Tools** are probably the best unsung heroes of Elements. Why? Simple: they are easy to use and are very effective visually.

The **Burn** and **Dodge** tools are electronic representations of what I did for years in a black and white printing lab. "Burning-in" a photo was a technique for making part of a print darker than the rest of the image—using something like a cardboard mask with a hole in it to make it happen. After the base exposure was done, I'd continue to expose the print—but only the bits of it that I needed to go darker—by holding the cardboard mask between the enlarger lamp and the photo paper. By gently moving the card mask so that the additional exposure only fell onto the the targeted area, I could manipulate the global exposure to that of a custom exposure. The dodging tool worked in reverse—a bit of card taped to some wire and held between the enlarger lamp and photo paper to stop light getting to parts of the print that would have otherwise come out too dark. When it worked, the results were good, but it was hit and miss and could never be repeated accurately. Then came Photoshop Elements, and my retouching life changed forever.

Before and after comparison: The lower image of the African elephant shows what you can achieve using these selective darkening/lightening brushes—add life to shady areas, while dramatically darkening other tones to add impact to the composition. The RAW image was underexposed in order to capture as much detail in the brilliant snowy peak (that can't currently be seen), which left the tones in the lower section of the frame rather dull looking and in dire need of attention! Let's see how we can improve the image.

All three tools work just like a paint brush. The brush tip has a variable size for different problem areas, a variable hardness, and a massive range of different shapes. But the real strength of these tools is in the tonal range that you can set them to operate in: **highlights**, **midtones**, and **shadows** (note that the **Sponge Tool** only has a **Saturate** and a **Desaturate** mode).

With these tools, I can "paint" darkness into the shadows, lighten the highlights, or increase the local color saturation of almost any part of almost any image. Here's what these tools can do:

- **Burn Tool**: Use this brush to darken the shadows, midtones, or highlights of your image. It's best to start with the **Exposure** setting at 10% or 15%—any higher and your brushing becomes hard to conceal. Choose a largish brush size, and a soft-edge brush tip to further conceal brush marks. The lower the **Exposure** setting, the more brush strokes you might need, but the more subtle the effect. Burning in the shadows has the most dramatic effect; burning in a highlight, especially one that's already nearly white, often makes the area look muddy because there's no tone there to actually burn in, so dial it back a bit. I start by darkening the midtones first, and only then do I move on to the shadows.

- **Dodge Tool**: Use this to lighten details in the shadows, midtones, and highlights. Trying to lighten details in dark shadows often makes the tones appear ghostly—not a good look. This brush works best if it's used to lighten/brighten midtones and highlights. Like the **Burn** brush, you should keep the **Exposure** set to between 5% and 10% to avoid over-brightening the highlights and clipping tones (thereby losing detail permanently). Lightening highlights and darkening midtones/shadows really pumps up local contrast.

- **Sponge Tool**: Use this feature to increase the saturation (richness) of color that's already in the file or to desaturate the color until it eventually turns black and white. This is useful when you want to knock back over-colorful parts of an image that are detracting from the subject matter.

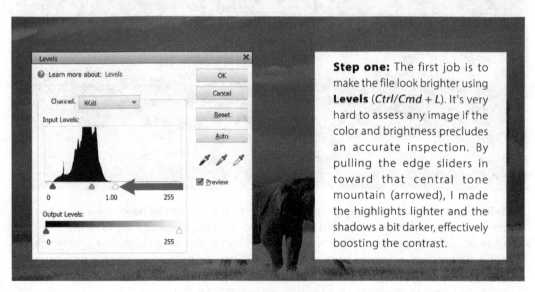

Step one: The first job is to make the file look brighter using **Levels** (*Ctrl/Cmd + L*). It's very hard to assess any image if the color and brightness precludes an accurate inspection. By pulling the edge sliders in toward that central tone mountain (arrowed), I made the highlights lighter and the shadows a bit darker, effectively boosting the contrast.

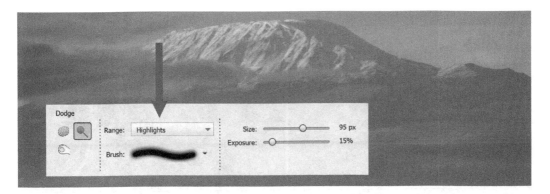

Step two: Then, I use the **Dodge Brush**, set to **Highlights**, to lighten the snow on Mount Kilimanjaro in the distance. For this job, I set **Exposure** to just 7% for the highlights—this sounds like almost nothing, but as the highlights are nearly white anyway, you can't afford to rush the lightening process. Set **Exposure** to a higher number and you'll see the white areas turning 100% white immediately, and once lost, there's no going back. 100% white means the tone is clipped—it's gone forever.

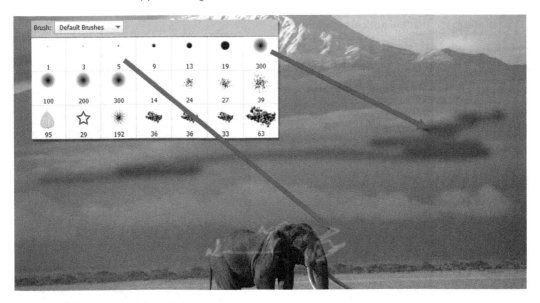

Step three: Be mindful with the **brushes** that you use for the job. And the **opacity** settings. Small, hard-edged brushes are not so useful because they can leave tell-tale marks, as you can see here. Soft-edged brushes work better as they tend to blend the retouching effect into the existing background more convincingly, especially with larger, softer brushes than you think you might need. In this illustration, I have deliberately used a brush that's too small with an exposure setting that's too high ("exposure" describes the speed of the tool – in this example, how fast it darkens the pixels). No matter how dexterous you might be with such a brush, if you use an **Exposure** setting that's too high, the brush marks always show.

Mastering Adobe Photoshop Elements 2023

Here's a close-up **comparison** of this old bull elephant, untouched on the left and dodged (carefully) on the right. I will never be able to lighten all the shadows on this subject because of the deep, late-afternoon shadows, but just lightening the already brighter parts of the pachyderm has made a noticeable difference.

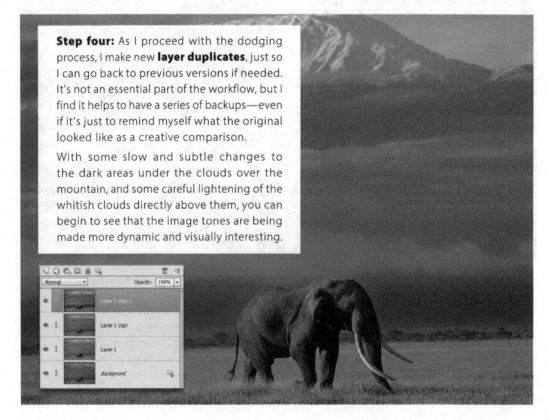

Step four: As I proceed with the dodging process, I make new **layer duplicates**, just so I can go back to previous versions if needed. It's not an essential part of the workflow, but I find it helps to have a series of backups—even if it's just to remind myself what the original looked like as a creative comparison.

With some slow and subtle changes to the dark areas under the clouds over the mountain, and some careful lightening of the whitish clouds directly above them, you can begin to see that the image tones are being made more dynamic and visually interesting.

Above: Here's the final dodged and burned version with significantly brightened clouds, warmer colors in the foreground savannah areas, and darker, more brooding clouds in the middle distance—which help to highlight the magnificence of Mount Kilimanjaro, Africa's highest mountain peak, in the far distance.

Tip:

- The **Burn** brush is possibly more useful than the **Dodge** brush tool. It works best when darkening existing tones, especially when set to **Midtones** or **Shadows**. However, it will not add tone to a bright highlight area.

- Burned-in highlights tend to go muddy when you over-burn these areas and are a sure sign that you have gone too far with your burning-in exercise.

- The **Sponge** Brush tool is used for enhancing or reducing just the color in the image. Colors under the brush tip saturate or desaturate (increase/decrease) depending on the type of brush tip (sharp edged or fuzzy), its size, and importantly, the flow setting. Treat the last setting like a speed control. The higher the number (on a scale between 0 and 100), the faster the effect (but the harder it is to control).

- Although technically a "brush," one thing the **Sponge** Brush tool will not do is add color where there was no color to begin with.

- Although Adobe provides several hundred brush shapes and sizes by default, you can also find more online. I have used brushes downloaded from `www.brusheezy.com` very successfully (more about this unique process in *Chapter 8, Additional Tools and Features.*)

Local Retouching: the Blur, Sharpen, and Smudge brushes

So many times, we use global editing tools in our work only to see that it's just a small part of the image that needs attention—not all of it. To this end, Elements sports a few excellent brush-based tools that work on **local adjustments**. You literally "paint" softness or sharpness into small areas of the image with complete control over how quickly the pixels under the brush tip are affected, and how soft the results might be.

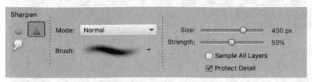

Three such tools are the **Blur, Sharpen**, and **Smudge** brushes. All three operate just like all other brush-based tools in that you can adjust the size of the brush (via a slider on the tool **Options** panel or by pressing the left/right square brackets), its efficiency (here, called **Strength**), and, of course, the softness/ hardness and shape of the chosen brush tip.

Blurring: I use this brush occasionally as it's good for small details—such as the stray shoots around this flower. I couldn't achieve the same depth of field effect using lens apertures, so I finished it off in Elements. This tool is easy to use, but it's not suited for softening large areas as it's likely to be very slow.

Tip:

- Don't expect instant results—all three are quite slow in their performance. You have to work at it a bit.
- Duplicate the photo layer so, once you have effected a change, switching that layer **On/Off** will allow you to quickly check whether it's working correctly or not.
- Use the **Strength** slider to make the effect progress quicker.
- Avoid over-use of the **Sharpen** brush as too much can ruin the result.

Sharpen Brush: I use the **Sharpen** Brush frequently because it's perfect for adding a dab of clarity to small areas, such as the facial features of this kookaburra. The version in the center is the best, the left-hand version is untouched, and the right-hand version has been over-sharpened.

Smudging: This tool is not as useful as the other two mentioned here—unless you really like messing with people's heads. As you can see, the smudging operation is quite destructive, so it's good for wild, crazy creations. However, if I need to create this type of effect, I'd choose the **Liquify** filter because it offers a far greater level of user control (see *Chapter 11, Troubleshooting and Additional Techniques*, for more on the **Liquify** filter).

Simple selections: Subject Selection

Here's another newish feature (first appeared in Elements 2020). It's called **Subject Selection** and is the simplest and easiest process you could imagine for doing exactly what it claims: selecting a subject. Here's how it works.

Step one: Choose your image, then open it in **Expert** mode. Go to **Select>Subject** (*Alt/ Opt + Ctrl/Cmd + S*) and sit back for five seconds to see the subject selected. Wham! It just happens—driven by Adobe Sensei (Sensei means *teacher* in Japanese), you'll get a pre-selected subject. I tried this with several picture examples where the subject stood out against the background. This AI-driven feature did the job pretty well—with about a 90-95% accuracy (around the "subject").

Not bad considering I did nothing to the images other than open the files then try the selection process. Yes, it is a selection tool "dumbed down"—there's no choosing the "right" tool. No tweaking or adjustments needed; it just does it.

> **Tip:**
>
> The **Select>Inverse** command can be incredibly useful because, as luck would have it, often the object you are trying to select is harder to *grab* than the background it's sitting on. If this is the case, it's best to select the background first, then choose **Select>Inverse**, which flips the original selection from the background to the object.

Above: In my example here, I desaturated the background, taking all the color out of it—it is noticeable, but nevertheless, the result isn't too bad. I constantly get asked if there is a quicker way to select an object in Elements, and until this feature came along, there really was no alternative other than using the selection tools mentioned in this section. It all took a bit of time and skill, but with the release of this selection feature, the process has become significantly easier—although as with all these AI-driven tools, if the original image is complex, your clean selection rate will drop...

Left: Here's an illustration of how well the selection process did with this shot. It's a tricky one—because of the woman's hair. Hair (and fur) is notoriously hard to select, even if the hair is blonde and the background dark. So, some of the fly-away bits were missed—the solution to this would be to either ignore it or retouch the errant hair out of the picture (quite hard). In fact, depending on what you do with the selection, you might never notice a few strands of hair missing from the selection.

Advanced Selections: Selection features

Before you even start manually selecting objects, it's vital to understand how to control the selection tools. Unlike the **Subject Selection** feature, which pretty much does all the heavy lifting for you, Elements has a wide range of manually operated selection tools that are designed for those tricky jobs that the AI-driven features can't handle.

Saving selections

One important feature that you'll find among the selection modifiers is the ability to save a selection once it has been finished, as shown in the following screenshot. For me, this is important because if you've spent time perfecting a selection, you don't want to lose it should you have a problem with the software or the computer, which might require a restart.

Elements has a dedicated selection menu at the top of the screen, and almost at the bottom of that pop-down menu, you'll find the **Save Selection...** command (**A** in the screenshot). Give the selection a memorable name in the **Save Selection** panel that opens (**B** in the screenshot) before clicking **OK** and moving on. If you plan on adding multiple selections to the same image file, it's probably worth naming your selections very specifically so that they can be easily identified later should you need to work on them again.

Save Selection is not the end of the story. To save it permanently, you must also save the entire file before moving on. When you do that, you'll notice that Elements forces you to save the file either in the Photoshop (`.psd`) or **Tagged Image File Format** (**TIFF**) file format (`.tif`). The other file formats discussed in this book, notably JPEGs, cannot contain additional information, such as selections, layers, paths, text, vector shapes, or masks.

Once the selection has been saved, you can close the image and move on to a different task. If you need to work on that selection once more, open the image, and, from the **Select** menu, choose **Load Selection...**. If there's a single selection saved in that file, you'll see it in the **Load Selection** panel, which means you can click **OK** to open it back into the image. If you have multiple selections, choose the correct one from the **Select** drop-down menu in the **Selection** panel. Remembering to save your selections will save you a heap of time and, more importantly, reduce your frustration levels by not having to recreate a selection from scratch.

Advanced Selections: Feathering

When you make a selection, the selection line around the subject is sharp. It's a little like a scrapbooking exercise where the subject is cut out of the page using a craft knife. We often don't want such a sharp line because your editing will become obvious. The answer is to use a feature called **Feathering**. This blurs the selection edge by a certain amount, dictated by the **pixel radius**. How much "feathering" you need is a hard thing to judge because the fuzziness of the selection line is also influenced by other factors, including file resolution.

Once you're happy with the modifications that you have added using **Mask view**, click back into **Selection** mode to view the traditional selection line of marching ants (as it's often described) before saving the selection and moving on.

Experience often helps you judge the feathering amount, although it's simple enough to experiment by starting with a 1-pixel radius. If that's not enough, undo the last action and try a different number. In this screenshot, the left-hand image was set to 5 pixels while the fuzzy line in the right-hand image was set to 25 pixels. This is too much because, with such a soft edge, any enhancement added to the sky would bleed into the edge of the building, creating a halo effect.

Tip:

One way to preview feathering is to swap whatever selection tool you are using for the **Selection Brush**. This has two modes: **Selection** and **Mask**. The **Selection** mode looks the same as all other selection tools. Its **Mask** mode represents everything that's not been selected as a red mask. This is one of the best ways to display the extent of the current selection, but it also works as a technique for modifying it.

Because this red overlay is in effect a mask, you can add to it using the **Brush** tool, or you can remove from it using the **Eraser** tool, much in the same way that we can add to or take from a **Layer Mask** using a black or white brush. Once happy with the modifications that you have added in **Mask** mode, click back into **Selection** mode to check the accuracy of the selection before saving the selection and moving on.

Too Much Feathering: This is what it looks like if your feathering selection is used too much—once a tone change is applied to the image (in this case, darkening using the **Levels** tool), you'll see a disturbing **halo** or glow around the selected objects (in this example, it's the roof line). Undo a few steps to just before you applied the feather, apply a smaller feather value, and try again, or use the equally useful **Refine Selection Brush** feature to reduce the feathering amount (below).

Advanced Selections: The Refine Selection Brush tool

The **Refine Selection Brush** is not technically a selection tool; rather, it's a feature designed to refine an existing selection. In this context, it *sort of* replaces the process of adding/removing from an existing selection by holding the *Shift* or the *Alt/Option* key while moving the cursor over the image.

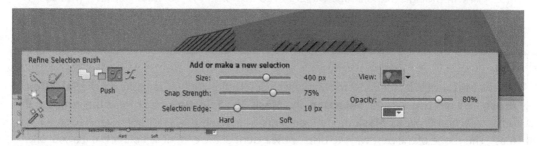

The **Refine Selection Brush** throws up the red mask overlay in the same manner as the **Selection Brush**, but under its **View** menu, you can also set this tool to show the selection on a black or a white background. If you don't like the overlay color, click on the color swatches button underneath the **Opacity** slider to change it to a different color.

Where the **Refine Selection Brush** out-features the older-style *Shift* or *Alt/Opt* keyboard shortcuts (to add to or take from an existing selection) is that its options not only include the ability to add to or subtract from the selection, but also the ability to push or move the existing lines in the selection. As with most of the other selection tools, you can, of course, change the size of the brush, as well as its softness, in order to give you greater control.

Advanced Selections: The Refine Edge tool

Another useful selection feature is called the **Refine Edge** tool.

Having made your initial selection, if you click the **Refine Edge** button in the **Options** panel, you'll see the selection view mode change to a white background. You can change this to a red mask background, a black background, or several other working *looks*, depending on how complex the picture is and how you like to view your selection work (as we'll soon see).

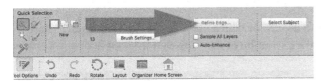

Refine Edge panel (below): Use this panel to perfect any selection. As all images are individual this panel provides you with the tools to customize selection accuracy.

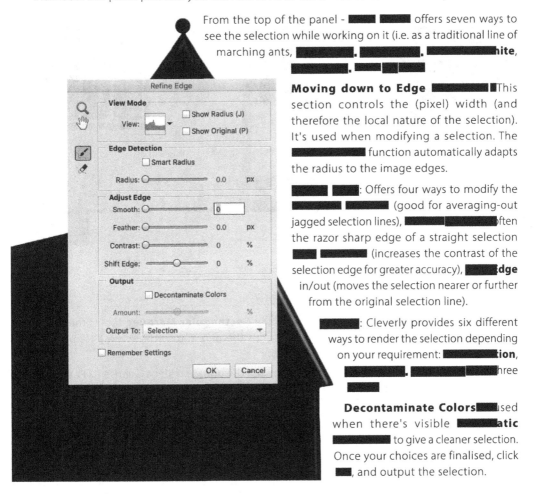

From the top of the panel - ▉▉▉ ▉▉▉ offers seven ways to see the selection while working on it (i.e. as a traditional line of marching ants, ▉▉▉▉▉. ▉▉▉▉▉. ▉▉▉▉▉▉hite, ▉▉▉▉. ▉▉▉▉▉).

Moving down to Edge ▉▉▉▉▉▉This section controls the (pixel) width (and therefore the local nature of the selection). It's used when modifying a selection. The ▉▉▉▉▉▉▉ function automatically adapts the radius to the image edges.

▉▉▉ ▉▉: Offers four ways to modify the ▉▉▉▉▉ ▉▉▉▉▉ (good for averaging-out jagged selection lines), ▉▉▉▉▉▉▉ften the razor sharp edge of a straight selection ▉▉ ▉▉▉▉ (increases the contrast of the selection edge for greater accuracy), ▉▉dge in/out (moves the selection nearer or further from the original selection line).

▉▉▉▉: Cleverly provides six different ways to render the selection depending on your requirement: ▉▉▉▉▉ion, ▉▉▉▉▉. ▉▉▉▉▉hree ▉▉▉

Decontaminate Colors▉used when there's visible ▉▉▉▉▉atic ▉▉▉▉▉▉ to give a cleaner selection. Once your choices are finalised, click ▉▉, and output the selection.

Advanced selections: the Marquee and Lasso tools

The **Marquee** Tool has two modes: **Rectangular** and **Elliptical**—with these you can draw a square, rectangular, elliptical, or circular selection shape. In this exercise, I want to shift the door in the following image to the right, copy and paste the left-hand window over the space left by the (moved) door frame, and finally, copy and paste an object from another image into the left-hand corner of this scene.

When making selections, it's important to appreciate that all selection tools work together—you can start with one, then if needed work with a second or third selection tool to complete the job.

Possibly the hardest task with selections is to determine which one is best for the job—here, I started with the **Rectangular Marquee Tool** to make a selection of this house's front door:

Step one: The door is roughly rectangular, so the **Rectangular Marquee** tool is the best starting point. As it's not 100% vertical (and there's the pink steps at the front), I dragged the marquee loosely around the edge of the door.

Step two: Because I've selected a bit more than just the door and steps, I chose to **Feather** the selection line. This feature (**Select>Feather**) softens the sharp selection edge so it can blend more discretely with whatever it's pasted over. How much feathering? With a 60Mp RGB file, I'd add anything between 8 and 20 pixels—if the number you add proves to be too soft (or not soft enough), undo the last action (*Ctrl/Cmd + Z*) and try another pixel amount.

Step three: I added a feather amount of 12 pixels (inset panel, left). As you can see in the **Layer** panel, on the top right, I have copied and pasted (*Ctrl/Cmd + C* then *Ctrl/Cmd + V*) the contents of the selection back into the same document. Because it lands onto its own (new) layer, it is independent of the background and, using the **Move Tool** (*V*), can be click-shifted to the right, to a new location.

Step four: Once the door has been relocated, there's another obvious visual problem—we can still see the original door. So, another rectangular selection was made over the metal wall—I used the same feather amount, which you can clearly see in the fuzzy edges. It too was copied and pasted back into the same image, then shifted under the pasted door layer to conceal the remains of the original door. Job done.

Step five: With the steel sheeting covering the original door, I noticed that the vertical corrugations didn't line up (left inset, arrowed). I used the **Transform** function (**Image**>**Transform**>**Skew**), which displays a bounding box around the object. By pulling the central right-hand edge **handle** down slightly (short arrow), I could line the pasted wall up better.

Step six: Selecting the left window frame was a little trickier. I used the **Polygonal Lasso** tool—perfect for this not-quite-rectangular shape. Click in a corner, then move to the next corner, click, and repeat. Five clicks and I had the window selected. Here, I've changed from the **Lasso** Tool to the **Selection Brush's Mask** view (in blue), as it's a great visual feature to check the accuracy of the selection. You can also edit this mask directly to modify the selection shape by brushing in, or out, more or less detail.

Step seven: With the window frame now accurately selected, it's a simple matter of copying and pasting it back into the same image—as I did with the door and the sheet metal section. Because I used the **Polygonal Lasso Tool**, the selection was quite tight around the object, so I decided that no feathering was needed.

As it panned out, the window pasted perfectly into the frame (below).

Step eight: Now, for something a bit more complex: to copy and paste an object from a different image into my tin shed picture. With this shopfront image open, I initially used the **Magic Wand Tool** to select the red waste bin. It's red, but it's also covered with stickers and graffiti, so it was hard to select "cleanly." Changing to **Selection Brush** and its **Mask View** mode (here set to blue), I proceeded to "clean up" the bits of the waste bin not already selected. In this clear-to-see view mode, it's a relatively easy task (see below).

Step nine: Once the selected bin has been copied, I switched to the tin shed picture and pasted it into the file. Once again, I used the **Transform Tool** to change its size to fit the scene. Then using the **Hue/Saturation** and **Levels** tools to make the object, taken from a different image, appear to have the same color, contrast, and brightness values as the host. The final image (below) had one final tweak added to it—I used the **Spot Healing Brush** to cover up/remove the vents in the newly copied window to make it look different from the original.

Advanced selections: the Magic Wand tool

The **Magic Wand** tool is one of the best selection tools because it selects objects based on their tones; plus, it's so easy to use. If I use the example of an image featuring a blue sky and a dark landscape, clicking on the blue sky with the **Magic Wand** tool will inevitably select everything that is blue, but if the sky fades from dark blue to light blue, as most skies do, you might find that **Magic Wand** only selects a band of color, not the entire sky. This is because the pixels that you click on represent a certain shade of blue. The tool will not automatically select every pixel that's blue. Its **sensitivity** (to the range of blues, in this example) is controlled by the **Tolerance** slider. The default value for this is 32, so if I were to increase the tolerance value to, say, 100, it would grab a lot more of the sky. If you set it to the maximum value, 255, the tool will select everything in the image, regardless of its color.

In this before and after example, I started with a regular snap that had a rather bleak, white sky—by selecting just the sky and adding several tone changes to it using **Levels**, I was able to make it appear far more dramatic with darker clouds, and by inverting the selection, I added more color saturation to the church and cemetery out front.

Step one: Choose the **Magic Wand** tool, check that its default is set to 32 in the **Tool Options** panel, and click once on the sky.

Step two: Here's how much **Magic Wand** selected in this image with one click—almost all the sky. By changing from **Magic Wand** to **Selection Brush**, then switching from **Selection** to its **Mask** mode, you'll instantly see what has been selected (the clear areas) and what has not been selected (the red mask areas).

Interestingly, the two small red areas in the top left and top right indicate that not all the sky has been selected—this is normal and easy to fix. In this example, the reason it is a slightly different tone from the rest of the sky (and therefore needs more attention when selecting) is that it has natural fall-off (that is, it has slight edge darkening), which is typically produced when using a wide-angle lens. The fall-off can be very subtle and hard to detect with the naked eye, but because it might only be a tiny bit darker, the selection process can still pick it out as being different.

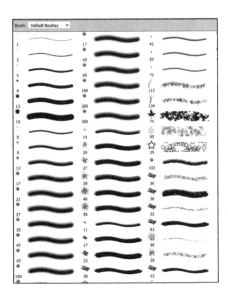

(Left) Here's a glimpse of Photoshop Elements' vast brush repository. What you see here is just what is labeled the **Default** brushes. There are a dozen more categories, including **Square** brushes, **Dry Media** brushes, and **Calligraphic** brushes. You can also download and install other people's brushes off the internet if you feel they have more to offer than the vast range seen here! Elements has more than 250 brush shapes and thicknesses.

Step three: While in this red mask mode, choose a suitably sized brush and use the **Eraser** tool to remove the easy bits of the mask first (that is, the top-left and top-right sections of the screen).

Productivity tip #1:
To draw, retouch, paint, or erase in a straight line, click at the start of your line, hold the *Shift* key down, move the cursor to the end of the (imaginary) line, and click a second time. The **Eraser** tool draws a straight line between click **A** and click **B**. Keep holding the *Shift*

key and click again. The straight erase line joins click **B** with click **C**, and so on. This works with all drawing, painting, retouching, and erasing tools. If the features you are erasing around are linear, consider using a *square* brush tip. There's an entire sub-menu for square brushes (and many other types of brush tip).

Productivity tip #2: Use the keyboard shortcuts *Ctrl/Cmd + +* and *Ctrl/ Cmd + -* to zoom in and out when erasing or retouching fine details (such as the sky under the church handrail). It's a lot faster than mousing over to the **Zoom** tool each time you want to enlarge something.

Productivity tip #3:
As you can see here, the point-to-point technique works well in tricky-to-select areas such as this. Note that the **Magic Wand** selection tool comes with a **Contiguous** checkbox (panel inset). If checked, the wand will only select pixels of a similar color if

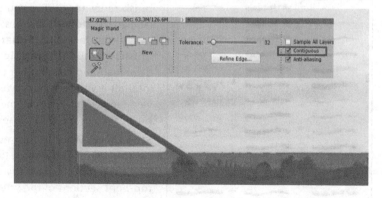

they are touching each other. Uncheck the **Contiguous** box, and it will select all the pixels that match that initial click. This can get you into a bit of (selection) trouble, so I suggest starting with **Contiguous** checked.

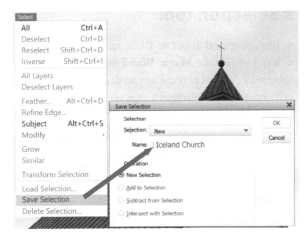

Step four: With all the red mask areas erased from the sky (and some mask areas extended using the **Brush Tool**), the next step is to save the selection. Go to **Select>Save Selection**, enter a suitable name, click 'OK' then save the file in the Photoshop or Tiff file format in case it is needed later.

If at the default of **32** it only grabs some of the sky, you can switch the tool to its **Add** mode, then click on a part of the sky it has not so far selected, and this is added to the original selection. To finish, keep holding the *Shift* key and click every missing part of the sky until it's completely selected.

My choice in this example is to start with the sky because it's easier to select. Once that's selected and saved, choose **Select>Inverse**, and the selection will flip into negative mode so that you now have the grass and church selected but not the sky. It can be very handy in all those situations where selecting the subject is harder than selecting the background.

Final Steps: Once your selection is nice and clean, it's time to make some adjustments to those selected tones in the image. Here, I used the **Levels** tool to add contrast—and therefore a bit more visual drama—to the original pale-looking sky. I wanted to make the lower part of the scene more colorful, so I used the **Select>Inverse** command to reverse the selection so that it was the church and green areas that were selected, not the sky. This enabled me to add some color using the **Hue/Saturation** tool.

Simple Selections: The Quick Selection tool

The **Quick Selection** tool certainly has a more instant appeal about it. Click and drag the cursor through the area that you want selected; it operates just like the **Magic Wand** tool, based on pixel color, while continually expanding its semi-automated selection process as you drag the cursor over different colored pixels. Because of its design, you'll note that this selection tool is very good at *snapping* to the edges of same-colored objects.

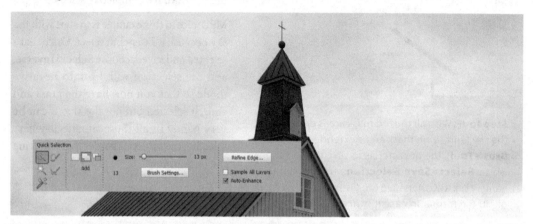

Note that the **Magic Wand** tool might also be fairly effective with this kind of selection subject, but it would probably need lots of additional mouse-clicking to scoop up all the tone variants, including shade, shadow, and other tonal inconsistencies, that every picture throws at us. In this example, it's the shading in the clouds that's hard to assess—those tones are hard to see with the naked eye, but nevertheless will appear a challenge to select evenly using a tool such as **Magic Wand**.

The Selection Brush tool

Photoshop Elements ships with a range of selection tools, all of which offer slightly different selection capabilities. Here's a neat one called, simply, **Selection Brush**!

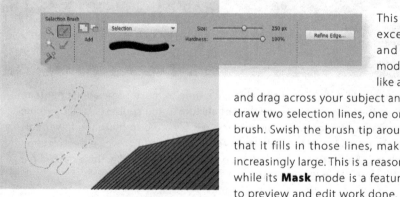

This tool features the excellent **Selection** and **Mask Viewing** modes. It operates just like a paint brush. Click and drag across your subject and it will appear to draw two selection lines, one on each side of the brush. Swish the brush tip around, and you'll see that it fills in those lines, making the selection increasingly large. This is a reasonably capable tool while its **Mask** mode is a feature I use frequently to preview and edit work done.

The Auto Selection tool

As with **Refine Edge Brush**, the **Auto Selection** tool is relatively new to Photoshop Elements. It combines the action of the regular **Lasso** tools with the **Auto Selection** functionality of **Quick Selection Brush**. What this means in practical terms is that if you want to make a freehand selection of a particular area using **Lasso**, once you let go of the mouse, having completed the selection as close to the edges as you can, the line snaps to the nearest edge of contrast.

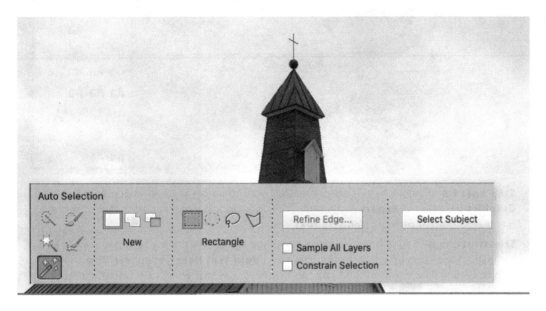

If you search for examples of how this selection tool is used, you'll probably find it's only applied to a certain type of image. The reason for this is simply that every image that requires a selection is very different from every other image—so no one selection tool is ideal for all selection tasks.

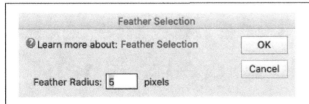

Selection tip:

How much feathering should you use? This is a hard question to answer, as there are so many variables: the resolution of the file, the selection size, the accuracy of the selection itself, and the final purpose of the exercise. I generally work with 20 megapixel images so begin with a feather of between 5 and 10 pixels. If I am blending an object into a background, I might choose a smaller pixel amount, especially if it's a tight selection. But if it's going to be going into a similar-sized document, I'd increase the feather to between 20 and 50 pixels. At the end of the day, it's always good to test a few different settings before moving on.

Basic Text: Text Styles

Step one: For absolute beginners, the easiest way to add text to an image is to use the **Graphics** panel in the **Expert** edit mode. Click once on this panel and from the drop-down menu at the top of the panel, choose **Text**.

Step two: Choose a style from the expansive range of examples in the type panel. Click into the main image area and you'll see the ubiquitous **Your Text Here** text appear. Now, the trick with this—and all versions of the **Type** tool—is to ensure that you click inside that text first, to make it active, then type your copy into the field. If, in your excitement, you click away from the text, Elements "thinks" you have finished and the line of text becomes set. It's no longer editable. Because text always occupies its own layer, it's simple to click back into the text field to make it active again, then start your typing.

Type tool tips: Even though these **Graphics Styles** are semi-automated for you, everything about them can be further modified: font size, font style, leading, text color, position, justification, and special effects, exactly as you would with a regular text editor such as MS Word or Pages.

Basic Text: The Type tool

Photoshop Elements includes a word-processing functionality, enabling text to be added directly to images and graphics. In fact, some of the more automated functions on offer are supplied complete with blank text boxes, ready for you to click and add your words of wisdom, so it's easy to do.

Step one: Choosing the **Myriad Pro Regular** font, I chose the **Horizontal Type** tool (as it is officially called), clicked once into the image, then typed in Stand up (hit *Enter*), comedian: (hit *Enter*), and then typed Vince Connolly to get this triple-deck text layout. The text is left-aligned, and the type layer is automatically placed at the top of the layer stack (inset panel).

Font size tip:

When you start using the type tool, you might notice that the text you've chosen appears very small or far too large. This might be because last time Elements was used, you chose a small or very large point size in the **Options** panel. But more than likely it's caused by the document's resolution setting. If you are typing into a 20 Mp image set to a 72 dots per inch (dpi) resolution, it will print 2 m x 1.5 m—huge. So if you add 12 pt text into a document that size, you'll understand why it looks so small. It's an easy fix: undo the last type layer, open the **Image Size** feature (**Image**>**Resize**>**Image Resize**), make sure that the **Resample** checkbox is **unchecked**, and change the resolution from 72 to 300 dpi. Save the file, select the **Type** tool once more, and when you add new text, it appears much larger in the main window because at 300 dpi, the new dimensions are a smaller 20 x 35 cm, so the 12 pt text looks larger. If the image is destined for social media, you need to resize the overall dimensions of the picture first to a suitable web resolution setting before you start typing.

Step two: Once you have the document set to the correct resolution for your application, it's time to format the text. To make changes to preexisting text, it first must be **selected**. This is where many newcomers might get into trouble. Selected text is highlighted in the opposite color—for example, black text is highlighted in white, and yellow text is highlighted in blue, as you can see above. It can look a little confusing.

Step three: In this step, I modified the text **style**—styles are variants of the same font; for example: **Italic**, **Regular**, **Semi-bold**, **Semi-italic**, **Bold**, **Black**, **Narrow**, **Light**, and **Extended**, and so on. Some fonts only have one style; others, such as **Myriad**, have a lot. The beauty of working with styles is that everything is the same font family, and the styles are used to add **emphasis** to words by making them light, italic, semi-bold, bold, and even black. It's also perfectly fine to use different fonts in the same document, although it's also best not to have more than two or three at any one time—which is why styles can be so handy for creative copywriters. In this example, I changed `Stand up comedian` to **Myriad Pro Light**, while `Vince Connolly` was changed to **Myriad Pro Bold**.

Design suggestion #1: To give you an idea of your choices in terms of **type styles**, here's a small sample of what's possible using a regular font such as **Myriad Pro**, from the top of the preceding screenshot: black, bold, semi-bold, regular, light, light condensed, light extended, italic, and italic semi-condensed. Your choice.

Step four: To emphasize text to a greater level, try using **Drop Shadow**. With the type layer as the **active layer** (highlighted in blue), navigate to the **Styles** panel, find the **Drop Shadow** submenu, and click on a thumbnail. This instantly applies a drop shadow to that layer.

Design suggestion #2: Leading is a useful design feature that you'll find on the **Type** tool's **Options** panel; use it to add or remove space from between lines of text, or even from between single words. By default, this is set to **Auto**, which normally works OK, but if you particularly want two lines of text to be closer together, manually enter a figure and adjust accordingly.

Design suggestion #3: Here's the leading reset to a smaller value than on the left. Use leading to close the space between lines of text as a group (changing all three lines of text in one hit) or select a single line, then change the leading on just that to push that line further away from everything above it. Note that you must select *all* the text, including any spaces in that line, in order for the leading to work.

Design suggestion #3: A text box can be created by dragging the **Type** tool cursor over the image to draw a box. When you release the mouse, start typing. The text is held inside the parameters of that box. This is handy if you have sourced a big bunch of text from a word-processing document. Create a text box, copy the content from the word-processing document, then paste it into the Elements text box.

Design suggestion #4: To select text that is currently being typed, use *Ctrl/Cmd + A* to select all. If the document has already been saved, then, with the **Type** tool selected, you need to first click inside the text once (to make it the active layer), then double-click the text to select a single word, or triple-click to select an entire sentence. If you're using a text box and want to select everything in that box, you will need to quadruple-click very quickly to select everything in that text layer.

Basic Text: Styles and effects

The **Type** tool allows users to apply the usual font styles and color to their text. But there's a lot more to using text than simply typing into an image.

With your text layer active (highlighted in blue), you can apply any of Elements' **Layer Styles** from the **Styles** panel that's located on the right-hand side of the main window. The most common style that's used with text is the **Drop Shadow**. Drop shadows are particularly effective for making text stand out from the page, especially if the background under the text is distracting.

Step one: Elements makes it easy to apply special effects. Choose **Drop Shadow** from the drop-down menu at the top of the **Styles** panel, pick one of the shadow "looks," and click its icon to apply the style to that particular layer. If you don't like this effect, try clicking another icon, and that new look will replace the old one. Using **Styles** in this way allows even novices to make their text productions appear professional in no time at all.

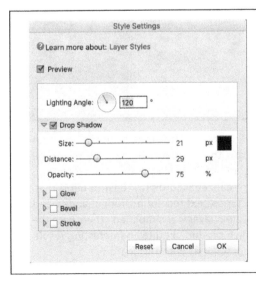

Step two: If you don't like a particular "look", modify it via that layer's **Style Settings**. Look at the layer that's supporting the effect - you'll see a tiny **fx** icon next to the text layer's description. Double-click the icon to reveal the Style Settings for that specific effect. Use the sliders to modify, in this example, the height (distance) of the shadow, as well as its **Size** and **Opacity**. You can also use this panel to add more effects, if needed.

Design suggestion #5: When trying out a new **Layer style**, do bear in mind that some of them, such as **Photographic Effects**, will only work on pixel-based photos and have almost no impact on text, and vice versa. Also, if you try to apply a drop-shadow effect on a full-frame image, it won't work because the photograph occupies the entire screen; however, if you were to apply a drop-shadow effect on an image that has been reduced in size, it will display a drop shadow. The trick with text is to experiment with some of the styles to see which suits your project best. Many of the styles that you see in Photoshop Elements have been with this software for a long time (more than 10 years), and so might appear somewhat dated.

Design suggestion #6: If you try out some of Elements' Filter Effects, you'll find that they don't work—unless first **simplified**. This means that the layer being used has to be converted into pixels first before the effect can be added. It's a simple process, and as you see here, Elements warns you so you can accept or cancel accordingly. Bear in mind that, once simplified, text layers lose their editability. So, typos, text recoloring, font changes, and extreme enlargement are no longer permissible. This text layer was simplified - then, with the type selected, I added a metallic gradient to it - which produced quite an interesting result. Elements provides hundreds of different creative possibilities with this feature.

Advanced Text: Custom Text

If you are looking for a special font to match a particular theme or character in one of your Elements projects, one thing you could consider is downloading a *custom font* from a site such as www.dafont.com. There are a lot of places advertising "free" stuff—I have never had any issues with this one, but I'd be mindful of what and where you click on some of the more disreputable sites online. I have been using fonts from Dafont for many years, and it seems pretty reliable. Here's how it's done:

Step one: Visit the site. Scroll through the pages or use the **Search** bar.

Step two: When you find a font to your liking, click the **Download** button. It's small and so downloads quickly.

Step three, left: Once downloaded—to your **Downloads** folder (Mac/PC)—locate the file and open it by double-clicking the downloaded file icon. It will open a window displaying what the font physically looks like.

Step four, left: In the upper left-hand side of this window, click the **Install** button. This will pop that new font into the shared font folder, which can then be accessed immediately (no need to restart).

Main image, lower left: In this example, I chose a font called **Papercuts**, which suited the Autumn in Japan theme of my book.

A word of warning: Not all the fonts I have downloaded and tried from the internet have worked once installed. I have about an 80% success rate—possibly because of compatibility issues—either way, seeing as they are free, I still think it's a good deal!

Keyboard shortcuts

As with most editing, you can lose sight of the image-making process and become too immersed in the more complex editing functions. Keyboard shortcuts are there to help spread the load, reduce **repetitive strain injury** (**RSI**), and generally speed up your workflow. I use the first three in the following list all the time. It's also beneficial for you to memorize some of the tool access keys (letters) to make it easier to jump from process to process. Some of these are shown here:

- *Ctrl/Cmd + J*: Duplicate the (active) layer.
- *Ctrl/Cmd + D*: Use this to deselect or remove any active selection.
- *Ctrl/Cmd + T*: Use this to transform objects on the active layer.
- *Ctrl/Cmd + E*: Merge down.
- *Shift + Ctrl/Cmd + E*: Merge (all) visible (layers).
- *O*: Burn, Dodge, and Sponge tools.
- *A*: Selection brushes (Quick Selection, Selection Brush, Magic Wand, Refine Selection, and Auto Selection).
- *L*: Lasso tools (Freehand Lasso, Polygonal Lasso, and Magnetic Lasso).
- *S*: Clone Stamp tool (also the Pattern Stamp tool).
- *J*: Spot Healing Brush and Healing Brush.
- *B*: Brushes (Brush tool, Impressionist Brush, and Color Replace Brush).
- *E*: Eraser brushes (Eraser, Background Eraser, and Magic Eraser brushes).
- *K*: Paint Bucket tool.
- *G*: Gradient tool.
- *Alt/Opt + Ctrl/Cmd + S*: **Enhance>Select Subject**.

Out of the hundreds of possible keyboard shortcuts published for this program, I consider the ones on this page to be the most important. They sum up the most practical features in this program, and once learned, will advance your understanding and editing proficiency tenfold.

Summary

In this chapter, we once more ramped up the depth of knowledge to present the best learning experience possible.

As you may well now be aware, it's possible to spend your entire working life immersed in the work of commercial photography and professional retouching. All the tools are here in Elements, but if you need to take the control you require to a higher level, this was the chapter for you, especially the sections on professional-grade retouching, selections, burning, dodging, masking, text, and graphics.

We also highlighted a couple of simple ways to make selections—Adobe is continuously attempting to incorporate AI into its semi and fully automated processes. In the case of its new **Subject Selection** feature, I think you'll agree it's a winner.

Having so many varied and powerful features at your disposal gives you a far wider range of creative options than just being able to add the odd preset effect to an image. If you can master this chapter, you'll be well on your way to becoming a retouching expert.

Coming up in the next chapter are plenty of in-depth sections for those who want more information about the power of illustration, graphics, drawing, and painting.

8
Additional Tools
and Features

Elements continues to grow and expand with every version released. While many of its newer features are more often concerned with operating efficiency many are also developed from the company's foray into artificial intelligence (AI). Some features might be automatic like the amazing **Moving Photos** feature, while others appear to have assimilated multiple complex operations into one easy to follow interface - like the fantastic 'Perfect' series (**Perfect Portrait, Perfect Landscape** and **Perfect Pet!**), **Move and Scale Object** and **Quote Graphic**.

What you'll find in this chapter is a list of great features - features that you might have never used if all you do with Elements is a bit of simple editing. As mentioned, most of these tools encompass some really complex actions - like selections, sharpening, chromatic aberration removal, smoothing, blending, re-composing, warping and even facial reconstruction (in the case of the **Open Closed Eyes** feature).

This is the power of Photoshop Elements - to write how to manually achieve what some of these processes offer would take several more chapters - and send most of you off to sleep. That's the genius of the program designers - by packaging these complex processes into a user-friendly interface with just one, two or maybe three buttons to get it all happening, Adobe effectively drags you up several skills levels - but without having to finish a university course!

> **What you'll learn from this chapter:**
>
> - Image Modes
> - Adjust Color Curves
> - Smart Brush
> - Paint Bucket tool
> - Gradient tool
> - Haze Removal tool
> - Content-Aware Move tool
> - Recompose tool
> - Extend Background feature
> - Move and Scale Object
> - Moving Photos
>
> - Quote Graphic
> - Convert to Black and White
> - Duotone Effect
> - B&W Color Pop
> - Old Fashioned Photo
> - Perfect Landscape, Portrait and Perfect Pet
> - Adjust Facial Features
> - Adjust Facial Features: Face Tilt
> - Open Closed Eyes

Image Modes

It's a feature found in all photo-editing applications but one that rarely gets a mention. Most photographers work in RGB mode—the color mode used by both the camera and the computer monitor. Professionals working in print (with Photoshop) will inevitably work in **CMYK** (**Cyan**, **Magenta**, **Yellow**, and **Black**) mode. We don't have this in Elements.

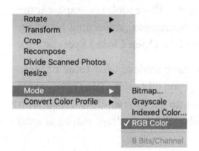

Most photographers will only ever encounter RGB mode, but occasionally might encounter a file that doesn't edit properly, so it pays to check its mode status. Choose **Image>Mode>RGB Color** (menu on the left) to convert it to a full-color file, or choose the 8-bit conversion option, when needed (Elements cannot handle high-bit-depth files—they must be converted to 8-bit in order to work properly). Other modes under the **Image>Mode** menu include **Grayscale**, **Indexed Color...**, and **Bitmap....**

Grayscale: RGB files have three color channels, while grayscale has one: grey. When you convert from RGB to **Grayscale**, expect the resolution to drop. In a regular 8-bit file, a grayscale image has just 256 shades of gray while RGB files have millions of colors.

Indexed Color: Common in the fledgling internet days. An indexed image allows you to limit the color range in a file, making it smaller and faster to display over slow connections.

Bitmap mode: The smallest—and least-used—of all image modes. Bitmaps are made from just two bits, black and white, so files are small. This is suited for simple graphic images. Bitmaps have a finite enlargability—so when it comes to graphics, they are not as useful as vectors.

Adjust Color Curves

It might come as a shock to some of you but Photoshop Elements is actually based on Photoshop CC. Of course, most of the features are unique to Photoshop Elements, but they have their origins in Elements' higher-end cousin **Photoshop**: **Levels**, **Hue/Saturation**, **Shadow/Highlights**, **Brightness and Contrast**, **Image Size**, **Canvas Size**—these are all identical to those in Photoshop.

And indeed, if you use a software plugin, such as **Photoshop Elements+**, you can actually open up and exploit legacy Photoshop features that are still present in Elements. One tool that's sort of part Photoshop and part Elements is called **Adjust Color Curves** (**Enhance>Adjust Color>Adjust Color Curves**).

The **Curves** tool in Photoshop is a useful feature and while **Adjust Color Curves** could be called the poor cousin, it's still a good feature with which to adjust the contrast in an image.

Photoshop CC is designed for those who know exactly what they want from an image—and what tools are needed to achieve that result. I'd argue that Elements can produce pretty much the same result, but the program's tools often differ in the sense that they come with a lot of "extras"—including help menus and presets. So, in **Adjust Color Curves**, you'll find a **Style** list (in red)—these are preset adjustments—**Backlight**, **Darken Highlights**, **Increase Contrast**, and so on. If this is not enough for a good result, use **Adjust** sliders in the center of the panel. What these are doing is displayed in the curves map on the right-hand side, with the shadows at the bottom left and highlights at the top right. In Photoshop, you adjust the image by click-pushing the actual curve line, whereas this Elements version is more preset-driven. It still works a treat. Its best feature, in my opinion, is that you can easily adjust both midtone contrast and brightness, which can produce a significant improvement to most images.

The Smart Brush

Here's an unusual tool—a special effects brush that works in tandem with a selection brush. Paint into an image and the brush finds contrast edges (around the subject), makes a selection, and fills it with whatever style of **Smart Brush** is currently set.

In practice, this works reasonably well—but, depending on the nature of the image chosen, the initial selection process can be quite flawed to the point where the effect it's filled with appears distinctly out of place.

That said, **Smart Brush** includes the **Refine Edge** utility—this allows users to soften, blur, widen, shrink, and smooth the brush selection edge to make the result look more realistic. Personally, I find this brush a bit too optimistic in what it tries to produce; everything is reliant on the efficacy of the selection process. But in this example, I was pleased with how well it did work.

The tool features more than 90 different effects, which are divided into 12 subsets to make choosing them a little easier. To get the most out of this tool, I suggest you start with simple images.

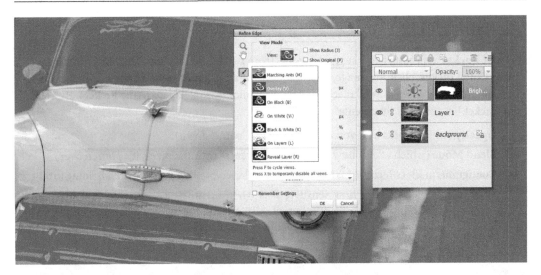

Step one: In this example, I first used the **Brighter Smart Brush** setting—essentially, this selected the roof of the car and lightened it. By combining the **Smart Brush** effects with the modification power of the **Refine Edge** utility (here showing as a red mask overlay), it's possible to make an accurate selection quickly. Obviously, the simpler the image, the easier it is to get great results with this feature.

Step two: Almost done—the second application was called **Old Paper** (a filter effect that's been in Elements for many years). I thought it suited the mood of the old 1950s car parked on a Havana side street. You can see the two associated **Adjustment Layer masks** in the layer panel: one for the brightness increase and the second for the **Old Paper** effect that's dropped into the mask. This is a fun feature!

The Paint Bucket tool

The **Paint Bucket** tool, as its name suggests, works like a real bucket of paint. Choose a color from the Toolbar **Color Picker**, click the image, and it will throw a bucket of color across the image. OK, so your beautiful landscape is now all black (or whatever color was picked up in the **Picker**). By default, **Paint Bucket** has several adjustments:

- **Opacity** (which works as if you are watering the "paint" down).
- **Blend Mode** (which affects how the paint color reacts with the pixels it's poured over).
- **Contiguous** mode (which means it only affects similar-colored pixels if they are adjoining to other).
- **Tolerance** (which dictates how sensitive it is when identifying similar-colored pixels over which it spreads). The default number of 255 means the paint covers the entire image regardless of what you clicked. Set to a smaller value, such as 15, and it only affects pixels that are very similar in tone to the ones initially clicked.

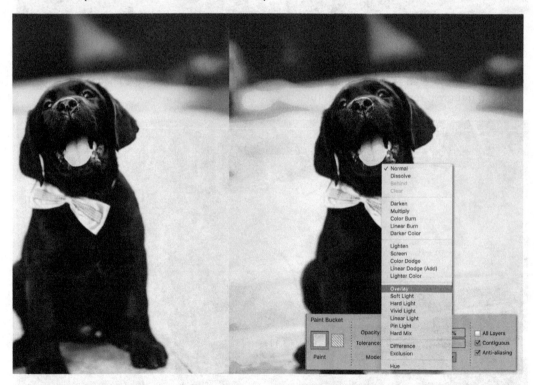

A good use for this tool that few people realize is its ability to *add contrast* or a *color tint* to an image, especially if it's black and white, as shown here. Set **Tolerance** to the max (255), **Opacity** to **10%**, and **Blend Mode** to **Overlay**; choose black from **Color Picker**; and then, click something that's already black in the image (the dog's body, in this example). Each time the image is clicked, you add 10% more black to dark areas. If it doesn't work as expected, uncheck the **Contiguous** checkbox (in the **Tool Options** panel) and see whether that improves the spread of paint. Using the **Overlay** blend mode ensures that the original tonal gradation of the picture shines through the black tone being added to the frame.

If I'm looking at an image that contains, say, a block of white, and I click on it, **Paint Bucket** instantly replaces white with whatever is set for the bucket. It won't go past the edges of the white block. If **Contiguous** is unchecked, it affects every white pixel in the file.

Another good use for this tool is to tint an image with color, or black and white (contrast). You can do this by going through the following steps:

Step one: Open the shot and choose a tint color (typically, photographers use this to warm up or cool down an image). I chose yellow from **Color Picker**.

Step two: Set the tool opacity (in this example I set it to **10**%).

Step three: Set **Tolerance** to the maximum (**255**).

Step four: Choose a **Blend Mode** setting from the tool **Options Panel** (I find that **Overlay** seems to work well). **Overlay** gives the paint a specific *translucence* so that the tones in the image are not hindered by adding opaque paint as they might be in real life.

With each click, the tint deepens by 10%. In this example, I tinted a black-and-white image of these old books with deep yellow—twice—to give a pale sepia effect (as shown in the center example), and three more times to warm it up considerably to produce a warmer, deeper sepia tint.

The Gradient tool

Another greatly underrated tool in Elements is the **Gradient** tool. The photographers among you that have used a graduated resin filter over the front of the lens from manufacturers such as **Cokin**, **Lee Filters**, and **B&W** will know what I am talking about.

You place the filter over the lens and position the darker part over the sky with the clearer section at the base over the landscape. This effectively reduces the sky's exposure, thereby balancing the often large exposure disparity that leaves us with an overexposed upper half and an underexposed lower half of the frame. Graduated filters come in different colors (such as orange to enhance sunsets or sunrises).

This tool in Elements comes with 16 default gradients and eight gradient subcategories, giving you a choice of 83 in total. I have only ever used two or three.

Step one: Here's a nice shot, complete with two figures silhouetted by a bright sunset. Click the **Gradient** tool icon (**Toolbar**) and then click the gradient thumbnail in the **tool's** options panel (highlighted in red) to open the complex-looking **Gradient Editor**. Because my **Color Picker** was already set to its default black background, you can see that the thumbnail, second from the left, is black, fading to transparent (highlighted in red in the image). Click once to select, then hit **OK**, and you are good to go.

Step two: If you use the **Gradient** tool immediately by click-stretching it vertically from the top to the bottom of the frame, it will deposit opaque pixels, which will look horrible. You first must change the tool's **Blend Mode** setting from **Normal Opaque** to **Overlay**. This is like thinning the paint so that the details shine though the color tint rather than being totally obscured by it.

Step three – technique: If you only drag the gradient a short way across the screen, the gradation will be very steep, and therefore quite noticeable—something you might not want. In this example, the gradient is so steep it looks like a mistake, which it is.

Here's a before-and-after comparison. On the left is the original file, and on the right half is the image featuring a gradient, applied twice, so that it's quite a dramatic color change from the original (alternatively, use a **Gradient Adjustment Layer**).

If you'd like to retain greater control, create a new layer (**Layer>New Layer**) and apply the gradient to that so it can be repositioned or the opacity of the layer can be adjusted. Make sure that **Overlay** is selected from the **Layers** panel drop-down menu; otherwise, it will look opaque. Another way of taking greater control over the gradient would be to add a **Layer Mask**, then paint black into the mask to modify the gradient—in this case, onto the couple sitting on the bench, the ocean, and the foreground.

The Haze Removal tool

Another great feature of Elements is its **Haze Removal** tool. This is a tool that's designed to boost the mid-tone contrast in your photos, and it works incredibly well on hazy, misty, steamy pictures where the clarity is suffering. You'll note, in the examples shown here, that once processed, the finished images also appear sharper. This is because the sharpening process is all about the **contrast differences** along subject edges, which is what the **Haze Removal** tool does, so it might not only fix the climatic conditions, but also make the scene appear sharper.

It's also beneficial on some black and white images and low-contrast images, and sometimes it's just good to add to a picture to add a bit of *punch*. Elements features two versions: one is the **Auto Haze Removal** tool, which does a credible job, but if it's control you need, it's best to go for the regular **Haze Removal** tool in the **Enhance** menu and use its sliders to perfect the effect on each image, one at a time.

The sample picture seen here is more a snowy-looking image than one that's suffering from haze. Even so, the sky is indistinct due to slight overexposure and the low cloud. Select **Enhance**>**Haze Removal...** from the **Enhance** menu.

Above: This is the easiest filter to play with. Use the sliders at the base of the self-contained filter panel to make adjustments. For some reason, this doesn't update your slider changes in the main window until the **OK** button is pressed, then it's too late. If you don't like the result, **Undo** then re-do the process. Easy. The finished image (**below**) is looking a lot stronger visually.

Above: Here's another use of the **Haze Removal** tool, where we are enhancing a slightly low-contrast (but not hazy) image. Because this feature adds mid-tone contrast, it's perfect for adding a bit of punch to the image. Of course, this doesn't work for all images, but when it does work, the result is quite impressive.

This feature keeps on giving: In this example, I have taken an old print that has been scanned and retouched, but its tones are still lacking in contrast. It's an ideal image to test the **Haze Removal** tool on. As is clearly visible in this before-and-after illustration, haze removal is also a good bet when it comes to adding contrast "punch" into scanned images. It doesn't work with everything, but it's certainly effective in this example.

The Content-Aware Move tool

A tool that might help fine-tune your **compositional skills** is the **Content-Aware Move tool**. Essentially, this is a large-scale **Healing Brush**, but instead of clicking repeatedly over an image hoping that it can copy, paste, and blend pixels over a problem area, this tool works on a much larger area. Draw around the object you want to move, drag the entire object to a new position, and release it—Elements will do the rest.

Here, *the rest* means assessing the pixels around the target site and then blending them into the background canvas. Some examples work much better than others.

Elements provides some control over the **Healing** action (via a slider), plus **Add** or **Subtract** modes, for the initial selection process.

After it has performed, however, I find I have to fine-tune the results with **Clone Stamp** or **Healing Brush** to tidy up some of Elements' visual mistakes. That being said, the **Content-Aware Move tool** is not a bad feature with which to recompose certain types of images, especially if it's applied to a photo where there's room for the moving and blending process to actually manoeuvre.

The sample image demonstrates this feature nicely because the object I want to move (the fishing boat) has plenty of (reasonably) uniform space around it (the ocean), which should make it easier for this tool to cover up the area once occupied by the boat.

Step one: Start by drawing a simple line around the object you want to move. It doesn't have to be accurate, but be careful not to include any of the object you are trying to shift (in this case, the fishing boat). Because the healing brush works by assessing the brightness and texture in the pixels around the target and source locations, it's important to work with a **simple image** rather than one that's busy.

Step two: Drag the object to its new location, and once you're happy with its position, click the green check mark.

Finished: You can see the result in this screenshot. Although there are some slightly uneven textures in the ocean where the boat once was, the result is acceptable (especially from an automated action). The boat in its new position is quite acceptable—but note in some cases, this target area might also need a little retouching to make it fit perfectly. Retouching with the **Spot Healing Brush** should help to further smooth the tones.

The Recompose tool

Another re-composition helper is the **Recompose tool**. Personally, I think its results can be very hit and miss, almost as if Adobe has bitten off more than it can chew.

We all have snaps in our libraries where we might wish the composition to be slightly different—people a bit closer to each other, landscapes a bit wider, or formats recomposed to a square shape, for example. The **Recompose** tool sets out to provide the solutions to these problems.

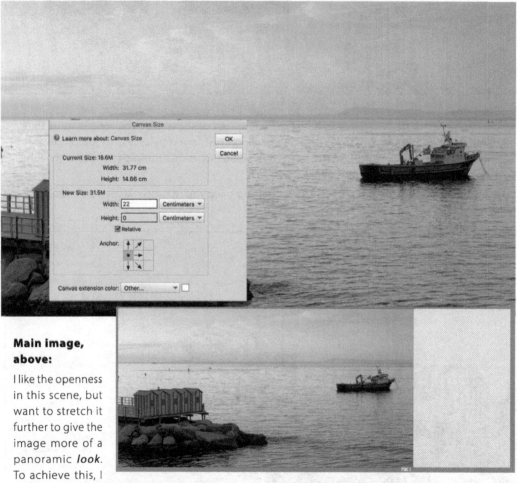

Main image, above:

I like the openness in this scene, but want to stretch it further to give the image more of a panoramic *look*. To achieve this, I need to add more to the right-hand side of the canvas using the **Canvas Size** feature (inset panel). I wasn't 100% sure how much extra real estate I was going to need, so I added a lot—if it adds too much, it's easy enough to crop any surplus off later. The new real estate appears as a checkerboard pattern, indicating that although that's now the new document size, it doesn't contain any pixels.

Step one: Note that there are two types of brush available: green and red. The green paintbrush is for preserving the shape of objects, while the red brush indicates that the selected pixels can be deleted. As you might deduce here, by using a big brush, you can paint over the objects in an image you want to keep and remove. If you make a mistake, use each brush's **Eraser** tool to fix the mask (a larger-sized brush makes the whole process a lot faster).

Step two: Once the regions are set, carefully grab one of the "handles"—in this example, it was the center handle on the right-hand edge that was dragged to the right in order to stretch the image to a wide panorama format (sometimes this "handle" is hard to see).

Final result: As you can see in the screenshot above, the stretched result is quite subtle. Although the final result wasn't quite as wide as I had originally hoped, if the image had been dragged any further to the right, the scene would have become distorted—compare this with the original 4:3 format image on the right.

Shooting tip:

Most of us shoot landscape format images—it's just easier to hold the camera in that position. I can guarantee, if you check your image library, 80% of your shots will be horizontal—maybe more. One of the best compositional tips I can pass on is this: when you shoot a frame, turn the camera 90 degrees and shoot it at a different orientation. Make this your shooting technique—it will ensure that, even if you end up throwing half your shots away because they don't work compositionally, at least you'll have that choice.

Extend Background feature

Although the **Recompose** Tool appears to be a fantastic answer to all those images that need a bit of compositional help, I find it clunky and hard to use. You might disagree, but I have to put a lot of effort into the process for any degree of success, and that means it's unlikely to get much use because there are plenty of other easier features to play with in Elements.

Launched in the previous version of Elements, I was pleased to see that the **Recompose** Tool had been reborn, as it were, as the **Extend Background** tool, located in the **Guided Edit** mode. A simpler, step-by-step version of the **Recompose** Tool was needed. And you'll be pleased to hear that it works really well.

Step one: Open a suitable image in Elements (note that it's best to choose a clear, sharp image with some clear space around the main subject—Elements needs these pixels to extend the canvas, so the better the quality of the original, the more realistic the result).

Step two: Open the **Guided Edit**>**Special Edits**>**Extend Background** feature. Note that you can choose to have the image displayed as a "before and after," or, to make it larger onscreen, just set the display to 'after').

Step three: Choose the final image size—this is slightly confusing, as there are so many to choose from: **Square, Instagram Post/Story, Facebook Cover/Event/Post, Twitter, Letter, or A4 or A3 Portrait or Landscape**. I worked with the largest option (**A3 Landscape**) for the two examples here, as the originals were high resolution 21Mp files.

Step four: Select the area you want filled (top, bottom, left, or right, or a combination). Go back and start again if the application fills the wrong part of the canvas or if the subject is distorted.

Step five: Choose **Autofill**, then watch the magic happen. If the photo contains lots of small details, the cloned result might not look convincing—you might have to practice with different images to get the hang of it. My first two results were outstanding. The hyena image looks good—although you can see some slight pixelation in the background—but overall it's a great result.

Tip: To stop the subject from being accidentally cloned with all this pixel black magic going on, you can add a **mask** by drawing into the image over the bits you want to keep pristine—here, it's in green (in **Extend** mode only).

The cheetah image was especially pleasing, as I extended the canvas to the right only, making the composition more dramatic. Another great tool, Adobe!

Move & Scale Object feature

It's not often that you get to experience a complex, automated photo-editing feature that's really exciting, but this is one of those times. In **Guided Edit** mode, under **Basics**, you'll find **Move & Scale Object**.

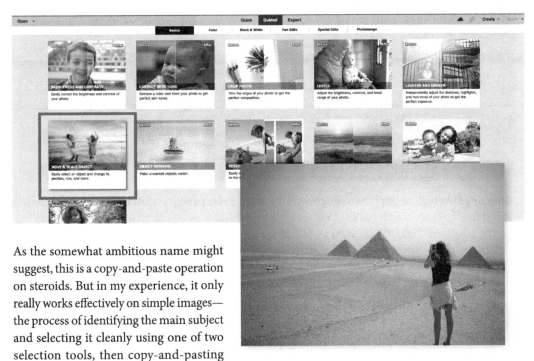

As the somewhat ambitious name might suggest, this is a copy-and-paste operation on steroids. But in my experience, it only really works effectively on simple images—the process of identifying the main subject and selecting it cleanly using one of two selection tools, then copy-and-pasting it elsewhere in the image, is both a complex operation and one that's fraught with potential editing problems. That said, I chose this simple shot of a woman photographing the pyramids in Egypt as an example. This feature is easy to use—just follow the onscreen instructions!

Photo manipulation woes

In 1982, the **National Geographic Magazine** got into hot water—the editors liked a proposed cover shot, but the pyramids were not in the right position for a vertical cover. So, the pyramids were moved. This caused quite a sensation among many purists, not to mention the photographer, who considered any pictorial meddling to be a bad idea.

Nowadays, the publication has strict rules about the degree of photo editing that can be applied to any story published. These rules do not apply to users of Elements!

(See more here: `https://www.nationalgeographic.com/magazine/2016/07/editors-note-images-and-ethics/`).

Step one: The feature offers two selection tools: **Auto Select** and the **Quick Selection** brush. I used the latter, as I find it easier to control. If your subject is not contrasty, "clean" selections can be tricky. As it was, my finished selection included some blue sky and a vehicle that was parked in front of the pyramid. I chose **Duplicate** (arrowed), which takes the selection, copies the content, then pastes it back into the file. Grab a corner handle to drag it out to go larger. Click the green check mark to OK the process.

Step two: The accuracy of your selection really becomes obvious once you enlarge the subject. I was not happy with the fuzzy skyline around the pyramids, as it didn't match—use the **Clone Stamp** or **Spot Healing Brush** tool to tidy up the digital deception—and it's job done!

Duplicate option: Editors at **National Geographic** will be running for cover when they see this. As an automated tool, this is an excellent feature, making it so easy to perform a complex selection and copy and paste operation with a high probability of success.

Not every picture works: In this shot, I tried to select and move the woman holding the dog. The selection result, on the right, was surprisingly good considering it's such a complex image. But once moved, the automatic healing cover-up process left a lot of smudgy-looking errors. You could use the **Clone Stamp** or **Healing** Brush tools to fix such errors, but in this example, it would probably take too long to get it just right.

Moving Photos feature

In **Photoshop Elements**, you'll find a few neat developments—many are connected with Adobe's continued development of **AI**. This is there to make the often-complex retouching processes appear easier to control, and in the case of the **Object Removal**, **Adjust Facial Features**, **Open Closed Eyes**, and the **Move & Scale Object** features, it works pretty well. Here's another one that I shall try to illustrate here, even though the end product is a video. **Moving Photos** (and the new 2023 Moving Elements feature) has bridged the gap between stills and moving pictures by supplying this cool GIF or MP4 maker.

Find a picture with a strong subject, open it in the **Moving Photos** feature (**Enhance>Moving Photos**), double-click the type of animation from the menu (inset, on the left), and sit back and let Adobe do its magic. And magic it is.

We have all seen the effect used in advertising campaigns and in some horror film genres in the eighties—where the subject stays relatively static, while the background shifts—forward or backward, to the left or to the right—now we can do it using our own images!

The process can be recorded as a **2D effect**—which means the entire picture zooms or pans the scene (this is also called the **Ken Burns effect** after the documentary filmmaker who used it so effectively that it was named after him).

If the switch is flipped to **3D effect**, the utility scans the image, selects what it perceives to be the subject, then animates the rest of the file to create the Burns effect. If you study the edges of the subject, you can see where the selection has been made, but I have to admit, it's pretty good—plus, of course, in an animated clip, the cool effect overrides any slight masking inconsistency.

Step one: Find an image, open it, and select **Moving Photos** (Quick/Expert>Enhance>**Moving Photos**).

Step two: Choose from one of the 22 animations (11 in 2D, 11 in 3D). Double-click the effect icon you want—then wait for it to fully process.

Step three: Click the **Export button (arrowed)**, and choose where it's saved to.

Step four: The next screen allows you to choose the **GIF quality**—plus, if you click **Advanced Settings** (highlighted), you can get into additional quality settings and file size output— important if this is destined for the web.

Quote Graphic feature

One feature I never expected to appear in Elements is this: **Quote Graphic**. But then, **Quote Graphic** is appropriate because it makes working with text both easy and very creative - especially when compared to the rather tricky-to-use **Type** Tool.

The idea behind this new feature is to make the job of working with text a little easier. You can work this a couple of ways: choose an image and add the text, graphics, and animations to it, or start from scratch and work with vector graphics and type on their own.

If you already have an image open, you can choose **Start with a Photo** and it opens in the special **Quote Graphic** window, as seen above.

There are plenty of possible artwork combinations here, from standard print sizes (vertical, square, horizontal) to the usual social media format options. Use your own images or use a stock one from Adobe and your own witty quotes, or one of those supplied.

Right: Two of the graphic menus from the **Quote Graphic** feature—there are plenty of options and because they are mostly vectors or Smart Objects, it does not matter how big or small you make them, the image clarity will always be excellent.

Step one (left): I chose one of the supplied Adobe stock shots and got this on my first attempt. It's a good example because, if this were a normal exercise using the **Type** tool, correcting this layout mess would be tricky unless you've had some prior experience. However, as you can see in this frame, the red-painted text box has corner handles. This means I can drag any corner to make it larger or smaller. Easy.

Step two: As with all transformations, once something has been resized, you need to hit the green **OK** button attached to the object that has been changed before proceeding. Everything in these little compositions can be changed—from text boxes to type styles, color, drop shadow color, point size, and more.

Step three (left): I dragged the graphic boxes one at a time around the frame to get better text positioning. If you change your mind and choose another graphic, it might automatically fit the scene, or you might have to jiggle it a bit, to get it positioned again. It's an easy, no-hassle process.

Step four: Most of the graphics have a color overlay, so the upper examples have a peachy color while the one on the left here is monochrome. You have no say in this; it just happens because that's the style Adobe presents. If you want it to look different, you'd have to edit it in **Expert** mode and start **Quote Graphic** again.

Step five: All of Elements' (many) graphics and clip art files can also be brought into play here.

Click to automatically drop one of these files directly from the menu into the main image, then click-drag to resize and reposition.

Step six: Aside from static graphics, **Quote Graphic** can also be **animated** (choosing from eight different movement styles). It's then saved as a GIF or MP4 movie file.

Convert to Black and White feature

The medium of black and white is favored by a lot of photographers—it evokes feelings of antiquity, style, and artiness in many different scenarios. The trouble is, if you ask a bunch of photographers how to convert a file into black and white, they'll come up with multiple different ways of doing it—some good, some great, some complex.

Elements makes the conversion process a little easier with it's own **Convert to Black and White** tool. Here's how it works:

Step one: Choose the **Convert to Black and White** tool (*Alt/Opt + Ctrl/Cmd + B* or **Enhance>Convert to Black and White**).

Step two: The **Convert** window opens and the image in the main edit space automatically converts into one of the black and white *recipes* on offer. With the introduction of higher-resolution monitors, the fixed-shape preview before-and-after windows are less relevant than the main image behind it.

Step three: Choose one of the preset recipes on offer: **Infrared Effect** (renders green foliage as white and blue skies as almost black, producing dramatic 'looks,' especially for landscapes), **Newspaper** (brightens highlights—good for copying text), **Portraits** (good general purpose conversion mode), **Scenic Landscape** (produces slightly contrastier, 'punchier' midtones) **Urban Snapshots** (generally produces the lowest contrast), or **Vivid Landscapes** (more midtone contrast than in the **Scenic Landscape** setting).

Convert to Black and White

OK
Cancel
Reset

Before   After

Undo
Redo

Tip

Select a style of black and white conversion. Each style uses a different amount of the red, green, and blue color channels of the original image to produce a specific look. Make further adjustments by moving the sliders below. Learn more about: Convert to Black and White

Select a style:

Infrared Effect
Newspaper
Portraits
Scenic Landscape
Urban/Snapshots
Vivid Landscapes

Adjust Intensity:

Red:
Green:
Blue:
Contrast:

Step four (above): Adjust the **intensity** of the black, white, and midtones using the sliders to the right of the recipes.

Step five: When you're satisfied, click **OK** and save the file.

When it comes to using this specific tool, I prefer to use the least contrasty conversion first (for me, this is usually **Urban Landscape**), click **OK**, then finish editing the contrast using **Levels**. Everyone has their own *best* way to make a black and white shot pop off the page.

Seven other black and white conversion techniques to try:

- In the **Hue/Saturation** tool, set the **Saturation** slider to **-100**.
- Convert the color mode from **RGB** to **Grayscale** (**Image**>**Mode**>**Grayscale**).
- Use the **Remove Color** tool (**Enhance**>**Adjust Color**>**Remove Color**, or *Shift + Ctrl/Cmd + U*).
- Use the **Black & White Effects** thumbnail in **Quick Edit** mode.
- Use the **Black and White Conversion** tool in **Guided Edit** mode.
- Use the **Monotone Color** menu from the **Expert**>**Effects** panel.
- Use a **Hue/Saturation** adjustment layer.

Duotone Effect filter

A duotone is a black and white image with an extra color added for effect. It's a feature that has been in Adobe Photoshop CC for many, many years. In fact, duotones have been popular with photographers when publishing high-end books of mostly black and white images. The Italian printing industry has one of the best reputations for producing such books, although now you can make your own with Elements. But this feature doesn't just stop at converting to black and white then adding color (which I guess is why it's called **Duotone Effect** and not just "duotone"). You can apply a gradient to the Duotone Effect, customize the color content of the duotone—in fact, you can have a lot of fun creating color images like never before.

Step one: Find an image, open it, move into the **Guided Edit** mode, and locate **Duotone Effect** under the appropriately named **Fun Effects** section.

Step two: Interestingly, this tool offers a wide range of crop sizes to begin with: **Instagram, Facebook, Twitter,** and so on. I chose a standard square crop.

Step three: Choose a color. It doesn't matter if you are not 100% happy with the color depth or saturation because this can be changed at any step.

Step four: Use the sliders to combine the percentages of the two colors. If it's not desirable, click back and choose a new duotone combo.

Step five (opposite page): Another option in this feature is to add a shaped mask—**circle, paint splat, diagonal, or square**—to the image as an overlay, combining part original and part duotone. I skipped this and went on to save the new version.

One problem I had with this new feature was in trying to stop—I liked so many of the monotone color versions that I found it exceptionally hard to pick the best. Oh well, what a luxury.

Duotone example #2: Here's another example, a completely different type of portrait that's already been heavily edited (left). However, a single-color duotone works very well on this image.

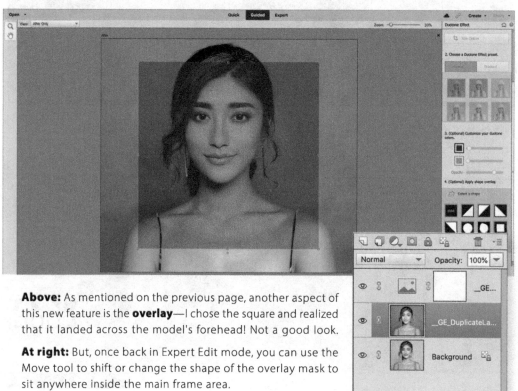

Above: As mentioned on the previous page, another aspect of this new feature is the **overlay**—I chose the square and realized that it landed across the model's forehead! Not a good look.

At right: But, once back in Expert Edit mode, you can use the Move tool to shift or change the shape of the overlay mask to sit anywhere inside the main frame area.

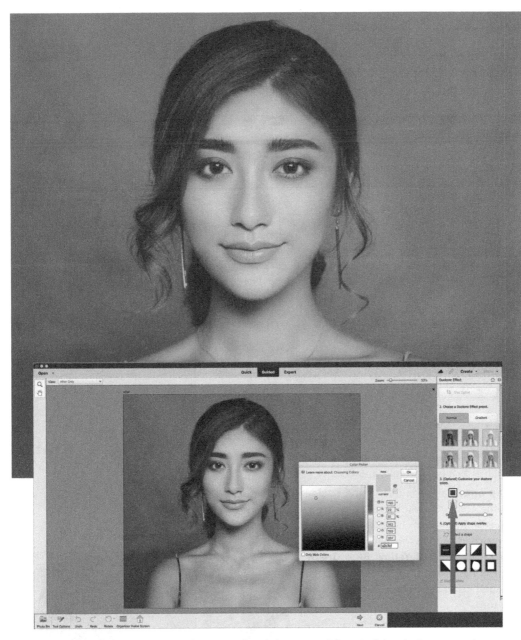

Color selection: Another nice feature is the ability to modify any of the six duotone colors on offer. Best practice would be to choose the one that fits closest to your idea of "perfection;" then, by clicking one of the squares to the left of each color slider (arrowed), you can pick another color from the **Color Picker (once picked, don't forget to click OK to activate the new color),** as well as varying its brightness—by adding more or less white and black to the combination. This is similar to the process that you'd experience if using Adobe Photoshop.

B&W Color Pop filter

Guided Edit Mode is, in this version of Adobe Photoshop Elements, a powerhouse of useful features. This one, **B&W Color Pop**, has been around for several versions—come to think of it, even some cameras have this feature as an inbuilt camera "look."

This is definitely one of the simpler **Guided Edits** on offer—it's only got four features or tools that you need to negotiate, and that makes it easy, simple, and fast.

Step one: Open the image and decide on the color you want to highlight (top screenshot, in red). I chose the yellow top of the child, as she's the main subject, but you can choose **Red**, **Yellow**, **Blue**, **Green**, or pick your own using the eye dropper if needed using the **Select Custom Color** button.

Step two: I liked the selection it made here (it was clean because there was no other yellow in the frame) so I didn't need to use the **Fuzziness** slider or the **Refine Effect** tool. I did whack in a heap more saturation, as I thought the initial knocked-back tint was, well, a bit weak. How's that for an (almost) instant visual hit!

Old Fashioned Photo filter

Black and white conversions, despite Elements having an easy-to-use **Convert to Black and White** feature (under **Enhance**), can be tricky—it's easy enough to do it, but to do it well, with a richness of tonality, takes a bit of skill. I have included this **Guided Edit** feature because it does a great job of tinting images—not just "sepia toning" but really offering a cool range of color tones that most would have never thought to create in the past. Now you can!

Step one: This first feature (outlined in red) borrows a few of the recipes from the **Convert to Black and White** tool under **Enhance** (such as **Newspaper**, **Urban**, and **Vivid**), allowing you to first off add a bit of contrast "kick" to the converted mono tones.

Step two: Adjust Tones affects the contrast—get it looking good, then move on to **Add Texture**. Most really old photographs actually have less grain and artefacts than we have now—even so, use the **Add Texture** slider to add grain/texture if you think it merits it.

Step three: Add **Saturation** (color intensity)—this adds the **Colorize** effect that you'd normally see in **Hue/Saturation**. I think this should be step two, so you can then adjust the sepia tones rather than waiting for the last step. Anyway, it produces a great result.

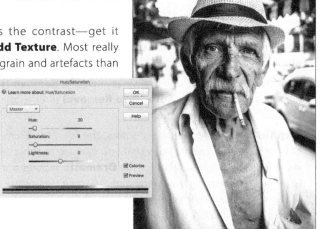

Mastering Adobe Photoshop Elements 2023

Perfect Landscape feature

This is a neat new feature to Photoshop Elements—and to be honest, I dismissed it immediately because I thought, "*OK, this is just going to be a fancy sky-brightening feature with, maybe, a diffuse filter effect.*" It really pays to check all of Elements' features in greater depth because, increasingly, you'll find some are now hosting sleek AI-driven features. This is no exception. You'll find **Perfect Landscape** in the **Guided Edit** edit menu under **Special Edits**. What does it do? This is a sky replacement tool, which is impressive on its own, so I'm a little curious as to why it has landed up being called **Perfect Landscape**. For me, "Sky Replacement" might have been a better name. Here's how it works:

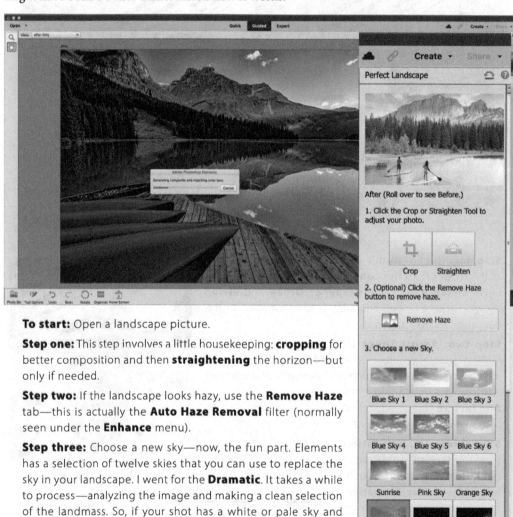

To start: Open a landscape picture.

Step one: This step involves a little housekeeping: **cropping** for better composition and then **straightening** the horizon—but only if needed.

Step two: If the landscape looks hazy, use the **Remove Haze** tab—this is actually the **Auto Haze Removal** filter (normally seen under the **Enhance** menu).

Step three: Choose a new sky—now, the fun part. Elements has a selection of twelve skies that you can use to replace the sky in your landscape. I went for the **Dramatic**. It takes a while to process—analyzing the image and making a clean selection of the landmass. So, if your shot has a white or pale sky and the landscape features snow-capped peaks, it is going to be come unstuck, as it's so hard to differentiate between similar shades of white.

Step five: Once the analysis has finished, you see how accurate, or not, the AI has been in finding a selection edge. This result was pretty good. Use the **Shift Edge** slider to expand or contract the selection to reduce, or preferably completely, hide any halo (arrowed).

Step six: Having adjusted the **Shift Edge** slider, that ugly halo has disappeared—the sky now "fits" into the landmass perfectly without a visible join. **Shift Edge** is an excellent feature. If it appears that the selection has actually grabbed some of the wrong bits of the picture, use the **Refine Edge Brush** tool (arrowed) to paint into the mask, adding or subtracting bits off of the selection until it's perfected. I had to fix a bit of mask error where the sky selection had bled into the snow on the mountain, but this was easily fixed.

Perfect Portrait feature

Elements now has three "Perfect" **Guided** edits—**Perfect Landscape**, **Perfect Pet** and **Perfect Portrait**. It's actually an amalgamation of not one, but 10 different editing tools, nicely lined up top to bottom in the panel on the right-hand side of the screen.

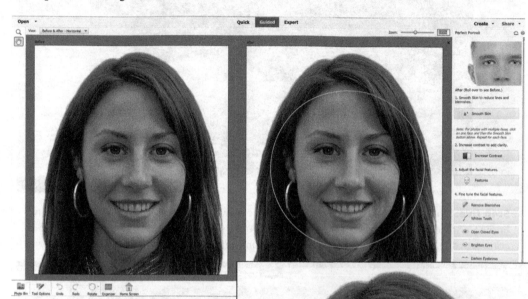

The advantage of a feature like **Perfect Portrait** is not so much that it works really well—it does—but rather that it brings all the features that you'd need to make a portrait appear perfect together in one panel. You probably won't use them all, but the relevant ones are all there in the toolbox. It's a bit similar to the toolbox a carpenter might take on a job—they're not necessarily going to use everything, but at least all situations are covered.

To use **Perfect Portrait**, open your image and run the feature (**Guided Edit**>**Special Edits**>**Perfect Portrait**). The first function to try is the **Smooth Skin** feature—as you see in the enlarged cutout (right), it might apply too much by default so reduce the effect using the slider (arrowed). Try the **Increase Contrast** feature to add a bit of "punch" to the tones (not needed in the example here).

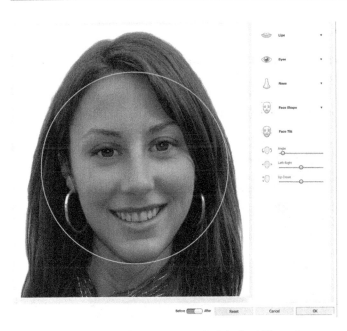

Left: Working your way down the effects list brings you to the **Features** button. This opens your portrait in the **Adjust Facial Features** utility, providing a further 19 options to modify the shape and orientation of the face. It's an awesome tool! **Remove Blemishes** uses the power of the **Spot Healing Brush:** This is perfect for removing/covering up small scratches, spots, and pimples. Works like magic.

The **Whiten Teeth** feature is a bit hit or miss. Actually, it's an auto "select and brighten" operation that's a little hard to control. In fact it's quite aggressive and often 'snaps' to select not just the teeth, but often part of the lips too, so I ignore it.

Open Closed Eyes, like Features, has been copied from the Enhance menu. Use it to replace closed eyes with eyes supplied by Adobe, or from your own images. Sounds too good to be true, but it really does work.

The **Brighten Eyes** tool is driven by the **Dodge** brush, and it also works a treat—but be careful not to overdo the effect!

Darken Eyebrows: Another excellent brush-based tool—driven by the **Burn** brush.

Add Glow: This is one of Elements' more obscure diffusion filters and, when used, can significantly lighten the face in particular. It's OK, but I thought it not vital for the example here.

Slim Down: This is a cheeky slimming tool. It simply narrows the width of the image size by a few percent. Repeat and it narrows again—so although the original proportions change the shape of the image, the subject does appear somewhat slimmer.

Perfect Pet feature

Following on from its **Perfect Portrait** and **Perfect Landscape Guided Edit** feature, Elements now sports a **Perfect Pet** mode. Don't laugh, it's actually quite good, encompassing tone changes with sophisticated retouching. Like most of Elements' **Guided** modes, it is a little limited, but it's also great fun—and fun is what editing images should be...

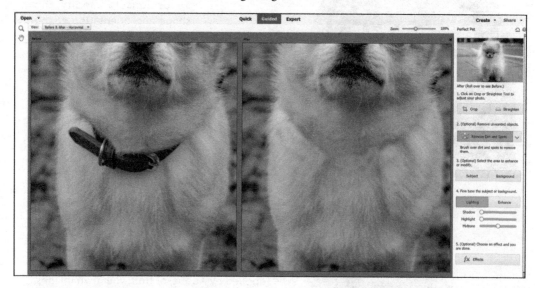

All Guided Edit features follow a step-by-step recipe—you start at the top of the list and work your way to the bottom before saving the work and moving to the next project (top, right).

After cropping and leveling the file (only if needed), move to the **Remove Dirt and Spots** function (actually **Spot Healing Brush** in disguise)—this is good for quickly removing small blemishes. I was amused to see the **Remove Collar and Leash** function—actually, this is the **Clone Stamp** tool, a very sophisticated retouching tool that enables you to copy and paste pixels from one part of the animal (that is, the fur near the collar) to cover up the collar (see *Chapter 7, Advanced Techniques: Retouching, Selections, and Text* for more on retouching tools).

Pet eye is usually greenish in color

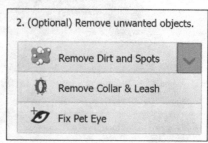

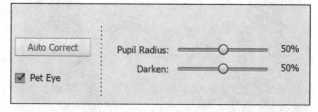

and if your pet suffers from this affliction, it can be removed, or at least concealed, using the **Fix Pet Eye** command! Click the **Fix Pet Eye** button, then carefully drag the cursor over one then a second eye—Elements autocorrects the eye color. You can fine-tune the settings using the **Pupil Radius** and **Darken** sliders. Again, it seems like black magic, but it actually works well.

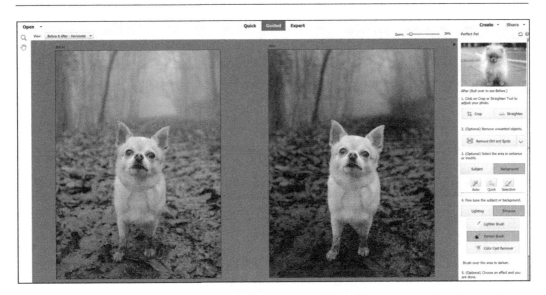

Once pet eye has been fixed, you can apply changes to the subject or to the background—Elements auto selects either with unnerving accuracy, leaving you to finish the process by choosing darker or lighter, or, as in my example here, I darkened the background, then desaturated it so it came out black and white. Great fun and simple to use...

Adjust Facial Features

This feature appeared in Elements a few versions ago. At the time, I didn't give it a second thought, but when I eventually tried it, I realized how amazing it was. Warning: your family photos might never look the same after trying this tool.

The clever **Adjust Facial Features** tool uses its AI to identify and isolate the facial area in a portrait. It isolates key facial elements, such as the eyes, nose, lips, and mouth, so they can be masked and edited separately. These sections can then be changed using a number of distortion techniques—Elements treats the pixels almost as if they were elastic, allowing you to stretch, expand, push, bend, and contract features accordingly.

Multiple faces: If there's more than one face in the snap, this is what Elements will present—a blue circle indicates the current or active face. To work on the other faces, simply click the circle to make it active, add your changes, then move on to the other faces in the line-up.

Work your way down the sliders on offer along the right-hand side of the window to improve or change the character of your subject.

I can't stress enough how effective this tool can be, provided that the portrait is taken relatively straight-on, facing the camera. Another consideration is resolution—the more pixels there are in the file, the better response and cleaner-looking final result you'll get. Images taken off the internet might also present issues, as they typically don't have enough resolution, and if there are any distractions elsewhere in the image, it might not lock onto a face and might refuse to work. When it does work, it can be great fun!

Here's a brief overview of how to get the most out of this innovative feature:

Step one: Open a suitable image (note: this works best with a **single portrait**, with the subject more or less looking directly at the camera. However, it will also work if there are multiple heads in the same shot—go from head to head, adjusting each one separately).

Step two: Choose the **Adjust Facial Features** tool (**Enhance>Adjust Facial Features**). The tool should automatically isolate the face in the picture, circling it in blue.

Step three: Use the sliders on the right-hand side of the screen to make your changes.

Step four: Click **OK** when you are happy with the edit and save the file. It's that easy!

Adjust Facial Features – Face Tilt

Since its first appearance a couple of releases ago, **Adjust Facial Features** has made its mark on the editing community. It works brilliantly to make slight adjustments to the human face—rounder eyes, thinner cheeks, and flatter-shaped eyebrows. Elements has taken the AI technology one step further with a new feature called **Face Tilt,** which you'll see at the bottom of the **Adjust** panel. Of course, like its parent **Adjust** feature, it only really works if the AI can identify a face, or faces, in the shot.

Then, using AI, and a fair bit of background selectivity and pixel manipulation, you can rotate the face area left/right, up/down, and at a rotational angle. Sounds crazy, no? I thought so, but soon discovered that it actually works.

Re-compose by warping pixels: I found this cute picture where both babies are not really looking at the camera—and, using this tool, managed to manipulate their angelic faces slightly toward the photographer.

The kid on the left-hand side was easier to persuade—while the child on the right also worked OK, but once turned, the face became very wide and fat. The mother would kill me if she saw it. I went back to the **Face Shape** option just above the **Face Tilt** controls, to make the bub lose a few pounds—and it worked a treat. The result was not quite as good as if I'd snapped them both looking down the barrel of the lens, but a significant improvement on the original nevertheless.

Image comparison: I think this was a good final result (below). Although clearly the effect is tempered severely by the quality of the raw material it's given, you couldn't get a better result using masks in the **Expert** edit mode—unless a huge amount of time was spent on retouching, something most of us don't have an excess of...

Open Closed Eyes feature

Another seemingly impossible editing feature that you'll see in Elements is its impressive **Open Closed Eyes** tool.

Sure, now I've heard it all—a software application that opens the closed eyes of your portrait subject? Well, don't laugh, it really works, and in most examples that I have tested, it works very well indeed, provided that you can find a pair of eyes that match the portrait sitter's eyes reasonably well. Why is this feature needed? If you have a bunch of portraits, but the one composition you really like has the subject blinking in it, you can use this feature to copy and paste the open eyes from another shot over the blinking eyes. You can also use it to replace one set of eyes with a second, different set of eyes. How good is that!?

Step one: Open the shot in **Quick** or **Expert** mode.

Step two: Choose the **Enhance>Open Closed Eyes** tool and wait for the utility to open in the main window (see the screenshots here).

If no replacement eyes are visible in that window, search for other portraits of that same person and bring them into the window by accessing **Folders**, the **Organizer**, or the **Photo Bin**. You can bring in any number of samples—even pictures of different people—to try, but clearly, for a sense of authenticity, you need to match the ethnicity, skin color, eye color, age, and possibly the sex of the subject to make this feature work convincingly.

Step three: Click on one of the thumbnail faces on the right-hand side of the **Open Closed Eyes** panel to see those eyes being pasted over the eyes of your subject instantly. The utility softens the edges of the selection so, providing the skin tones are roughly similar to the target, the process ends up being almost seamless. Brilliant fix!

Eyes now open: Here's a quick fix that seems to work really convincingly. I used one of the sample sets of eyes to get this result. With a bit more testing, this could be better if I'd had a wider range of samples to choose from. As with most AI-driven tools, you might run into trouble if the source (eyes) or the target portraits are not 100% clear. If the face is not looking directly at the lens, or if it is obscured by contrasty lighting or even out-of-focus objects, the auto function might refuse to cooperate, and therefore, the process might not work. Even so, this is still a terrific feature to try, especially if you love taking pictures of people!

Keyboard shortcuts

- Image Modes: **Quick/Expert Edit>Image>Mode**
- Adjust Color Curves: **Enhance>Adjust Color>Adjust Color Curves**
- Blur, Sharpen, Smudge: **Tool Bar>Enhance** (*R*)
- Eraser: **Tool Bar>Draw** (*E*)
- Smart Brush: **Tool Bar>Enhance** (*F*)
- Paint Bucket: **Tool Bar>Draw** (*K*)
- Gradient Tool: **Tool Bar>Draw** (*G*)
- Haze Removal tool—**Enhance>Haze Removal** (*Alt/Opt + Ctrl/Cmd + Z*)
- Content-aware Move tool: **Tool Bar>Modify** (*Q*)
- Recompose tool: **Tool Bar>Modify** (*W*)
- Move & Scale Object: **Guided Edit>Basics**
- Quote Graphic: Create menu
- Convert to Black and White: **Enhance>Convert to Black and White** (*Alt/Opt + Ctrl/Cmd + B*)
- Duotone Effect: **Guided Edit>Fun Edits**
- B&W Color Pop: **Guided Edit>Black and White**
- Old-fashioned photo: **Guided Edit>Fun Edits**
- Perfect Landscape: **Guided Edit>Fun Edits**
- Perfect Portrait: **Guided Edit>Fun Edits**
- Adjust Facial Features: **Enhance>Adjust Facial Features**
- Adjust Facial Features: Face Tilt: **Enhance>Adjust Facial Features**
- Open Closed Eyes: **Enhance>Open Closed Eyes**
- Moving Photos: **Enhance>Moving Photos**

Summary

In this chapter, we have explored some of Photoshop Elements' "other" features. By this I mean those features that are not part of mainstream editing but are still notable—for their ease of use, productivity, and visual impact.

By now we should all be familiar with processes such as using the Camera RAW utility, controlling brightness and contrast adjustments using **Levels**, and manipulating color intensity using the powerful **Hue/Saturation** feature.

But there's a great deal more to explore in this application, so hopefully this chapter has inspired you to look further afield—into all the additional menus, panels, and processes—and then to experiment with some of the very cool features that you will have discovered.

In the next chapter, we look forward to an adventure into the world of **graphic design**. Although this program began life as a simple JPEG photo-editing program, it's evolved into a sophisticated image editor and asset management application. What many do not know is that Elements also comes packed with a wide range of sophisticated graphic design and illustration tools. So many, in fact, that there's enough for a book on these alone.

We will be studying the benefits of working with graphics tablets and harnessing the power of the **View** menu—essential to all as well as the equally handy **Eraser Tools**. We then move on to look at how to get the most from Elements range of pens and brushes before highlighting some of the graphic department's more fun features. These include the **Cookie Cutter**, the **Color Replacement Brush**, the **Impressionist Brush** and various **texturizing effects**. But this chapter is mostly all about graphic design - learn basic freehand drawing techniques, how to include vector art into your projects, create custom greeting cards - and finally bringing it all together with **scrapbooking** projects, **custom brushes** and **photobashing** techniques. You are going to be busy!

9

Advanced Drawing, Painting and Illustration Techniques

In this chapter, we will look at some of the more *esoteric* design functions that you'll find in Elements. I use the word *esoteric* simply because these features are more graphic than *photographic*, more illustrative than *documentary*. However, as you'll see here, these features can be used to create impressive standalone designs, or they can be incorporated into your day-to-day photography projects to produce outstanding results.

As you'll see in this chapter, it's not so hard to push your experience into the field of basic graphic design—and if that's not your interest, we'll also look at some of Elements' creative brush effects, tools such as the cool **Impressionist Brush**, and even learn how to work with **custom brushes**, create **scrapbooking pages** and get into **photobashing projects**.

Topics that we will learn in this chapter:

- The View Menu
- The Eraser Tools
- Using Brushes: Controlling brush behaviour
- Brush and Pencil tools
- Cookie Cutter Tool
- Color Replacement brush
- The Impressionist brush
- Basic drawing techniques
- Working with Vector Graphics

- Vector Graphics: Custom Shape tool
- Text Graphics
- Adobe Vectors: Greeting card project
- Custom vector illustrations
- Filter FX: Texturizing and Artistic Effects
- Scrapbooking techniques
- Collages: Auto page layout
- Custom Brushes
- Technique: Photobashing
- Using a Graphics Tablet

The View menu

Before you start any design project, it's important to have **layout** and **line-up** tools at your disposal. That's mostly the job of the **View** menu. The menu repeats some of the keyboard shortcuts we've already mentioned elsewhere in this book, notably the **Zoom in** and **Zoom out** functions (*Ctrl/Cmd + +* and *Ctrl/Cmd + –*, respectively). These are important because, as a picture editor, you need to constantly go in close to retouch, then zoom out to see the global effect, then go in close again, then zoom out again, on a regular basis. Alternatively, you can use *Ctrl/Cmd + 0* (zero) to **fit the image** to the main screen—another handy shortcut. Zooming to **Print Size** will show you how large an image will print. If you have adjusted the file resolution so that it matches the output requirement (in the **Image Size** panel), this should provide accurate feedback on the finished display size.

Open the very useful **grid** directly from the **View** menu or use *Ctrl/Cmd + '*.

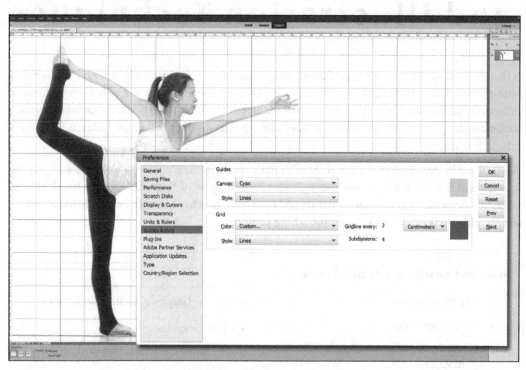

Above: In this screenshot, I am modifying my grid via the **Preferences** panel (*Ctrl/Cmd + K*). Once open, choose **Guides and Grid** tab and change the **Grid** frequency and color to suit your working requirements. Here I set it to displays in red, at 25% intervals, with four subdivisions. This produces a clearer-looking grid with an easy-to-see vertical and horizontal center line.

Rulers are self-explanatory (*Shift + Ctrl/Cmd +R*), I use them all the time—but **Guides** are less obvious. A **Guide** is a moveable line used to help position multiple elements in a document. Guides can be positioned anywhere on the main screen, vertically or horizontally—you can have as many Guides that you need for the design job. To create a Guide, move the cursor over either the vertical or horizontal ruler then click, hold and drag into the main screen, and a Guide magically appears. Need multiple Guides? Drag them off the ruler one at a time. To remove Guides, either drag them off the screen and into the ruler, or choose **View>Clear Guides**. Change Guide color via the Preferences, same as the Grid.

Tip:

When drawing a straight line, either horizontally, vertically, or at 45 degrees, do so while holding down the *Shift* key. This locks the tool into drawing on one of those three axes only, making the process of alignment that much easier and quicker.

Snap To is another handy feature, especially if you are using Elements for page layout or design and need to precisely align multiple elements (i.e. text boxes, images, or other graphic elements). Position a guide somewhere on the page, then drag each element one by one into the vicinity of the guide—provided that **Snap To** is turned on in the menu, it will "snap" or stick to the guide as if magnetic. I use this feature constantly because it works so well. If you are working on a project where positioning elements freehand is necessary, turn **Snap To** off so as to specifically stop those elements sticking to Grids or Guides.

127 Tottenham Court Road
London WC 1

In this screenshot, you can see the **Rulers** and the **Guides** (red) in action. Guides can be accessed by using this shortcut: *Ctrl/Cmd +;)* These design aids are brilliant for lining up text and image layers for precise positioning. (Note: Guides and Grids do not print.)

The Eraser tools

Before computers, graphic design studios used a range of analog drawing tools such as pens, pencils, brushes, and charcoals. They also used a range of *erasers* to remove mess, mistakes, and drawing errors. Photoshop Elements also has a range of eraser tools, the most useful being the **Eraser Tool**. Use this to remove excess pixels when blending different pixel layers together, for example. The **Eraser** Brush works with all brush tips, and if used on the **Background Layer (the bottom one in the layer stack)**, it will always erase to the background color (which will be white by default). If you are erasing on a duplicated layer, it will reveal the pixels on the layer immediately beneath it.

The **Eraser** Tool has three brush modes: **Block, Brush**, and **Pencil**—although I think the **Brush** setting is the best for most retouching tasks, as it's the softest and most controllable. The speed of the erasing process is controlled by the **Opacity** slider in the **Options Panel**. Set it to 50% and you'll have to go over the layer twice to remove all the pixels.

Background Eraser is also a useful tool because it functions based on the brightness of the pixels being clicked. Click the background and drag the cursor though the image. It should erase only those that are close in color to the initial click, leaving other colors untouched.

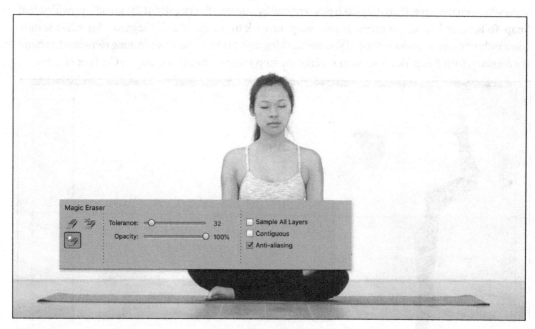

Step one: In this example, I chose to use **Magic Eraser** because the background I want to change is even in tone. All that's needed is to choose the **Magic Eraser** tool, check the **Tolerance** and **Brush** size settings, and then click the image. As **Contiguous** was not checked in the **Options Panel**, though it selected all the background, it missed the space between the woman's arms and body. An understandable mistake but easy enough to fix either by trying again with **Contiguous** checked or by holding the *Shift* key and clicking on the bits initially missed.

Use the **Tolerance** slider to increase/decrease how much latitude its color selection has. Its efficiency, like many tools in photo editing, relies on the type of file being edited as much as the capability of the tool used.

Step two: Magic Eraser, as the name might suggest, "magically" removes same-colored pixels once clicked. If the background is just a single color, it's an efficient tool. If the background is composed of many different-colored pixels, one of the other two eraser tools might do a cleaner, more accurate job.

Check the document to ensure all the correct bits have been selected. Hold the *Shift* key and click again to scoop up any missed pixels. Note that the **checkerboard pattern** indicates transparency—there are no pixels present.

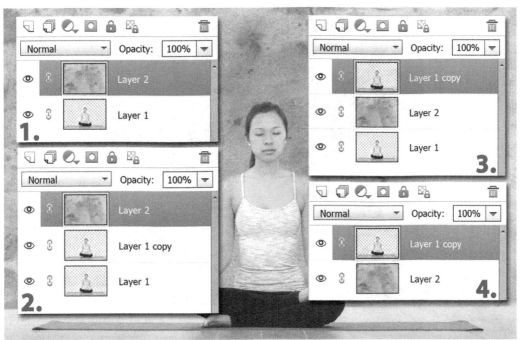

Step three: In this last step, I opened a textured wall image from my picture library and copied and pasted it into the document. It was the same resolution as the yoga image, so it pasted in at the same size above the figure (**1**). To get the background texture **behind the figure**, I had to duplicate the yoga layer (**2**), then drag the texture layer from the top to in between the two yoga layers (**3**), then delete the bottom yoga layer (**4**), as it was effectively hidden and was therefore no longer needed.

Using Brushes: Controlling Brush behavior

Though Elements is mostly a photo editing program, many of its tools rely on the use of a brush—**Dodge**, **Burn**, **Healing**, **Clone**, and **Smart** are all examples of brush-based tools.

These retouching brush tools are not the only brushes available. Elements contains a wide range of real (read 'digital') brushes used to paint, sketch, draw, and illustrate, either by brushing over an existing picture or by starting from scratch with a blank canvas.

Elements allows the user to change the characteristics of each brush—the shape, orientation, opacity, color, pressure, and appearance, which we'll look at here.

Above: With the assistance of a graphics tablet (inset), and a lot of skill, you can create a wide range of impressive illustrations using the creative tools in Photoshop Elements.

To modify your brush characteristics and behaviors, open the **Brush Settings** panel by clicking the tab on the tool **Options Panel** (arrowed).

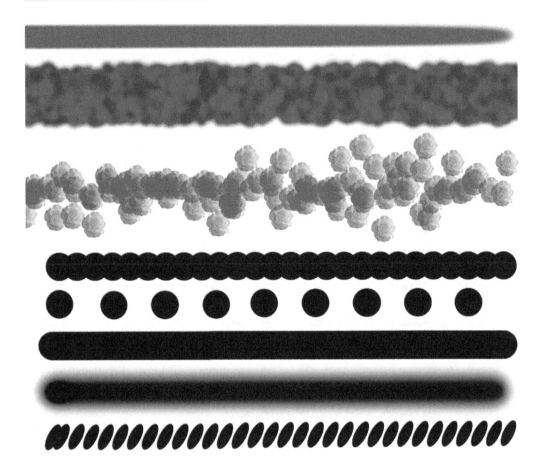

The Brush Settings panel has a bunch of adjustment terms that might sound quite alien to a photographer; if you are not sure what each does, read on, or better still, test each one to see how it affects the look of your work. Settings include (from the top):

Fade - The paint fades to nothing after a set pixel length.

Hue Jitter - This setting splits a single selected color into different hues based on that color or it mixes foreground and background colors (in this case red and blue). The higher the Scatter number the more the dots are spreads around the canvas.

Scatter - I chose a rose from the Special Effects brush collection and scattering set to 50%.

Spacing - A painted line is really a succession of closely-placed dots—increase spacing and that line breaks up into individual dots.

Hardness/Softness - A hard-edged brush has 'sharp' edges. Reduce the hardness setting to soften that edge (soft-edged brushes are perfect for seamless retouching).

Roundness - As the name suggests, changes the brush tip from round to elliptical.

Brush and Pencil tools

To get the best from this application, you really need to be adept at drawing with the mouse or a **graphics tablet**. These devices are perfect for artists and designers because they substitute a pen for the mouse—the same size and shape as a real pen (see the section on graphics tablets in this chapter).

Elements has three types of brush tool—the **Brush Tool**, the **Impressionist Brush Tool**, and the **Color Replacement Tool**:

- The **Brush** Tool looks and works like an electronic version of a paint brush: choose a color from **Color Picker**, pick a brush tip from the 300+ on offer, set the size and opacity, and draw. Instead of using **Normal**, you can paint in a different **Blend Mode**, depending on how you'd like the brush pixels to blend into the layer pixels. With skill and the right brief, artists can create impressive-looking artworks.

- **Impressionist Brush** is fun because it (sort of) clones your image and turns it into large, fuzzy brush strokes, producing what passes for an impressionist look. Broaden your impressionist style using the **Advanced** button, which provides more brush strokes, tolerance settings, and so on.

- The **Color Replacement Brush.** This relies on applying a color change effect to similar-colored pixels. So, if I want to replace blue with red, provided that all the blue pixels are the

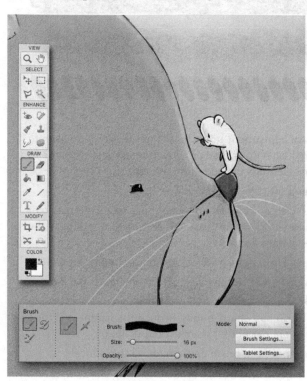

same (color) value, it will work well. But we all know that digital images are composites of different colors—so use the **Tolerance** slider to make it more or less lenient when it's making a color change. Increase the tolerance and it will apply the change to lighter and darker shades of blue. There are different brush styles, four different **Blend** modes (**Color** works best), and the **Contiguous** checkbox.

• The **Pencil** tool, alone on the **Tool Bar**, draws in much the same way as a regular pencil, with variable size, opacity, Blend Modes, and an **Auto Erase** feature (which draws the Background Color over the Foreground Color). But, unless you are a skilled artist working with a graphics tablet, it's very hard to work accurately or creatively with this tool.

The Cookie Cutter tool

The **Cookie Cutter** tool is a cropping tool that works just like a baker's cookie cutter. Drag a custom shape over your image and the cutter removes any pixels that are not inside the cutter shape - there are hundreds of shapes to choose from.

Some of the cutting shapes are great fun—I particularly like the rough-edged photo **Crop Shapes** because they produce a completely different photo edge from the normal standard rectilinear photo edge.

Above: Here's a classic **Crop Shape** effect. You'll find the Cookie Cutter on the Tool Bar, sharing space with the regular **Crop Tool** and the **Perspective Crop** tool (a feature that combines cropping with perspective correction).

Choose your cutter shape, then click and drag somewhere in the image. This takes a bit of practice, both in the dragging action and image choice but, as long as you have not pressed the OK (green) button at the edge of the cropping marquee to action the process, it can be repositioned and re-shaped as much as needed.

Right: This is another **Cookie Cutter** shape—a heart. This tool is excellent for scrapbookers and all the family.

Color Replacement brush

You could have a lot of fun with this feature—applying the color change effect to similar-colored pixels so that Elements covers the area with a color wash. How much it changes is mostly influenced by the **Tolerance** slider.

Main image: I repainted the tops of the three women in just a few minutes with the **Color Replacement** tool. I thought that this was a pretty good result.

So, for example, if I want to replace blue with red, provided that all the blue pixels are the same value, the tool works well—but we all know that life in the digital editing realm is never like this, so that's why there's the **Tolerance** slider. This makes Elements a bit more or less sensitive when it's applying a color change. Increase the tolerance and it will apply the change to lighter and darker shades of blue. You have different brush styles to choose from: four different **Blend Modes** (I find **Color** works best), and the inevitable **Contiguous** or **Discontiguous** checkboxes.

The Impressionist Brush

Impressionist Brush is fun as it *sort of* copies your image and paints it directly back into the canvas with large, fuzzy brush strokes, producing something that passes for an impressionist *look*. You can broaden that *look* using its **Advanced** button, which takes you to a range of other brush stroke options, **Tolerance** settings, and more. I'm not sure what *Edouard Manet* or *Claude Monet* might have thought of this process, but with the right image plus textured inkjet paper to print on, the effects can be quite splendid.

I generally set **Impressionist Brush Tip** to a large size when painting the background, but make the brush smaller when working on the details—otherwise, the photo will just look out of focus or blurred. Another technique is to duplicate the layer first, apply the impressionist brush to the top layer, and then, with the **Eraser** tool (set to a low opacity of around 20%), carefully erase some of the top layer to reveal the *real* image beneath.

Basic drawing techniques

Now, let's learn a few drawing basics that anyone can achieve, starting by using a neat point-to-point drawing technique to create a **perfect square or rectangle** using any of the brush-based tools in Elements. In fact, this technique also works with all Elements retouching and drawing tools.

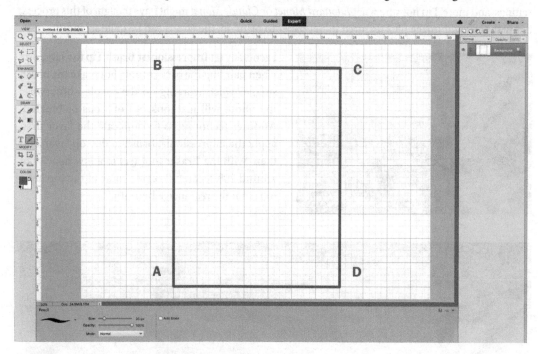

Step one: Turn on the **Grid** (**View>Grid** or *Ctrl/Cmd* + ').

Step two: Choose a drawing brush (such as the **Pencil** or **Brush** tool).

Step three: Mouse-click once on point **A**.

Step four: Hold *Shift* and mouse-click point **B**. The pencil line joins point **A** to **B** in a straight line.

Step five: Hold *Shift* and mouse-click point **C**. The pencil line joins point **B** to **C** in a straight line.

Step six: Hold *Shift* and mouse-click point **D**. The pencil line joins point **C** to **D** in a straight line.

Final step: Hold *Shift* and mouse-click point **A**. The pencil line joins point **D** back to point A.

(Note that this point-to-point drawing technique works with all the **Eraser**, **Sharpen**, **Smudge**, and **Blur brushes**—as well as the **Burn**, **Dodge**, and **Sponge** tools).

Now, let's learn how to draw the **perfect circle** using the **Elliptical Shape** tool and the **Elliptical Marquee Selection** tools.

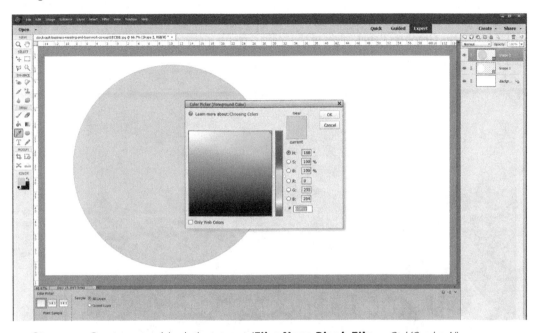

Step one: Create a new blank document (**File**>**New**>**Blank File** or *Ctrl/Cmd + N*).

Step two: Choose the **Elliptical Marquee Selection tool**—normally, you'd click and drag in the new canvas to draw the shape, but it's hard to get it precisely symmetrical dragging this freehand.

Step three: Hold the *Shift* key, then click and drag in the canvas. The *Shift* key locks the proportions off, giving you a perfect circle.

Step four: To add color, I picked the **Paint Bucket** tool, chose a suitable color from the **Color Picker** (as shown above) off the **Tool Bar**, and clicked once inside the marquee. You can also recolor a selection using the **Edit > Fill Selection** command. Also note that you though can make a perfect circle using the **Ellipse** tool—it cannot be color filled using the Paint Bucket, you must choose the color before drawing the circle or ellipse first.

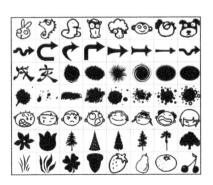

Custom shapes: If you are a bit challenged with a pencil or brush, you'll be pleased to read that Elements has a huge range of vector shapes located under the **Custom Shape** tool—everything from a plain circle to Chinese characters, animals, ragged photo edges, and much more. (There are 548 to choose from—all are arranged under different subheadings, such as animals, arrows, banners, crop shapes, and symbols.)

Working with Vector Graphics

Photoshop Elements is not Adobe Illustrator by any stretch of the imagination, but it does contain a reasonably good range of **graphic elements** that can be added to images to enhance their design—these are located in the **Graphics Panel** (right of the main screen).

The illustration above was made from the range of (free) graphics available through Photoshop Elements—encompassing backgrounds, frames, symbols, and images. All elements have to be downloaded from the Adobe servers first, but as they are vectors, file sizes are small so it takes no time at all.

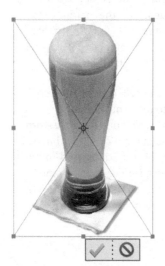

At left: Vector graphics can be reduced or enlarged significantly without loss of quality—just grab a corner handle and drag in or out. These graphics fall into the following groups:

- Graphics that can be added to existing semi-automated creative projects, such as **Photo Book** and **Greeting Card**, found under the **Create** menu. These features include a big array of downloadable content ranging from **backgrounds** and **picture frames** to **clip art** objects and preset **text styles**.

- Then there are those that are designed to add benefit to single images—graphics such as **text boxes**, **copyright logos**, **arrows**, **lines**, **speech bubbles**, and **shapes**.

Vector Graphics: Custom Shape tool

Elements' graphics are all **vectors**, which means that they are made up from a mathematical formula rather than pixels. Because of this it means they are **infinitely scalable**, compared to a pixel-based image that can only be enlarged by around 50% before it begins to look soft.

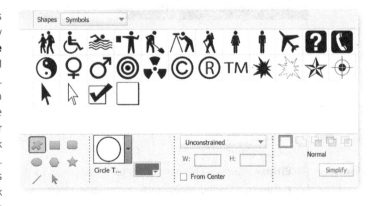

Copyright stamp: Here's the perfect example of how a simple **Custom Shape** graphic can be used. Here, I chose the copyright stamp. Use this stamp when posting your work in the public domain to deter theft or if submitting work to a potential new client. The copyright symbol was added to a separate blank layer (panel inset, main pic above) then saved as a Photoshop file, thus preserving the two layers. To send this to a client, I'd save the file as a JPEG, in which case, Elements automatically flattens all layers into one background layer, making it impossible to remove the stamp.

Text graphics

Adding text to an image using the text tab on the Graphics Panel is as easy as select, drag and drop (into your open image). You do have to finalise the process by clicking in the Your Text Here sentence to add your own words, but the font, color, bevel, shadow, and—in some cases—texture are already loaded into the design. It's so much easier and quicker than doing using the more traditional Type tool on the Tool Bar.

Aside from the vector-filled **Custom Shape** tool we looked at on the previous pages, its Options Panel offers seven other shapes that can be useful in a number of different applications. These tools include:

Rectangle shape - Drag in the canvas area to draw a square or rectangle. It automatically makes its own layer to sit on. Its Opacity can be adjusted in the Layer Panel. (Double-click layer to open Color Picker to change color).

Rounded Rectangle - Similar to above, but the shapes have rounded corners—it's a style thing.

Ellipse - Similar characteristics to above—use to draw circles or ellipses.

Polygon - Similar characteristics to above, but polygon shaped.

Star - Similar characteristics to above, but star shaped.

Line - Click, hold, and drag to draw a line. Adjust thickness, color, and length via the Options Panel. Can be converted into a neat **arrow graphic**.

Shapes can be helpful to photographers and designers, for example by adding a rectangular shape under text to make it more legible, or by using the **Line** tool to direct the viewer to salient points in an illustration. It's not PowerPoint, neither is it Adobe Illustrator, but these tools provide an excellent starting point for those wanting to take their photographic design into a significantly more commercial arena.

Adobe Vectors: greeting card project

As we have already seen, Photoshop Elements comes packed with **vector clip art** that you can use in your various projects. Actually, these assets are not in the Elements application when it's first downloaded, but every time you pick a vector item from the **Graphics** panel, it will automatically download from Adobe. Since these are vector graphics, their size is tiny, so they take no time to download. Vectors are made from mathematical formulae and not pixels. Photographs are made up of individual pixels, so they take up a lot more space.

To appreciate just how easy vectors are to work with, let's make a **custom greeting card**:

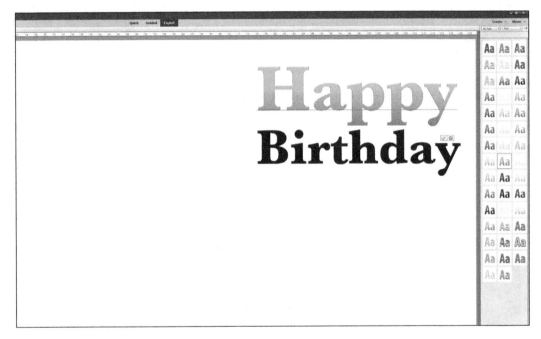

Step one: To make your own custom greeting card, create a new document (**File>New>Blank Document**). Before you start the design process, I recommend that you search for envelopes that match your cards. It's annoying if you go ahead and design a card and then find that no one makes envelopes to match the size of the card (yes, it's happened to me a couple of times). Find an envelope, measure its proportions, and create a new document that's twice its width or height, depending on whether you want the fold line at the top, or on the left-hand edge of the card.

Step two: You can add some nice preset text effects using the **Text** sub menu in the **Graphics** panel. Double-clicking the text style from the listing on the right-hand side immediately adds it to the document open on the page as `Your Text Here`. Click inside this text to type in your own greeting.

Step three: As an example, I chose **Backgrounds** from the drop-down menu, which is at the top right in the **Graphics** panel, and chose one of the thumbnails to automatically download and install it into my document (one problem I have with this otherwise good feature is that it's hard to see what the design looks like. But then, because it's only a small file, you can try one, and if it's no good, undo and try more).

Step four: If textured backgrounds are not your thing, you can also drag entire designs, plus picture window frames, into your custom artwork. It's a bit hit and miss because some of the designs look different once they're in place. If this happens, undo, and try another style before saving and printing it on your local inkjet or laser device. I chose a picture frame to slot under the **Happy Birthday** text—then added a picture in the space provided to further personalize the design.

Custom vector illustrations

Photoshop Elements has an amazing range of **vector tools**—shapes, text, and more. The beauty of these forms is that, since they are essentially made up of nothing more than a mathematical formula, they occupy very little space, and can be resized to any size with no loss of quality.

In these illustrations, I am making a design for a book on Japanese food, experimenting with a custom font (**Paper Cuts**, downloaded for this project), as well as vector shapes as text boxes, plus a range of special effects, such as **Drop Shadows**.

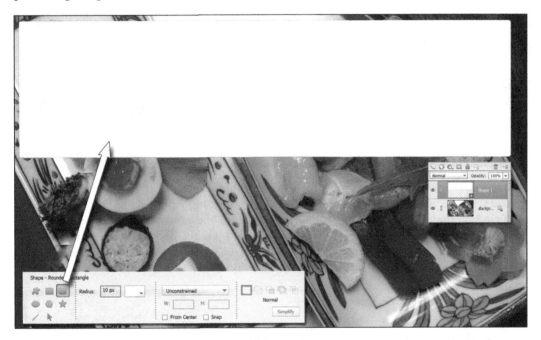

Step one: In this example, I'm using scalable vectors to create a simple page design for a book on Japanese food. I have the main image open and have chosen a rounded edge panel as a starting point.

Choose **Custom Shapes** from the **Tool Bar**, select the **Rounded Rectangle Tool** (*U*), then click, hold, and drag into the image to add this vector shape to the document. It will go into its own layer automatically. Note that it doesn't matter whether this is appearing at the right proportion or size because it can be resized at any time.

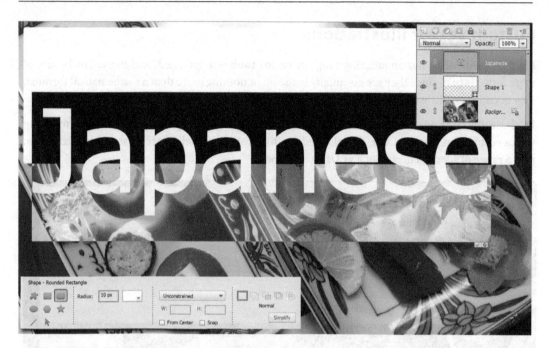

Step two: I added the first text layer. There are now three layers in this file: the background food shot, the vector shape layer, and the type layer at the top. At this stage, the font is just the default font. I changed the default font to a custom one called Paper Cuts (from a free site called `www.dafont.com`), which suits the Japanese theme. Note that the **Rounded Rectangle** tool acts like a text box, into which text can be typed. This can be rather restrictive, especially if you're using a non-standard font, as I was here.

Step three: In this instance, I created the new type layer by clicking in the main image away from the **Rectangular** panel, then dragged it to the top, ensuring that it was independent of the vector panel beneath it.

Step four: I duplicated both text and vector layers. This is a handy shortcut—by duplicating these layers, I don't have to go back to the **Tool Bar**, select the **Custom Shape** tool, choose the **Rounded Rectangle** tool, and draw another shape or text layer. It's quicker to duplicate what you already have and then adapt the duplicate.

Step five: I've dragged both newly duplicated layers to the bottom of the page using the **Move** tool, and with the **Type** tool, edited the copied text layer so that it reads **Kaiseki** (an exquisitely presented traditional Japanese multi-course lunch or dinner). This process is much faster than trying to create a new rounded rectangle panel plus a new type layer.

Step six: To make the design more retro, I transformed the rectangular shapes. *Ctrl/Cmd + T* puts the vector layer into **Transform** mode (confirmed by the appearance of corner handles around the shape). Right-click inside the transform box to access the menu to change from **Scale** to **Distort**, **Skew**, or **Perspective**. I used **Distort** because it allows you to drag one corner only—which I did to reshape the rectangular proportions, as you can see below.

Step seven: I duplicated the vector and text layer one more time to add the third text component to the design. Double-clicking the vector layer thumbnail brings up the **Color Picker**, allowing you to add any color you like to that panel:

Step eight: Adding color to the text is a slightly lengthier process. Select the text first, then choose a color from the **Options** panel. Or click on the **Color Picker** and add a color from there.

Finishing off: In the final stage, I added a small black drop shadow to the three text elements on their separate layers, just to lift them very slightly off the background color. Drop shadows are always a good feature to use if the text is not 100% legible—you'll find these features located in the **Styles** panel.

Vector graphics – key points

- Infinitely scalable, with no loss of clarity
- Contain smoother edges than pixel-based images
- Small file sizes—fast to save and download from the Internet
- Excellent for web use
- Excellent for photo books, illustrations, school projects, and much more

Filter FX: Texturizing & Artistic Effects

Photoshop Elements has a staggering range of **filter effects**, so many it's often hard to know where to start or stop. Some filters are quite obscure and seemingly hard to use—possibly because they are legacy features from years ago. You'll also discover that while some, like the **Mosaic Tiles** filter (demonstrated below) get a bit lost in all the picture detail, others work quite dramatically. To make the most of these filters here's some working advice:

- Consider the end product. Some filters look good onscreen, but once printed the effect might be lost. One solution is to increase/decrease the filter intensity and test again.

- Intense filter effects can flatten the contrast. After applying, try using **Brightness and Contrast** or **Levels** (*Ctrl/Cmd + L*) to inject contrast back to the image.

- Sometimes it's more effective to increase both the contrast and color saturation before adding a filter effect to counteract the softening effect some filters create.

- I get the most from filters that can be merged or blended back in the original image, thus creating a mix of real and effect (illustrated here).

- Choose simple compositions for best results.

Above: Under the Texturizer menu, you'll find six different patterns to choose from (this one is called **Mosaic Tiles**). Though quite effective, at certain resolutions the effect is lost and replaced by a drop in contrast and a loss of detail. This is common with many of the filters on offer. Adding color and contrast before or after the filter effect is applied can make it appear better. Though, with this filter, the size of the effect (size of tiles, depth of grout, etc.) has to be perfect for the viewing size. This means you might have to redo the filter a few times before getting it to display at its best for your end product.

Above: This is quite a simple picture, two Balinese dancers, so the filter (**Palette Knife**) does a good job of blurring reality. As you can see in the inset picture, I have cranked all three sliders to the maximum.

Below: Another nice graphic effect, **Fresco**, adds drama to the tone, although it is much darker than the original so you might have to add some brightness back into the frame.

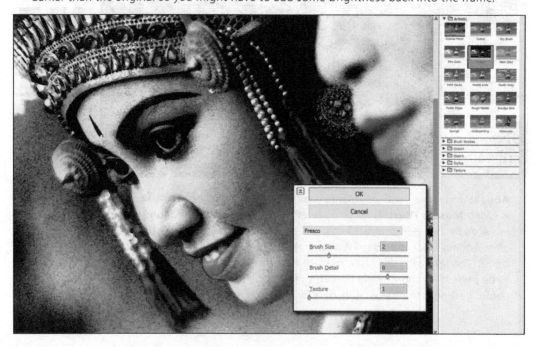

Above: My aim with this demonstration is to show how effective a partial filter effect can be in highlighting other parts of an image. Here's what I did to make the picture you see opposite:

Step One: Open your photo.

Step Two: Choose a nice diffusing filter effect. Apply to image and repeat if more diffusion is needed. I used two different filters in this example.

Step Three: Making sure you have the top layer active (highlighted in blue), pick up the **Eraser Brush** (*E*) on the **Tool Bar**, set the **Opacity** (speed that this erases) to about 25% and, with a soft-edged brush, start removing the pixels around the woman's face. As you do this it reveals the original photo in the background. This is really a **Pseudo layer masking effect** (see *Chapter 6, Advanced Techniques: Transformations, Layers, Masking, and Blend Modes*) but can be most effective in producing a mix of reality and graphic effects.

At right: Another neat way to work with filter effects is to blend a filtered image (on the top layer) into a non-filtered image (on the background

layer. In this example I added a strong **Charcoal** filter to the top layer then swapped the Layer Blend Mode from **Normal** to **Overlay** to produce this strong graphic effect.

Scrapbooking techniques

Scrapbooking, the art of combining photos, clip art, found objects, text, textures, backgrounds, and random objects to tell a story, is both great fun as well as being extremely creative. And it's a cinch to achieve using Photoshop Elements.

So, how do you get started?

Here are the skills needed:

- Adding basic tonal edits to selected photos (i.e. **Auto Smart Fix**, **Levels**)

- Cutting bits out of photo using one of the selection tools (**Magic Wand** and **Quick Selection Brush**).

- Pasting image elements into a master page (Basic copy and paste)

- Sourcing (free) clip art

- Adding text to the document

- Changing image shapes (**Transformation**)

- Manipulating Layers

Collages: Auto Page Layout

If you want a quick result don't go past this excellent Elements feature that you'll find under the **Create>Photo Collage** menu. All that's required to arrange a collection of images across a page is a bunch of photos and one of the templates displayed on the right hand side of the **Organizer/Editor>Create>Photo Collage** page.

Cut and Paste Technique

Being able to select a part of an image and place it into another image before resizing it to fit artistically is a fundamentally important part of picture creation. Providing the image 'bits' are easy to select, the process is quite easy. Let's have a go:

Step One: Open an image file and create a new page (**File>New Blank Document**) to your required size.

Step Two: Depending on the complexity of the image, choose an appropriate selection tool: **Magic Wand** or **Selection Brush** would be my first choice.

Step Three: Click-draw over the object you want to copy. Note **All** selection tools can be combined, so if you start off with the **Magic Wand** and then feel that the **Lasso** tool might be better, just swap tools and hold the **Shift** key down to **Add** your initial selection to the new selection (you can also choose the **Add to Selection** mode from the **Options Panel**, at right).

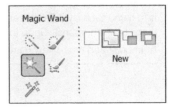

Step Four: Fine tune your selection by using the **Adding to Selection** or **Subtract from Selection** options.

Step Five: Happy with the selection? If it's a hard edged object (i.e. masking tape) copy the content of the selection (**Edit>Copy** or *Ctrl/Cmd + C*), open your new document file, and paste the selected contents into it (**Edit>Paste** or *Ctrl/Cmd + V*). If the selected object is soft-edged, consider adding a small **Feather** (softness) to the edge of the selection before copying (**Select>Feather**).

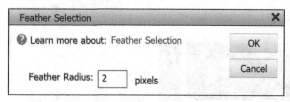

If you think you will use a selected asset again, it's a good idea to save it as a separate file so you don't have to reselect it each time it's needed. Do this after copying the selection by creating a new file (**File>New>Blank File**). Ignore the size dialog panel (i.e. click **OK**) then paste the content of your copied selection into it (**Edit>Paste** or *Ctrl/Cmd + V*) then save it with a memorable name for later use.

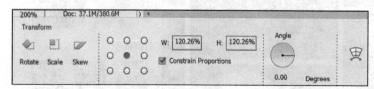

Step Six: Depending on the resolution difference between the source and target files, your pasted content might be too large or small.

This is easily fixed using the **Transform** command. Choose **Image>Transform>Free Transform** (or *Ctrl/Cmd + T*), then grab one of the small 'handles' that appear in the image corners and drag in or out depending on whether you want to shrink or enlarge the file. Clicking the green check mark (lower right hand side of the **Transform** box) executes the shape change.

Step Seven: Mouse over the outside of a corner handle to go into **Rotate** mode to swivel the entire image where needed.

Step Eight: Save the file—each time you paste an image into the master document, it automatically makes a **new layer**, thus retaining its editability. When saved, it will automatically default to the Photoshop format (`.psd`) unless you specifically want to use Tiff (`.tif`) files (which also preserve the layer integrity). Move on to the next copy-and-paste operation.

Naming Layers

Sometimes adding multiple assets into a single document can be confusing. One technique that helps is to name each layer. This is particularly useful if the object on that layer is small so it can't be seen easily in the Layer thumbnail. Go to the layer in question, double-click in the text field to the right of the image thumbnail, and type a new name into the layer.

Assets, Assets, Assets

Once you start creating your own photo fantasies it's a good idea to build up a library of assets—those images that are useful shared across a range of different projects—from background textures to water splats, brush marks, masking tape, and much more.

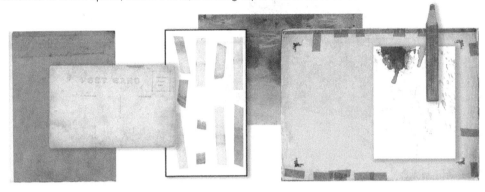

Saving Assets with Transparent Backgrounds

Often, you might need an object to have empty space around its edges like this old postcard scan I downloaded from a free art site. It has a cream background which I want to remove. Here's how it is done:

Step One: Open the photo and duplicate the layer (**Layer 1 copy**).

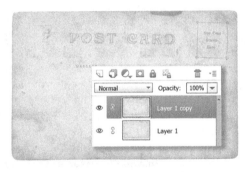

Step Two: Using an appropriate selection tool, select the object in question. (Sometimes it's easier/quicker to select the background if it's plain like with this example, in which case ignore Step Three).

Step Three: Choose **Select>Inverse**—this command flips your selection from the object over to everything else but the object.

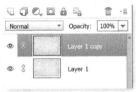

Step Four: Press the *Delete* key. This removes all those pixels in the flipped selection. (You can just make out the chequerboard pattern around the post card in the top layer.)

Step Five: Before saving the file, delete the base layer—you'll now see just the postcard in the file with a chequerboard surround, indicating no pixels or transparency. Save this as a Photoshop (`.psd`) file to protect this transparency or, save it as a PNG (`.png`) file—these are smaller than Photoshop files, and are perfect for scrapbooking as they preserve background transparency.

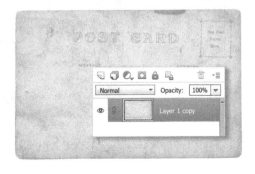

Mastering Adobe Photoshop Elements 2023

Design Your Own Scrapbook Pages

Once you are familiar with the select, copy, paste and transform regime, designing your own scrapbook pages should be relatively easy. Let's look at the steps involved in making the first page:

Step One: I suggest you locate your assets for the first page and open them in the **Expert Edit Mode**. Then create your Master page (**File>New>Blank Document**). A typical scrapbook format is 12 x 12 inches (that's 304mm x 304mm). **Above:** With the master page highlighted in the main edit window, click and then drag/push an image thumbnail from the Photo Bin at the base of the page into the main window. Once done, resize it using the **Transform** command (**Image>Transform>Free Transform** or *Ctrl/Cmd + T*). Click **OK** and move on.

Step Two: Repeat this process with all your other photos, background and any other other assets being used. Use the **Move Tool** (*V*) to Transform and reposition/resize everything to your satisfaction.

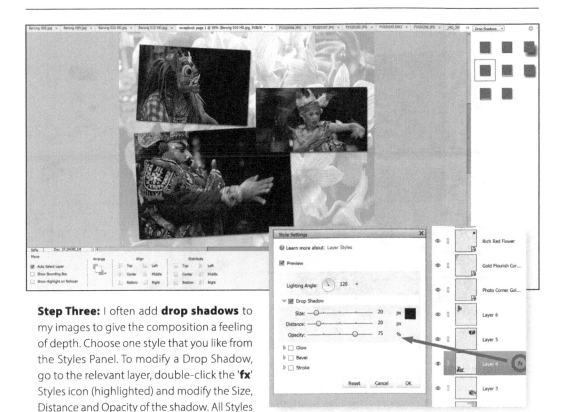

Step Three: I often add **drop shadows** to my images to give the composition a feeling of depth. Choose one style that you like from the Styles Panel. To modify a Drop Shadow, go to the relevant layer, double-click the **'fx'** Styles icon (highlighted) and modify the Size, Distance and Opacity of the shadow. All Styles can be edited in this Style Settings panel.

Using Supplied Assets

Most people I demonstrate Photoshop Elements to have never fully explored its massive range of **clip art assets**—understandable, I guess, if you only edit photos. But for scrapbookers, this asset library is both huge and very handy. Here I am going to use one of Elements' many backgrounds to add some texture and character to the scrapbook master page. To grab a background, first bring up the Graphics Panel either from the Window drop-down menu or by clicking the Graphics tab, at the bottom right of the Panels stack.

Use one of the two drop-down menus at the top of the Graphics Panel to select Backgrounds, and then simply drag a thumbnail into the main image. You might have to wait a few seconds as it is downloaded from Adobe. If it's not the right size simple simply Transform it to a new size. Easy!

Further assets:

While looking through the **Graphics Panel**, you might also download things like text panels, name plates, embellishments, edge filigree art, shapes—you name it, the range is staggering— enough for most avid scrapbookers. And if you need something a bit different you can always search online as there are a lot of very good sites giving away loads of free stuff (always exercise caution when downloading from unknown sources!).

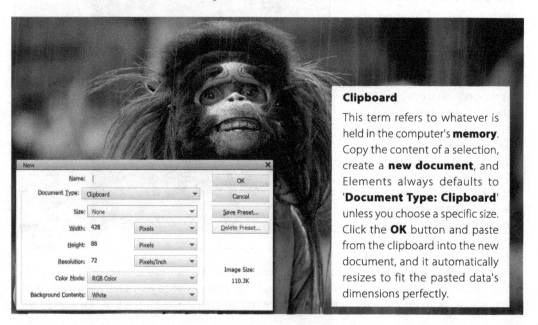

Clipboard

This term refers to whatever is held in the computer's **memory**. Copy the content of a selection, create a **new document**, and Elements always defaults to '**Document Type: Clipboard**' unless you choose a specific size. Click the **OK** button and paste from the clipboard into the new document, and it automatically resizes to fit the pasted data's dimensions perfectly.

Custom brushes

Readers might be a little surprised to learn that Elements can be customized with a range of features, from third-party plugin software to custom brushes.

A custom brush is a tiny piece of software that describes the shape of a brush—it might be a traditional artist's style brush or it might be a brush tip made from a picture, as you'll see here. There are hundreds of (free and paid) brushes available online for download. Why would you bother? As there are more than 300 brushes already in Elements, I think you'd need to be after a very specific brush type to justify an online search. But, as mentioned, some brushes are made from pictures and it's this fact that opens up an entirely new set of options.

The following illustrations describe the process of looking for, locating, loading, and then using custom brushes to enhance your images. Sometimes, this might just be the addition of something small—a tiny cloud in an otherwise cloudless sky—or, at the other end of the scale, something more dramatic, such as lightning bolts striking the Earth.

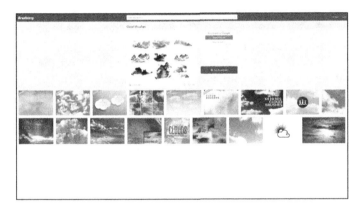

I often use a site called Brusheezy.com as it has some fantastic **free brushes**—plus it seems to be 100% reliable (although please always be careful about exactly what you download off the internet!). This is a partial screenshot taken off the website after searching for "cloud" brushes. There are dozens to choose from.

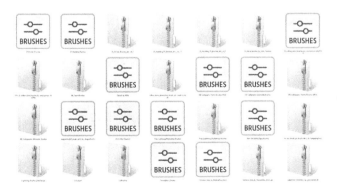

Left: This is the contents of my computer's **Downloads** folder—I download a lot of different brush sets to experiment with! Here, you can see that some are in zipped folders waiting to be used, while the black and white icons named **BRUSHES** are the unzipped .abr **format** brush sets waiting to be loaded into Elements for use in a project.

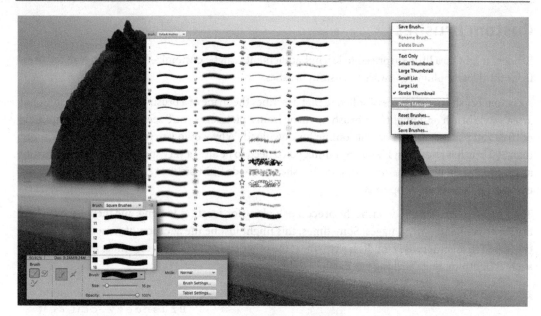

Step one: Make your search for "free Photoshop brushes" online. Most are designed for Photoshop—but they seem to work perfectly with Elements. Choose a sample, hit the download button, and note that it downloads into your downloads folder (Mac or PC).

Step two: Choose the **Brush tool** from the **Tool Bar** and from the brush style pop-up menu, click the tiny icon in the top right of the pull-out panel. In the illustration above, I have imposed the full brush panel, complete with a pop-out menu (upper right). You can choose **Load Brushes...** from this menu or, as shown here, import new brushes via the **Preset Manager** (see below).

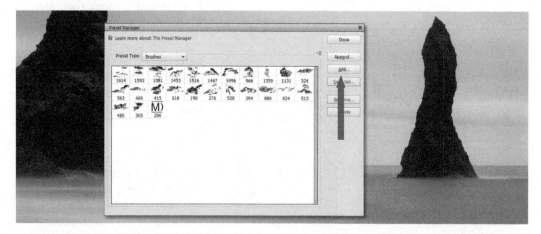

Step three: This is **Preset Manager** (it holds and manages all Brushes, Swatches, Gradients, Styles, Patterns, and Effects). To import a new brush, press **Add** (arrowed), navigate to the **Downloads** folder, find your newly downloaded brush file, and click **Open**. It loads into this window. No need to do anything else—but you can rename brushes, or entire brush sets, from this panel and delete those that you don't like or don't think you'd ever use in order to simplify your (growing) collection.

Step four: These cloud brushes are made from photos (of clouds) scaled down in size, rendered black and white, and saved in a special `.abr` file format using Photoshop. Note that brushes can also be made in Elements:(**Edit**>**Define brush from Selection)-** but this is quite a complex process especially if you are time-poor. There are enough free brushes available to keep the average enthusiast busy for years. The installed cloud brushes are large (brush width is denoted in pixels displayed under the brush thumbnail). These can be made smaller or larger, as is done with any brush in Elements, either by changing the pixel width in the **Tool Options** panel, or by tapping the left and right square brackets (smaller/larger). If you click and drag, as you would when creating a brush stroke, the cloud image drags across the canvas, creating a smeared line, which isn't what's wanted here. Click once in the picture to add a single image, not a brush stroke. Here, a single click has placed a cloud image over my seascape. The cloud is realistic but its positioning is not. (You can also add a cloud to a new (blank) layer so it can be repositioned easily.)

Step five—try another brush from the brush set: In this example, the selected cloud brush is smaller than the previous illustration so the single cloud appears to fit neatly between the two rock stacks, exactly where you might expect to find a cloud—in the sky. In this example, I reduced the opacity of the brush slightly (to 85%) before clicking in the picture to make it blend better with the tones in the original sky.

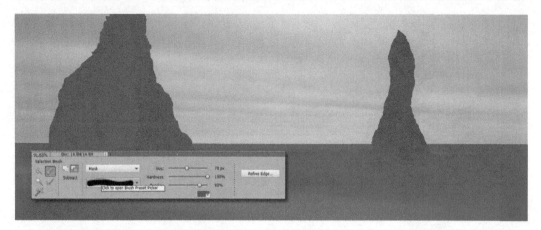

Step six: One way to make this *fake* cloud appear more realistic is to **integrate it** behind the subject—in this example, behind the two dark rocks.

Because the sky was pale in the original, I can easily select it using the **Magic Wand** tool. Doing so means that if I now stamp my cloud brush into that sky area, the image will only appear in the sky, not on top of the dark rocks sticking up into the scene. This is because they are protected by the selection (this screen grab shows the extent of the selection in (red) **Mask** mode). **Mask** mode in Elements is the same as Quick Mask in Adobe Photoshop and is a terrific way of checking the accuracy of the selection. The red mask can also be edited using a brush to extend the mask or with the eraser brush tool so that you can trim bits off it.

Below: With the final cloud stamp in position behind the selection, the finished image looks 100% more realistic—effectively created with just one brush click!

Technique: Photobashing

Photobashing is a relatively new term which applies to the art of fast and effective illustration—blending (compositing) photos with clip art, 3D assets, paint techniques, backgrounds, textures, and more. Typically, photobashing is used to prepare concept art for a client prior to commissioning a job, or to follow how a project is developing. Photobashing is used extensively within the game development market where the 'look' and feel of a scene, for example, needs to be extremely accurate before it can be translated into a 3D environment.

It's therefore handy to be able to produce a quick result by employing existing images and textures, rather than having to create a full image or storyboard which might take hours to physically draw from scratch.

The trick with this technique is in being able to blend or composite your various elements so the finished result appears natural, and of course this applies at all levels of expertise. Scrapbookers tend to spend little or no time matching lighting, resolution, color, and contrast between their picture elements—that's the 'look' of a scrapbook whereas, for photobashers, it's just the opposite.

Here's what you need to get photobashing:

- A good personal image library
- Access to royalty-free stock images, textures and backgrounds
- An eye for lighting: direction, color and contrast
- An understanding of: cut and paste, layers, masking and selection tools
- Experience using the Burn and Dodge Brush Tools
- Experience using the various Brush Tools

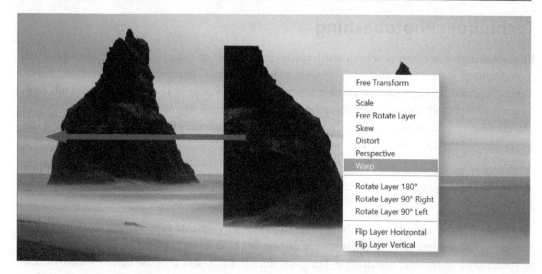

Step One: Possibly the hardest part of photobashing is selecting the right images to play with. Check the lighting direction, image contrast, and resolution for each image. In this example I chose an ocean scene with relatively low contrast. Using the **Magic Wand Tool**, I selected the large rock stack (easy selection as it's mostly black), then copied and pasted it back into the same canvas before pushing it off the edge of the frame to the left. Make extensive use of the Transform command (menu inset). To make the ocean stack blend into the sea better, I softened its base by dragging a fuzzy-edged **Eraser Brush** (set to 25% opacity) across the base several times. This process 'nibbles' away some of the pixels, leaving a more convincing soft edge. Unless you know exactly what you are doing with a project, consider working with **Layer Masks**; their non-destructive nature make them ideal for this kind of illustrative work.

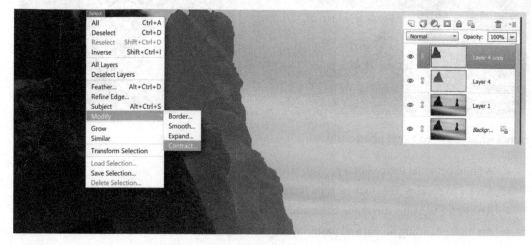

Tip: When making a selection, especially around irregular objects, try shrink-wrapping the selection (i.e. by a pixel or two) using Elements' **Select>Modify>Contract** feature (If you have selected the background, then use **Select>Modify>Expand**). Another trick is to give the selection a tiny (soft-edged) **Feather** (one or two pixels only) to slightly blur the selection line (**Select>Feather**).

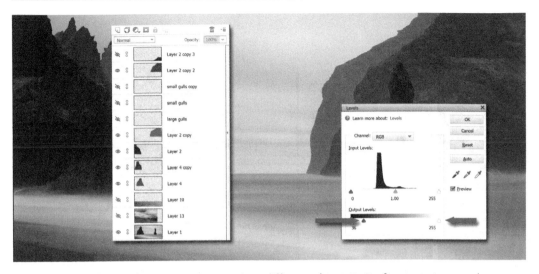

Step Two: When splitting an image up into different elements it often pays to copy layers; here I have selected both ocean stacks, copied them, then changed their shapes using the **Transform>Distort** and the **Transform>Warp** command.

Step Three: To give the composite a sense of depth, I used the **Levels** tool to lower the contrast on the elements at the back of the scene, going on the basis that the further away something is, the fainter it appears.

Step Three: Time to start importing new elements. Here's a new ocean pasted into the canvas—it needs to be dragged down the Layer stack so it appears behind the rock outcrops rather than covering everything else in the frame.

Step Four: As the imported seascape has a near-flat horizon line, it was easy enough to cut the sky using a slightly Feathered rectangular marquee.

Step Four: Now's the time to introduce a few more elements—a brooding sky plus a bunch of seabirds, all saved onto their own transparent layers so they can be re-positioned and re-colored when needed. The accuracy of your selections is directly influenced by the size that the finished product is reproduced at.

Hint: A big picture requires a lot of care when cutting out any subject. Sourcing art that has already been cut out and saved with a transparent background, like this Viking figure here, will save you heaps of time.

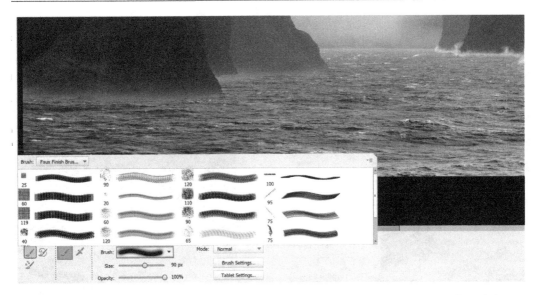

Step Five: As is sometimes the case, I found that a third party brush tip produced the best sea spray effect (downloaded from a Site called **Brusheezy**). To load a new brush into Elements go to Edit>Preset Manager>**Add**, then navigate to where the brush set has been downloaded to, click it and you are good to go. **Append** on the same Manager panel adds new sets to an existing collection so you can save, for example, a whole bunch of similar brushes in the 'master' set.

Step Six: I created a new layer for the seaspray, then took time working with different brush sizes and brush opacities to get the look of surf smashing into rocks just right. (Note: This is quite time consuming and hard to get 'perfect'. A graphics tablet would make the process easier and faster).

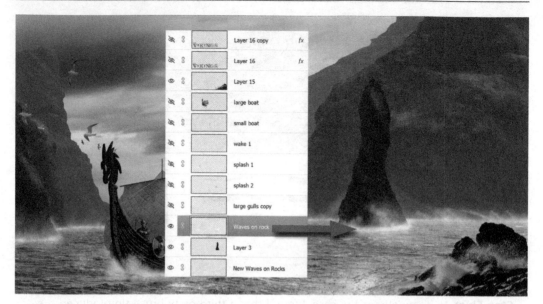

Step Six: I have added this illustration of a Viking longboat (copyright free image) onto its own layer, resized it, then added a seaspray brush effect just on the boat layer. With so many elements, it pays to **name your layers** - the (arrowed) layer is described as 'Wave on rock' - this saves a lot of confusion. It's also good practice to turn various layer visibilities **Off** to keep track of exactly which layer is being edited (Note: The red line through the eye indicates that the layer's visibility is **Off**).

Step Seven: More elements have been added: an illustration of a Viking warrior (from `www. pexels.com`) plus a small rocky outcrop (for her to stand on). This needed resizing (using the fantastic **Warp Transform** feature) and edge softening (soft **Eraser Brush Tool**) to get it to blend a bit better. Contrast on the rocks is far too heavy so that was also modified using the **Output** scale of the **Levels** tool (*Ctrl/Cmd +L*) to flatten out the contrast a bit.

Step Eight: The rock outcrop looked weird so I used an Eraser Brush to soften and blend it into the ocean behind it. Adding seaspray perfected the illusion. The warrior's face is illuminated from the left which also looks wrong so I used the Burn Brush Tool to darken the midtones and shadows slightly. In my opinion it's one of the best retouching tools in Elements.

Step Nine: After darkening the warrior's face a bit, I added some 'typical' Viking makeup (thanks to the TV series for that) using a brush called **Starburst** in the Assorted Brushes set (inset). I set the brush size to cover the face, chose the color, opacity (25%) then, choosing the **Linear Dodge** Blend Mode, kept tapping the mouse till the color was strong enough. Drag the mouse in a painting style and the unique shape is lost and you end up with just a smear. Not such a nice outcome.

THE VIKINGS
THE VIKINGS

Although it was not in my initial plan, I added this title, 'The Vikings', using a custom font downloaded from the 'net called **Tarantino** (see section on **custom fonts** in *Chapter 7, Advanced Techniques: Retouching, Selections, and Text* to learn how this is loaded). Having typed the title, I duplicated the text layer, then added an Elements **Wow Chrome** effect (**Styles>Wow Chrome**). This effect is pretty cool but it still needed a color tint, which is where the duplicated text layer came in. I changed it to a gold/orange color, then changed the Layer Blend Mode from **Normal** to **Multiply**, producing the look I was after; in this illustration I have separated the color text from the chrome effect text layer so you can see the components.

Final thoughts: One of the trickiest things about photobashing, blending a range of disparate elements into a single cohesive illustration, is in knowing when it is finished. I spent a lot of time tweaking the brightness and contrast of the individual landmass layers to perfect the depth in the scene. Painting in the seaspray was also a time consuming process, along with selected **Burn** and **Dodge** operations on the various picture elements; as mentioned, a graphics tablet would have made this a lot easier

Using a graphics tablet

We have already discussed several uses for the **Brush** tool, notably in creating **layer masks**, in previous chapters (See *Chapter 6, Advanced Techniques: Transformations, Layers, Masking and Blend Modes*), but it can also be used as a real *brush*. To do this, you really need to be very adept at drawing with a mouse, or you might consider buying a **graphics tablet** or **graphics monitor**.

Tablet devices are perfect for artists because, instead of drawing with a mouse, you use a **pen stylus**, which is roughly the same size and shape as a *real* pen, and draw onto the tablet as if it were the screen itself. Interestingly, tablets are also available as graphics monitors—digital screens onto which you can draw—but they are significantly more expensive.

Tablets come in a staggering range of sizes, though the larger the better since they provide more drawing accuracy and features. But even a $50 model will serve you well. One leading name in tablets is **Wacom**, which produces a complete range of products, from entry-level to expensive $700+ professional versions. If you just need a different and more accurate way to control your mouse actions, it's probably best to invest in a small or medium-sized tablet, from a less-expensive company, such as **Huion**, which might set you back only $30 or so.

Bluetooth-enabled models are slightly more expensive than non-Bluetooth models. If you can survive with a USB cable connection, you could save $40 or so. Larger models (8.5 x 5.5 inches and up) are easier to use because the active part of the tablet reflects the size of the screen more accurately. At the top end of town are tablets specially designed to work with real paper. Clip your favorite paper to the tablet and use the electronic stylus to either trace or draw through the paper to create an electronic file. Expect to pay over $600 for one of these bad boys.

If your work is 100% reliant on your penmanship (and your boss is OK with buying one for you), consider the top-of-the-range monitor tablet—essentially a 4K screen that you draw, design, and animate on. These are beautiful products, but at $1,000+ for a top-of-the-range model, they might be out of the price range of most enthusiast photographers. Wacom is possibly the most costly brand, but there are plenty of less pricey players coming into this market, so prices for these devices are dropping.

Tips for getting the best from a graphics tablet:

Buy the largest one you can afford—the larger the surface, the closer it is in relation to what you see on screen.

More expensive tablets have programmable buttons to aid in productivity.

Make use of the **Tablet** menu in Photoshop Elements' **Brush Options Panel**.

Unless you have incredible manual dexterity, a graphics tablet is never a complete replacement for the mouse.

Keyboard shortcuts

Here's a list of some of the best (or most appropriate) keyboard shortcuts for this chapter:

- Create a new document: **File>New>Blank Document**.
- Zoom in: *Ctrl/Cmd* + "+".
- Zoom out: *Ctrl/Cmd* + "-".
- Fit image to page: *Ctrl/Cmd* + *0* (zero).
- **Grid** (repeat the same to remove it): (*Ctrl/Cmd* + *'*).
- Show and hide the Guides: (*Ctrl/Cmd* + *;*).
- Use this keyboard shortcut to temporarily hide the selection line of marching ants. Repeat to show it: *Ctrl/Cmd* + *H*.
- Puts any object on a layer into **Transform** (resize) mode: *Ctrl/Cmd* + *T*.
- Hold the *Shift* key down while drawing with the **Elliptical** tools, **Rectangular** tools, or any of the Custom Shapes to lock the proportions.

Summary

So far in this book, we have discovered how this software application not only produces some outstanding results on regular image files, but also that it can be used very effectively as a graphic design and illustration tool.

We have discovered that working with vectors can be a completely different experience from pixel-based photos because, as we saw in this chapter, vectors can be infinitely scalable—while raster images cannot.

What's more, even if you have no desire to become the world's best designer, you can still use Photoshop Elements to produce simple artworks, add special filter effects to images, add text to your projects, and take your editing capabilities to the next level with custom brushes.

In the next chapter, we'll look at finalizing the edited image by starting with a recap on the best **resolution settings** for social media and the printed page, saving images specifically for the web, several methods for **sharpening images**, exporting the files, singly or en masse, (a feature called **Process Multiple Files**), plus a section on how to broaden your editing capabilities even further using third party **plug-ins**.

10

Exporting Work, Sharpening, and Plug-ins

Having successfully navigated the often-complex world of advanced editing and illustration using Photoshop Elements, this chapter is all about setting up those images to achieve the best results when **exporting your work** to online resources, to print or into a third party software application called a **plug-in**.

To start this chapter, we look at uploading image files to various social media sites and blogs: **Instagram**, **Facebook**, and **Flickr**. We'll also cover the complex subject of **printing** to an inkjet printer, dealing with the often confusing printer page setup, as well as how to maximise image quality online while maintaining fast download speeds using the **Save for Web** feature. We also take a look at various ways to enhance **image** sharpness, before looking at the fascinating opportunities offered by third party applications called **plug-ins**.

Finally we look at Elements' **Export as New Files** feature as well as its amazing auto batch tool – **Process Multiple Files**.

What you'll learn from this chapter:

- Posting online: web and blogging
- Posting online: Facebook
- Posting online: Instagram
- Posting online: Flickr
- Inkjet Printing: general features
- Inkjet Printing: Page setup
- Images online: Save for Web feature
- Sharpen tools: Unsharp Mask

- Sharpen tools: Shake Reduction tool
- Sharpen tools: High Pass sharpening
- Sharpen tools: General sharpening filters
- Third party software: working with Plug-ins
- How plug-ins work
- Export as New Files feature
- Process Multiple Files feature

Posting online: web and blogging

Online display is typically 72 **dots per inch** (**dpi**), a standard resolution for everything online. Since this is a **fixed number**, the more pixels there are present in the file, the larger, physically, it will be displayed.

However, most websites (and blogs) have a finite size for displaying images, which is partly impacted by the design intent, the speed of the internet connection, and storage space, but, ultimately, by the company offering the service. I use **Google Blogger**, which is free. It offers several image display sizes, topping out at only 640 pixels wide for the largest image view—at the default of 72dpi.

So, if the resolution (number of pixels) in your file exceeds the number needed to display an image at its best, it's essentially pixels wasted. Extra pixels don't add quality and may well slow the onscreen display—and potentially turn your audience off.

If you use a commercial site, such as **Google Blogger** (pictured), the file size is automatically restricted in the upload process. But if it's your own domain, you can technically upload files of any size, although there's likely to be little benefit.

Note also that uploading full-resolution images might tempt less-upstanding members of the public to steal your work by downloading the high-quality file and using it in some way for their own profit. It happens.

Later in this chapter, we will discuss using the **Save for Web** utility, a feature that's designed specifically to optimize file sizes as well as download and display speed.

So, if your images are destined for the web (you might have your own domain and website), the ultimate size (resolution) of your images is essentially in your hands—you decide their dimensions and how much optimization has to be added to each file to produce the fastest download speeds at the best image quality.

Posting online: Facebook

According to Facebook guidelines, *high-resolution* images can be as large as 2,048 pixels (wide). This dimension will produce the best visual result—even if Facebook's **automatic compression algorithms**, which are added to every upload, are heavier than most people might be comfortable with. Unfortunately, there's nothing you can do about the compression level. If the images don't look as good as you hoped, try re-editing them and upload them again—this only takes a few minutes. Facebook is the world's largest repository of images; so, with something like 300 million images uploaded **every day**, I'm surprised that its compression algorithms aren't more aggressive.

One typical method of reducing the resolution of an image that is destined for posting on a personal website or social media would be to use the **Image Size** tool (**Image>Resize>Image Size**). This is fine for one or two images, but tedious if you are uploading a lot of work. You can, of course, upload a full-resolution image directly to Facebook but, if there are a few to upload, this is going to use a lot of bandwidth and time. If you want the fastest uploads, resize everything to fit the exact display proportions first. I usually size images a bit larger than the recommended size (for example, 2,500 pixels wide).

This is what happens if the JPEG compression added to a file is too much—it produces softness, lack of color, and low sharpness compared to the original in the preceding screenshot.

Posting online: Instagram and Flickr

As another ever-growing repository of image and video data, **Instagram** recently increased its standard image resolution requirement to 1,080 pixels per square inch. It's not much, considering the original resolution of most cameras is 24 million pixels or more, but this has been an attempt to keep up with the ever-higher screen resolutions coming onto the market. When I first started writing about imaging technology, a 17-inch screen was a big deal. Now, if it's not 22, 24, or even 30 inches wide, it's considered old technology. 4K and 5K screens are pretty much standard, with higher-resolution **8K screens** just around the corner.

As one of the world's largest image resources, **Flickr** is ever-changing in terms of its online resolution requirements. Currently, you may still upload high-resolution files to this site, but you can elect to set the online display resolution of those files to a maximum of 2,048 x 1,463 pixels, should you wish. Again, the real danger of uploading full-resolution files while having them in the public domain is that it might attract unsavory characters wanting to download and use your work for free (see the *Process Multiple Files* section in this chapter). Some folk are happy to do this, but if you are hoping to make a commercial business from your photography, only upload low-resolution, copyright-stamped versions, and store the best, high-resolution work on external drives or use a cloud-based service such as **Dropbox**.

To get your images out of Elements and uploaded to a **Flickr account**, it might be best to have the image open (and preferably edited) on the desktop. Then, find the **Flickr** tab from the **Share** drop-down menu in **Editor** (note that you can also upload directly to Flickr from **Organizer**):

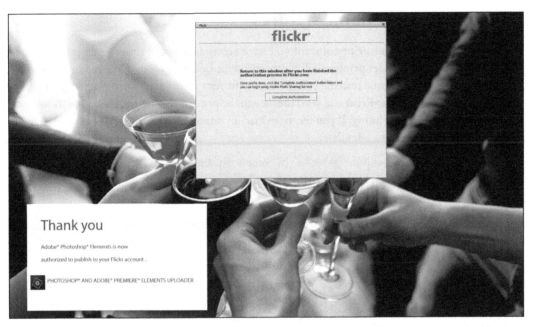

If you have never done this before, you'll have to first authorize the connection between Flickr and Elements. Just agree to all of the conditions and you'll get a thank you from Adobe once it's completed. The process takes a few seconds. Click **Complete Authorization** in the Flickr panel (top, center panel), and you are good to start uploading images directly into your Flickr Photostream.

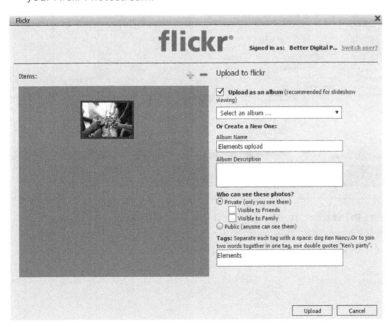

Left: The upload process is easy from here on. Select one or more images, then select an album to display them on Flickr, or create a new one for everything to go into. Then, add a description, if needed, elect who can or cannot see the images, add Tags if needed, and hit **Upload**.

Inkjet printing: general features

Elements is well equipped for print output if you have access to a laser printer or an inkjet device (note that photo-quality inkjet printers will always produce better photographic quality than laser printers). If you have spent time resizing your images to fit your favorite paper sizes, then it's an easy process to choose **Print>File>Print** and send the data to the printer. As a bonus, Elements allows you to queue multiple files for printing. If you forgot to load an image into this queue, it's easy enough to add (and subtract) images at a later date.

To get an idea of both its capabilities as well as its complexity, the following screenshots illustrate the various steps needed for a regular home print, plus all of the many options it includes. Let's go over these now:

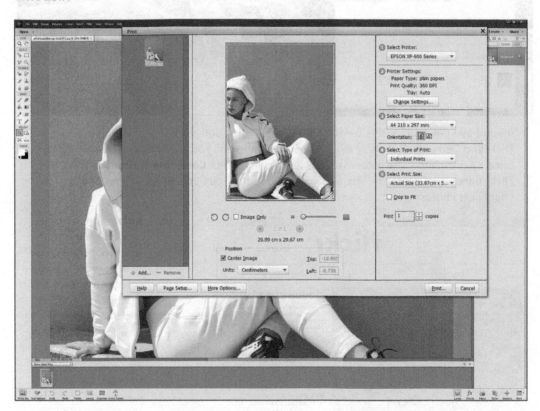

Above: This is the Elements **Print** panel for Windows. I think it is overly complex, confusing, and poorly designed. There are too many windows, buttons, options, and hidden settings—this is very confusing when all you want to do is print a photo!

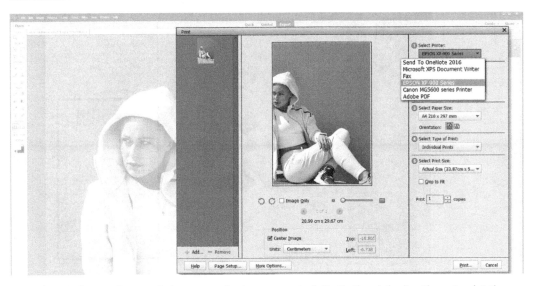

Select Printer: If you only have one device connected, that's the default; otherwise, hit the drop-down menu and select the appropriate print device (Note: If you have recently replaced a printer, the software driver for the old one will still show up in this list unless you take the time to delete it).

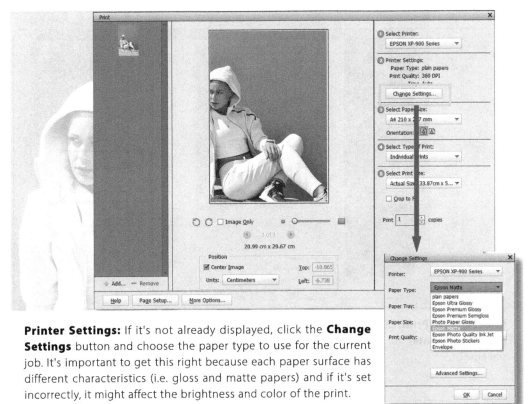

Printer Settings: If it's not already displayed, click the **Change Settings** button and choose the paper type to use for the current job. It's important to get this right because each paper surface has different characteristics (i.e. gloss and matte papers) and if it's set incorrectly, it might affect the brightness and color of the print.

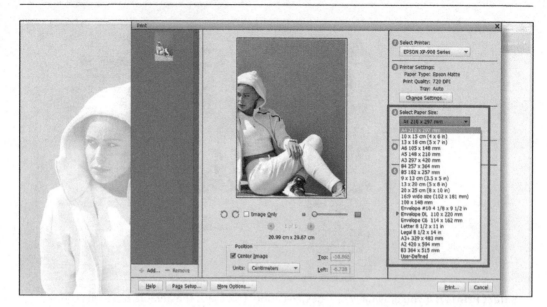

Select Paper Size: This is a no-brainer, but I'm always mildly surprised at how easy it is to just press the print button in a hurry, only to find it was set to 5 x 7 inches and not **A4**, so I have to start over. Also, check the paper orientation (**Landscape** or **Portrait**) in order to match the image being printed.

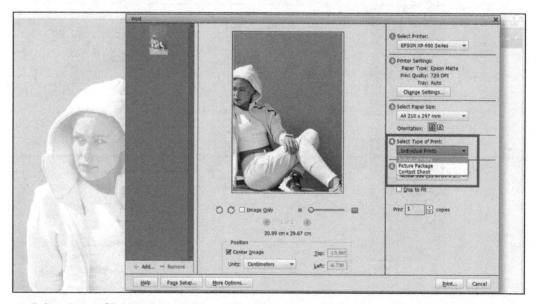

Select Type of Print: Most photographers will expect to fill the page with one image (choose **Individual Prints**) but Elements offers two other options, as you can see in the following screenshot.

Picture Package: This function arranges multiple photos onto a single page according to the layout chosen from **Select a Layout**. There are only four layouts for A4 paper—two-up (127 x 178mm), ten-up (55 x 91mm), two-up (100 x 148mm), and 16 assorted sizes (a true package). Other paper sizes have a different number of options available.

Contact Sheet: One of my favorite features because it mimics the traditional photo darkroom contact print format. It adds as many images as you want to each page (actually, you can only add up to nine columns, which makes the images about the size of a postage stamp). You can also include the date, caption, and file name of each image on the sheet, if required. In all of these printing modes (**Individual**, **Package**, and **Contact Sheet**), if you add more images than can fit on one page, Photoshop Elements adds another page so that everything fits—a very nice touch.

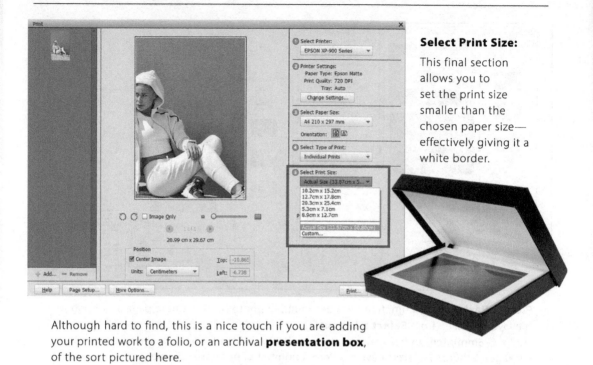

Select Print Size:

This final section allows you to set the print size smaller than the chosen paper size—effectively giving it a white border.

Although hard to find, this is a nice touch if you are adding your printed work to a folio, or an archival **presentation box**, of the sort pictured here.

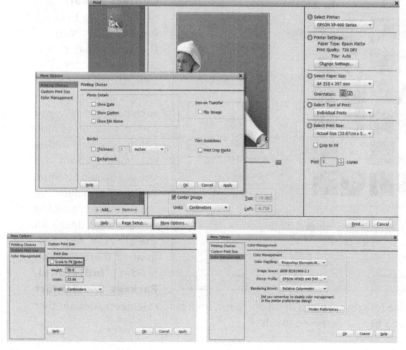

More Options:

This button reveals **three more panels** for adding photo details and a border, checking **Scale to Fit Media** (custom sizes), and using **Color Management** (set this so that Photoshop Elements manages colors). It's where you'll find the **Scale to Fit Media** checkbox. Now, you are finally ready to click the **Print** button!

Inkjet printing: Page Setup

This button takes you to the printer software, where you can also set the paper size, paper type, and other printer-specific features, such as two-sided printing, borderless printing, checking ink levels, and turning the printer's color management software to **Off** (it's always better to let Photoshop Elements handle the color management):

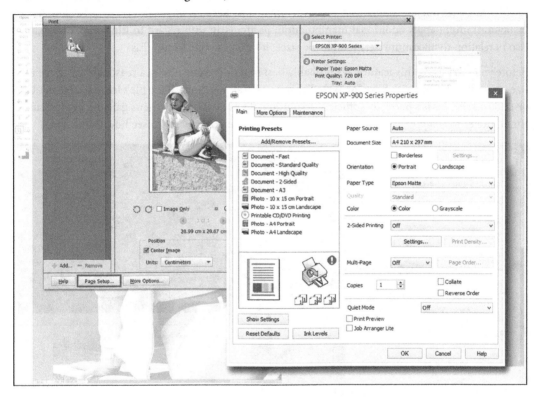

This is the printer's software—offering a range of more options, as if we don't have enough already. Options include printer maintenance (important), paper source, orientation, and paper type. You'll find that the user settings are a great feature that allows you to save all your settings so they can be recalled next time you make a print. You can then save user settings for glossy paper, matte paper—even different ink types and final print sizes.

Archival printing: When inkjet printers first hit the consumer market in the late 80s, we all jumped for joy because, almost overnight, we had taken control of a major part of the photographic process; print production. However, aside from poor resolution, early units used inks that faded in months. Today, it's possible to buy inkjet printers that, in combination with **archival ink** and **acid-free paper**, produce full-color, high-resolution results guaranteed not to fade for 100+ years. A remarkable achievement in a very short period of time. The best archival inkjet printers come from Epson and Canon, although there are dozens of companies producing excellent quality archival media.

Images online: Save for Web

Photoshop Elements comes with a feature called **Save for Web** (**File>Save for Web**), a slightly simplified legacy feature that was passed down from Adobe Photoshop. You would use this feature to specifically fine-tune image output so that it performs optimally on web-based media, such as blogs and websites. Note that although this is an excellent process for perfecting web-bound images, uploading to some social media sites might produce a slightly different quality because those sites (such as Facebook and Instagram) might apply additional manipulation, particularly with regard to **file compression**, but also in relation to maximum permissible file sizes. It's easy enough to test this.

Before you start using this feature, it's probably best to reduce your files to a reasonably manageable size before fine-tuning with **Save for Web**. For most web applications, if the file's longest edge is 1,000 or 1,200 pixels, this is a perfectly sufficient resolution. It's not too big but, then again, it's not too small either. (Refer to *Chapter 3: Increasing or Decreasing file size: Resampling* to see how this is done).

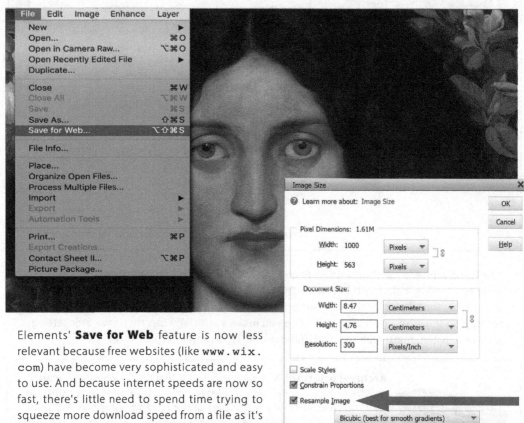

Elements' **Save for Web** feature is now less relevant because free websites (like www.wix.com) have become very sophisticated and easy to use. And because internet speeds are now so fast, there's little need to spend time trying to squeeze more download speed from a file as it's already more than fast enough. Before importing files to the utility, it's usually best practice to work with small files (i.e. 10-20MB) otherwise the **Save for Web** utility will slow down. This example was huge, over 100MB, so I resampled the file to a more manageable size before importing it to the **Save for Web** utilty.

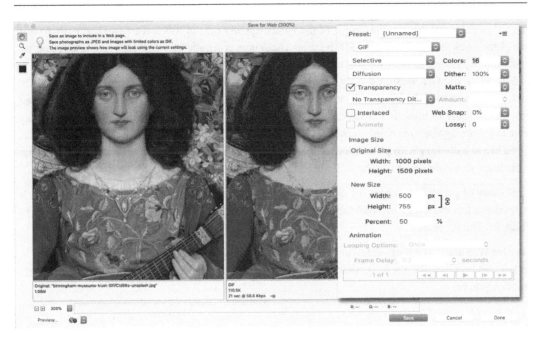

Settings: Here's the twin-screen configuration with the untouched version on the left, and the processed reduced-color GIF file on the right. Display speeds are listed at the base of the image, while the file format, compression, dithering, and color size are adjusted either through the drop-down preset menu, on the top right-hand side of the screen, or by setting the edit parameters manually using the sliders and menu choices. You can also use this utility to reduce its file size, if you haven't already done so. I'd use this file reduction panel if I were only processing a couple of images; otherwise, I'd use the **Process Multiple Files** function to bulk-reduce image resolution first because it's so fast (you'll see how this works later in this chapter).

In the right-hand pane is a **GIF preview**, set to just **16 colors**. The image is looking spotty—but the display time is very fast. Everything in this technology is a compromise.

The **Save for Web** panel has a number of presets to get you started if the process of editing for the web is a new concept. Elements provides presets for saving GIF, PNG, and, of course, JPEG files, all of which can be set to different compressions and/or dither amounts (dithering is a clever computer technique where adjacent pixels are blended to create colors that might not be normally visible in the often-limited color range offered by GIF files—the more dithering, the larger the file size).

By choosing one of these presets, you'll see how much impact an additional compression, dither amount, optimization, or scan will have on the saving process. These options vary depending on which file format you are using. The time it will take to display using a range of internet speed samples can be adjusted from an excruciatingly slow 28 kilobytes per second to figures of around two megabits per second, depending on the resources available or the client's requirements.

The following is another good example of the varied-quality output this feature can serve up. In this case, I have set the file format to **GIF** because the image is simple and contains few colors and no gradation. By choosing only **64** colors and adding a dither amount, the original (JPEG) file size is 1.5MB, while the GIF version is only 48KB. In practice, what dithering does is merge the pixels in such a way as to hide the blockiness some GIFs suffer from when their color palette has been pared down to the bare minimum. I suspect that many of these features are not as important now as they were five years ago before cable internet became an accepted default for many consumers. Of course, if you live in a country with poor internet speeds and access, you'll find these tools helpful. Note that in reality, you would never use the GIF file format for images.

The beauty of preparing images for use on the web is that, even if you've never done this before, it only takes a few minutes to upload the new material and, if it doesn't look good, it's quick enough to undo, fix, and replace.

Save for Web also has a sensible feature called **Preview**, which shows you what the image looks like in an internet browser. For the best results, it's best to test your processed images on different browsers and computers:

The idea behind working with this tool is to tinker with the settings that are available so that you get the fastest possible download speed without (too much) loss of image quality. It also gives you a great opportunity to swap between those (three different) file formats that produce, according to your settings, significantly different results. These can be accepted or rejected depending on the type of image, the placement on the web page, and the application of the web page (such as a personal portfolio, professional services, commercial shop front, or social media page).

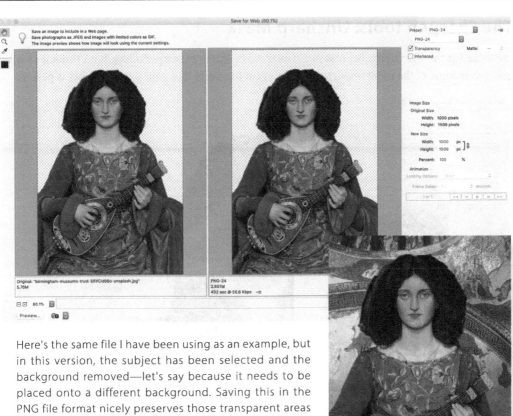

Here's the same file I have been using as an example, but in this version, the subject has been selected and the background removed—let's say because it needs to be placed onto a different background. Saving this in the PNG file format nicely preserves those transparent areas (the chequerboard pattern). If this is saved as a JPEG, those transparent edges would be filled in with white (by default), so it has to be in PNG format to preserve transparency—when it's super-imposed on a background, it will fit seamlessly, as seen on the right (both Photoshop and TIFF files also save transparency but both would produce files that are too big for internet use).

Web file formats:

JPEG is the best format for displaying photographs.

PNG24 is also a good format for photography. The PNG24 format comes into its own when you are saving transparency—for example, with a ripped, uneven edge effect, or a circular logo. PNG files save the image and the transparency around the image, so when it is placed on a color background, the transparency is replaced with the background color.

GIF is the format to use for displaying line art and illustrations that feature large areas of flat color and sharp detail and text. Animated images are also saved in GIF format.

PNG8 is an alternative to GIF in that you can set the number of colors it uses and therefore restrict file size accurately.

The Sharpen tools: Unsharp Mask

We looked at the sharpening process in *Chapter 3, The Basics of Image Editing*, but I think it's worth going over some of the more important points again to ensure that your output quality is perfect.

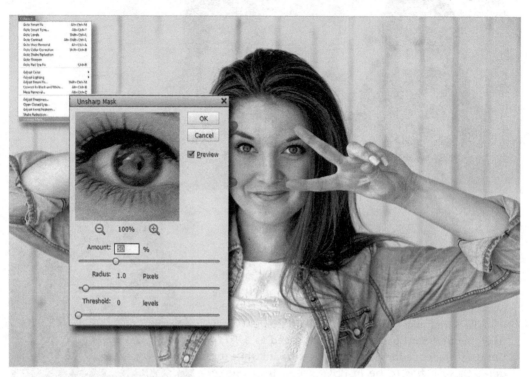

The regular **Unsharp Mask** filter from the **Enhance** menu has three sliders and a small preview window:

- The **Amount** slider is the amount of enhancement that's added to the edges of the contrast.
- The **Radius** slider controls how much attention is spread either side of the contrast edge.
- The **Threshold** slider has the effect of blending or softening the contrast edge.

If the **Amount** and **Radius** sliders are increased too much, the sharpening effect looks very gritty and unpleasant to the eye. Adding a **Threshold** amount will help to soften the overall result.

Unfortunately, the downside of using this particular filter is that it's not possible to control the unsharp mask. We can do this in the **Camera RAW** window.

Note: To get the most out of files destined **for print**, you can actually over-sharpen a file by 20%, or more. This counteracts the image softening experienced when ink is applied to paper...

The **Unsharp Mask** filter, as shown in the previous screenshot, is accessed via the **Enhance** drop-down menu and is quick and easy to use, but it doesn't give you the same level of control you get with the **Detail** panel in **Camera RAW**.

If you open your picture in the **Camera RAW** editing window, Elements offers a far superior way of controlling the sharpening process. If you are editing a RAW file, this sharpening process is part of the normal procedure, but if you're working on a JPEG, TIFF, or PSD file, you must open it in the **Camera RAW** window using **File>Open in Camera RAW**.

Once the image is open in **Camera RAW**, go to the **Detail** tab, and note that the sharpening panel has the same **Amount** and **Radius** sliders as the **Unsharp Mask** filter from the **Enhance** menu. Note that it also has **Detail** and **Masking** sliders. Here's how to get the best results from this feature:

Unsharp Mask for non-RAW files: To open any file that's not a RAW file in the **Camera RAW** window, use **File>Open in Camera RAW**. This works for JPEG, TIFF, and PSD files. Set the **Amount** (of sharpening) and **Radius** sliders as you would have done using the regular unsharp mask filter. Of course, holding down the *Alt/Opt* key while using the **Masking** slider will reveal the extent of the sharpness mask—and, of course, you can also use **Camera RAW**'s excellent **Noise Reduction** filters on these non-RAW files as well.

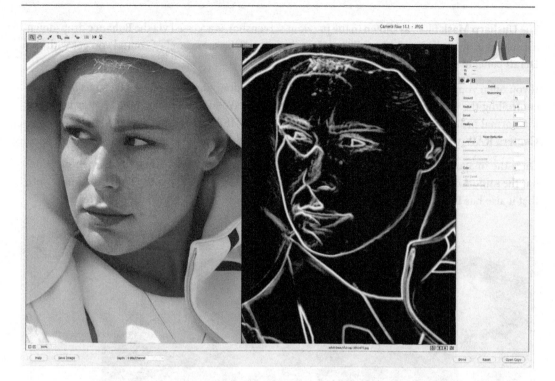

Viewing the mask: By holding the *Alt/Opt* key and then shifting the **Masking** slider (red dot) at the same time, you'll see the black and white mask appear on the main screen. For a portrait, you probably want to move the slider to the right, to a point where the smooth skin areas are all black—this indicates that no sharpening will be applied to that area. As you can see in this screenshot, I have shifted the **Masking** slider to the right-hand side. This effectively restricts the spread of the sharpening effect to only the white regions (which means you should only sharpen the parts of the image that benefit most from it). In a portrait, there's little or no reason to sharpen open areas of skin because it can produce quite unflattering textured results. As soon as the *Alt/Opt* key is released, the mask is hidden, and you'll see the sharpening effect applied to the real image, especially if you enlarge that image beyond 100%, in the original version.

Another tip: Hold *Alt/Opt* while shifting the **Details** slider so it displays the added texture/detail emphasis it applies to the edges of the subject. Use this to fine-tune the mask effects further.

One problem you'll encounter when sharpening images is, if the file has been exposed using a high ISO number (such as 1,600 ISO+), chances are any sharpening will also increase the visual presence of **digital noise**, which is never a good look. Underneath the **Sharpening** panel, you'll find the **Noise Reduction** settings—use these to help reduce the unflattering effects too much noise produces.

Digital photos generally suffer from two kinds of noise: **luminance** and **color**.

Luminance noise is essentially graininess that appears in high-ISO images. Note that many cameras have built-in **noise reduction filters**, which are designed to reduce the negative effect of shooting at high ISO ratings. Some of these filters are quite effective; but, to be honest, I usually prefer to reduce the amount of noise using Photoshop Elements because it's easier to see what you are doing on a large computer screen. Once a camera has passed its noise reduction filter over the file, that's it—you can't reverse the process.

The second type of noise is color noise, and this produces an ugly, multi-colored pixelation, mostly in the dark, shady areas of the final file. We typically shoot at very high ISO numbers when the lighting is poor, and because noise is created by under-exposure; this is why we can see a lot of visual problems in photographs taken indoors, at night time, in the early morning, and anywhere you experience poor lighting.

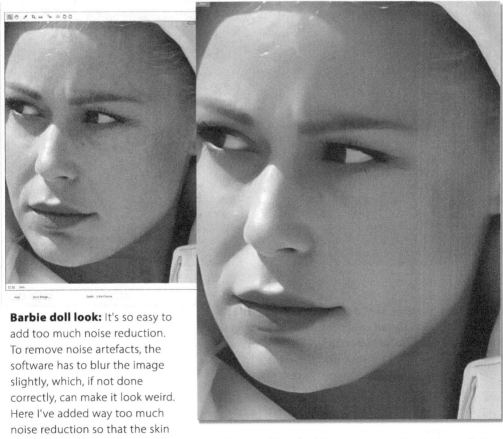

Barbie doll look: It's so easy to add too much noise reduction. To remove noise artefacts, the software has to blur the image slightly, which, if not done correctly, can make it look weird. Here I've added way too much noise reduction so that the skin tones appear surreal, but the subject has also lost all her freckles, texture, small wrinkles and all definition in the hair.

When you look at the **Noise Reduction** panel underneath the **Sharpening** panel, you'll note that only the **Luminance** and **Color** sliders are active. As soon as you shift that **Luminance** slider to the right, the **Luminance Detail** and **Luminance Contrast** sliders become active. Shift the main slider first to reduce the grittiness created by the noise, then fine-tune the results using these other two sliders. In reality, their effectiveness is very subtle, but persevere and they might reintroduce more detail into the image without increasing the noise.

If your image suffers from color noise, something my Canon files are particularly prone to exaggerating, then try shifting the **Color** slider to the right. This effectively turns the color speckling into black and white noise, something that most photographers can live with compared to ugly color-noise pollution.

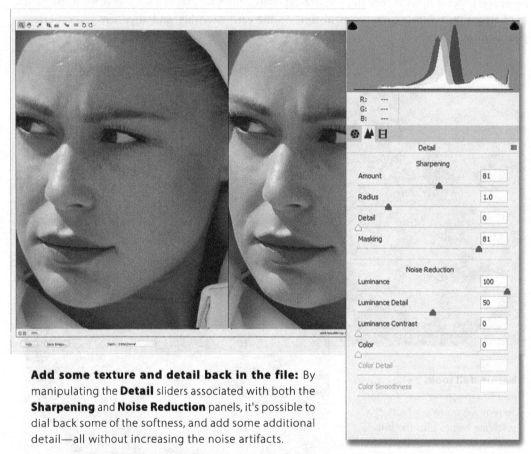

Add some texture and detail back in the file: By manipulating the **Detail** sliders associated with both the **Sharpening** and **Noise Reduction** panels, it's possible to dial back some of the softness, and add some additional detail—all without increasing the noise artifacts.

Of course, images are not all the same and will require a different amount of sharpening and treatment. I find that using the mask feature goes a long way in illustrating, in a very black and white way, how the sharpening process works and, more importantly, precisely where it is directed.

The Sharpen tools: Shake Reduction

As the name suggests, **Shake Reduction** (**Enhance>Shake Reduction**) is included in the sharpening toolbox and targets those pictures that are not 100% clear. I've always been a bit suspicious of tools like this because, let's face it, if the image is really unsharp, there's little we can do to reverse the problem. This tool allows you to select a portion of the image onto which shake reduction, a processor-intensive process, can be imposed (inset screenshot below). In the example shown here, I think it actually works well (improved on the right-hand side), but it won't work quite so well on all blurry images. Its efficiency depends on the degree of shake, and the area the problem covers in the file. But don't take my word for it—try it yourself and see whether it works on your images.

The Sharpen tools: High Pass sharpening

Another useful way of applying sharpness to an image is to combine a fairly obscure filter, **High Pass,** with a layer Blend Mode. The **High Pass** filter applies a mid-gray mask over the image, which highlights differences in edge contrast—much like the masking feature we saw in the **Unsharp Mask** tool. The gray areas are exempt from sharpening while the lighter edges that you see in the gray field get sharper. If you really want your images to *pop*, try this using the **Hard Light** blend mode, although **Soft Light** and **Overlay** also work.

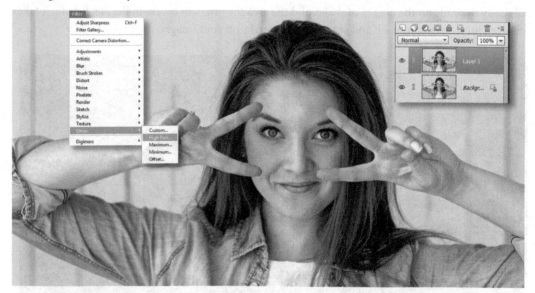

Step one: To achieve this technique, first duplicate the layer (**Layer**>**Duplicate**) and choose the **High Pass** filter from the **Filter**>**Other** menu.

Below: This is what the **High Pass** filter looks like at a value of 10 pixels. Weird. In essence, the popping effect we are about to see is added to the parts of the image that are not mid-gray—essentially, the highlighted edges of the subject only.

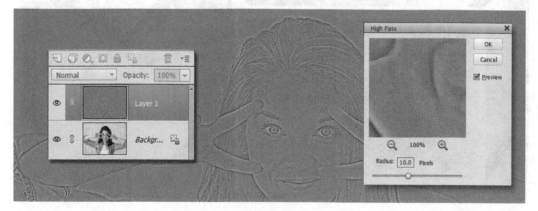

Step two: Change the duplicated layer's blend mode from the default, **Normal**, to **Overlay** or **Soft Light**, or even **Hard Light**. The former produces quite an abrupt change and **Soft Light** often produces the best, most natural result, while **Hard Light** is dramatic.

Comparison (below): In this sample, I added the **Overlay** blend mode to the left-hand pane and left the right-hand side as the original to compare the look that was created. This is a simple and highly effective way to add a lot of visual drama to your work.

The Sharpen tools: Sharpen filters

Elements has several other places where it's possible to add sharpness to an image. This includes the **Quick Edit** mode, the **Guided Edit** mode, and the **Adjust Sharpness** control under the **Enhance** menu in the **Expert** mode. All three work well but can be a little heavy-handed, and, of course, somewhat lacking in control, which is one good reason to use the better-featured unsharp Mask or adjust sharpness tools.

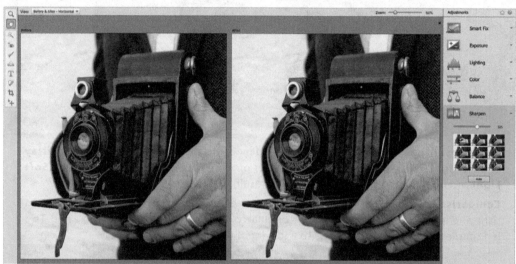

General sharpening: Here are screenshots of two filters that you'll find in Photoshop Elements: the **Sharpen** feature (top) in the **Quick Edit** mode and, at the bottom, the **Sharpen Photo** panel, located in the **Guided Edit** mode.

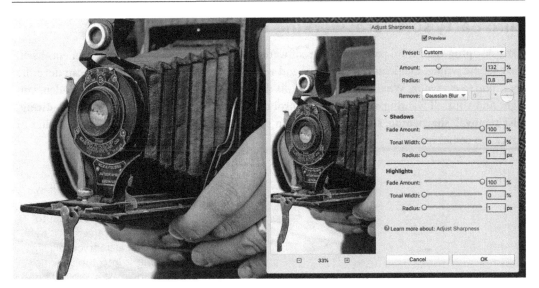

Adjust Sharpness feature: I rarely use any of the auto sharpen filters because they don't offer much control. Even the **Sharpen** feature in **Guided Edit** mode is quite aggressive and hard to temper without the luxury of a mask. But if you want a quick sharpening fix, try the **Adjust Sharpness** panel (under the **Enhance** menu). It's simpler than the **Unsharp Mask** tool (in **Camera RAW**). Use the **Amount** slider to increase/decrease the degree of contrast added to the edges, the **Radius** slider to control how wide that edge contrast is, and the **Remove** menu (which features **Lens blur**, **Gaussian blur**, and **Motion blur**) to mitigate the often-harsh effects of the sharpening process. The tool also provides scope to modify the sharpening effect in the shadows and highlights via the drop-down menu at the bottom of the panel, but in reality, its efficacy is almost negligible.

Final thought: I never fully understood why Adobe always left the sliders in features such as **Adjust Sharpness** with a scale that ran off the map. By dragging **Radius** to the right, you create an ugly halo. Avoid over-compensating like this at all costs.

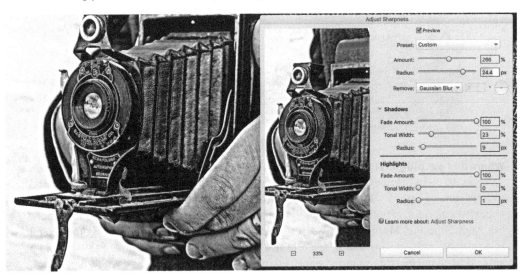

Mastering Adobe Photoshop Elements 2023

Third party software: working with Plug-ins

I like using **plug-ins**—third party specialist software apps—that operate from within Elements itself. Don't get me wrong, Elements is a powerful and very capable graphics package but it can never be everything to everyone. When your editing skills develop and your creative horizons broaden, you might find yourself wanting a little extra control over certain processes such as **portrait editing**, **noise removal**, **sharpening**, **selections**, and even special **visual effects**. And that's where a plug-in application comes in...

How to install a plug-in

Download the plug-in application and follow the installation instructions. It should take just a few minutes. If, for any reason, auto installation doesn't work, you can install it by physically copying the plug-in from your digital download and pasting it into the specific Plug-Ins folder within the master application itself (at left).

Where do I get plug-ins? There are hundreds available online, ranging from simple one-button 'freebies' to quite complex plug-ins for photographers, designers, and artists. Note that even though most plug-ins are labelled **Photoshop Plug-ins**, they will work perfectly when imported into Adobe Photoshop Elements; indeed many also work in non-Adobe applications like Paint Shop Pro. **Main pic:** This is the sort of photo transformation you might expect to get from a plug-in. This one is called **Moku Hanga** ('woodblock' in Japanese) and when applied to an image adds a ragged edge, a paper tint, surface texture and wood block 'look' to the tonal areas of the picture.

How a plug-in works:

Once the plug-in has installed correctly, restart Elements and test it. Open a suitable photo (this image was snapped in the nocturnal house at a local wildlife park—it was so dark I had to boost the ISO way past my normal comfort zone to ISO12,800, so the noise in the image is very pronounced!

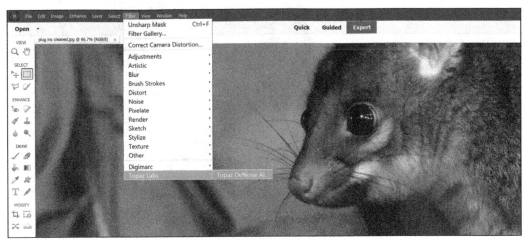

Step 1: Open the image, then, from the **Filter** drop-down menu, click the name of the appropriate plug-in to start it. In this example I'm using the **Denoise** plug-in from **Topaz Labs**.

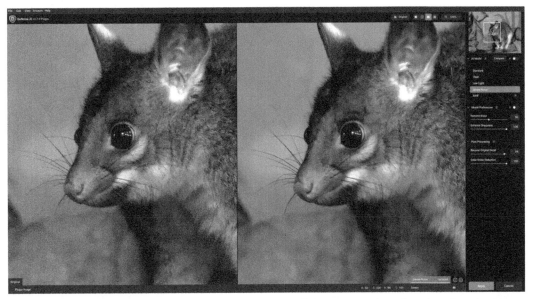

Step 2: Once the plug-in is started you lose sight of Elements and work within the plug-in software itself. Denoise has a range of presets: RAW, Standard, Clear, and Severe Noise, all of which can be further modified if needed. Some plug-ins have hundreds of possible processing combinations, making it tricky to decide on which is best. In this case you can usually save your own favourite combination as a preset to use later.

Step 3: Once you have finished removing the noise, click **Apply** and the software applies your custom settings to the file, in this case, making a significant improvement over the very noisy, 12,800 ISO original.

TIP: When dealing with sharpness and noise reduction it's sometimes hard to actually see how well the application has performed—if it's not the expected result, I then repeat the process, but using different settings. Often one of the plug-ins' presets are a good place to start, especially if you've not used the plug-in before. But it's only that: a start, so be prepared to adjust everything to get it just right.

Above: The final result, while slightly softer, has had most of the ugly noise removed, making it look as if it were shot at a far lower ISO setting. Don't forget, you can always add a little **sharpening** if the softening effect of noise removal becomes apparent.

What are the 'best' Plug-ins?

The best plug-in is the one that works best for you—there are so many to choose from, both free and paid. Here are a few to consider:

DXO - Color Efex Pro, Silver Efex Pro, HDR Efex Pro, Sharpener Pro).   www.dxo.com

Exposure Software - Snap Art, Eye Candy.   www.exposuresoftware.com

Flaming Pear Software - Special effects.   www.flamingpear.com

Jixi Pix Software - Moku Hanga, Grungetastic (to name just a few).   www.jixipix.com

On1 - On1 Effects 10 and many more.   www.on1.com

Portrait Pro - A must-have for wedding and portrait photographers.   www.portraitpro.com

Topaz Labs - Adjust AI, DeNoise AI, and more.   www.topaz.com

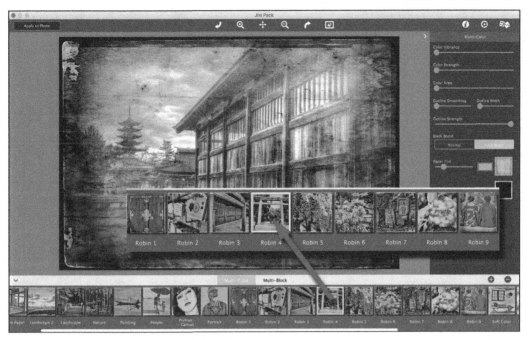

Above: Grungetastic from **Jixi Pix** - Some plug-ins have too many parameters like edge sharpness, texture overlays, paper color, ageing FX and more, and it makes it very hard to choose the best result. When I find a combination I like, I save it as a **preset**, so I can use it again in the future—it saves a lot of time. **Below: Moku Hanga** or Japanese woodblock effect from Jixi Pix.

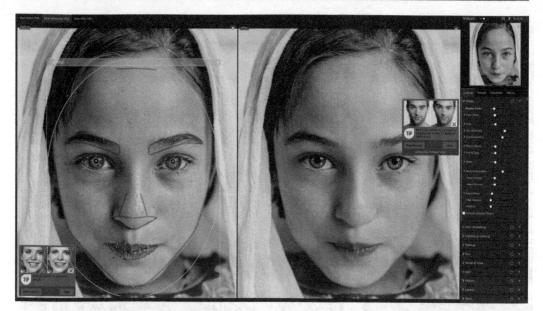

Above: For wedding and portrait photographers, this is a must-have plug-in. **Portrait Pro** analyses the image, identifies it as male/female and young/old, then tailors its improvement suggestions accordingly. You can make more than 150 different adjustments to any portrait to produce the perfectly edited image.

Above: One problem I sometimes experience when using a plug-in is the sheer number of results available. In the example of this portrait of a Balinese dancer, I wanted to add a graphic effect and ended up with more than ten versions that I really liked. Settling on one was a hard ask. Plug-ins can offer a range of creative possibilities that you'd never have thought of before and they add to the creative potential of the user.

Exporting work: Export as New Files

Resizing images one at a time in order to upload them to Facebook, Instagram, or another social media site is one technique that works well for a few images at a time. But if you have a lot of material you'd like to resize, and need it done fast, the Organizer's **Export New Files** tool might be your best option.

It has many advantages. You can export a lot of images to a specified location, add a common name to all exports, change the file format, and even choose a specific image dimension. It takes around 2 minutes to export 200 images—so it's fast.

As you can see from the preceding screenshot, this feature is handy because it works right out of the Organizer (there's no need to open images in the editor first). It also allows you to add more to the **Export as New Files** window if you missed a few, then all that's needed is to change to the preferred file format (such as PNG or TIFF), choose a desired resolution, set the location where the exported images get saved to, and click **Export**.

It's a very neat little utility but one concern is that you can't save it at the best resolution to upload to Facebook (2,048 pixels). **Export as New Files** goes as high as 1,280 x 960 pixels. As a workaround, it's possible to use the **Custom...** feature at the bottom of the drop-down **Size and Quality** menu. Enter 2,048 and 1,150 pixels. Note that this is never going to work 100% of the time because, although 2,048 is the correct measurement for the longest edge, the short edge will vary with every different camera file (because cameras have different-shaped sensors). If it's clearly distorting your exports, then turn to the **Process Multiple Files** utility (see next section) and reduce the images that way.

Exporting work: Process Multiple Files

I don't think **Actions** (prerecorded edit processes that can be played on a batch of other files) in Photoshop Elements is a very strong feature, because every action recorded originates from Photoshop CC (you cannot record actions in Elements). The ones that come with Elements work (there are 20 in all) but if you download any of the thousands available online, they might not work because its toolset is quite different. Have a look for yourself—you'll find the **Actions** panel under the **Window** menu (as shown in the following screenshot).

Process Multiple Files, on the other hand, works brilliantly for many automated editing operations. For example, you can use it to **change the file format**, **reduce the file size**, and **add unique names** to files. And, as its name might suggest, you can use it to process a couple of files, or a few hundred in one go. Provided that it's set up correctly from the outset, you'll find that it's a handy tool that performs extremely quickly.

Features offered by **Process Multiple Files** include the following:

- Renaming files
- Resizing files
- Converting files into a different format
- Adding a range of quick-fix edits
- Adding a caption or a simple **watermark**

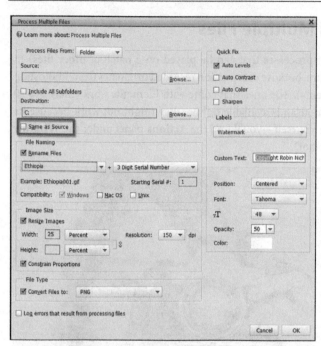

Step one: I put all of the images to be resized into the same folder, and then run **Process Multiple Files**, resetting the image size to a maximum of 1,000 pixels along the longest edge (this figure varies depending on your quality requirements).

Before you start the utility, you must first tell it where the originals are, and where the processed versions are to be saved. I think it's important to have two distinct folders for this: the **Source** and **Destination** folders (highlighted here in red).

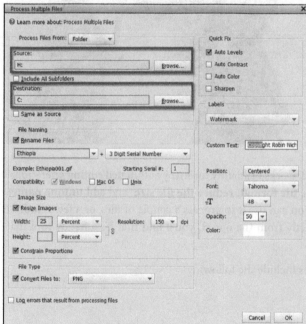

Step two: Having set the source and destination locations, check the boxes for the processes required—**Process Multiple Files** will work on files that are already open, or you can take them from a specific folder. In my workflow, I typically edit my pictures, save them to a specific folder, and then create a new, empty folder on the desktop, which is used to store the processed files (I put them on the desktop so that they can be accessed easily). I mostly use this to **resize** image files and to save them in a different format (usually JPEG) but you can also apply **tonal changes** and even add a **watermark**. Hit the **OK** button and you are done.

Same as Source means that your processed image files end up in the same folder as the originals. I have two problems with doing this. Firstly, I'm always nervous about accidentally overwriting the originals, and secondly, once done, you might have 400 originals and 400 edited files—which then have to be separated. It's far quicker to have them delivered, once processed, into a prearranged folder.

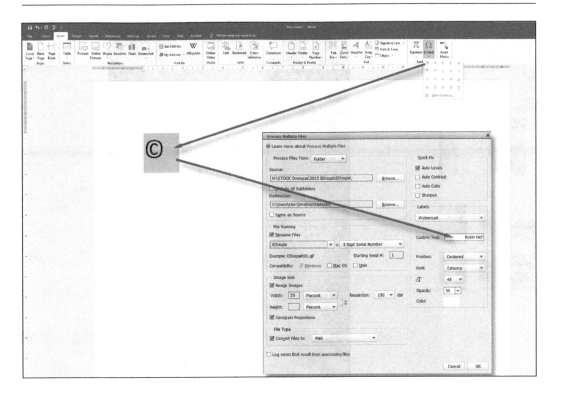

Adding a copyright stamp: This is another good feature that's highly useful for photographers (but a little difficult to control). Note that the tiny field into which you type your personalized copyright message can contain more characters than it can display (even if the field appears full, you can continue typing—but bear in mind that if you add too many characters, they will be cut off).

By default, the program adds 50% opacity to the custom text—you can set it to a slightly lower opacity if required so that your copyright warning doesn't obscure the impact of the image. To add a copyright symbol, I use MS Word (the symbol is pictured in the preceding image), but there are a number of other ways to find and place this symbol that I won't go into here. On a Mac, use the **Opt + G** keyboard shortcut for the copyright symbol.

Copyright stamp not fitting the image?

This is what happens when the files being processed are different resolutions. The copyright stamp has been set for the original high-resolution files, but there were some smaller-resolution files in there too—these are not big enough to accommodate the overlay. Verticals also suffer from the same issue—in this case, it might be best to run **Process Multiple Files** twice, once on horizontal files and once on vertical files.

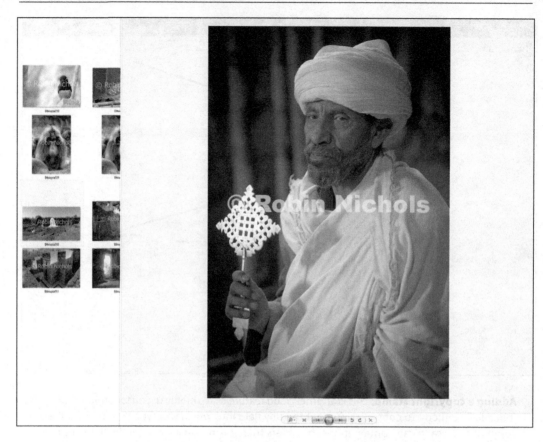

Correct copyright icon size: This is what your result should look like (this display is Windows Photo Viewer): a big copyright statement through the middle of the frame, making it hard for even a skilled picture retoucher to steal your work. From experience, I know that it's quite hard to get the copyright stamp in the right proportion to the images—we all have different camera sensors and mostly work using differently proportioned images. I experimented several times before I got the percentage reduction correct, then again a few times to get the text point size at an agreeable height. **Process Multiple Files** is very fast so it takes no time at all to figure it all out.

Tip:

For down- or upsizing files, the options offered in this panel include **Inches**, **Pixels**, **Centimeters**, **Millimeters**, and **Percent**. For my own workflow, the best option is to choose **Pixels** because I can then reduce everything to a maximum pixel width of 1,000.

Unfortunately, you will run into trouble doing this if your folder contains vertical and horizontal files (because they'll come out at different sizes). If this is the case, either put your vertical pictures into one folder and your horizontal pictures into another and run the **Process Multiple Files** feature twice, or choose to reduce both vertical and horizontal images by a percentage. Elements opens, processes, and saves your files quickly—processing 100 images will only take a few minutes at most.

Keyboard shortcuts

Here are a few handy keyboard shortcuts that fit nicely with the topics we discussed in this chapter:

- **Export as New Files**: *Ctrl/Cmd + E.*
- Change resolution and image size: **Image>Resize>Image Size or** *Alt/Opt + Ctrl + I.*
- **Change Canvas Size**: **Image>Resize>Canvas Size or** *Alt/Opt + Ctrl/Cmd + C.*
- Copy, resize, name, and format change images in bulk: **File>Export as New Files (Organizer)**.
- Copy, resize, name, add tone changes, file format changes, add a copyright stamp, and export in bulk: **File>Process Multiple Files**.
- Send the current image to a local printer: **File>Print or** *Ctrl/Cmd + P.*
- Optimize the image for best online web display: **File>Save for Web** or *Alt + Shift + Ctrl + S* (PC) and *Opt + Shift + Cmd + S* (Mac).
- Open non-RAW files in the **Camera RAW** editor: **File>Open in Camera RAW or** *Alt/Opt + Ctrl + O.*
- Used in conjunction with a layer blend mode to make image sharpness *pop*: **Filter>Other>High Pass**.
- Add mid-tone contrast to remove haze and mist and to make tones *pop*: **Enhance>Haze Removal** or Alt/Opt +Ctrl/Cmd + Z.

Summary

Exporting your work is the final process of the Elements workflow. In this chapter, we have summarized resolution by looking at the different settings that are required for a range of social media and print spaces. We also looked at the features Elements offers for preparing images for export, including **Save for Web**, **Sharpening**, and exporting to various places on the computer and cloud. Don't forget to try the excellent **Process Multiple Files** feature—this is one of those often-missed little gems that can be used to really speed up output.

Our next chapter looks at what to do if your editing goes wrong - featuring sections on: **File Saving** issues, how to re-instate a **Catalog**, search for **missing files**, adjust dates for different time zones and how to exploit the excellent **Find** menu.

There's also a section on how to make files larger (a process called **Resampling**), how to fix incorrect color, and how to perfect skin tones.

The final sections deal with **altered reality** - adding **lens flare**, correcting lens distortion, creating a fake **depth of field** effect, changing eye color and finally the mother of all manipulation tools - the **Liquify filter**!

There's also a section about how to add new pixels to a file (resampling), how to fix grossly overexposed or underexposed images, how to make blurry images appear sharper, and how to copy and paste body parts from one image into another using the amazing Photomerge **Face Swap** utility.

11
Troubleshooting and Additional Techniques

Nothing ever goes entirely as planned when shooting pictures, which is why we use Photoshop Elements to help fine-tune things such as **composition**, **color**, and **image clarity**. But even then, things can still go wrong when wrangling any software.

Adobe does a great job of updating the security and stability of Photoshop Elements on a regular basis, but even though almost everything in this industry is updated or replaced every few months, it's not surprising that problems can arise from time to time.

In this chapter, you will find the solutions to some of the most common image editing problems, including catalog issues, lost files, and poor color results. The last section profiles a bunch of really great **additional techniques** - correcting **lens distortion**, **depth of field effects**, **adding lens flare** and having fun with the fantastic **Liquify filter**.

What you'll learn from this chapter:

- File-saving issues
- Finding lost or disconnected files
- Using the Find menu
- Adjusting dates for different time zones
- Reinstating your catalog
- Resolution issues: adding pixels
- Color Issues: Fixing skin tones
- Remove Color Cast

- Altered reality: Correcting lens distortion
- Altered reality: Adding lens flare
- Altered reality: Creating depth of Field FX
- Altered reality: Changing eye color
- Altered reality: using the **Liquify** filter
- Using the Help menu

File-saving issues

I see many photographers lose their entire image collections from time to time—it can be very frustrating, for me as a teacher and, of course, for them, as they have no idea what happened or where everything disappeared to! However, there are several ways to prevent this kind of disaster from happening.

Firstly, don't just click **OK** whenever asked—it pays to look at the **Save** or **Save As** panel in respect of where it's going to save your precious stuff to.

That said, Elements will always save an existing file in the same location where it was opened from—so if you just saved something then wonder where it went, take a look in the folder where it was originally saved.

If you open a holiday snap, via Organizer (let's say it was originally imported from a folder called Vacations), then edit it, and choose **Save** (**File>Save** or *Ctrl/Cmd + S*), where did it go? It went back into the Vacations folder, so that's a good place to start looking.

The **Save As** panel also has the option of saving the edited version back into the Organizer. If you are harnessing the power of this file browser, it makes a heap of sense to keep this checked at all times. Elements also has a habit, sometimes annoyingly, of forcing files to be saved **as a copy**—not something I'd prefer in most cases. In fact, I usually want the application to deliberately overwrite the file as it's updated, rather than having five or six versions of the same image—even though I'd only ever use the latest version. It's an inbuilt protection mechanism on Adobe's part so that those who are not paying attention 100% of the time don't do what I just mentioned: overwrite files.

> Note: If you had the option to **Save to the Cloud** in the 2021 Elements release you might also note that it disappeared in the following year - happily it's back in this new version, in both the Organizer and the Expert Edit modes. Registered users get **2Gb free cloud storage** plus access to several project editing tools (i.e. Collage and Slideshow) in its online Web Browser.

Finding lost or disconnected files

Elements keeps all your original files, plus all your edited material, displayed in the Organizer—but only if you ask it to by checking the **Include in the Elements Organizer** box in the **File>Save As** window. That's the theory, but as we all know, in real life, things rarely go 100% to plan. Pictures can get corrupted, get lost, or just go missing. The following are a few strategies to initiate if you can't find images you thought were already imported and part of Elements' Organizer.

On any typical day, you might see a missing file or two in the **Media** area of **Organizer**. In my experience, Elements is very good at finding these errant files, providing it has the time (that is, you don't cancel the search prematurely) and that it is still in existence (that is, the image has not been deleted or renamed).

Check the Organizer: If your image was originally imported into the **Organizer**, but has disappeared for whatever reason, you will still be able to see its **thumbnail icon** in the main **Organizer** window—even if it's just a question mark. Despite the fact that the original image might be *missing*, Elements remembers what the file's name was and immediately searches for it. Double-click the thumbnail for the missing file and you'll see the following **Elements Organizer** screen: **Searching for missing file**. It might take a few minutes, or more, but providing that the missing file has not been deleted, it will be located.

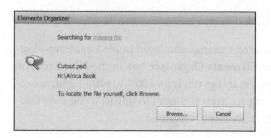

Double-click the thumbnail to let the **Organizer** know you want to enlarge the file to full size. If it's lost the **connection** to the original file, you'll see this **Search** panel appear. If you leave it long enough, Elements will find that missing file—providing the original is still on your drive. Elements' ability to locate lost files makes it one of the best picture-editing programs.

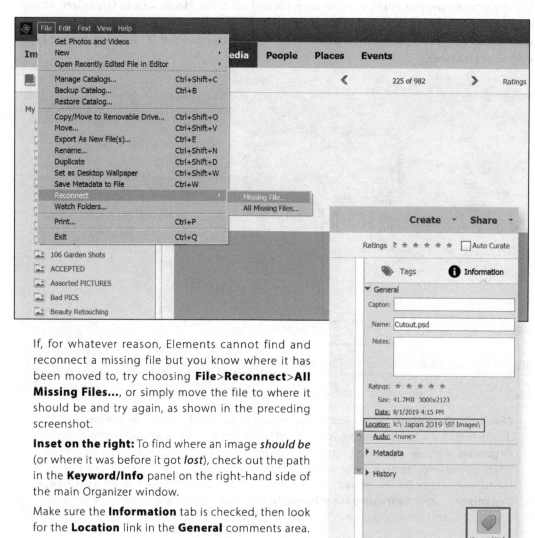

If, for whatever reason, Elements cannot find and reconnect a missing file but you know where it has been moved to, try choosing **File**>**Reconnect**>**All Missing Files...**, or simply move the file to where it should be and try again, as shown in the preceding screenshot.

Inset on the right: To find where an image *should be* (or where it was before it got *lost*), check out the path in the **Keyword/Info** panel on the right-hand side of the main Organizer window.

Make sure the **Information** tab is checked, then look for the **Location** link in the **General** comments area.

Using the Find menu

The **Find** menu is perhaps the most useful tool in the arsenal of search functions found in Elements. With this drop-down menu, you can search through the following categories:

- **Metadata** (including camera and shooting details)
- **Media Type** (such as photos, video, audio, projects, and items with audio captions)
- **History** (including **Imported on**, **Emailed to**, **Printed on**, **Exported on**, **Shared Online**, and **Used in Projects**)
- **Caption**
- **Filename**, including the following:

  a) **Version Set**

  b) **Stack**

  c) **Untagged items**

- **Visual Search** (including visually similar photos and videos, objects appearing in the photo, or duplicate photos)
- **Saved Searches**

You can even search for an image using terms such as **Items with Unknown Date or Time**, **Untagged Items**, or even **Items not in any Album**:

Tip:

Although mentioned at the start of this book, it's worth reiterating the point—when Adobe states that you "import" assets into the Organizer, what it actually does is create links to your files wherever they might be stored. Nothing is physically moved or copied into the Organizer; instead, it's just linked to wherever the files have been stored. This is a good thing if you ever have to reinstall the program because of a computer malfunction or hardware issue. But it can be bad if you habitually move or rename files using only the computer's finder system (Mac or PC), and not through Elements itself. Avoid doing this because it will create lost files—Elements can usually find them providing the name is the same but why waste time? Do everything either before you import into Elements or through Elements itself, and you should be good to go.

Mastering Adobe Photoshop Elements 2023

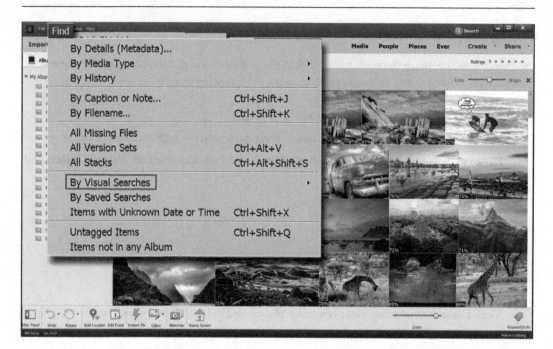

In the preceding screenshot, I searched for images that were visually similar to the one I originally picked. The result was immediate, finding and ranking the other three files that were near-identical in a few seconds. Although the image of a man and his dog on a surfboard has an 82% visual match to the original landscape, that is not considered a close match. When considering the distance between Elements' successful choices (the three most similar landscapes and *the rest*), an 82% match is actually far down the list. The **Find** menu has a very comprehensive list. Personally, I find the *visually similar* search quite useful. It doesn't get it right all the time, as you can see in the preceding example, but when it does get it right, it can save you a heap of time.

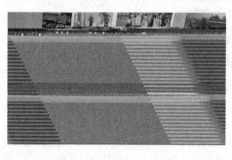

Damaged files?

Occasionally, you might have an issue with a damaged file. This can happen for any number of reasons but the result is the same: Elements cannot read the file, so you don't get to edit it.

Damage can occur if the memory card is interrupted while photos are downloading from the camera, if the camera itself gets damaged, or if the file loses its name. If the card has been compromised, try downloading data recovery software (on the internet), or take it to a data recovery service (which is expensive). Damage also occurs because the filename has been changed. Simply finding the file (via the computer browser) and renaming it—making sure the file format suffix is correct (`.jpg`, `.tif`, `.psd`)—might be all it takes to bring it back to life.

Adjusting dates for different time zones

One thing that's going to mess up a photo search is if the date is set incorrectly on your camera. If you fail to set the proper date, the results of the Elements search will be inaccurate, because it'll be hunting for a different date.

Even if the date on your camera is set correctly, you must also be aware of time travel! Traveling across a different **time zone** will also throw your searches into a state of confusion. Traveling north or south is not the issue, but moving from east to west can confuse any search parameter.

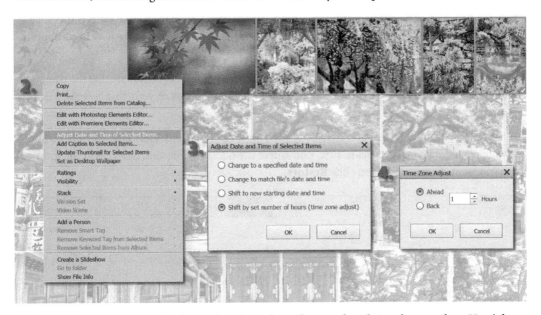

The date of an image file can be changed in Photoshop Elements by editing the metadata. Here's how:

Step one: Select the files with dates you want to change in the Organizer.

Step two: Right-click the images, and from the pop-out menu, choose **Adjust Date and Time of Selected Items**....

Step three: In the **Adjust Date and Time of Selected Items** dialog panel that opens, select the fourth option: **Shift by set number of hours (time zone adjust)**.

Step four: In the **Time Zone Adjust** panel that opens, set the time difference based on the **Ahead** or **Back** options.

Now, you should be able to find those glorious sunset shots you took from that Hawaiian beach rather than pictures of relatives waving you off at the airport the day before you arrived!

Reinstating your catalog

The catalog is saved to a computer's hard drive by default, although it can be saved to any drive, even a removable one.

Catalogs should be **backed up** on a regular basis (use the **Organizer>File>Backup Catalog** command to do this), preferably to a removable drive or even to the cloud. Never back up to the same drive that you use to run Elements from because that wouldn't really be a true backup. Always back your catalogs up to a different drive.

I know the prospect of backing up is boring, but trust me, you only have to lose everything once—whether to a mechanical or electronic failure, or even a virus—to fully appreciate how important the simple process of backing up can be.

So, how do we reinstate a catalog if we suffer data loss? The first thing is to make sure that the computer is 100% virus- and problem-free. There is no point in risking the loss of your data a second time if the computer is not fixed.

Plug in the drive containing the backed-up copy, start the **Organizer**, and select **File>Restore Catalog**. This will present you with two fields: first, find where the backup is located, navigate to the location where you want it reinstated, then click **Restore**.

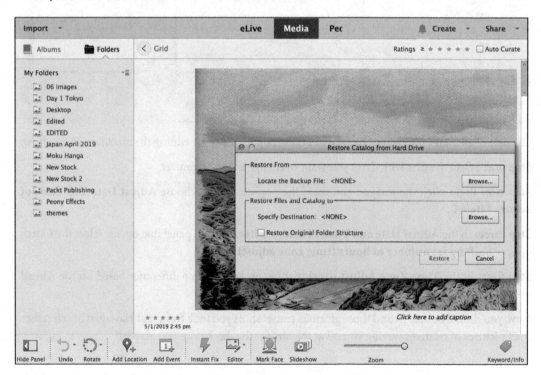

If you just want the catalog restored to where it was initially installed by default, select the **Restore Original Folder Structure** checkbox.

Resolution issues: adding pixels

Occasionally, you might have to deal with pictures that don't have a high-enough resolution for the task you have in mind. For example, let's say you are preparing a family photo album but soon discover that some of the older photos that were scanned from the originals are too small; the images can't be enlarged past the size of a matchbox without them appearing soft and fuzzy.

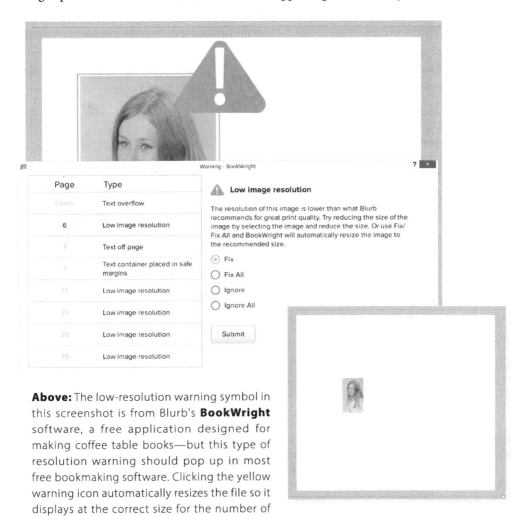

Above: The low-resolution warning symbol in this screenshot is from Blurb's **BookWright** software, a free application designed for making coffee table books—but this type of resolution warning should pop up in most free bookmaking software. Clicking the yellow warning icon automatically resizes the file so it displays at the correct size for the number of pixels in the file. The resolution for print is 300 dpi. In this example, my scanned file is on par with the size of a postage stamp (inset)—not the size I'd envisaged for my book. It needs to have additional pixels before it can be printed larger, which should also stop that annoying warning sign in the book's software from popping up.

Much of the free software available for producing digital book products has in-built warning symbols that appear as soon as you over-enlarge an image on a page. These warnings are there mostly to protect the company from complaints that the images being used are low resolution. You could, of course, still complain, but the defense for the book company is in the low-resolution **warnings** that appear in the original book file.

Luckily, Photoshop Elements has an amazing feature called **resampling** that allows you to add pixels to or subtract pixels from image files that need resizing. However, note that the quality of a resampled file is directly determined by the size of the original file. If the original is only a tiny 2 megapixel internet image, for example, you can only increase its size by 5 percent or so before the quality deteriorates (that is, it will look softer). But if the original image is from a 20+ megapixel camera, you can probably double, or even triple, its size and still produce a clear, sharp-looking result.

Resample the file: Although you can enter almost any enlargement figure, results are not always guaranteed. In this example, I checked the **Resample Image** checkbox at the bottom of the **Image Size** dialog panel (**Image>Resize>Image Size**), then added what I thought was a more appropriate pixel width for the book. Note that this updates the file size, which gives you a good idea of whether the image will be big enough for the page in question. In this example, the image changed from 400 pixels to 1,600 pixels wide, which was enough to boost the overall file size from 0.75MB to 4.6MB.

Because a large percentage of new pixels were added to a low-resolution original, the resulting file doesn't look entirely sharp, but it's a better result than having to reduce the file to the size of a postage stamp. Note that you can also sharpen the file to compensate for any softness introduced by the resampling process.

Remove Color Cast

You could also use the **Remove Color Cast** tool to achieve a similar skin color improvement —although this feature is not quite as flexible as it lacks those **Tan, Blush**, and **Ambient Light** sliders.

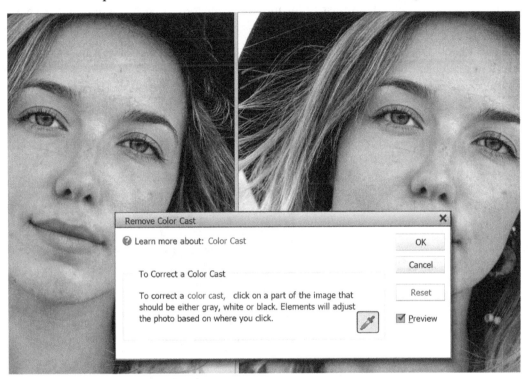

Essentially, any tool designed to adjust the color by taking a sample from the image itself is based on the **White Balance** feature, which you'll find scattered about the application in one form or other.

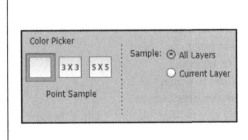

Tip:

'*Click on a part of the Image*'. It's a clear instruction but the information Elements receives from a single random click might not be accurate enough to get a reasonable result. To improve results, try right-clicking and from the pop-out menu choose to average out the sample with either a 3 x 3 or 5 x 5 pixel array. This might well produce a more reliable and realistic result.

Fixing Skin Tones

Getting the skin tones in a portrait 100% correct is always tricky. Factors such as memory (the photographer's), computer monitor calibration, and printer calibration can all play a role in not producing the best result. The **Adjust Color for Skin Tone** tool can help you produce the best color—and what's more, it's simple and fast to use.

Step one: Choose the **Adjust Color for Skin Tone** tool (**Enhance>Adjust Color>Adjust Color for Skin Tone**) and follow the onscreen panel instructions. It's simple to use.

Step two: Click on the skin tones, and if it corrects the color nicely, either click **OK** and save, or make further tweaks using the **Tan**, **Blush**, and **Ambient Light** sliders. Although your subject might look like they have a slightly tanned complexion, the skin tones in the image are a blend of different colored pixels—from yellow to ochre, brown, gray, and even red (inset)—with a specific but complex distribution, so one random *click* might hit the wrong-colored pixel and give a disappointing result. Persevere!

As with most aspects of image editing, adjustments to tone and color values can be wasted if your computer monitor is not correctly calibrated. If the screen is not displaying accurate color, then you'll risk poor results once the image is output to another device such as a printer (see *Chapter 2, Setting Up Photoshop Elements from Scratch*, in the *Color Management Options* and *Screen Calibration* sections).

Altered reality: Adding lens flare

Years ago I read that this filter effect was actually developed during the production of George Lucas' **Star Wars** movie because the vision being created by his company, Industrial Light and Magic, was too 'clean'. Adding lens flare, traditionally an optical lens fault, was added to give some of the scenes a higher sense of reality. I was transfixed!

Above: Lens Flare is one of Elements' many hidden gems; you'll find it at: **Filter>Render>Lens Flare**. Choose a point source for the light and a lens focal length and that's all you need. It works really well on images that have been shot more or less into the sun as this adds to the veracity of the flare.

Left: The original image was shot late in the day, hence the white sky, which makes it a good candidate for this particular filter treatment.

Altered Reality: Correcting lens distortion

Sadly, even if you pay a lot of money for a lens, it is going to distort the image. As a general rule, the wider the lens' angle, the more it might distort the image—perspective changes, verticals lean inwards, people's faces appear almost caricatured. The more you might pay for a lens, the less it is likely to distort, but they all do and thankfully, Photoshop Elements has a tool, located in the Filters menu called **Correct Camera Distortion**. It should be called Correct Lens Distortion but, well, it works so let's not get too pedantic about its correct nomenclature.

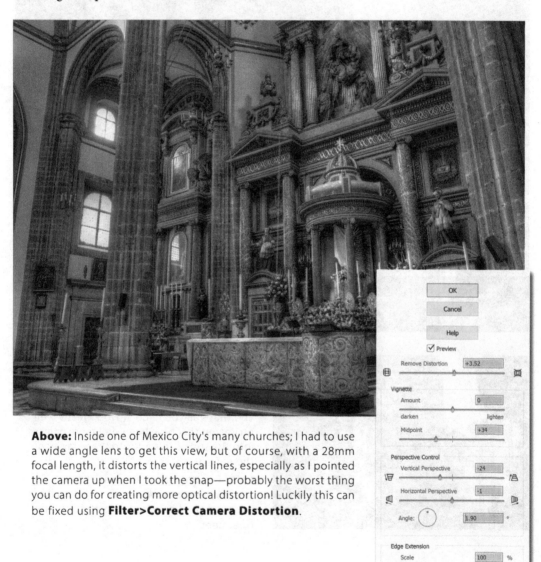

Above: Inside one of Mexico City's many churches; I had to use a wide angle lens to get this view, but of course, with a 28mm focal length, it distorts the vertical lines, especially as I pointed the camera up when I took the snap—probably the worst thing you can do for creating more optical distortion! Luckily this can be fixed using **Filter>Correct Camera Distortion**.

Above: This is the optically corrected version—a far more accurate depiction of the actual scene (as far as I can remember). One thing to bear in mind is that when radically bending pixels to correct optical distortion, you will most likely lose pixels around the edges, especially so if you don't stand at right angles to the subject (which I certainly didn't here). You are unlikely to be able to fully correct the shot. Nevertheless this is still a good result.

Right: If you are not interested in correcting lens distortion, you can of course add a 'correction' to a portrait to make

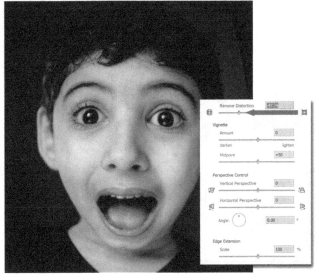

a caricature—in this example, instead of removing the lens distortion, I added it by pushing the **Remove Distortion** slider to the left (arrowed), creating an over-the-top barrel distortion effect. Your family snaps might never look the same again!

Altered reality: Creating depth of field FX

Most photographers I know love to shoot at wide open apertures to produce an extremely shallow depth of field. Unfortunately lenses with 'fast' apertures (i.e. f1.4 or even f1.2) cost a lot of money, but there's an easy way to simulate this 'look' using a combination of the **Lens Blur (Filter>Blur>Lens Blur)** feature, layers, and the **Eraser Brush Tool**.

Top: Open the image and duplicate the layer. Choose **Filter>Blur>Lens Blur** and add the desired amount of blur to the layer. The amount might need a bit of trial and error to get right. Once done, take the **Eraser Brush Tool**, set it to a soft tip, and an opacity of around 20%, and erase the (soft) pixels from the areas you want to look sharp. To add a greater depth of authenticity, fade the erasing action off towards the edges of the sharp bits so there's a gradual shifting from soft to sharp detail, as you'd see with a wide aperture photograph.

Altered reality: Changing Eye Color

We have all seen this in our lives: the subject's eyes have changed color—this could be created live using colored contact lenses or done in post using Photoshop Elements. This technique can be varied at all stages to give different results, from very subtle to outrageously graphic. Here's where to start:

Step One: Open the image and duplicate the layer.

Step Two: For this to be visually more effective I converted that new top layer from full color to black and white using the **Convert to Black and White** feature (**Enhance>Convert to Black and White**, or *Alt/Opt + Ctrl/Cmd + B*). I nearly always go for the **Scenic Landscape** preset as it's not very contrasty (compared to the Newspaper preset, for example) so it's more likely to retain all the highlight details.

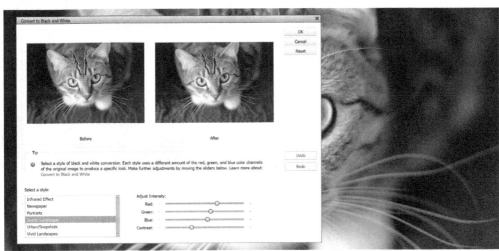

Step Three: Rather than spend money on expensive contact lenses which the cat would never tolerate, it's easier to paint in a new color using the regular **Brush Tool**, but also to use the **Soft Light Blend Mode** (arrowed) rather than the default '**Normal**' setting. Soft Light is semi-transluscent so it allows the grey tones in the photo to filter through the layer.

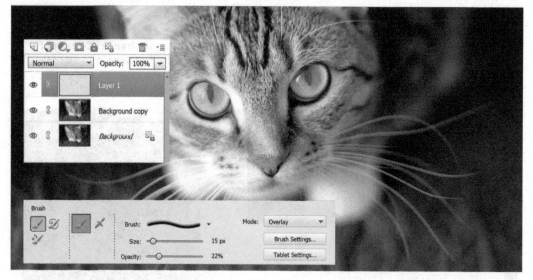

Step Four: I also added a **new blank layer** to the file—that's where the painted eyes are going. The reason for this is if I make a slight error and cover the cat's fur, I can easily trim off the excess later with the Eraser Brush. With the brush tip set to **Overlay** Blend Mode, I added a little yellow to the eyes (brush opacity set to 20%).

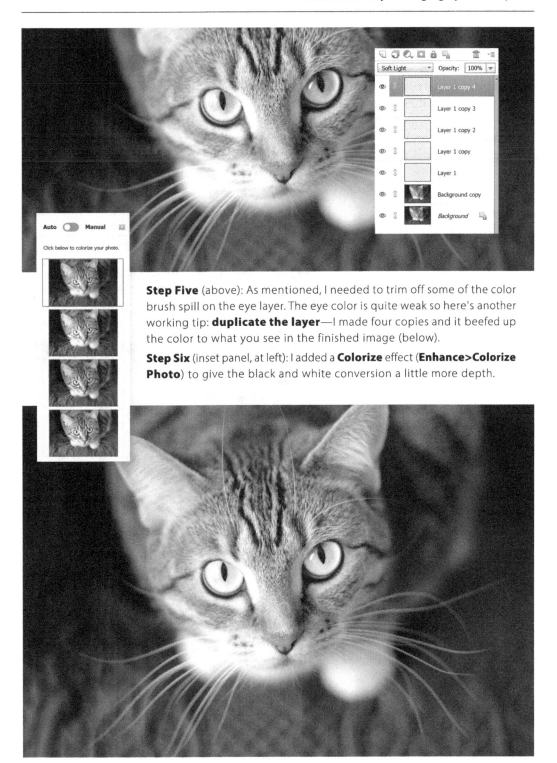

Step Five (above): As mentioned, I needed to trim off some of the color brush spill on the eye layer. The eye color is quite weak so here's another working tip: **duplicate the layer**—I made four copies and it beefed up the color to what you see in the finished image (below).

Step Six (inset panel, at left): I added a **Colorize** effect (**Enhance>Colorize Photo**) to give the black and white conversion a little more depth.

The Liquify filter

Fashion photographers, wedding photographers—anyone photographing people for a living—will love this filter. **Liquify** turns your digital file into a malleable, liquid pool of pixels that can be pushed around as if they were wet oil paints. Its original purpose was to change the physical attributes of models—thinning faces, fixing broken noses, and enlarging eyes. While the fantastic **Adjust Facial Features** tool (under the **Enhance** menu) does a terrific job, **Liquify** offers far greater control over the entire image, whether it's a face or full body.

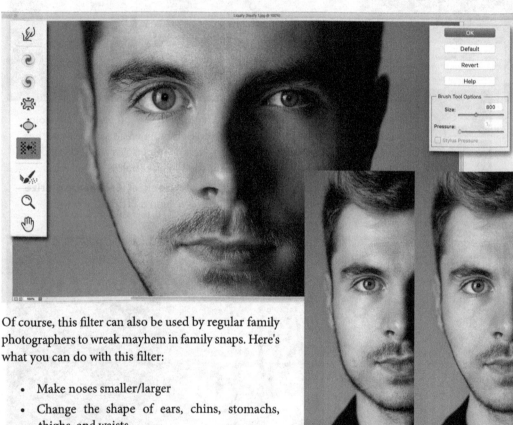

Of course, this filter can also be used by regular family photographers to wreak mayhem in family snaps. Here's what you can do with this filter:

- Make noses smaller/larger
- Change the shape of ears, chins, stomachs, thighs, and waists
- Change expressions
- Bend reality

Its tool bar (above left) includes:

- **Warp tool:** This is very much like the **Smudge** brush—but better.
- **Twirl Clockwise:** Rotates pixels clockwise as you hold down the mouse button or drag.

Above: In this quick example, I thinned out this man's face using the **Shift Pixels** tool and made his eyes slightly larger using the **Bloat** tool. Nothing too dramatic, but enough to make his face appear slightly thinner.

Meaner or leaner? This boxer image was a slightly different challenge for **Liquify**—in this example, I wanted to make him appear a little more menacing, so I bent his nose, lowered the brows, added a curl of the upper lip, and made the eyebrows a little thicker, particularly on the right-hand side of the face.

- **Twirl Counter Clockwise:** Rotates pixels counter-clockwise as you hold down the mouse button or drag.
- **Pucker:** Moves pixels toward the center of the brush area as you hold down the mouse button or drag.
- **Bloat:** Moves pixels away from the center of the brush area as you hold down the mouse button or drag.
- **Shift Pixels:** Moves pixels perpendicularly to the stroke direction. Drag to move pixels to the left, and *Alt*-drag (*Option*-drag in macOS) to move pixels to the right.
- **Reconstruct:** Fully or partially reverses the changes you've made.

  (You will find this impressive filter under **Expert>Filter>Distort>Liquify**.)

Using the Help Menu

Under the **Help** menu, you'll find a number of areas of interest, including the following:

- **Photoshop Elements Help**
- **Getting Started**
- **Key Concepts**
- **Support**
- **Video Tutorials**
- **Forum**

As you can see, Elements directs its users to an amazing array of instructional videos. They might not specifically address your exact requirement, but they do provide a starting point for anyone who needs help with their editing.

Summary

I trust that this penultimate chapter has helped answer any residual questions you might have about the features found in Adobe Photoshop Elements. This chapter has covered most of the basic and commonly encountered problems in the software, although I must add that many of the technical problems that used to plague Elements (and there were a lot) have been ironed out almost completely.

From my own experiences, I think you'll find that any problems you come across derive from either incompatibilities with your computer operating software (Mac or PC), or problems encountered during the download process. Luckily, every new version seems to be increasingly stable.

While teaching, I often found students not paying full attention when saving importing or files, resulting in them being unable to locate their latest work. Adobe has mostly solved this issue as well—you can't just close your computer without first saving your work (thank goodness), and if you edit a file then save it and the wonder where it went, it's good to know that it always goes back to where the original was filed. And if you are still not 100% sure, you can always use the handy **File>Open Recently Edited File** command—this has got me out of trouble on many occasions!

We also took a look at some of Elements slightly more esoteric features such as **Remove Color Cast** and **Adjust Color for Skin Tones**, both offshoots from the **Auto Levels** command that work surprisingly well. We then delved into the world of altered reality with the Lens Distortion filter, fake depth of field effects, eye color manipulation and the awesome **Liquify** filter.

You should now be well versed not only in how to perfect your digital creations but also in how to create believable fantasy images at the drop of a hat.

In the final chapter, we will summarize Elements' common features: all of its tools, panels, filters, menus, and project opportunity features. Treat it as the ultimate reference point if you ever need a bit more information about the tools and features in this amazing application.

12

Feature Appendix

This appendix features a summary description of every **important tool**, **panel**, and **feature** to be found in this amazing photo-editing program. There's also a comprehensive overview of all the major menus along with the items that you'll find displayed there.

Bear in mind that not everything you find in this application is 100% perfect, so I have also endeavored to add my personal thoughts on the usefulness of some of the tools and features to prevent people who are new from wasting time by choosing inappropriate tools—or the wrong tools for the job. Though this chapter is by no means comprehensive (that would require another book), it's designed to shed additional light on the workings of this multifarious and powerful editing application.

Treat it as a **quick reference section**. If you are trying to achieve a specific effect, look, or result, use these pages to provide inspiration and the right tool or process for the job at hand.

As a quick reference, here's a brief listing of the topics covered in this appendix:

Home Screen

Organizer: Import button

Organizer: The five view spaces

Quick Edit mode: Tool bar

Quick Edit: Adjustments

Guided Edit mode: Basics, Color, Black and White, Fun Edits, Special Edits, and Photomerge

Expert Edit mode: Tool bar (including: View, Select, Enhance, Drawing, Modify, and Color tools)

Drop-down menus: File, Edit, Image, Enhance, Layer, Select, Filter, View, Window, and Help

The Panels: Layers, Effects, Filters, Styles, Graphics, Actions, Color Swatches, Histogram, History, Favorites, Navigator, and Info

Create menu: Slideshow, Photo Collage, Photo Prints, Quote Graphic, Photo Book, Greeting Card, Photo Calendar, Instant Movie, Video Collage

Share menu: Email, Twitter, Flickr, Vimeo, YouTube, Facebook, and PDF Slideshow

Home Screen

Start by double-clicking on the Elements icon on your Windows PC or Mac to open the Home Screen.

This screen acts a gateway into the various parts of Elements itself. Firstly, it provides creative inspiration by offering examples of its features through Auto Creations, a clever AI-driven feature that presents examples of its features using your own images automatically selected from the **Organizer**. This includes slideshows, **Pattern Brush**, **Painterly**, **B&W Selection**, **Depth of Focus** effects, collages, and special text effects. The Home Screen also features web inspiration links, a list of previously viewed files, and three shortcuts to open the **Organizer**, **Editor**, or **Video Editor**.

Organizer – Import

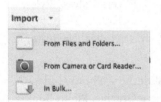

This big button, at the top left of the **Organizer** window, is pretty much where it all starts. Use this to bring images into the Photoshop Elements database (called the **catalog**). Note: Elements never actually copies the original files into the program—it just imports thumbnails and metadata, while forming links to the original files.

There are several ways to do this: **Import from Files and Folders**, from **Camera or Card Reader**, from **Scanner**, or **In Bulk**. (You can also import files using the **File>Get Photos and Videos** command.)

Organizer—its five view spaces

Media: This is the central window in which you see all of your photos, music, video, and graphics files stored in the catalog. Use it as a base—but further sort and categorize your images by placing them into **albums**.

Media	People	Places	Events

People: If you decide to analyze your image database, Elements can file your photos based on the people it identifies in each image. It's a clever feature that seems to work well.

Places: An internet-reliant viewing mode that's geared toward photographers with GPS-enabled cameras. Images appear on a Google world map according to the coordinates sourced from the file's metadata. This is a nice feature for anyone embarking on a road trip, or perhaps researching travel. This feature is not supported by versions older than Elements 2020.

Events: Use **Events** to group your images based on the date. This is handy if you need quick access to files that were shot at specific times. If they are travel snaps taken in a different time zone, remember to change the date in each file to make searching more accurate.

Albums: Albums can be created inside the general media area to hold specific groups of images. They are an effective way to further subdivide your files into more manageable quantities—rather than having everything display together in the one **Media** window.

Folders: The folder view displays the computer's folder hierarchy. Only those folders that feature already-imported images appear in this display.

Auto Curate (checkbox, top right of the main screen)**:** Turn this on to see what Elements regards as the top 50–500 *best* images (you select from how many). Good luck with that!

Keyword/Info: An essential panel in the Organizer as it displays the basic metadata for each file, along with the history (that is, the edits). The **Tags** part on the same tab displays any keywords or tags that have been attached using Elements or, indeed, another applications.

Quick Edit mode: Tool bar

This tool bar shares many common features that are also found in Expert Edit mode, including Zoom, Hand, Quick Selection, Red Eye, Straighten, Type, Spot Healing, Crop, and Move. One that is unique to this tool rack is the curious **Whiten Teeth** tool.

Whiten Teeth (*F*)**:** This tool produces a *select-and-brighten* effect. If you click and drag across teeth, or anything else that might need a bit of brightening, it selects the area (based on edge contrast) while adding a brightness boost. This isn't a good substitute for regular visits to your dentist.

> **Tip:**
> The letters in brackets, for example, (*Z*), denote the **keyboard shortcut** letter for that tool, or group of tools.

Quick Edit: Adjustments

On the right-hand side of the **Quick Edit** space, you'll find this handy tone-fixing utility.

It features the **Smart Fix (pictured below)**, **Exposure**, **Lighting**, **Color**, **Balance**, and **Sharpen** tools, all of which can be adjusted using a slider or by clicking on one of the nine thumbnails under each subheader. It's easy to use and produces good results.

Every tool in this application has its own **unique settings** that can be used to modify that specific tool's efficiency. If you find that the tool you are working with doesn't work as effectively as you had hoped it would, simply open the corresponding **Options** panel at the bottom of the screen and adjust the settings to make it work more effectively.

(The small semi-circular arrow icon at the top of this, and most other Elements processes, is for resetting the image back to its original state. The **?** icon takes you to Adobe's online community **Help** section.)

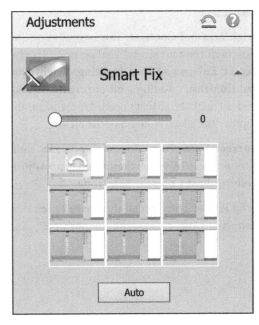

Mastering Adobe Photoshop Elements 2023

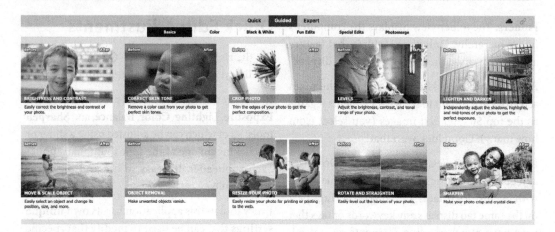

Guided Edit mode

The Guided Edit mode offers 53 step-by-step editing processes—from a basic color fix, to far more sophisticated processes, such as **panorama stitching**, **tilt-shift**, and **watercolor** effects. It's a neat feature that works very well—plus it's a good place to look for image-editing **inspiration**. This excellent edit space is subdivided into the following subsections.

Basics

Brightness and Contrast: This has got to be the most useful edit for most digital photos. (Also in **Expert>Enhance>Adjust Lighting>Brightness and Contrast**.) Adding a bit of brightness and contrast might be all that's needed to significantly improve the visual strength of the picture.

Correct Skin Tone: Fixes color casts and inconsistencies. Also in **Expert> Enhance>Adjust Color>Adjust Color for Skin Tone**.

Crop Photo: Trim bits off the image to remove distractions and improve the composition.

Levels: Easy-to-use and powerful contrast and brightness adjustment tool—an essential feature. Also in **Expert>Enhance>Adjust Lighting>Levels**.

Lighten and Darken: A simple feature, though in my opinion, it's not as effective as **Levels**.

Move and Scale Object: This has an auto select, copy, retouch, and paste function that works effectively. This is a logical development of the next feature, **Object Removal**.

Object Removal: A very impressive feature that automatically removes objects from a scene using Adobe AI and the **Healing Brush** tool. All you have to do is draw roughly around the offending item and it disappears as if by magic.

Resize Your Photo: A quick way to resize any image file.

Rotate and Straighten: A basic, self-explanatory function for leveling off images.

Sharpen: A simple process designed to add clarity, especially if the image is to be printed.

Vignette Effect: Adds a darker edge around the image to emphasize a central subject.

Color

Enhance Color: Uses the powerful **Hue/Saturation** feature to boost color. Essential.

Lomo Camera Effect: Creates a cool high-contrast "look," and a heavy vignette effect. A nice effect.

Remove a Color Cast: Good for correcting unpredictable or weird color.

Saturated Film Effect: A simple, one-click color booster. Easy to use, and effective.

Black and White

Black and White: Simply converts a color shot to black and white. Also try the **Convert to Black and White** feature in the **Enhance** menu.

B&W Color Pop: The same as above but it retains a single color, which you choose, as a special effect. Produces strong visual results without requiring much previous experience.

B&W Selection: The same as above, but in this version, you select an area of color to retain (could be single or multiple colors).

High Key: Great, graphic result.

Line Drawing: As above, producing a distinctive graphic-looking visual effect.

Low Key: Good for dark, extra-moody shots.

Fun Edits

Peek Through Overlay Add the illusion of a shallow depth of field with moveable overlays.

Double Exposure: Blend one picture into another for a neat 60s look.

Duotone Effect: A new effect that creates a two-color look in any image. It's been in Photoshop CC for decades but this new version is easier to use and very effective for making creative monocolor looks.

Effects Collage: A simple but effective way to split an image into "parts," such as a diptych (two panels) or triptych (three panels), each with a different visual effect applied to them. Easy to use as everything is automated and clever.

Meme Maker: An easy way to create a neat graphic for Instagram or Facebook.

Multi-Photo Text: The same as the **Photo Text** effect, except this edit uses a different image for each letter of the effect. You need to have a range of different images ready so one can go into each separate letter in the design.

Old Fashioned Photo: Combines a graphic photo effect with a sepia-toning "look," as well as some texture overlays.

Out of Bounds: A 3D effect that looks cool—but you'll find that it only works with selected subjects in very specific images.

Painterly: Add rough brushstroke effects to any image file. Especially good if you print the image onto watercolor or textured inkjet paper.

Partial Sketch: Converts the photo into a graphic, monochromatic line drawing, with some of the original color showing through the layer. Very illustrative.

Pattern Brush: A new feature that automatically selects the main subject in the frame, then adds a graphic pattern to the background and, amazingly, behind the subject. Effective.

Photo Text: Fill text with any image for a bold, graphic look. Works best with bold, extra bold, or very heavy, wide fonts.

Picture Stack: Adds a nice "stack o' prints" look to any collection of images. An AI-driven feature that produces a strong visual result in seconds. A real time-saver.

Pop Art: Remember Campbell's soup tins and Marilyn Monroe posters from the 60s? This produces a similar Andy Warhol-type screen print and posterization effect. Nice.

Puzzle Effect: Splits an image into a jigsaw "look" using a simple graphic overlay.

Reflection: This effect is designed to appear as if the lower part of the frame is water or glass, into which the top part of the image is reflected. Does not work on all images.

Shape Overlay Effect: A fun feature using the **Cookie Cutter** tool. Use this to add a bit of a scrapbooking design feel to your projects.

Speed Effect: Adds a sense of movement using a **Motion Blur** filter.

Speed Pan: Adds a blur to the left and right, simulating the look of a panned shot.

Zoom Burst Effect: Makes it look like you zoomed into the subject with the lens at the time the shutter was pressed.

Special Edits

Depth of Field: Selects part of a photo and makes it blurry to create the look of selective wide-aperture, shallow-focus effects.

Extend Background: A simpler version of the Recompose tool. Excellent for seamlessly adding backgrounds—works well.

Frame Creator: Adds a graphic frame to any picture.

Orton Effect: Adds a heavy soft-focus effect to the image. It looks a bit 70s, but nice anyway.

Perfect Landscape: A new feature that allows you to replace any sky easily, while cleaning up the landscape using the **Straighten** and **Crop** tools, plus the **Auto Haze Removal** tool and the **Spot Healing Brush**—sounds complex, but this is anything but, plus it produces robust results.

You'll also find the **Auto Haze Removal** feature under the **Expert>Enhance** menu.

Perfect Pet: Quite a good, multi-featured tool for brightening up your family pet photos—includes retouching and a highly effective auto subject selection.

Perfect Portrait: Great for flattering any portrait sitter. Easy to apply and a very useful tool.

Recompose: Uses the Photomerge engine to push and scale (user-protected) parts of an image to produce a different composition.

Replace Background: A semi-automated select-and-replace feature. If you don't have the best background, Elements provides a few samples. Works optimally with simple images—the more complex the image is, the harder it is for the AI to select the "right" bits.

Restore Old Photo: A bit of a powerhouse feature involving 11 different processes to make an old snap or scanned print look like it was shot yesterday.

Scratches and Blemishes: Uses the retouching **Healing Brush** and **Spot Healing Brush** tools to refine and retouch any image to make it look professionally edited. Excellent features.

Text and Border Overlay: Adds a graphic border over your photo.

Tilt-Shift: Produces over-the-top softness in parts of the image, which in turn gives that wonderful close-up look that makes a full-size subject appear as if it's really a miniature figure. A popular feature in most video editing suites—now available here for still shooters.

Water Color Effect: A lovely overlay filter effect used for adding a bit of extra creativity to any shot. Good to use if you go on to print the created art on watercolor inkjet paper, or similar.

Photomerge

Photomerge Compose: Use this tool to select and transfer a person or object from one picture to another. It's a simple process where you (roughly) draw a line around the subject and the software automatically selects the subject (that is, a figure), and copies, pastes, and blends it from one picture to another.

Photomerge Exposure: Elements' nearest equivalent to a high dynamic range effect (HDR). Combines multiple exposures of the same shot to produce an image that contains a wider tonal value than is possible with a single snap. In this context, dedicated HDR software applications would do a far better job.

Photomerge Faces: Use like Photomerge Compose. Select one face from a picture and paste it on top of another face in a different shot. Good for group shots where not everyone is smiling in every scene, for example. But the trick is you must remember to take multiple versions of the same group so you can find suitable "replacements."

Photomerge Group Shot: The same as Photomerge Faces, but designed for groups of people.

Photomerge Scene Cleaner: Shoot multiple frames of a busy scene (preferably without moving the camera), then remove some of the people by copying and pasting selected empty spaces over the populated parts of the scene. Sounds complex but it's easy to do and works remarkably well.

Photomerge Panorama: Works brilliantly by lining multiple snaps of a scene up to produce a seamless panorama. Sections of the panorama must be shot with a good 20% overlap, with the same exposure and focus point, to get the best results. (Photomerge only works if you remember to shoot multiple frames in the field!).

Expert Edit mode: Tool bar

Tools on the **Tool bar** are divided into six groups, each pertinent for specific picture-editing tasks: **View**, **Select**, **Enhance**, **Draw**, **Modify**, and **Color**.

VIEW tools

Zoom tool (*Z*): Use **Zoom** to click and enlarge your image in the main screen. Note that you can also do this by using the keyboard shortcut: *Ctrl/Cmd + +* or *Ctrl/Cmd + -*.

Hand tool (*H*): Use the hand tool to move the image around the main screen. It only works when the image is enlarged bigger than the main screen. If you are working with any other tool at the time and need to reposition your image in the main window left/right or up/down, hold the *Spacebar* and the **Hand cursor** appears, allowing you to shift the image. When the *Spacebar* is released, the tool you were originally using reappears.

SELECT tools

Move tool (*V*): Perhaps the most useful tool in Photoshop Elements. Use it to click, hold, and reposition images, objects, or text in multi-layered files. Also used to reposition/distort the same when using the Transform Tool.

Rectangular Marquee tool (*M*): Used for making quick rectangular or square selections. Once drawn, only the pixels inside that selection can be altered. Those outside the selection are protected. To cancel a selection, choose **Select>Deselect** or *Ctrl/Cmd + D*. To draw a perfect square, hold the *Shift* key while clicking and dragging in the image. To move the already-made selection, click immediately inside the marquee (the selection line) and drag it to reposition the *live* selection. Also use this tool to crop an image—by drawing the rectangular marquee first, then choosing **Image>Crop**.

Elliptical Marquee tool (*M*): Make non-rectilinear selection ellipses or circular selections. Holding the *Shift* key while drawing a selection locks the tool into drawing a perfect circle.

Lasso tool (*L*): The Lasso tool is exactly that: click, then drag the cursor to draw a line around any subject. As it's a freehand operation, accuracy is quite hard to maintain. If your editing style requires you to work with selections frequently, I would recommend purchasing a **graphics tablet**, a device that almost completely replaces the (clumsy) mouse with a pen-shaped electronic stylus—making it far easier to execute fine and accurate brush strokes.

Polygonal Lasso tool (*L*): This selection tool is particularly good for selecting geometric shapes because it operates on a **point-to-point** basis. Click once, reposition the cursor, click a second time, reposition the cursor, and click a third time, and so on until you join up at the start point. Each time you mouse-click, it pins a straight selection line to the canvas—so drawing a square selection takes just five clicks.

Magnetic Lasso tool (*L*): This is also a freehand-style selection tool—except for the fact that the selection line's *qualities* are designed like a magnet that sticks to the edges of objects, by way of its edge contrast. So, if you're selecting a black object on a white background, it will work seamlessly with little or no real draftsmanship required. As long as you follow the outline of the object roughly, it will snap to the object outline automatically for you. The *magnetic* "stickiness" of the tool can be increased/decreased depending on how defined the contrast edge in the subject is.

Magic Wand tool (*A*): An all-time favorite for most picture editors because its selection capabilities are based on the color of the pixels clicked. Vary its effectiveness by increasing or decreasing the **Tolerance** levels so that it selects a wider, or narrower, range of the color that was initially clicked.

As with all selection tools, if you hold the *Shift* key while clicking in an image, each subsequent click *adds* to the overall selection. If you over-select something (because the **Tolerance** is set too high), you can subtract from the selection by holding the *Alt/Opt* key while clicking. **Magic Wand** shares space with the excellent **Selection Brush**, **Quick Selection**, **Refine Selection**, and **Auto Selection** tools.

ENHANCE tools

Red Eye Removal tool (*Y*): By clicking and dragging a small selection marquee (square shape) over the offending red eye, Elements *looks* for red pixels and turns them gray—essentially converting the effect to gray-eye, even if your subject has green or blue eyes. But gray eyes are far more preferable to red eyes. Note that this tool also has a check button for removing (greenish) pet eye.

Spot Healing Brush (*J*): This is the most useful of all the retouching tools because it's easy and effective to use. Choose a brush size, move the cursor over the blemish, and click once. Elements copies the pixels from around the outside of the brush and pastes them inside, virtually covering up the blemish in the original image. It works like magic in most retouching situations, providing the blemish is not too near other strident details, such as the hairline, in which case, it might copy unwanted items such as hair into the target area. Making the brush smaller usually solves this problem.

Healing Brush (*J*): This works just the same as **Spot Healing** brush, except that you must first select where the "good" pixels are coming from (**Spot Healing** brush always takes them from around the brush shape). Delineate a source area by holding the *Alt/Opt* key and clicking in a *good* area of the image. This *tells* Photoshop Elements where you want to copy pixels from. You then shift the cursor over the area to be repaired and click a second time to paste and blend the copied pixels over the damaged pixels. This is especially useful if the source area is a long way from the area requiring repair. For larger repairs, click, hold, and move the brush freehand over a larger area, before releasing the mouse to instigate the fix. The larger the brush size, the further afield Elements looks for a good source area, which increases the possibility of copying inappropriate details, as well as good stuff. Always keep an eye on the source area while retouching.

Smart Brush tool (*F*): A clever, AI-driven, *all-in-one* tool. The brush operates as a selection tool, detecting the edges of the object you want to transform, while automatically adding to that selection one of the visual effects available (these are chosen from the extensive menu: lighting, nature, portrait, tints, black and white, special effects, and many more). Success relies on your object having a defined edge that the selection tool can identify. If it goes over the bounds of the image, you can modify the selection by painting in reverse mode, or fine-tune the effect using the **Refine Edge** feature, located in the tool's **Options** panel.

Detail Smart Brush tool (*F*): The cousin to **Smart Brush**—it relies on your painting and drawing skills to refine the AI selection process. I find this tool hard to use. Again, a graphics tablet would make this a lot easier to use.

Clone Stamp tool (*S*): The **Healing Brushes** blend color and tone from the "source" into the "target area." **Clone Stamp** does not blend— what you see is what is copied, although you can adjust the opacity of the sample process. If you need to repair some lighter-colored pixels, for example, it's important to find some equally light-colored *good* pixels to use as your source area, otherwise the transfer of pixels in the copy-and-paste operation will be visible. Use this tool, with **Opacity** set to a very low number, to copy and paste good pixels over the bad pixels in very transparent layers. It takes considerably longer doing this, but it's also easier to cover your (retouching) tracks, and can give you a more professional-looking result.

Pattern Stamp tool (*S*): This is similar to the **Clone Stamp** tool, but instead of copying and pasting pixels from the same or even a different image, this tool applies textures. I think it has limited application in photography, but I can see it being an asset for designers and web builders.

Blur tool (*R*): As its name suggests, use this brush-based tool to add softness to critical areas of your images. This tool is useful for blurring small areas, but works slowly if you try and apply it to a large area with a big brush on a high-resolution image file. For bigger jobs, I'd use a selection and one of the blur filters.

Sharpen Brush (*R*): This works in the opposite direction to the **Blur** brush in that you can paint in some sharpness to small, brush-sized areas of a picture. It's useful for fine-tuning portraits, for example, but it's easy to go too far with this—doing so produces a jarring, pixelated look. Use with care.

Smudge tool (*R*): This effects brush allows you to push pixels around as if they were made of wet paint. It works well, but if the image file is low resolution, manipulating the pixels makes the image appear defocused and blurry—the higher the resolution in the original file, the better the results. A more effective alternative might be to use the **Liquify filter**.

Dodge tool (O): This (along with the **Burn** and **Sponge** tools) is one of the *unsung heroes* of the image-editing world because it allows you to make significant tonal changes to parts of the image without the need for complex selections or masks. It's an adjustable brush-based tool that allows you to *paint* lightness into three distinct tonal ranges: the **highlights**, **midtones**, and **shadows**. How fast this effect materializes is controlled using the tool's **Exposure** slider.

Burn tool (O): This adjustable-sized brush works in the opposite direction to the **Dodge** tool. The **Burn** tool allows you to *paint in* darkness to three distinct tonal ranges: the **highlights**, **midtones**, and **shadows**. How fast this occurs is controlled using the **Exposure** slider. These tools produce the best results by choosing a low exposure setting. The slower the process goes, the less noticeable it will be in the finished product.

Sponge tool (O): This brush-based tool operates by increasing or decreasing the saturation (color intensity) over which the brush passes. You can increase the color, or decrease it, to the point where it turns black and white. Note that it'll only have an effect if the original contains visible color information—it won't work, for example, if you try and increase the saturation of a sky that looks white because it has been overexposed and contains no color.

DRAW tools

Brush tool (B): Not surprisingly, this (paint) **Brush** tool works just like an artist's brush. Choose a color from the **Color Picker** at the bottom of the toolbar and start painting. For the best results, use a graphics tablet.

Impressionist Brush tool (B): As its name might suggest, this clever tool copies the pixels over which you brush and represents them, in one smooth action, in a blurred, impressionistic style, hence the name. You can choose from a range of impressionist brush stroke styles. Works best on images with simple content.

Color Replacement tool (B): This brush-based tool allows you to choose one specific color in the image, and by choosing a second color from the color picker, you can simply replace the color that was initially picked from the picture with the new color that's been chosen from the Tool bar. Quite an effective tool.

Eraser tool (E): As its name suggests, this tool is used to erase pixels from any image. It is especially useful for jobs such as cutting objects out of a background, removing bits missed by a selection, or blending images together from different layers.

Background Eraser tool (E): Another type of selection tool that works on the edge contrast in the image—you set the parameters with the brush's **Size** and **Tolerance setting**. Set it up, then click and drag just away from the object you want the background removed from and it removes the background pixels while hopefully leaving the subject intact. I find this tool hard to control. You be the judge. You can work in **Contiguous** or **Discontiguous** mode. Much of its success relies on the type of image you try it out on.

Magic Eraser tool (E): I suspect that this tool is based on the same pixel-grabbing design as the **Magic Wand** selection tool, except that, instead of selecting pixels, it removes pixels based on their color. You can adjust its efficiency using the **Tolerance** slider. I find this a lot easier to control than the **Background Eraser** tool.

Paint Bucket tool (*K*): This feature has been in Photoshop Elements forever, and is used, as its name suggests, to slop *paint* (color) over the image. Like most of Photoshop Elements' tools, how far the paint spreads across the canvas (the image) is controlled using the **Tolerance** slider, the **Contiguous** check box, and the tool's **Blend Mode**. And by changing its **Opacity** value, you effectively water the paint down. I use this tool quite a lot to *throw* a color wash over an image if I want to give it an old, faded, or different emotional feel. You can also use it in conjunction with an **Adjustment Layer**, or a mask, to darken, lighten, or color select parts of an image file. It's a very handy yet under-utilized feature.

Gradient tool (*G*): This is used both as a photographic tool and for graphic design applications. Click and drag the gradient line through the image in any direction to apply it over the picture—in combination with the tool's **Blend Mode** and the **Opacity** slider. Photographers use this feature in the same way as they might a **graduated neutral density filter** that fits over the front of the lens, specifically for landscapes and for artists to re-color images. It can be especially effective with black and white files. This is another under-utilized Elements tool in my opinion.

Color Picker (*I*): This is a tremendously useful, but nevertheless underrated, feature in Elements. Use the eyedropper (in conjunction with the **Info** panel) to sample the brightness levels in any part of your image, specifically to check the density of the shadows or highlights. Also, use this tool to sample colors from within the image and load them into the **Color Picker**.

Custom Shape tool (*U*): This tool shares space with the **Rectangle** tool, the **Rounded Rectangle** tool, the **Elliptical** tool, the **Polygonal** tool, the **Star** tool, and the **Line** tool. All of these are **vector shapes** (so, not made from pixels) and can be applied to photographs, or used solo, as part of a design or illustration. Since they are vectors, they can be enlarged or reduced with no loss of quality. Use shapes as text boxes or design elements. Use the **Custom Shape** tool itself to apply features such as a copyright stamp to pictures. There are 560 different shapes (yes, I counted them all) to choose from under the following submenus: **Animals, Arrows, Banners and Awards, Characters, Crop Shapes, Dress up, Faces, Flowers, Foliage and Trees, Food, Frames, Fruit, Music, Nature, Objects, Ornaments, Shapes, Signs, Symbols, Talk Bubbles,** and **Tiles**. Phew!

Horizontal Type tool (*T*): Use this feature by clicking into the main window and typing in order to add text to a photo or blank document. Its features mirror those of a typical word-processing application. Text is placed on its own individual vector text layer, which can be edited independently of the image into which it has been placed. It's a highly useful feature.

Pencil tool (*T*): Use this in exactly the same way as you would a regular artist's H (hard) pencil (although this tool does not have the softness or shading capabilities of the real thing). Works best in conjunction with a **graphics tablet**.

MODIFY tools

Crop tool (*C*): Click, hold, and drag inside an  image to draw a **crop marquee** around the bits you want to keep. Click **OK**, and the pixels outside of this marquee are deleted from the file. Use this tool to recompose a shot at the editing stage. The **Crop** tool can be used to rotate an image, as well as cropping it. It can also be used to add a **border** to an image—first by dragging the **Crop** tool to the extremities of the image, then, in a second action, pulling the edges of the **Crop Marquee** off of the image and onto the surrounding pasteboard area. When you click **OK**, that section between the edge of the image and the pasteboard becomes a color border. Choose a color from the **Color Picker** before you create the border.

Recompose tool (*W*): A relatively new addition to Photoshop Elements, the **Recompose** tool uses the power of **Photomerge** (originally designed to stitch panoramas together) to bring separate subjects closer together or further away—in the same frame. It's somewhat tricky to use and, like many of the fully automated tools in Elements, it doesn't always produce good results because every picture is completely different from the previous one. It's worth a try though.

Content Aware Move tool (*Q*): This is a select, copy, and paste tool. Draw a generous line around the subject (the **Source**) that's to be moved and drag the entire selection to a new location (the **Target**). Using Elements' content-aware AI, it analyzes the **Target** area and blends the copied pixels into the new background. In my experience, this doesn't work as convincingly as a manual copy, paste, and blend adjustment, but if the situation is right (if there are enough pixels in the **Source** area), it does the job beautifully.

Straighten tool: This tool is used to level all of those photographs that have uneven horizons. Click, hold the mouse, and drag the ensuing *line* across the real horizon in the shot, and when you release the mouse button, the image rotates to make the line you drew 100% on the level. Amazingly, this also works for vertical lines.

COLOR Picker

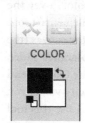

Color Picker: This feature, located at the base of the **Tool** bar, allows you to change the color of the **Foreground** and **Background** color palettes. Pressing *D* on the keyboard resets the **Color Picker** to its default black foreground/ white background state. Pressing the *X* key swaps black with white, foreground and background.

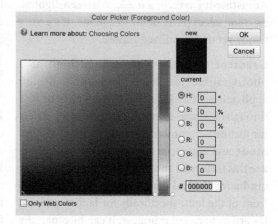

Use this feature to select a color whenever using any of Photoshop Elements' brush tools, pencils, drawing tools, **Paint Bucket**, and anything else that requires coloring in. Note that, instead of clicking the small color square at the base of the **Tool bar** and then choosing a color from the **Color Picker** panel (as in the following screenshot), you can move the cursor off of the panel and over the image to choose a tint from the image.

Drop-down menus

(**Quick and Expert Edit** modes only)

File menu

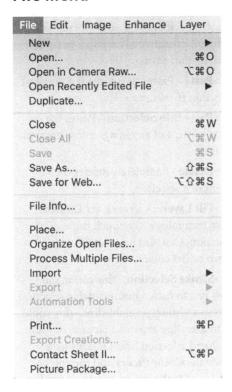

Use this important menu to do the following:

- **File>New** - Create a new, blank document, and a new image from the clipboard.
- **File>Open** - Open a file from a hard drive (*Alt/Opt + Ctrl/Cmd + O*).
- **File>Open in Camera RAW** - Force-open **non-RAW** files in the **Camera RAW** utility.
- **File>Open Recently Edited File** - Locate the last 10 or 20 recently edited files without having to navigate through the usual file structure.

- **File>Duplicate** - Copy the currently open image and rename it, if needed.
- **File>Close** and **File>Close All** - To close single pictures (*Ctrl/Cmd + W*), or groups of pictures (*Alt/Opt + Ctrl/Cmd + W*), with one action.
- **File>Save** - To **Save** your progress (important—*Ctrl/Cmd + S*).
- **File>Save As** - To save your progress and to rename/relocate the file (**File>Save As...**, or *Ctrl/Cmd + Shift + S*).
- **File>Save for Web** - To save a file and specifically optimize it for best/fastest display on the web (*Alt/Opt + Shift + Ctrl/Cmd + S*).
- **File Info** - To access file information—metadata, GPS, audio information, IPTC, and camera data.
- **Place** - Place images as layers inside other images (especially useful when working with **Smart Objects**).
- **File>Organize Open Files...:** To organize already-opened files.
- **File>Process Multiple Files** - To batch process files in bulk—a great productivity feature. Change the size, name, and file format and add copyright information, automatically.
- **File>Import** - bring data in from other devices such as a scanner.
- **File>Export** (usually grayed out unless Elements is working with a third-party plugin).
- **File>Automation Tools** (usually grayed out unless Elements is working with a third-party plugin).
- **File>Print** - Provides access to the Elements **Print** panel and, eventually, the printer software.

- **File>Export Creations** - Grayed out unless used for exporting Elements .pse or project files, such as a photobook.
- **File>Contact Sheet II...** and **Picture Package** - used to create and print multiple images in specific page layouts.

Edit menu

This is an important menu because it gives you multiple undo/redo commands. In fact, Photoshop Elements allows you to go backward as much as required. Also, try using the *Ctrl/Cmd + Z* (undo) and *Ctrl/Cmd + Y* (redo) keyboard shortcuts.

Also use this menu to copy and paste data into an image or to do any of the following:

- **Edit>Revert** - Return the file to its pre-edited state (*Shift + Ctrl/Cmd + A*).
- **Edit>Copy** - Copies the content of a selection (*Ctrl/Cmd + C*).

- **Edit>Copy Merged** - this copies the contents of a selection plus any layers in the document by merging them, then copying the result (*Shift + Ctrl/Cmd + C*).
- **Edit>Cut** - deletes the content of a selection (*Ctrl/Cmd + X*)—although it can be pasted back into the same document, or a different document, if needed, but only before further saving.
- **Edit>Paste** - Pastes the (copied) content of a selection (*Ctrl/Cmd + V*).
- **Edit>Paste Into Selection** - Pastes the copied content of any image into a premade selection.
- **Edit>Delete** - completely deletes the content of a selection.
- **Edit>Fill Layer...** - Uses clever **Content-Aware** technology to retouch the area of a selection. Can also be set to fill with a pattern or flat color.
- **Edit>Stroke Selection** - this command allows you to turn a non-printable selection line into a visible, printable line. This could be a fine keyline around a picture, or even a freehand selection line. Options here include the **Color Picker** and the choice to add the **Stroke** inside, outside, or in the middle of the selection line. Can be set to any pixel width.
- **Edit>Define Brush from Selection** - Use this to copy a selected part of any image to convert it into a brush tip saved in the brushes library.
- **Edit>Define Pattern from Selection** - The same as above except the selected area is defined as a pattern rather than a brush tip.
- **Edit>Clear>Clear History, Clipboard Content, or All** - Use this to clear the content saved as the **History**, or data stored in the clipboard, or both (good to use if

your computer has limited RAM or a full hard drive and it begins to play up or go slow).

- **Edit>Color Settings** - To adjust the (global) **color settings** (*Shift + Ctrl/Cmd + K*).

- **Edit>Preset Manager** - Where your brush presets, color swatches, gradients, and layer styles are kept and "managed."

- **Edit>Start Dictation** - Used in conjunction with speech recognition software.

Image menu

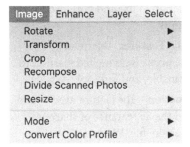

In this menu, you'll find all of the functions that apply directly to the image:

- **Image>Rotate** - An extensive menu used to manipulate the orientation of the file: **Rotate 90 deg left/right**, **180 deg**, **Custom**, **Flip Horizontally**, and **Flip Vertically**. Also used to rotate individual layers—**90 degrees left/right**, **180 deg**, **free rotate**, plus **Flip Layer Horizontally/Vertically**. It also has two other commands: **Straighten and Crop Image**, plus **Straighten**. I find both functions alarmingly inaccurate—but it really depends on how the subject in the frame is aligned.

- **Image>Transform** - A superbly important part of image editing. *Ctrl/Cmd + T* allows you to change the size, proportion, or perspective of any object on a layer—this is a valuable function that you'll use a lot.

- **Image>Crop** - If you make a selection, then choose this item, it crops everything not selected off the file.

- **Image>Recompose** - This is a menu shortcut to the **Recompose** tool (*W*) found under the **Modify** section of the Tool Bar.

- **Image>Divide Scanned Photos** - this is very similar to scanner software in that it permits you to scan multiple pictures in one (scanner) pass, then use this menu command to split that single scan file into multiple files—one for each print scanned.

- **Image>Resize** - Use **Image Size** to change the number of pixels in a file (*Alt/Opt + Ctrl/Cmd + I*), and use **Canvas Size** (*Alt/Opt + Ctrl/Cmd + C*) to add pixels to the image **canvas** (the border around the image).

- **Image>Mode** - Use this to set/change the image mode (that is, **Grayscale**, **RGB**, **Indexed color**, and **Bitmap**).

- **Image>Convert Color Profile** - Used to change the color image data from one setting to another (advanced).

Enhance menu

In this powerhouse menu, you'll find all of the features and tools you need to improve the tones and clarity of your creations:

- **Auto Smart Fix** (*Alt/Opt + Ctrl/Cmd + M*).
- **Auto Smart Tone** (*Alt/Opt + Ctrl/Cmd + T*).
- **Auto Levels** (*Shift + Ctrl/Cmd + L*).

- **Auto Contrast** (*Alt/Opt + Shift + Ctrl/Cmd + L*).
- **Auto Haze Removal** (*Alt/Opt +Ctrl/Cmd + A*).
- **Auto Color Correction** (*Shift + Ctrl/Cmd + B*).
- **Auto Shake Reduction**
- **Auto Sharpen**
- **Auto Red Eye Fix** (*Ctrl/Cmd + R*).
- **Adjust Color** - Includes: **Remove Color Cast, Hue/Saturation** (very useful—*Ctrl/Cmd + U*), **Remove Color** (*Shift + Ctrl/Cmd + U*), **Replace Color, Adjust Color Curves, Adjust Color** for **Skin Tone**, and **Defringe Layer**.
- **Adjust Lighting**—Includes **Shadow Highlight**, **Brightness** and **Contrast**, and the useful **Levels** (*Ctrl/Cmd + L*).
- **Adjust Smart Fix** (*Shift + Ctrl/Cmd + M*).

Enhance	
Auto Smart Fix	Alt+Ctrl+M
Auto Smart Tone...	Alt+Ctrl+T
Auto Levels	Shift+Ctrl+L
Auto Contrast	Alt+Shift+Ctrl+L
Auto Haze Removal	Alt+Ctrl+A
Auto Color Correction	Shift+Ctrl+B
Auto Shake Reduction	
Auto Sharpen	
Auto Red Eye Fix	Ctrl+R
Adjust Color	▸
Adjust Lighting	▸
Adjust Smart Fix...	Shift+Ctrl+M
Convert to Black and White...	Alt+Ctrl+B
Colorize Photo...	Alt+Ctrl+R
Haze Removal...	Alt+Ctrl+Z
Adjust Sharpness...	
Smooth Skin...	
Open Closed Eyes...	
Adjust Facial Features...	
Shake Reduction...	
Unsharp Mask...	
Moving Elements...	
Moving Overlays...	
Moving Photos...	

- **Convert to Black and White** (*Alt/Opt + Ctrl/Cmd + B*).
- **Colorize Photo** - Uses Adobe AI to select and colorize parts of a black and white or color image. Excellent new feature with an auto and manual override feature.
- **Haze Removal** (*Alt/Opt + Ctrl/Cmd + Z*).
- **Adjust Sharpness**
- **Smooth Skin** - Uses Adobe AI to isolate the facial features before adding a soft smoothness. This is mostly hands-free, producing a satisfying result in portraits.
- **Open Closed Eyes** - Both this and the next feature rely on automated facial recognition (Adobe AI). Fun to use and both produce effective results.
- **Adjust Facial Features** - Manipulate a face as if the pixels were melted plastic. An awesome, capable, and fun tool.
- **Shake Reduction** - The feature used to add contrast and the appearance of sharpness back into a shaky file. Works OK.
- **Unsharp Mask** - The best tool for making your not-so-sharp images appear crisper and clearer.
- **Moving Elements** - Select, then animate parts of a photo. Excellent feature for social media.
- **Moving Layers** - A new feature producing animated graphics over an image. Easy to use, effective for social media.
- **Moving Photos** - A new feature that takes a single image, automatically selects the subject, then animates either the background or the subject in a number of different ways—the resulting animation is then saved as a GIF.

Layer menu

Not surprisingly, everything pertaining to the use and the modification of **layers** is found under this menu:

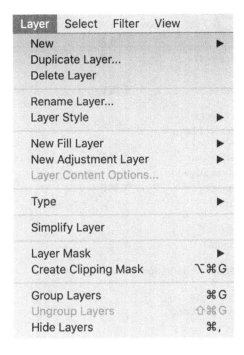

- **Layer>New>Layer** - This simply adds a new (blank) layer to the **Layers** panel (*Shift + Ctrl/Cmd + N*).

- **Layer>New>Layer from Background** - converts the background layer into a regular layer.

- **Layer>New>Group** - Creates a new (empty) **group**—this is a method to tidy up a busy layer panel by placing common layers together into a folder (as a group).

- **Layer>New>Group from Layers:** Collects all selected layers automatically into one group.

- **Layer>New>Layer via Copy** - this takes the entire content of a layer or the selected part of a layer and converts it into a new layer (*Ctrl/Cmd + J*).

- **Layer>New>Layer via Cut** - The same as the previous command but by removing the cut layer rather than copying it (*Ctrl/Cmd + Shift + J*).

- **Layer>Duplicate Layer...** - Copy (duplicate) an existing (selected) layer.

- **Layer>Delete Layer** - Delete a selected layer.

- **Layer>Rename Layer** - Give the layer a specific name (important if you have a lot of layers in the document, or if the content on that layer is very small).

- **Layer>Layer Style** - A feature such as a drop shadow, bevel, stroke, or emboss effect. Can be applied via this menu or by clicking the **Styles** panel. Use this command also to modify layer styles. Style "recipes" appear attached to the layer in the **Layers** panel—where they can also be modified.

- **Layer>New Fill Layer** - A **Fill Layer** can be a flat color, a gradient, or a pattern.

- **Layer>New Adjustment Layer** - Adjustment layers are non-destructive edits that can be customized through their attached layer mask. Adjustments include **Levels, Brightness/Contrast, Hue/Saturation, Gradient Map, Photo Filter, Invert, Threshold,** and **Posterize**.

- **Layer>Type** - this general menu command allows access to the **Type** layer—you can change an existing **Type** layer from horizontal text to vertical, manage the fonts, and access the cool **Warp Text** feature, which allows you to bend and distort lines of text. Ideal for making non-linear logos and other creative text designs.

- **Layer>Simplify Layer** - this command converts the content of a layer—which might be a smart filter or vector text—into regular pixels. Also available by right-clicking the appropriate layer in the **Layers** panel.

- **Layer>Layer Mask** - this feature allows you to work with a layer mask. The same features are available by right-clicking the layer in question (advanced).

- **Layer>Create Clipping Mask** - Hides areas of the active layer, based on the transparent pixels of the layer below (*Alt/Opt + Ctrl/Cmd + G*—advanced).

- **Layer>Release Clipping Mask** - removes the effect of the clipping mask without deleting it.

- **Layer>Make a Layer Group** (advanced).

- **Layer>Hide Layers** - a handy shortcut to temporarily hide a layer—*Ctrl/Cmd + ,*.

- **Layer>Arrange** - a command to re-arrange the layer order. I think it's far easier to drag the layer to a new position in the **Layers** panel itself.

- **Layer>Merge Down** - Use the keyboard shortcut (*Ctrl/Cmd + E*) to merge the selected layer with the layer beneath it.

- **Layer>Merge Visible** - this works like the previous command except that all visible layers are merged (*Shift + Ctrl/Cmd + E*).

- **Layer>Flatten Image** - Flattening an image discards all hidden layers, and fills transparent areas with white. You don't need to flatten a file until all editing has finished. Flattening a multi-layered file reduces its file size.

Select menu

As its name suggests, this menu contains everything to do with **selections**. Use its features to do the following:

Select	Filter	View	
All			⌘ A
Deselect			⌘ D
Reselect			⇧ ⌘ D
Inverse			⇧ ⌘ I
All Layers			
Deselect Layers			
Feather...			⌥ ⌘ D
Refine Edge...			
Subject			⌥ ⌘ S
Modify			▶
Grow			
Similar			
Transform Selection			
Load Selection...			
Save Selection...			
Delete Selection...			

- **Select>All** – A very handy command—select an entire image or the content of a selection, prior to you pasting it somewhere (*Ctrl/Cmd + A*).

- **Select>Deselect** - this effectively kills off the current selection (that is, turns it off—*Ctrl/Cmd + D*).

- **Select>Reselect** - used to bring the previous selection back into the image (*Shift + Ctrl/Cmd + D*).

- **Select>Inverse** - use this to flip your selection into a negative state. An excellent technique if your subject is hard to select but the background is not (*Shift + Ctrl/Cmd + I*).

- **Select>Feather** - this is an integral part of the selection process—to **feather** the edge means the sharp selection line is made softer.

- **Select>Refine Edge** - no selection is ever 100% perfect, so use this mini-utility to modify that selection edge.

- **Select>Subject** (*Alt/Opt + Ctrl/Cmd + S*) – An impressive new feature using AI to find and select the subject of the image. If the subject is clear, it works well.

- **Select>Modify** – Opens up a range of very useful selection modification features such as **Border**, **Smooth**, **Expand**, and **Contract**. Vital tools for perfecting the accuracy of a selection.

- **Select>Grow** – As a selection modifier (makes the selection larger by a set pixel amount).

- **Select>Similar** – A selection modifier that selects pixels of a similar tonal range to those of the current selection.

- **Select>Transform Selection** – A handy tool for adjusting the size and shape of an existing selection.

- **Select>Load Selection** – Allows you to import (or load) an already-saved selection.

- **Select>Save Selection** - this is an important command—it allows you to preserve your selected work (in the TIFF or PSD file format only).

- **Select>Delete Selection** - this is a selection modifier allowing you to take the previously saved selection out of the file. Used particularly if you have a lot of updated or modified selections in the file. Delete the ones that are no longer in date or relevant.

Filter menu

There are too many filter tools to mention here. Under the **Filter** menu, you'll find a huge range of filter **special effects**, some of which are designed to lend an artistic look to your work. I use filters for jobs such as blurring pixels (depth-of-field effects) and some for distorting, sketching, stylizing, adding texture, and even for adding more digital noise. All filter effects can be used globally or simply applied to a smaller part of the image once they're confined inside a **selection**.

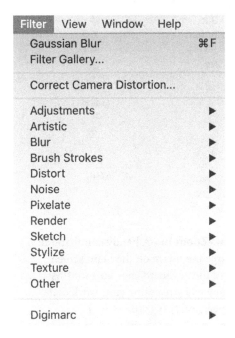

Correct Camera Distortion - Separate from the rest of the filters, **Correct Camera Distortion** is designed for correcting lens distortion. Use this to add or subtract optical errors, as well as creating a vignette and adjusting perspective.

View menu

The tools that are found inside the **View** menu are used principally to line up, arrange, enlarge, or reduce the image size that you're currently viewing. Note that none of these overlay *helpers*, such as **Grid**, **Rulers**, or **Guides**, will show once the images are printed or uploaded to the internet. They are merely there in order to assist your page layout and design:

View	Window	Help	
New Window for Untitled-1			
Zoom In			⌘ =
Zoom Out			⌘ –
Fit on Screen			⌘ 0
Actual Pixels			⌘ 1
Print Size			
Selection			⌘ H
Rulers			⇧ ⌘ R
Grid			⌘ '
✓ Guides			⌘ ;
Snap To			▶
Lock Guides			⌥ ⌘ ;
Clear Guides			
New Guide...			

- **View>Zoom In** - A handy command to enlarge the image on the main screen. Learn the keyboard shortcuts for this as they will streamline your workload immeasurably (*Ctrl/Cmd + =*).
- **View>Zoom Out** - The opposite to the previous action (*Ctrl/Cmd + -*).
- **View>Fit on Screen** - another excellent shortcut to learn (*Ctrl/Cmd + 0*).
- **View>Actual Pixels** - Enlarges the image to pixel level (*Ctrl/Cmd + 1*).
- **View>Print Size**

- **View>Selection** - Hides the selection line temporarily (*Ctrl/Cmd + H*—a handy shortcut to learn and use when you're working with selections, but don't forget to turn it back on again, with *Ctrl/Cmd + H*).
- **View>Rulers** - another essential tool for any document designer (*Shift + Ctrl/Cmd + R*).
- **View>Grid** - set the grid parameters (size, color, and frequency) through the application preferences (*Ctrl/Cmd + '*).
- **View>Guides** - a great helper for lining objects up. To find a guide, turn the **Ruler** on and drag the mouse out of the ruler margin into the image. Drag back into the ruler to get rid of it (*Ctrl/Cmd + ;*).
- **View>Snap To** – Makes the grid and guides sticky or *magnetic*, making it easier to align multiple objects quickly and accurately.
- **View>Lock Guides** - handy if, having spent time arranging a layout, you want to prevent accidental shifting of the guides (*Alt/Opt + Ctrl/Cmd + ;*).
- **View>Clear Guides** - simple—removes all guides.
- **View>New Guide** - places a new guide in the image—it's far, far easier to drag a new guide off the ruler.

Window menu

In this drop-down menu, you'll find references to all of the panels inside Photoshop Elements. These include the following:

- **Window>Actions** – An Action is a prerecorded editing process that can be played back on single or multiple files. Actions are recorded in Photoshop CC so not all actions copied (from online resources) will work in Elements.

- **Window>Adjustments** – Useful and easy **Quick Edit** special effects and tonal fixes.

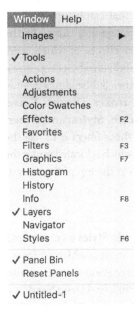

- **Window>Color Swatches** – Useful for setting, saving, and reusing text and painting colors.
- **Window>Effects** – Excellent bunch of preset effects—inspirational (*F2*).
- **Window>Favorites** – Drag often-used features here so that they can be found and used again quickly without having to hunt through all the menus.
- **Window>Filters** – Too many to mention here—hundreds of filters and creative possibilities (*F3*).
- **Window>Graphics** – Access to Elements' hundreds of downloadable graphics (*F7*).
- **Window>Histogram** – The histogram refers to the tonal distribution throughout the image.
- **Window>History** – Calls up all the actions performed since the last save. Click on a previous state to "go back in time" in relation to the edits applied to that file.
- **Window>Info:** Used to measure pixel brightness (among other metrics), irrespective of screen calibration. An excellent little helper (*F8*).
- **Window>Layers:** An important panel for all multi-image and text-based image projects.
- **Window>Navigator:** When working on a highly zoomed-in image, use **Navigator** to keep an eye on exactly where it is in the image that you are looking/working.
- **Window>Styles** - provides access to the **styles**; press *F6* or go to the panel directly, at the bottom right-hand side of the screen.
- **Window>Panel Bin:** All open images are visible in this pop-up bin area.
- **Window>Reset Panels** – Use this if your desktop is awash with panels and you need a fresh start.

(If the name of the panel has a checkmark next to it, it's open somewhere on the desktop. If there is no checkmark, it's closed.)

Help menu

The **Help** menu provides a shortcut to the online Adobe help manuals, as well as subjects such as the following:

- Tips for getting started
- Key concepts

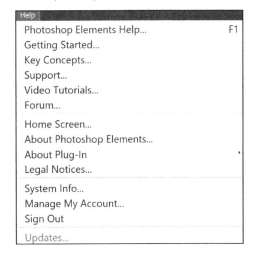

- Support
- Video tutorials online
- Adobe forums
- Updates
- A direct link to your account settings
- Panels overview

The Panels

(Quick and Expert Modes)

Layers panel

This is possibly the most important panel in this program, especially if you're working with multi-image files or images with text (because different image elements can be placed onto separate layers). In some of the more complex operations offered by Photoshop Elements, this panel is hidden unless you specifically search out its advanced mode. (It's hidden because, since that process might involve a very complex list of functions, having everything visible might be a recipe for disaster. Deleting, moving, or renaming any one of those layers might prevent the (prerecorded) action from being completed.)

Effects panel

As its name might suggest, this panel is all about choosing a special "look" to apply to a pixel-based **image**. From Elements 2022, the panel is split between Classic effects ("looks" from previous versions) and Artistic, 30 new "looks" that can be added globally or, using the auto select feature, to the subject only, or background only. Works really well!

Filters panel

Like the **Effects** panel, this panel offers a wide range of special effects that can be applied in a range of ways to your image files. Also like the **Effects** panel, these filter effects, of which there are more than 300, are subdivided by a drop-down menu inside the main panel. Subheadings include **Artistic**, **Blur**, **Brush Strokes**, **Distort**, **Noise**, **Pixelated**, **Render**, **Sketch**, **Styles**, and **Other**. Another way to access these filters is to use the excellent **Filter Gallery**, which is located under the **Filter** drop-down menu at the top of the screen.

Styles panel

Like the previous two panels, **Styles** incorporates a number of special effects, most of which are legacy items from the early days of Photoshop Elements. This is the panel where you'll find **Drop Shadows**, **Bevels**, **Image Effects**, and **Photographic Effects**. Other subheadings include **Complex**, **Glass Buttons**, **Inner Glows**, **Inner Shadows**, **Outer Glows**, **Patterns**, **Strokes**, **Visibility**, **Wow Chrome**, **Wow Neon**, and **Wow Plastic**. Some of these can be applied directly to images while others work especially well on text layers. They can also be used to create graphic effects if you're designing web pages or creating vector art.

Graphics panel

This panel perhaps has more than all of the other panels put together (with more than 1,500 downloadable assets). To give you an idea, you can use the **By Type** drop-down menu at the top of the panel to display the numerous options a little more clearly. **By Type** includes **Activity**, **Color**, **Event**, **Mood**, **Object**, **Seasons**, **Style**, and **By Word**.

The right-hand drop-down menu features headers that read **Backgrounds**, **Friends**, **Graphics**, **Shapes**, and **Text**. Note that these need to be

downloaded first before you can incorporate them into a project. They are vector clip art files, so they are very small and are ready for use almost immediately.

Actions panel

An **Action** is a prerecorded set of instructions for a specific editing process, such as a resolution change, brightness adjustment, or file format change.

Actions are created (recorded) using Adobe **Photoshop CC** and can be replayed on a single image, or in bulk. Since many **Actions** are recorded using functions that are not present in Photoshop Elements, you'll find that, if you download and import new **Actions** (from the internet), it's more than likely they'll not function correctly. Adobe has included the same prerecorded **Actions** as a *starter pack* in Elements for years—which would suggest to me that they are no longer worth pursuing, because most of the Photoshop CC-recorded actions will not work in Elements. Some actions are designed to reveal features in Elements that are normally hidden, such as the **Curves** tool.

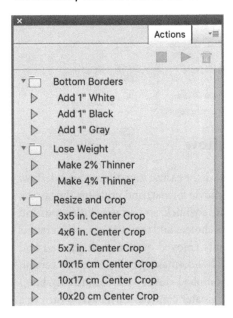

Color swatches

Adobe supplies Elements with a range of **color swatches**, which can be treated like a student paint box. Each swatch has a range of different colors. You can choose from **Photo Filter Colors**, **Web Hues**, **Web-Safe Colors**, **Web Spectrum**, **Windows**, or **macOS**. Alternatively, you can create and save your own **custom swatches** for specific jobs.

More tabs

Histogram panel

The **histogram**, that curious *mountain range* depicting where in the image the tones sit in relation to absolute black and absolute white, is a very handy tool. At a glance, you can tell whether an image is overexposed or underexposed.

History panel

History contains a list of all the steps and mouse clicks that are made while editing an image. Everything is recorded in a linear fashion, so it's entirely possible to go back in time to a previous edit state in order to re-work a specific part of the edit process. It doesn't allow you to combine different states—once a state has been deleted, everything later than that is also lost.

Favorites panel

Store frequently used clip art, filters, effects, and text, by dragging the effect thumbnail into this panel. This is a huge time-saver because everything is in one place for fast access.

Mastering Adobe Photoshop Elements 2023

Navigator panel

This small panel displays a large thumbnail of the image that's displayed in the main screen. If this is enlarged beyond the bounds of the screen, it clearly displays the proportion of the enlarged image that's currently visible as a bright red rectangle. Click in this shape to shift your view of the enlarged image. This is useful when you're editing highly enlarged images because it allows you to navigate around the image far faster than if using the regular scroll bars.

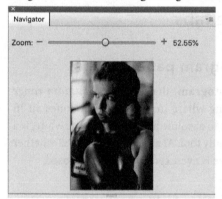

Info panel

Use this panel to measure the brightness or darkness of any part of the image that's displayed on the main screen. It doesn't matter what tool you happen to be using at the time—mouse over the area of concern and the **Info** panel will give you an RGB (brightness) readout.

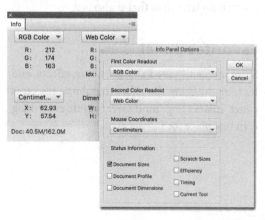

If you have just edited the picture and then read the **Info** panel, it cleverly displays both the before and after RGB readout values together. This is a very useful tool, especially for all of those photographers whose monitor is not 100% calibrated. As seen here, this little panel (plus the opened, larger **Options** panel for **Info**) is chock-full of other display information if and when needed, including: **Scratch Sizes**, **Document Sizes**, **Efficiency**, and **Current Tool**.

Create Menu

(**Organizer and Editor**, left and right)

Slideshow

This is one of the easiest ways to create a slideshow (in MP4 movie format) and probably the fastest. Because it's so quick, you get very little input and a few style choices and that's it. Previous versions of Elements enjoyed quite a sophisticated and feature-rich slide-making utility. This new version has been dumbed-down—it's fast and easy, but if you want greater control, you'll have to turn to a third-party application.

Photo Collage

This is an amazing feature that takes a bunch of images and assembles them into a nicely designed collage. To achieve this the traditional way, that is, using layers and masks, would take a long time. This feature takes a few seconds. Brilliant.

Photo Prints

This is a feature that links your Elements output to a local printer. Options include **Local printer** (single prints), **Picture Package** (a set of differently sized pictures all on one sheet of paper), or **Contact Sheet** (multiple images arranged in a grid across the page).

Quote Graphic

Quote Graphic provides the tools to make a photographic illustration or a purely graphic image incorporating any kind of short text message (hence the name) using a range of clip art graphics and animations so the file is exported as a GIF file for social media or video usage.

Photo Book

This feature allows you to add multiple images to a preset page layout—you choose the number of pages and the design, which is then downloaded from the Adobe servers. Populating the pages is as simple as drag and drop.

Greeting Card

A rather dated-looking set of preset card designs mark this feature as one that hasn't been upgraded for many years. That being said, it is easy to use and produces reasonably good results. With a little experience, anyone could produce a far better, more personal design by doing it manually.

Photo Calendar

This feature runs in a similar fashion to the Greeting Card utility—choose a style and design, download it from the Adobe servers, and drag and drop your images from the Photo Bin into the monthly pages. To finish, print this on a local printer and get it bound at a local office services outlet. Many other companies, most notably digital photo-making businesses, produce far superior products.

Video Story

A slightly more serious and complicated video-editing feature (than the Instant Video feature), this was designed, as its name suggests, to tell a story, thereby incorporating text and graphics with your video clips. Again, this is a brilliant, entry-level video widget.

Video Collage

This is another beautifully designed utility that allows you to make a split-screen, multi-clip video with virtually no prior experience of editing clips. A great design that works well.

Share menu

(Organizer and Editor)

Email

Link your email account with this utility to attach images easily and efficiently.

Twitter

Sign up, then upload your images directly to the Twitterscape.

Flickr

Sign up, then load images directly into your Flickr Photostream or be more specific and target a specific Flickr folder.

Facebook

Sign into FB and upload your images directly.

Vimeo and YouTube

Both of these features are only relevant for video—linking your Vimeo and YouTube accounts to provide a direct link between the two features makes posting so much simpler.

PDF Slideshow

Here, you can add multiple images in the PDF slideshow window. Then, the software binds it all together into a universally readable PDF file that can then be distributed via email, a blog, website, disk, or USB media.

Glossary

Artifact

Optical distortion within an image caused by (too much) image compression. Filters in Elements can be used to minimize the negative aspects of this ugly occurrence.

Bit depth

The amount of data in a digital file. The higher the bit depth, the more potential you have, especially for editing. Files have to be reduced in bit depth for printing as most printers have limited capabilities.

Bitmap

A method of storing digital information by mapping out an image bit by bit. The density of the pixels determines how sharp the image resolution will be.

CMYK (Cyan, Magenta, Yellow, Black) color

The color space used for commercial offset printing. CMYK is also a common working color space for inkjet, laser, and dye-sublimation printers.

Color Calibration

The process of regulating the color on a computer monitor so that what you see onscreen is an accurate representation of what was captured by the camera.

Color Space

The range of colors that can be reproduced on a computer monitor or in print. The most commonly used color spaces for digital imaging are the baseline RGB and wider-gamut Adobe RGB (1998).

Compression

Used to make image files physically smaller on disk. There are two types of compression: lossless and lossy. TIFF and Photoshop files can be compressed with no loss of quality, while JPEGs, because of their native compression, are lossy.

Depth of field

A measure of how much of an image, apart from the main subject, remains in focus, in the background and the foreground. Depth of field is controlled by the aperture, the focal length of the lens, and the subject distance. A large aperture has a shallow depth of field—a smaller (for example, f22) aperture records a much deeper focus.

Digital Negative (DNG) is a free RAW file format produced by Adobe. It's regarded as being a "universal" RAW file though many photographers consider the 'native' RAW file produced for a specific camera model to produce the best quality, something that's almost impossible to prove either way.

Dots Per Inch (dpi)

Dots per inch describes the proximity of the pixels to each other. The closer the dots, the more detailed the image. A typical dpi for print is 300 dpi, while online it's considerably less, at 72 dpi. Dpi is the same as ppi (pixels per inch) and lpi (lines per inch).

EXIF

An abbreviation of Exchangeable Image File, this is the metadata your camera records in an image file. It provides information about the camera settings. This includes date, time, camera make and model, resolution, aperture, shutter speed, ISO, and GPS (if available).

Gamma

The brightness curve of the color spectrum as displayed (or reproduced) on a computer monitor, printer, or scanner.

HDR

HDR, or high dynamic range photography, is a technique for surpassing the somewhat limited exposure range of cameras. By shooting a scene with several different exposures, then combining them using dedicated software, you can create an image with a far wider tonal range than if it were just the one shot. Photomerge Exposure is one example of this technique (Guided Edit mode).

Histogram

The chart or "mountain range" you often see on the back of a camera and in the **Levels** tool. The horizontal axis represents the tonal range of an image, expressed in values of 0 to 255: 0 = black, 255 = white. The vertical axis indicates the number of pixels in the image that match that particular tonal range value.

Image Resize

A software feature for changing the pixel dimensions of an image file. Changing the size up or down also changes the resolution of the image. But if it includes a resample—a process where pixels are added to or subtracted from the original image—the resolution (dots per inch) remains the same.

JPEG

A lossy compression file format that keeps file sizes relatively small and is easily transferred via email and the web. The smaller the file is compressed, the more ugly visual artifacts become noticeable.

Kilobyte

1,024 bytes make 1 kilobyte, written KB, which refers to the size of an image file. This relates to the amount of image data in the file.

Megabyte

1,024 Kilobytes, written MB, 1,024 kilobytes make a megabyte, written MB, which is a term that describes file size or media capacity, such as hard drives. The number refers to the amount of information or image data in a file or how much information can be contained on a memory card, CD or DVD, hard drive, or disk.

Megapixel

A standard unit of measurement for DSLR camera resolution. Generally, the more megapixels, the better the image detail.

Noise

The appearance of unwanted color artifacts in digital images. Noise increases with sensitivity, so it is more visible in images taken with higher ISO ratings.

Overexposure

The result of recording too much light, producing a lighter image. It can usually be corrected with software, but if it is dramatic, data might have been fatally lost ("clipped").

Pixelization

The negative breakup of an image file that has been enlarged to a point where there are not enough pixels to create a clear picture. Most software adds a type of diffusion that helps smooth out the lack of pixels, which means the image appears soft rather than just pixelated.

Pixel

Pixels are the tiny dots that make up a digital image. The resolution of digital images is measured in the number of pixels that make up the width and height, for example, 6,000 x 4,000 (this equals 24 megapixels).

PNG

Portable Network Graphic, a type of image file format used on the World Wide Web. Its most notable feature is the ability to preserve transparency, making it ideal for irregular-shaped objects that have to encompass a preset background color or texture.

PSD file (.psd)

This is the Photoshop file format used by Elements and many other applications. Typically used to store both picture information as well as details of any masks, selections, or paths that might be in the file. It's a good general format and is totally lossless.

RAW file

A RAW file is a complete download of what your camera's sensor "sees" before it is processed in the camera. RAW files take longer to write to the memory card and occupy more storage space. They allow more flexibility and options in post-processing.

RGB (Red, Green, Blue) color

RGB is an additive color model in which red, green, and blue light is added together in various ways to reproduce a broad array of colors for representation and display as images on computers and other digital devices.

Saturation

The depth of color tones in an image. Too much is termed "heavily saturated" while not enough is described as being "muted." No saturation produces a black and white image.

TIFF file (.tif)

Another almost universal file type. Like the .psd format, TIFF files can contain additional information, such as selections and layers. TIFF files can be compressed by up to 25% losslessly.

Tonal Range

A photographic term used to describe the quality of color and tone ranging from an image's darkest shadow through to the brightest highlight details, including all of the transitions in between.

Vignetting

A technical term for when the barrel of a zoom lens becomes visible on an image—usually in the form of dark corners. Darkening the edges of a photo is also a very effective way to emphasize the central subject in post-production.

White Balance

Digital cameras need a reference point for white in order to render all the colors of the spectrum naturally. This is called the White Balance and it can be calculated automatically in-camera. If it gets it wrong, you can set it manually, choosing from a preset range of "recipes," such as **Fluorescent**, **Sunlight**, **Cloudy**, **Flash**, and **Indoors**.

Packt.com

Subscribe to our online digital library for full access to over 7,000 books and videos, as well as industry leading tools to help you plan your personal development and advance your career. For more information, please visit our website.

Why subscribe?

- Spend less time learning and more time coding with practical eBooks and Videos from over 4,000 industry professionals
- Improve your learning with Skill Plans built especially for you
- Get a free eBook or video every month
- Fully searchable for easy access to vital information
- Copy and paste, print, and bookmark content

Did you know that Packt offers eBook versions of every book published, with PDF and ePub files available? You can upgrade to the eBook version at packt.com and as a print book customer, you are entitled to a discount on the eBook copy. Get in touch with us at questions@packtpub.com for more details.

At www.packt.com, you can also read a collection of free technical articles, sign up for a range of free newsletters, and receive exclusive discounts and offers on Packt books and eBooks.

Other Books You May Enjoy

If you enjoyed this book, you may be interested in these other books by Packt:

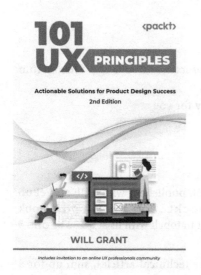

101 UX Principles, Second Edition

Will Grant

ISBN: 978-1-80323-488-5

- Work with user expectations, not against them
- Make interactive elements obvious and discoverable
- Optimize your interface for mobile
- Streamline creating and entering passwords
- Use animation with care in user interfaces
- How to handle destructive user actions

Adobe Illustrator for Creative Professionals

Clint Balsar

ISBN: 978-1-80056-925-6

- Master a wide variety of methods for developing objects
- Control files using layers and groups
- Enhance content using data-supported infographics
- Use multiple artboards for better efficiency and asset management
- Understand the use of layers and objects in Illustrator
- Build professional systems for final presentation to clients

Packt is searching for authors like you

If you're interested in becoming an author for Packt, please visit `authors.packtpub.com` and apply today. We have worked with thousands of developers and tech professionals, just like you, to help them share their insight with the global tech community. You can make a general application, apply for a specific hot topic that we are recruiting an author for, or submit your own idea.

Share your thoughts

Now you've finished *Mastering Adobe Photoshop Elements 2023, Fifth Edition*, we'd love to hear your thoughts! Scan the QR code below to go straight to the Amazon review page for this book and share your feedback or leave a review on the site that you purchased it from.

https://packt.link/r/1803248459

Your review is important to us and the tech community and will help us make sure we're delivering excellent quality content.

Best Wishes,

Robin Nichols

Index

Download a free PDF copy of this book

Thanks for purchasing this book!

Do you like to read on the go but are unable to carry your print books everywhere?

Is your eBook purchase not compatible with the device of your choice?

Don't worry, now with every Packt book you get a DRM-free PDF version of that book at no cost.

Read anywhere, any place, on any device. Search, copy, and paste code from your favorite technical books directly into your application.

The perks don't stop there, you can get exclusive access to discounts, newsletters, and great free content in your inbox daily

Follow these simple steps to get the benefits:

1. Scan the QR code or visit the link below

https://packt.link/free-ebook/9781803248455

2. Submit your proof of purchase
3. That's it! We'll send your free PDF and other benefits to your email directly